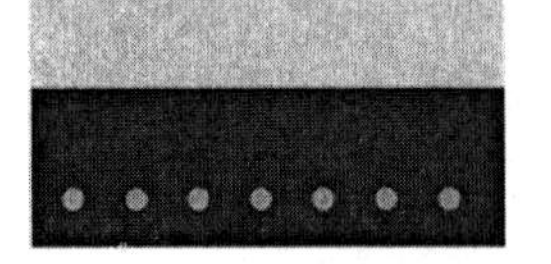

AMERICA'S RELIGIOUS TREASURES

A SPIRITUAL HERITAGE TRAVEL GUIDE

AMERICA'S RELIGIOUS TREASURES

Text by Marion Rawson Vuilleumier

Illustrations by Pierre DuPont Vuilleumier

Harper & Row, Publishers
New York Hagerstown San Francisco London

Dedicated to the Memory of
Our Parents

Walter and Ethel Rawson
and
Pierre and Marie Vuilleumier
who left
a spiritual legacy
to their children

For information address Harper & Row, Publishers, Inc., 10 East 53rd Street, New York, N.Y. 10022. Published simultaneously in Canada by Fitzhenry & Whiteside Limited, Toronto.

FIRST EDITION

Designed by C. Linda Dingler

Library of Congress Cataloging in Publication Data
Vuilleumier, Marion.
America's religious treasures.

Bibliography: p.
Includes index.
1. United States—Description and travel—1960–
—Guide-books. 2. Churches—United States—Guide-books.
I. Title.
E158.V84 1976 917.3'04'925 76-9342
ISBN 0-06-068940-4
ISBN 0-06-068941-2 pbk.

---

76 77 78 79 80 81 10 9 8 7 6 5 4 3 2 1

CONTENTS

Within each section the contents are arranged chronologically by states as America's spiritual heritage developed. Within the states, contents are arranged both chronologically and geographically for the convenience of the traveler.

There is a map at the beginning of each state write-up. The numbers on the maps that are within circles indicate the location of sites described in the body of the book. Numbers without circles show the location of sites listed in the appendix.

ACKNOWLEDGMENTS

Appreciation is expressed to the Departments of Tourism and the State Libraries in the 50 states for supplying materials and suggestions for subjects to be included in this book.

We also thank staff members at the individual sites who provided detailed information and guided us when we visited.

Denominational officials of the various religious institutions have been of inestimable help.

In addition, appreciation is expressed to the following individuals:

ALABAMA David De Jarnette, Mound State Monument, Moundville; Rev. Lambert Gattman, Ave Maria Grotto, Cullman; Faye Herring, State Bureau of Publicity, Montgomery; Mrs. David Turner, Marengo County Historical Society, Demopolis.

ALASKA Mrs. Jetret Petersen, Kenai Historical Society; Sister Victoria, Russian Orthodox Diocese of Sitka and Alaska, Sitka.

ARIZONA Brother Leon Carr, Franciscan Renewal Center, Phoenix; Gary Howe, Tumacacori National Monument.

ARKANSAS Jerry Bedford, Heifer Project Fourche River Ranch, Perryville (also to Rosalie Sinn of Plymouth, Mass. who supplied information on the Ranch); N. Lee Cate, Mt. Sequoyah Assembly, Fayetteville; Gregorio Carrera, Arkansas Post National Memorial.

CALIFORNIA Ursula Bond, Vedanta Society, Hollywood; Brother Lew, Franciscan Fathers, Santa Barbara; Joyce Carter, Riverside Municipal Museum; Katherine Hart, Last Supper, Santa Cruz; Rev. Trevor Hoy, Berkley Center for Human Interaction; Kristin Kontilis, Mission Inn, Riverside; Roy Patchen, Oakland Mormon Temple; P. T. Schellhas, Pacific School of Religion, Berkley; Rev. Harvey Tafel, Wayfarer's Chapel, Palos Verdes; Dr. and Mrs. Alfred Gilbert of Napa and Prof. and Mrs. Linton Seaverns of Angwin.

COLORADO Betty Charles, Mesa Verde National Park; David Kirwin, Young Life International, Colorado Springs; Alice Lucas, The Navigators, Colorado Springs; Colonel M. A. Madsen, United States Air Force Academy, Colorado Springs; Lena Riedel, Colorado Council of Churches, Denver.

CONNECTICUT Mrs. Miles W. Daley, Cornwall; Liane Mosher, Cornwall Bridge.

DELAWARE Rev. Myles Edwards, Immanuel Episcopal Church, New Castle; Thelma Williams, Division of Historical and Cultural Affairs, Lewes; Sophie Luoma, New Castle Board of Trade.

DISTRICT OF COLUMBIA Henry Mastroni, National Presbyterian Church and Center; Dr. Muhammad Rauf, The Islamic Center; Carol Hetzell, General Conference Seventh-day Adventists.

FLORIDA Glenn Couvillon, Florida Dept. of Commerce, Tallahassee; Dorothy Woolley, Bibletown, Boca Raton; Rev. Robbins Ralph, Florida Conference United Church of Christ.

GEORGIA Gary Ford, Callaway Gardens, Pine Mountain; Father Augustine, Monastery of the Holy Spirit, Conyers; Roger Durham, Midway Museum; Patricia Hall, Georgia Historical Commission, Atlanta; Mary Arthur, St. Paul's Episcopal Church, Augusta; Dana McGahee, Ocmulgee National Monument; Sharon Alexander, County Chamber of Commerce, Calhoun.

HAWAII Roselle Howell, Wananalua Congregational Church, Hana; Rev. Edith Wolfe, United Church of Christ; Rev. T. Ichinose, Soto Mission, Honolulu; Lindy Boyes, Hawaii Visitors Bureau, Honolulu; Orlando Lyman, Lyman House Memorial Museum, Hilo; Father Edward Fleming, Kailua Kona; Jerry Shimoda, City of Refuge National Historical Park; Honaunau; Yvonne Del Rio, Pearl Harbor Memorial United Church of Christ.

IDAHO Martha Cook, First United Methodist Church, Boise.

ILLINOIS Jack Weck, Shrine of Our Lady of the Snows, Belleville; Rebecca Myers, Bishop Hill Memorial; Beatrice Robertson, Cahokia Mounds Museum, East St. Louis; Earle Searcy, Dept. of Business and Economic Development, Springfield; Robert Ray, Vivekananda Vedanta Society, Chicago; Georgia Lyman, Rockefeller Memorial Chapel, Chicago.

INDIANA Paul Stabile, St. Meinrad Archabbey and Seminary; Betty Flohr, North Christian Church, Columbus; Kenneth McDowell, Church of the Brethren, Nappanee; James Ahr, Division of Tourism, Indianapolis; David McCoy, Our Sunday Visitor, Huntington; Norman Temme, Valpariso University; Shirell Fox, Anderson College; Marjorie Gratz, First Christian Church, Columbus; Dr. Elton Trueblood, Yokefellow Institute and Thomas Mullen, Earlham College, Richmond.

IOWA Cliff Lee, Council Bluffs Chamber of Commerce; Madeline Roemig, Amana Heritage Society; Lauretta Mintzmyer, Herbert Hoover National Historic Site, West Branch; Marion Nelson, Vesterheim Norwegian–American Museum, Decorah; Rev. Dennis Haas, Grinnell College; Norval Smith, William Penn College, Oskaloosa.

KANSAS John Pearson, Bethany College, Lindsborg; Regis Hickey O.S.B. St. Benedict's Abbey, Atchison; Clyde Ernst, Rice County Historical Society, Lyons; Mrs. A. N. Wiltz, Shawnee Mission; John Wickman, Dwight D. Eisenhower Library, Abilene.

KENTUCKY Preston Slusher, The Book of Job, Pineville; James Thomas, Shakertown, Pleasant Hill; Mrs. A. H. Proffeit and Lou Delle McIntosh, Old Mulkey Meetinghouse, Thompkinsville; Stephen Sebert, Yokefellows at Shakertown, Harrodsburg; Keithel Morgan, Abraham Lincoln Birthplace National Historic Site, Hodgenville; Julia Neal, Shakertown, South Union.

LOUISIANA Rev. James Savey and Elisabeth Dart, Grace Episcopal Church, St. Francisville.

MAINE Dorothy Corey, Lady Pepperrell House, Kittery Point.

MARYLAND Rev. John Tierney, Basilica of the Assumption, Baltimore; Frank Krastel, Old Bohemia Historical Society, Warwick; McKinley Coffman, Brethren Service Center, New Windsor; Ann Morgan, Mt. Vernon Place United Methodist Church, Baltimore; Father Alagia, Manresa–on–Severn, Annapolis.

MASSACHUSETTS Elspeth Miles, Old Ship Church, Hingham; Byron Rushing, Museum of Afro–American History, Boston; Paul Chapman, Packard Manse, Stoughton; A. W. Phinney, First Church of Christ, Scientist, Boston; David Little, Essex Institute, Salem; Jan Bauer, Plimoth Plantation, Plymouth; Richard Molloy, Mary Baker Eddy Museum, Brookline; Dorothy Freeman, Salem; Rabbi Albert Axelrod and Jeffrey Osoff, Brandeis University, Waltham; Rose Marie Knott, Atlantic Union Conference of Seventh-day Adventists, South Lancaster; Rev. Cyril Wismar, Marblehead.

MICHIGAN Kathryn Thornberry, Lunds Scenic Gardens, Maple City; William Murdoch, Holland Chamber of Commerce; Ralph Martin, Word of God, Ann Arbor; Rev. Thomas Dominiak, Catholic Shrine, Indian River; Robert G. Wheeler, Greenfield Village and Henry Ford Museum, Dearborn; Eleanor Gillen, St. Joseph's Shrine, Brooklyn; Harold Coolman, Ludington Area Chamber of Commerce; Nancy Pflug and John Williams, *New Covenant Magazine*, Ann Arbor; Robert Matson, Cranbrook Educational Community, Bloomfield Hills; Mrs. Henry McCall, Old Mission Women's Club, Traverse City.

MINNESOTA Joan Olson, Saint Olaf College, Northfield; Darralu Lindholm, Augsburg College, Minneapolis; Nancy Lindberg, Bethany Fellowship and Missionary Training Center, Minneapolis; Melanie Ohman, Gustavus Adolphus College, St. Peter; James Dock, Augsburg College, Minneapolis; Thom Woodward, St. John's University, Collegeville; Sharon Anderson, Cathedral of Our Merciful Saviour, Faribault.

MISSISSIPPI John Mohlhenrich, Natchez Trace Parkway, Tupelo.

MISSOURI August Sueflow, Concordia Historical Institute, St. Louis; Martha Gaddy, Vedanta Society, Saint Louis; Rev. Monsignor Rowland Gannon, Saint Louis Cathedral; Sister M. Erskine, Shrine of Blessed Philippine Duchesne, St. Charles; Beverly Holsman, Winston Churchill Memorial, Fulton; Stephanie Kelley, Saints Auditorium, Independence; A. E. Whatett, Missouri–Independence Museum; Brother Aquinas Nichols, Conception Abbey; Rev. William Ripley, St. Paul's Episcopal Church, Ironton; John Moad, School of the Ozarks, Point Lookout.

MONTANA Father Joseph Shirey, St. Ignatius Mission, Ronan.

NEBRASKA Judy Ely and Aliane Flanigan, City of Bellevue Historic Buildings; Mrs. Al Werthman, St. Cecilia's Cathedral, Omaha; Rev. Otis Young, First–Plymouth Congregational Church, Lincoln.

NEVADA Marshall Humphreys, Mormon Station Historic State Monument, Genoa.

NEW JERSEY Madeline Lancaster, Springfield Historical Society; Norman Thomas, New Brunswick Theological Seminary; Herbert Butcher, Friends' Meeting House, Trenton; Edith Joseph, State of New Jersey, Trenton; Dierdre Thomson, Old Tennent Presbyterian Church.

NEW MEXICO Brother David Gerates, Benedictine Monastery, Pecos; Rev. Mark Short, Jr., Glorieta Baptist Assembly; Dan Murphy, Gran Quivira National Monument, Mountainair; Fabian Chavex, Jr., State of New Mexico, Santa Fe; Rev. Dennis Walker, Episcopal Church of the Holy Faith, Santa Fe; William Schart, Aztec Ruins National Monument; R. M. Ab, Mission of St. Francis of Assisi, Ranchos de Taos; Rev. Joseph Cubells, Holy Family Church, Chimayo.

NEW YORK Margaret Carmen, Bowne House, Flushing; Annette Rohan Quaker Meeting House, Flushing; Elder Greg Whittaker, Cumorah Mission, Rochester; Kenneth Hasbrouck, Huguenot Historical Society, New Paltz; Beatrice Loennecke, Plymouth Church of the Pilgrims, Brooklyn; Hazel Ryder, The First Church in Albany; Robert Williams, Collegiate Reformed Protestant Dutch Church, New York City; Helen Je, Middle Collegiate Church, New York City; Marie Carlson, Marble Collegiate Church, New York City; Joseph Horan, State of New York Travel Bureau, Albany; Reformed "Old Dutch Church," Kingston; Johann Christoph Arnold, Society of Brothers, Rifton.

NORTH CAROLINA Phil Royce, Chowan College, Murfreesboro; Charles Pennington, Field of the Wood, Murphy; Donald Taylor, Tryon Palace, New Bern; George Calhoun, Thyatira Presbyterian Church, Salisbury; Leeming Grimshawe, Church of St. John in the Wilderness, Flat Rock; Philip Hudson, The Sword of Peace, Snow Camp; Robert Cole, Brevard Music Center; Mittie Linney, Third Creek Presbyterian Church, Statesville, René and Enes Durand, The Waldensians, Valdese.

NORTH DAKOTA Marie Desrosiers, Pembina State Historical Museum.

OHIO Rev. Heth Corl, Wyandott Indian Mission Church, Upper Sandusky; Rev. Juniper Cummings, Our Lady of Consolation, Carey; Ruth Flere, National Shrine of Saint Dympha, Massillon; Judith Sheridan, Ceauga County Historical Society, Burton; Edna McKenzie, Rankin House, Ripley;

P. M. Virtue, Gnadenhutten Historical Society; Ginny Stark, Hebrew Union College, Jewish Institute of Religion, Cincinnati.

OKLAHOMA Grace Fields, Indian City U.S.A., Anadarko; La Verda Evans, St. Luke's United Methodist Church, Oklahoma City.

OREGON Joe McKay, St. Paul Mission; Rev. Horace Batchelder (of Plymouth, Mass.), Atkinson Memorial Church, Oregon City; Swami Aseshananda, Vedanta Society of Portland; Craig McCroskey, Oregon Historical Society, Portland.

PENNSYLVANIA Mary Kay Stunkard, Harmonist Historical and Memorial Association, Harmony; Harold Myers, Pennsylvania Historical and Museum Commission, Harrisburg; Joy Crink, Philadelphia Yearly Meeting of Friends; Rev. John Stoudt, Schwenkfelders and other groups, Fleetwood; Sidney Rosenberg, Beth Sholom Congregation, Elkins Park.

RHODE ISLAND William and Ruth Richardson of Barrington, Newport Historical sites.

SOUTH CAROLINA Jean Smith, Kahal Kadosh Beth Elohim, Charleston; Ray Sirmon, South Carolina Dept. of Parks, Recreation and Tourism, Columbia; Bob Harrison, Bob Jones University, Greenville.

SOUTH DAKOTA Harold Moore, Buechel Memorial Museum, St. Francis.

TENNESSEE Hillard Brown, Jr., Christus Gardens, Gatlinburg; Ruby Wray, St. Mary's Church, Nashville; Kenneth Miller, Tennessee State Planning Office, Johnson City; Catherine Avery, Downtown Presbyterian Church, Nashville.

TEXAS Carolyn Ericson, Stone Fort Museum, Nacagdoches; Lois Ferguson, Word Books, Waco; Richard Pierce, Texas Highway Dept. Travel Development, Austin; Happy Shahan, Alamo Village, Bracketville; Jane Glidewell, Harris County Heritage Society, Houston; Rev. William Cody, Laity Lodge, Leakey.

UTAH Dan Rosenhan, Latter Day Saints Church Graphics Library, Salt Lake City; Reed Olsen, Box Elder Tabernacle, Brigham City.

VIRGINIA William Dunstan III, *Virginia Cavalcade Magazine*, Richmond; Rev. Howard Mueller, Abingdon Episcopal Church, White Marsh; Sylvester Putnam, Booker T. Washington National Monument, Hardy; Barbara Crews, Alexandria Tourist Council; Jim Embleton, Association for Research and Enlightenment, Virginia Beach; James Bailey, Blandford Church Interpretation Center, Petersburg; A. Robbins, Jr., Merchants Hope Church Foundation, Hopewell.

WASHINGTON Marta Brooks, Pioneer Village and Willis Carey Historical Museum, Cashmere; John Winchell, Whitman Mission National Historic Site, Walla Walla; Bette Meyer, Park & Recreation Commission, Olympia; Frank Green, Washington State Historical Society, Tacoma; Donald Richardson, Travel Development Division Washington State, Olympia; Thomas Mayer, Washington State Library, Olympia; Rev. Martin Goslin, Seattle.

WEST VIRGINIA Larry Frye, Bethany College; Gladys Hartzell, Historic

Shepherdstown; Lucille Skaggs, Old Stone Presbyterian Church, Lewisburg; Carl White, Mother's Day Shrine, Grafton; Rev. Charles Roth, Church of the Good Shepherd, Grafton; Mary Jenkins, Department of Archives and History of West Virginia, Charleston.

WISCONSIN Father Robert Perkins, Grotto Shrine and Wonder Cave, Rudolph; Mrs. A. M. Rasmussen, Ephraim; Mary Jane Koehl, First Unitarian Society, Madison; Stephen Gmur, New Glarus Historical Society.

WYOMING David Crosson, University of Wyoming Library, Laramie.

PREFACE

The Discover America Travel Organizations and the United States Travel Service have recently created nine distinct vacation sections in this vast "land of many lands." We gratefully use eight of these sections in the organization of our travel guide. It has enabled the presentation of a multitude of religious landmarks in an orderly fashion. Within the sections, the arrangement of states chronologically in order of their settlement enables the reader to follow the development of our spiritual heritage.

Out of the profusion of religious communities, buildings, and shrines that could be mentioned, we have chosen those where the traveler will find something of interest to visit and where it is convenient to travel and find lodgings. Since more and more public transportation is being used, those areas near cross-country bus lines or Amtrak routes have been highlighted. Additional sites in the 50 states are listed in the Appendix.

Obviously all of the spiritual heritage sites in the nation could not be given in these pages. Therefore we have tried to make a representative and varied selection, one which will portray vividly the richness and depth of spiritual fiber. Hopefully readers will be encouraged to embark on further voyages of discovery.

The volume is intended to be used in conjunction with road maps and travel guides, such as the AAA Tour Books, so that detailed directions, lists of accommodations, entrance fees, if any, and time schedules for historic sites have not been included.

National, state, and local historical and religious representatives have been most helpful in providing information and illustrations to enrich the book. The American Automobile Association materials have been of great value. Also, the secretarial expertise of Miss Marian Logan has made manuscript preparation much easier. To all of these we are extremely grateful and hereby pay tribute.

Marion and Pierre Vuilleumier
West Hyannisport, Massachusetts
March 1976

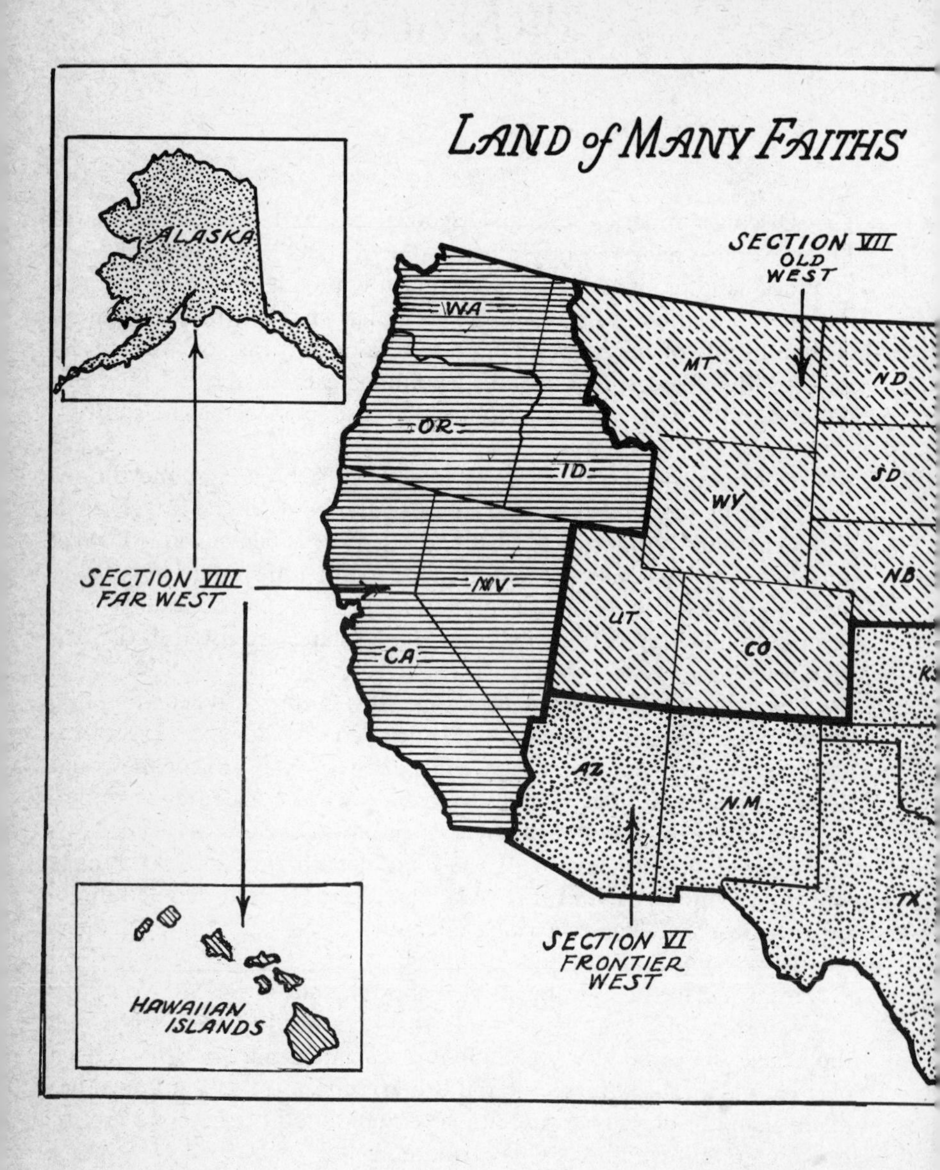
LAND of MANY FAITHS
ALASKA
SECTION VIII
FAR WEST
HAWAIIAN
ISLANDS
SECTION VII
OLD
WEST
SECTION VI
FRONTIER
WEST
WA
OR
ID
NV
CA
MT
WY
UT
CO
ND
SD
NB
AZ
N.M.
TX

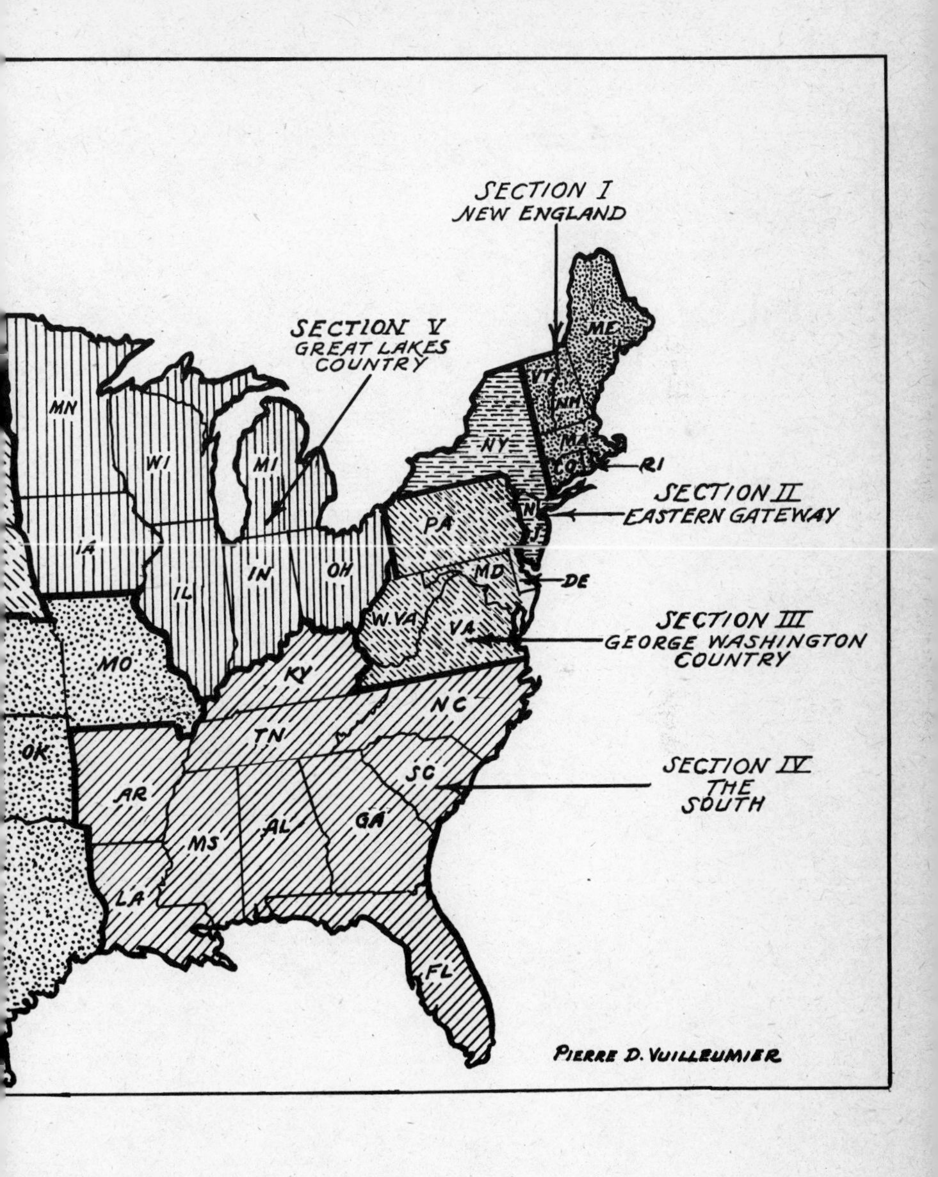
SECTION I
NEW ENGLAND
SECTION V
GREAT LAKES
COUNTRY
SECTION II
EASTERN GATEWAY
SECTION III
GEORGE WASHINGTON
COUNTRY
SECTION IV
THE
SOUTH
MN
WI
MI
IA
IL
IN
OH
MO
OK
AR
LA
MS
AL
TN
KY
GA
SC
NC
FL
W.VA
VA
MD
DE
PA
NY
NJ
VT
NH
ME
MA
CT
RI
PIERRE D. VUILLEUMIER

INTRODUCTION

Over four centuries ago, this great and tumultuous land of ours lay quiet and serene, save for an occasional storm crashing and thundering across its face. From the blue Atlantic with its contoured frame of sandy beaches and salt-sprayed rocks to the majestic Pacific edged with cliffs and mountains, it was verdant and gentle, except where snowy peaks thrust high beyond the clouds. In the north the land pressed on to infinity, and in the south arid deserts and lush bayous fringed a gentian gulf.

Green was the backdrop of this tapestry, occasionally flecked with tan, wherever the native people lived and loved, respecting and protecting the land that mothered them, and worshiping the Great Spirit.

Then from the southeast, sharp-prowed galleons wafted by the wind hesitantly nudged the shore. Spanish explorers accompanied by men of God disembarked and sought to penetrate this fascinating but alien land. Gradually they pushed west, some evangelizing, some brutalizing, drawn by rumors of glittering riches and the challenge of the unknown. Splashes of gold and blood-red began to color the tapestry.

Not long afterward, if one reckons time in centuries as this vast land does, other ships approached the northeast from England and France. One, storm-tossed and exhausted, reached the New England shore. It was filled with Pilgrims exiled from a hostile homeland and seeking peace and freedom to worship God as they chose. As they put down roots and began a sturdy settlement, the blues, grays, and maroons of their garb and the browns of their thatched houses blended into the pattern.

Like two giant pincers, the settlers moved westward from their eastern beachheads. They were met by travelers from the Orient and by migrants over the Bering Straits. People of all colors and all faiths merged into a muted rainbow.

Soon America was multihued, with occasional strands drawn from Chinese and Japanese settlements clustered around unique temples.

Religion was a primary cause that led men and women to this virgin territory. One could be free, they thought, from persecution. There would be room and time to establish community as it should be. So they came from Alpine peaks and Russian plains, from English moors and Moravian colonies. Then more groups were spawned by this land as people moved on to found new faiths.

Today we have the rich tapestry of a great religious heritage undergirding our country. It is all around us. Some of the strands are visible and remembered, like the Baptists of Rhode Island, the Quakers of Philadelphia, the Mormons of Utah, and the Roman Catholics of St. Augustine and the southwest. Others are not so obvious, but still can be searched out and recalled, like the Shakers of New Hampshire and Kentucky, the Seventh-day Baptists of Ephrata, Pennsylvania, and the Rappites of New Harmony, Indiana.

Now is a good time to reflect on the religious heritage that has helped make the United States a great nation. It will take a lifetime, though, to search out the many places where this greatness began. Perhaps in so doing we may recapture the hopes of those pilgrims who in the last four centuries gave strength and richness to the American Dream.

I.

NEW ENGLAND

MASSACHUSETTS

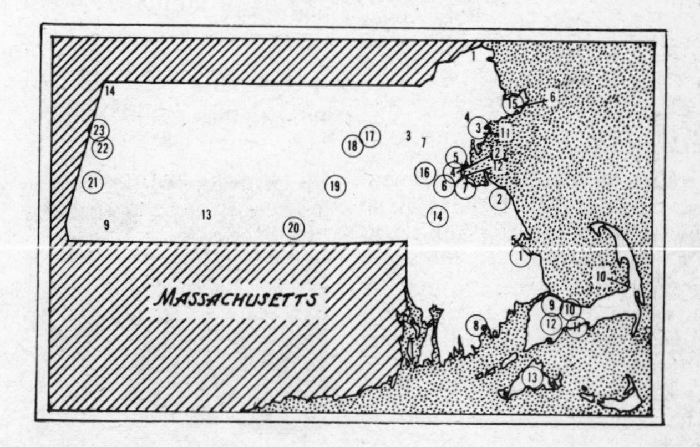

The tiny Pilgrim band that arrived in Plymouth Harbor on the forbidding winter day of December 21, 1620, held high a torch of pure faith sparked by their interpretation of the Holy Bible. Known as Separatists, they had fled England after being ejected by its state church. Unable to create in Holland the church they had envisioned, they left for the New World.

The Virginia area was originally planned to be the setting of their Great Experiment. Here a New Testament model church could be established. Bible truths could rule all of life and a community of believers could, without outside interference, follow the will of God.

Since provisions were low and winter was upon them, Plymouth was destined to be their home. In this "hideous and desolate wilderness," said Governor William Bradford, "What could now sustain them but the Spirit of God and His Grace."

After a tenuous hold that first winter when famine and fever took half the number, the colony put down roots. Indian friends like Supreme Sachem Massasoit and guide Squanto, assisted the survivors and shared their first Thanksgiving.

Plymouth soon spawned satellite towns as newcomers arrived. A decade later the Pilgrims were joined by the Puritans in Salem and Boston. Thus the Pilgrims were the first of a host of arrivals who established communities for religious reasons. The eastern part of the Commonwealth has a profusion of shrines reminding us of our religious heritage. A traveler can spend many days there and still not see them all.

East Central Massachusetts

(1) PLYMOUTH

Halfway between Boston and Cape Cod and just off double-barreled Route 3, Plymouth is a good starting point for a tour of Massachusetts and indeed all of New England. This community is the first permanent settlement north of Virginia.

Plymouth Harbor and Town

Drive directly to the shore on Water Street and climb Coles Hill for a panoramic harbor view. Stand by Cyrus Darlin's statue of Massasoit and imagine that great chieftain's feelings as he [might have] watched the full-sailed *Mayflower* enter the Bay. To the south is ancient Plymouth Rock, covered by a portico, where allegedly the Pilgrims first stepped ashore. Ahead, rising serenely at anchor is *Mayflower II*, a replica of that gallant, tiny ship which carried the crew and 102 colonists to these shores.

After visiting both these national shrines and the Pilgrim House replica by the shore, walk up Leyden Street (originally First Street), site of the first settlement. The many house markers record the site of Pilgrim homes. Continue to the street's head where two churches, the First Parish Unitarian and the Church of the Pilgrimage (Congregational and United Church), both rightly claim *Mayflower* roots. Beyond is Burial Hill, site of the old fort, of the old powder house, and of many Pilgrims' graves. On the stone for Governor William Bradford are these words: DO NOT BASELY RELINQUISH WHAT THE FATHERS WITH DIFFICULTY ATTAINED.

Other historic sites like the Jenney Grist Mill, Harlow Old Fort House, Howland House, Spooner House, Sparrow House, Mayflower Society House, and Plymouth Antiquarian Society illustrate how these spiritual ancestors of ours lived. The Plymouth National Wax Museum makes this history live.

Don't skip Pilgrim Hall, one of the oldest public museums in America and the only place where you can see a fine collection of actual Pilgrim artifacts. The manuscript collection here is extensive and researchers come to it from all over the world.

Plimoth Plantation

After you've exhausted the sites, but hopefully not yourself, drive 2 miles south on Route 3A to Plimoth Plantation, a re-creation of the first settlement that was on Leyden Street. The site of 100 acres contains the original first street, an eastern village, and working exhibits—by the costumed staff—of the crafts and household tasks of the Pilgrims. Do enjoy first the introductory movie.

Pause in the Old Fort Meeting House, the heart of the settlement, where decisions were prayerfully made in all areas of daily life. Along with the Mayflower Compact, this procedure of government by the will of God was the basis for much of our later governmental documents, including the Declaration of Independence and the Constitution of the United States.

Hopefully you've planned a several-day stay in one of Plymouth's very fine modern motels or in the nearby campgrounds. Then you can visit other historic places like the Forefathers' Monument, the 81-foot-high memorial completed in 1888, and the Miles Standish State Forest.

(2) HINGHAM

First Parish Church

On the way to Boston is Hingham and the Old Ship Church, so called because the roof structure is similar to the construction of old wooden ship hulls. One of the oldest continuously used wooden church structures in the country, it was erected in 1681. The pulpit with sounding board, the pews, and the galleries were added in 1755. [In Hingham, too, you might want to stop at the Old Ordinary, home of the Hingham Historical Society and a restored hostelry dating back to 1680.]

(3) SALEM

Though Boston will tempt you, you should visit Salem next on this spiritual heritage tour, for this was the second major settlement in the Commonwealth that was made by religious dissenters from England.

Settlers built homes as early as 1626 at Naumkeag, as Salem was originally called. It became an official settlement when Tobias Endicott arrived with 100 newcomers and a patent in September of 1628. The first Congregational Society in America was organized here on August 6, 1629, after another large company of planters arrived. Rev. Samuel Skelton was elected pastor and Rev. Francis Higginson, teacher. The famous Salem Church Covenant was then adopted: "We covenant with the Lord and one with another, and do bind ourselves in the presence of God to walk together in all his ways, according as he is pleased to reveal himself unto us in his blessed word of truth." At this time the community was renamed Salem, the ancient name for Jerusalem.

The Salem community was the capital of the settlement until 1630 and remained the focal point of the "Bible Commonwealth" for some years. Its first meeting house, erected in 1634, was the earliest built for Congregational worship by a church formed in America. Since town and church were intertwined, the structure was used for both religious and secular purposes.

Several other religious movements had their beginnings here. The first

Prayer Book service in New England, for example, was held here by Church of Englanders John and Samuel Brown in 1629.

Around the year 1634, Roger Williams, pastor of First Church, expressed belief in separation of church and state and insisted on the rights of conscience thus incurring the displeasure of the magistrates and other clergy and forcing his subsequent banishment in 1636. He escaped south, eventually reaching Rhode Island, where he founded the Baptist Church in America.

In 1812, the first missionaries sent from America to foreign lands left Salem. Two years earlier, the first Sunday school in America was established in nearby Beverly.

Salem not only helped create the Bible Commonwealth, but also played a fundamental role in launching the tragic hysteria against witches. In 1692, accusations were made which led to witchcraft trials and the hanging of 14 women and five men. Another man was pressed to death. Though some religious leaders assisted in ferreting out the witches, calling them "tools of Satan," others decried this mass phenomenon. Some publicly repented afterward.

Witch House

Route 1A leads directly to Salem Center, and running parallel to it is Essex Street. At No. 310½, is the forbidding-looking Witch House, scene of some of the witchcraft examinations. Built in 1642, it was the home of Jonathan Corwin, judge of the Witchcraft Court. Dark wood, peaked gables, and small diamond-shaped windows of leaded glass create a somber effect. A witchcraft frenzy erupted when five girls, who were practicing palmistry and magic, became hysterical. A physician who was called pronounced them bewitched. Boston had been trying witches for some time, and this was like a spark to a tinderbox. Soon many hastened to accuse others, in order not to be accused themselves. One can imagine the stern cross-examinations that took place here.

(4) BOSTON

When John Winthrop arrived on the *Arabella,* June 12, 1630, he carried a new charter and had already been elected governor. Altogether 17 vessels

Witch House

arrived that year carrying 1,000 colonists, their supplies, and their livestock. Seeing before him an already settled community, Winthrop scouted the surrounding area, finally choosing Boston as the site of his settlement.

Boston, originally called Shamut (Sweet Waters), was first settled by an Anglican clergyman, William Blackstone (or Blaxton). Then John Winthrop and his colonists arrived in 1630, calling their settlement Trimountaine, for the area's three hills. Only the highest, Beacon Hill, still remains. The town was renamed Boston, after Boston in Lincolnshire, England, on September 17, 1630.

Like other towns in the Bay Colony, the Boston settlement surrounded a meeting house situated in a central common pasture. Designated at first as a cow pasture and a training field, Boston Common is now one of the country's oldest public parks.

The meeting house was used for both worship and civil assembly.

The first town meetings handled both church and civil affairs, for residents were both church members and town voters. As more settlers arrived who did not profess church membership, however, the interesting legal structures of church and parish developed. Vestiges of these linger anachronistically into this century, sometimes complicating modern church life.

Boston Common

A trip back in time to religious beginnings in Boston should start at the Common with the ancient burying ground and the first footsteps of the Freedom Trail.

Begin your visit at the corner of Tremont and Boylston streets. Here is a tiny graveyard where a number of prominent citizens, including Gilbert Stuart, noted portrait painter, are buried. Take a stroll (brisk or slow according to the weather) through the adjoining gardens, where one can ride on the lovely Swan boats, then go back through the upper Common by the State House.

African Meeting House

One of the oldest standing black church buildings in the United States is found at 8 Smith Court on Beacon Hill. Originally built to function as both a religious and an educational center, the African Meeting House was instrumental in encouraging the growth of the black community on the north slope of Beacon Hill in the 19th century. The Federal-style structure was built by free blacks in 1806, when they resisted the white policy of seating blacks in galleries without an adequate view of the minister and out of sight of the whites. The church is sometimes called the Abolitionist Church, since it was the place where William Lloyd Garrison founded the New England Anti-Slavery Society in 1832. It is presently being restored by the Museum of Afro-American History.

Swedenborgian Cathedral

Also east of the State House is the Church of the New Jerusalem. An outgrowth of teachings of the Swedish religious genius Emmanuel Swedenborg, this denomination is also often referred to as the New Church. Boston soon became an area headquarters for the movement begun here in the early 1800s and the city now has a Swedenborgian Library, Bookstore, and School of Religion.

Park Street Church

Down Park Street and adjacent to the city headquarters of the Paulist Fathers is this impressive Congregational church erected in 1809, built on the site of an old granary. During the War of 1812, brimstone was stored in the basement of the church, giving the site the name Brimstone Corner. Here, on July 4, 1832, the song "America" was first sung. Browse among the headstones of Old Granary Burying Ground where many of historic Boston's notables are buried.

King's Chapel

Continue on Tremont Street to the corner of School Street where the first Anglican building was erected in New England in 1686. The present massive structure was built in 1754. Inside you will see the royal governor's box and other reminders of pre-Revolutionary days. The church is now Unitarian. Outside in the burying ground are the graves of Gov. John Winthrop and Rev. John Cotton who shaped the Bible Commonwealth.

Old South Meeting House

Continue to the corner of Washington and Milk streets where a beautiful colonial structure is a reminder of the close church and state relations in early Boston. The first meeting house was built on this site in 1669. The present building, erected in 1729, was the scene of gatherings to protest English domination. During the Revolution, the British used the building as a riding school. Later it was restored and there are many relics reminding one of that turbulent era. (Across the street, at 17 Milk Street, is the site of Benjamin Franklin's birthplace.)

Old North Church

On Salem Street is the oldest church building in Boston, the Old North Church, dating back to 1723. Here the signal lanterns warning of the British advance to Concord and Lexington were displayed by Paul Revere. A restored organ and one of the earliest peals of bells are among the historic artifacts.

Trinity Church

Now leave the center of old Boston and proceed up Boylston Street to Copley Square. Here is architect Henry Hobson Richardson's beautiful stone Romanesque church. Phillips Brooks, immortalized with a statue outside, was one of its most noted ministers, and is remembered also as author of the words of the carol, "O Little Town of Bethlehem." Other places of interest in the square are the Boston Public Library designed in Italian Renaissance style and containing many early manuscripts and art treasures, including the Abbey paintings of the Holy Grail.

Christian Science Center

Continuing west on Huntington Avenue, you will find the headquarters for worldwide activities of the Christian Science religion. Situated on 15 acres, the center includes the original Mother Church and an extension, with dome rising 224 feet. Publishing activities began in 1908 when the *Monitor* was founded by Mary Baker Eddy as a daily newspaper. The Society also publishes the *Journal, Sentinel, Herald,* and the *Quarterly,* as well as books and pamphlets in as many as 34 translations. The *Quarterly* contains Lesson-Sermon citations that are read in each Christian Science church. Since the church does not have pastors, the *Science and Health, Key to the Scriptures*

and the *Quarterly,* along with the *Bible,* are keys in teaching.

During a tour of the publishing house be sure to see the unique Mapparium, where the visitor literally steps inside a 30-foot globe of the world.

Outside again, you will be impressed by the new administration building, colonnade, Sunday school building, and reflecting pool.

First and Second Church of Boston

On the corner of Marlborough and Berkeley streets stands an unusual modern structure which has arisen from the ashes of an older one. Attached to the earlier façade and tower is a sweeping modern church with concrete amphitheater. Inside is a large lobby with art displays, flanked on one side by a small theater (one of the homes of Boston Repertory Theater) and on the other by a breathtakingly beautiful sanctuary with jutting balconies and organ pipes used decoratively. Its historical roots spring from the first Puritan church in 1630, with Rev. John Wilson, minister. It is now Unitarian-Universalist.

Ramakrishna Vedanta Society

At 58 Deerfield Street stands a center resulting from the teachings of the Hindu mystic Sri Ramakrishna. Through a life of rigorous spiritual practices, in his native Calcutta area, Ramakrishna attained a high spiritual state in tune with Vedantic (or Hindu) tradition. His many followers spread his teachings after his death. One disciple, Swami Vivekananda, represented Hinduism at the World's Parliament of Religions in Chicago in 1893. His successful lectures and classes caused creation of the Ramakrishna Order and its Mission for social service and education.

The Boston Society was formed in 1941 and the Society moved into this permanent residence overlooking the Charles River in 1942. A chapel and library are also open to visitors.

(5) CAMBRIDGE

Settled in 1630 and first called Newtowne, this community was early noted for education. Puritans and Pilgrims felt an educated ministry was of primary importance, so in 1636 the General Court allotted £400 for a "school or colledge." It was here also that the *Whole Book of Psalms,* known as the *Bay Psalm Book,* was printed by the English Colonial Press. Cambridge continues today to be a center for academic and cultural pursuits.

Harvard University

The oldest college in the English colonies, Harvard was founded in 1636 to prepare young men for the ministry. It wasn't named Harvard until 1638, when 31-year-old Rev. John Harvard died and left his library of 400 books and his fortune of £780 to the fledgling school. From these small beginnings has developed one of the most distinguished universities in the world.

On the Heritage Trail walking tour you will find the Memorial Church in historic Harvard Yard. This slender-spired Colonial structure is a center for interdenominational activity. The Harry Elkins Widener Memorial Library, which is the center for university collections, has on display a Gutenberg Bible as well as early records of religious work with native Americans during the Colonial period.

M.I.T. Chapel

A short ride down Massachusetts Avenue and in the midst of the world-renowned scientific community of the Massachusetts Institute of Technology is an unusual chapel built in 1955. A striking cylindrical structure designed by Eero Saarinen, it gives the visitor an amazing effect of retreat from daily concerns. A shallow moat surrounds the windowless building, and light reflecting upward from the moat makes changing patterns on the interior walls.

(6) BROOKLINE

Mary Baker Eddy Museum

At 120 Seaver Street, an impressive 100-room mansion is filled with manuscripts, books, and memorabilia of the life of Mary Baker Eddy, the founder of the Christian Science Church. The huge brownstone structure was moved here from Marquette, Michigan, in 1903 by the Longyear family, who in 1926 established a foundation in her memory.

The Longyear Historical Society has responsibility for six historic sites in Massachusetts and New England related to the life of Mrs. Eddy.

When Mrs. Eddy experienced a Divine Healing, she received a new sense of Life and of God, which caused her to write in 1875 *Science and Health, with Key to the Scriptures.* From an initial following in Lynn, Boston, and Chicago, the church she founded became worldwide, with the Mother Church in Boston.

Greek Orthodox Center

Here at Hellenic College and Holy Cross Seminary is an educational center for the Greek Orthodox Church. Headquarters for one of the 13 dioceses in the country, it also has a library and is the center for activities of citizens of Greek extraction.

(7) QUINCY

United First Parish Church (Unitarian)

Just south of Boston, on Hancock Street in the city's center, is the impressive Greek Revival structure designed by Alexander Parris and built in 1828. Granite was donated by John Quincy Adams. The interior is massive and stone memorial plaques line the walls. Visitors may go below into the crypt and see the simple graves of two of our country's presidents, John Adams and John Quincy Adams, and their wives.

Southeastern Massachusetts

(8) NEW BEDFORD

A swing around this section of the Commonwealth should begin with this city, which was once the greatest whaling port in the world. It is still one of the east coast's largest fishing ports.

Seaman's Bethel

On Johnny Cake Hill, next to the Whaling Museum of the Old Dartmouth Historical Society, stands Seaman's Bethel, a small house of worship dedicated in 1832.

Referred to by Herman Melville in *Moby Dick* as the "Whaleman's Chapel," he continued: "and few are the moody fishermen, shortly bound for the Indian or Pacific Oceans, who failed to make a Sunday visit to this spot." Inside are 23 cenotaphs, memorializing sailors lost at sea, the earliest in 1818 and the latest in 1934. The vestry is known as the "old salt box," for it resembles a ship's hold in which fish were preserved and parallels the concept of the church as a "preserving place for men redeemed of every race."

Sandwich Friends Meeting

(9) SANDWICH

Follow Route 6 east along the coast, and over one of the spectacular bridges at the Cape Cod Canal, to the little town of Sandwich. Dating back to 1637, it was the first settlement of the Cape. Continue down the ancient King's Highway (today's Route 6A) which runs just north of the town's center with its white Colonial church, Shawme Pond, old grist mill, and Hoxie House, oldest on the Cape. At Spring Hill Road, turn left and watch for an ancient Quaker Meeting House on a knoll in the woods, surrounded by the peaceful Friends burying ground.

Sandwich Friends Meeting

Established in 1654 when Friends were receiving a cool welcome, this is the oldest continuous Quaker congregation in America. Church membership and voting privileges were synonymous in the first years of the religiously based colony. Town officials were perplexed when these new residents refused to contribute to the support of meeting house and minister.

The movement began in England in 1648 when George Fox, a weaver's son, having had an inward experience of the Holy Spirit, began to witness to this Inner Light. The Society of Friends that resulted dates to 1652 when Fox "brought convincement" to the household at Swarthmore Hall in Lancashire. Quakerism, as it began to be called, was feared by the Church of England because it minimized the liturgical and teaching functions of the ordained ministry. Persecution in the mother country as well as missionary zeal of the converts brought Quakers to Boston, where the Puritans and Separatists also disapproved of them. At first, Quakers were refused entrance when they came by ship, and a law was enacted against them. When adherents persisted, they were imprisoned. Finally four were hanged before protests succeeded in diminishing the persecution.

When Quakers came to Plymouth Colony, they settled on the Cape and were more humanely treated. Soon 17 families comprised this congregation. The present building, erected in 1810, is the third on the site. Sheds for horses and buggies, as well as an ancient cemetery, surround the simple two-story wooden structure. The plain sanctuary is divided in half by an amazing pulley-and-ship's-wheel contrivance located upstairs. A partition was lowered during separate business meetings of men and women.

(10) WEST BARNSTABLE

Continuing east in picturesque Route 6A, one travels by salt inlets and Sandy Neck, with its mammoth sand dunes. A marker locates the site of the first communion when an entire parish arrived at the Great Marshes of Barnstable. A stone foundation farther along marks the site of one of the earliest meeting houses.

West Parish Meeting House

West Parish Meeting House

Go south on Route 149 and you will come to the earliest Congregational church in America. Founded in 1616 in London, its members escaped harassment by traveling to Scituate in 1634. Then, in 1639, when Barnstable was founded, the parish settled in the Great Marshes.

When the east and west precincts of the town were established in 1717, this colonial meeting house was erected. The entrance on the broad side, and high pulpit with sounding board, testify to Puritan influence. Box pews, great oak timbers, and substantial three-sided balcony make it a must for anyone on religious pilgrimage.

(11) CENTERVILLE

Craigville Conference Center

On the southern side of Cape Cod, behind the half-moon curve of Craigville Beach, lies a tiny century-old village begun in 1872 as a Camp Meeting Ground by the former Christian denomination. On Christian Hill, at the head of the Village Green, is the Tabernacle. It retains this name, meaning tent church, because the sides open wide on summer Sundays giving one the sense of worshiping outdoors. A redwood chancel and Hook and Hastings tracker organ, plus conference side rooms, make it an ideal spot for conferences and retreats.

The Tabernacle, Craigville Conference Center

Old Indian Church, Mashpee

(12) MASHPEE

Old Indian Church

Proceeding westward on Route 28, one passes the old Indian church and its burying ground with headstones for Chief Big Elk and Deacon Zacheus Popmonet. The oldest church building on Cape Cod, it was built in 1684 on Briant's Neck in Santuit, where Richard Bourne, missionary to the Upper Cape Indians, held services. In 1717, the church was moved to its present site and has since been remodeled and renovated twice.

Originally Congregational, the church became Baptist under the leadership of the native American preacher Rev. Joseph (Blind Joe) Amos. Commemorative services are held here on special occasions meaningful to the Wampanoag people, whose town is Mashpee, and where many Wampanoags live today. This and Gay Head on Martha's Vineyard are two of the Indian heritage towns in the Commonwealth.

(13) MARTHA'S VINEYARD

A pleasant ocean trip is by ferry from Woods Hole to the offshore islands Nantucket and Martha's Vineyard. Though both are replete with history and fascinating to visit, Martha's Vineyard has two spiritual-heritage areas not to be missed.

Oak Bluffs Camp Meeting Grounds

The Methodists came to the Vineyard in 1835 and established a summer camp meeting. Tents eventually gave way to tiny houses with varieties of gingerbread decorations. The huge Tabernacle is the setting for religious services and entertainments each summer. It's a real treat to walk through the cottage colony, see 300 Victorian Gothic cottages, and enjoy the spiritual and cultural programs offered here.

Christiantown

On the western side of the island is a reminder of the first native inhabitants. When Governor Thomas Mayhew purchased the island in 1641, his son, Thomas, Jr., a clergyman, became concerned with carrying the gospel to the local tribes. He learned their language and established several congregations. Eventually, in West Tisbury a "Praying Indian" town called Christiantown was created.

Visitors may see the Indian church within which is a library. The small wooden-shingled building is open summers and is surrounded by an ancient burying ground. From there, on the road to Indian Hill, travelers may see a monument dedicated to the natives. About 16 miles away is Gay Head, the present Indian town, located near the famous Gay Head cliffs.

(14) STOUGHTON

Packard Manse

As you leave this area, go northwest on Routes 25 and 24. In an average New England town on a quiet street is Packard Manse, a very unaverage community, dedicated to promoting a deeper encounter with Jewish and Christian traditions. Here and in a satellite center in Roxbury, 17 people seek to bring belief and action together in their various callings. Established in 1957, and dedicated to reconciliation, the center spans all gaps from affluent to poor.

Ecumenical conferences with noted leaders, a gift shop selling handwork of Third World people and staffed by volunteers, and participation in worthy movements anywhere in the world, make this center a unique microcosm of Christianity in action. The gift shop is at 583 Plain Street in Stoughton and provides a consumer with a shopping facility that benefits the poor worldwide.

Northeastern Massachusetts

(15) GLOUCESTER

An interesting trip to spiritual-heritage sites in the northeastern section begins at Gloucester, another town settled in 1623 and long associated with fishing.

Our Lady of Good Voyage Church

Facing the sea from a high position between the twin towers of this Roman Catholic church stands a statue of Our Lady. In her left arm she cradles a full-rigged schooner. Her right hand is raised in blessing. Portuguese fishermen came early from the Azores to join the fishing fleet. Many remained and formed the nucleus of this congregation. Each year there is a blessing of the fleet and a memorial service for the fishermen lost at sea.

Berlin Chapel, Brandeis University

 WALTHAM

Brandeis University Chapels

On a 20-acre campus overlooking the river is one of the nation's youngest universities. Founded in 1948, the school's growth has been phenomenal. Named for the late Supreme Court Justice Louis Brandeis, it is the only Jewish-sponsored nonsectarian university in the country.

On the campus are three chapels designed by Max Abramovitz. The university's three chapels were dedicated to the reverence and understanding of the Jewish, Protestant, and Roman Catholic faiths. The chapels are placed around a heart-shaped reflecting pool and the façades are of glazed brick. Berlin Chapel (Jewish) is in the form of a sacred scroll. Bethlehem (Catholic) and Harlan (Protestant) Chapels are shaped like an open Bible. Although an outstanding architectural attraction, they are far more significant as an integral part of the fabric of the university.

Central Massachusetts

 HARVARD

Fruitlands Museums

Turning westward, as the early colonists did, the route goes slightly north on Route 110. On Prospect Hill Road is Fruitlands, where Bronson Alcott, father of Louisa May and a leader of the Transcendentalist movement, made an unsuccessful attempt to found a new religious community with social overtones in 1843. The restored 18th-century farmhouse contains objects belonging to the Alcott family as well as to Emerson and Thoreau.

On the site also is an Indian museum, a picture gallery of 19th-century itinerant artists, and an old Shaker house where exhibits of Shaker handcrafts, furniture, and other products point up the workmanship done in these unusual communities.

The Shakers, or "The United Society

of Believers in Christ's Second Coming (the Millennial Church)," began in England. Ann Lee Stanley (known as Mother Ann Lee) had been converted by Shaking Quakers. Such were her piety, trances, and visions that others as well as herself were convinced that Christ's Second Coming was occurring through her. In 1774, she came to America with eight followers, who included her husband and her brother.

Settling in Watervliet, New York, she began a communal-type-living community which soon spread. Between 1830 and 1850, the church numbered 6,000 persons living in 19 communities. One was in this Harvard-Shirley area. Shaker villages were idyllic. Clean functional buildings, graceful practical furniture, wonderful gardens and herbs as well as a place where wants of life were abundantly supplied drew many followers. Two of their most distinctive features were the call to celibacy and the group dance in worship.

(18) LANCASTER

A few miles south is this town, which sheltered Shakers originally, but now other groups predominate, particularly the Seventh-day Adventists.

Atlantic Union College

One of the schools of the Seventh-day Adventists, Atlantic Union College is also the site of Adventist meetings. The student body has grown in numbers through the years and there is now a pleasing country-like campus.

First Parish Church

On the town common stands this Unitarian church, a National Historic Landmark. Built in 1816 of Lancaster brick and slate, this is considered one of the most beautiful ecclesiastical structures in the country. Designed by noted early architect Charles Bulfinch, it contains a handsome pulpit, a Paul Revere bell and a church-artifacts exhibit.

(19) WORCESTER

Armenian Church of Our Saviour

Founded in 1890, this is the first Armenian Apostolic church to be established in America. Christianity was proclaimed the national religion of Armenia in A.D. 301 and it has remained so during centuries of domination. Massacres and persecutions in 1895 brought great waves of immigrants and some augmented the membership of this congregation.

The church, designed in the Armenian tradition, is built of brick. A central tower rises over lesser towers, much like the first Armenian cathedral built near Mt. Ararat early in the 4th century. Some 90 congregations now have about 275,000 members in this country.

(20) STURBRIDGE

Old Sturbridge Village

Farther west, where the Massachusetts Turnpike and Route 20 cross, there is a remarkable re-creation of a New England farming village of 150 years ago. Visitors can step back in time in this 200-acre, 40-building site and see how Americans worked and worshiped then. Dominating the Green, in back of the Liberty Pole, is the white-spired meeting house which was used mainly for worship but also for town meetings. Originally the Baptist Church in Sturbridge, built in 1832, it was moved to the village and restored. Box pews, center pulpit, oak-grain wooden finish, and two of the original chandeliers give this building an authentic aura.

In the village also is an old Quaker meeting house which was built in 1796 in Bolton. Given by the Society of Friends, it was moved to the village and restored. A two-story structure painted stone gray, it is typical of the plain, unadorned Quaker buildings. Inside are a three-sided gallery and elders benches that face the congregation.

Western Massachusetts

STOCKBRIDGE

First Congregational Church

Charter members of this church were Mohican Indians who, through their Chief Konkapot, arranged for a mission to be established in 1734. Rev. John Sergeant was first minister and he instructed in Christianity as well as teaching the children to read and write. The Mohicans deeded land to the Colony and a house of worship was erected with dedication in 1739. Sergeant's successor was the celebrated Rev. Jonathan Edwards. Field Chime Tower, which plays each summer evening, was erected in 1878 on the site of the first mission.

PITTSFIELD

Temple Anshe Amunim

Continue north to Pittsfield nestled in the hills. Here you will find a most unusual contemporary structure of award-winning architecture. A large cantilevered block design incorporates the activities of education, social activity, and worship. Huge boulders symbolize the rocky character of Mt. Sinai. A circular dome in the sanctuary reveals nature as created by the Almighty. Hebrew characters on the exterior mean "People of Faith."

In 1654, Jews fled from Portugal to New York City. This Portuguese-speaking group formed a congregation. Then in 1658, 15 Jewish families came to Newport, Rhode Island, from Holland. By 1800, American Jewry probably did not exceed 2,000 or 3,000, and only a few large cities had congregations. This congregation, established about 104 years ago, is part of the Reform movement which arose about the mid-1850s, in which the religious nature, as opposed to the national character, of Judaism was emphasized.

HANCOCK

Shaker Village

On Route 20, 5 miles west of Pittsfield, is a restored religious community which for 180 years was operated by the Shakers. Settled in 1780, the village has 19 buildings containing furniture, labor-saving tools, stove, and household items of exquisitely simple designs for which these people are famous. An amazing building is the 1826 Round Stone Barn, also a laundry, machine shop, and an 1820 Sisters' Shop, dairy, weaving and herb displays. Vacated in 1960 by the Shakers, 11 of the buildings may be visited.

RHODE ISLAND

Though New Hampshire and Maine had earlier settlements, Rhode Island, the tiniest state in New England, was next settled for *religious* reasons. Those fleeing from Puritan strictness created a tolerance that lead to a state of great religious diversity.

First to flee here from Boston was that individualistic bull-riding cleric, William Blackstone. Then in 1636, Roger Williams settled Providence, after having been banished from Massachusetts for his "heretical" beliefs of separation of church and state and freedom of conscience. Here he founded the first Baptist church in America.

Two years later Anne Hutchinson, ousted from the Bible Commonwealth for her antinomian views, settled Portsmouth along with her husband and a few friends. In 1639, some of these settled Newport, including William Coddington who would later become an influential Quaker.

A more radical religious individual, Samuel Gorton, who had worn out his welcome in Boston and in Plymouth, founded Warwick.

Roger Williams, seeing the necessity for legalizing and protecting the new colony, sailed to England where he gained a patent for "Providence Plantations" in 1644. On his return, he guided the four towns into a federal commonwealth which jealously guarded the principles of religious liberty and separation of church and state, the first government in modern history to make these tenets cardinal principles of its corporate existence.

Thus Rhode Island was open and welcoming to other religious exiles. Quakers, not accepted by the northern colony, were the first to come in 1657. Here they established a base for their missionary operations and later, in 1672, hosted their founder, George Fox, on a visit to America.

The first Jews arrived from Holland in 1658. Then, Anglicans, who also did not find a welcome in Puritan settlements, arrived in 1695.

The established church of Massachusetts had its eyes on this neighboring colony and its amazing multiplicity of religious strains. Apparently feeling compelled to see that their faith was represented, they sent a mission to Newport in 1695.

In this religious melting pot, there are varieties of spiritual heritage shrines, beginning with the site of Roger Williams's home in a park on Main Street and his grave and monument on Congdon Street.

(1) PROVIDENCE

First Baptist Church

The Baptist denomination had begun in England in 1612, with a church at Spitalfields, just outside London. Originally part of the Separatist movement, members had concluded that baptism was not for infants nor by sprinkling but, ought to be undergone by choice "by diping ye Body into ye Water, resembling Burial & riseing again."

This oldest Baptist church in America, as well as the oldest of any denomination in the state, was founded by Rev. Roger Williams of Salem and others of like persuasion from Boston. Endeavoring to establish a new order in harmony with New Testament teachings, the small company adopted baptism by immersion. In March 1639, Ezekiel Holliman, who had been a member of Williams's Salem church, baptized Williams, who then baptized ten others. Adopting no creed, they offered to all men "distressed of conscience" the priceless boon of soul-liberty.

Meeting at first in homes, the members had no meeting house until 1700. A second, built in 1726, preceded the present commodious and graceful structure built in 1774-1775 on North Main Street, approximately ¼ mile south of the original site. It was built larger than needed, in order to accommodate Brown University commencements. The unusually beautiful steeple rises 185 feet and is modeled from designs by James Gibbs, a pupil of Sir Christopher Wren. It was built on the ground in telescopic sections by ship's carpenters who were idled by the shipping blockade imposed by the English during the Revolutionary War.

Beneficent Congregational Church

Colloquially referred to as Round Top, this early Greek Revival building on Weybosset Street was organized as the First Congregational Church in 1743 with Rev. Josiah Cotton as minister. The Massachusetts Bay Colony had noted the variety of religious persuasions harbored by their southern neighbors and, in 1721, wrote to inquire "if the preaching of our ministers in Providence might be acceptable." The answering epistle thundered of "wolves in sheep's clothing" but nevertheless soon the church was "gathered and constituted."

The first meeting house was erected in 1744 when a group of parishioners cut timbers and erected a rude church on this spot. The present church building was dedicated January 1, 1810. Its congregation early emphasized ecumenicity and pioneered in senior-citizen housing.

(2) PORTSMOUTH

Heading south on Route 114, travelers will come to another historic village, settled in 1638 by Anne Hutchinson and her adherents. They first landed at Founder's Brook. On Pudding Rock is a bronze tablet with a copy of their Portsmouth Compact. Founders Memorial Grove is a pleasant reminder of that first event.

(3) NEWPORT

No trip to Rhode Island religious shrines would be complete without at least a day spent in Newport, home of several major faiths. Their shrines, beautifully restored and in use, are set in the middle of a thriving community. Settled in 1639 by William Coddington and John Clarke, it became a colonial seaport and still gives that effect, with its streets of restored buildings. Though it has an elaborate resort section with magnificent estates like Belcourt Castle and The Breakers, its original spiritual heritage still predominates.

Friends Meeting House

At 30 Marlborough Street is a reminder of the Quakers, who received refuge in 1657 in Newport when they were refused entrance to other colonies. The earliest part of the old structure dates to 1699, which makes it one of the earliest Friends' structures in America. The north ell, built in 1704, is known as the ship room because of its construction and is now a museum.

Tauro Synagogue

At 72 Tauro Street is the oldest synagogue in America and a National Historic Shrine. Sephardim Jews came to Newport from Spain and Portugal as early as 1658 and were joined later by Ashkenazim Jews from Central and Eastern European countries. Eventually the two groups mediated their traditional differences and formed one congregation, now the Congregation Jeshuat Israel. It was named for Abraham Tauro, an early leader and benefactor. The synagogue was built in 1759. An earlier synagogue, in New York, was demolished and the Tauro remains today the oldest synagogue in the country. The interior designed by Peter Harrison, is acclaimed as an architectural masterpiece. George Washington attended services here and later wrote: "May the children of the stock of Abraham . . . continue to enjoy the goodwill of the other inhabitants; while everyone shall sit in safety under his own vine and fig tree."

Trinity Church

"A supreme and matchless reminder of colonial America," this church is the fourth to have been established north of the Mason-Dixon line. Organized in 1698 largely by Huguenots who had fled persecution in France and by colonists loyal to the Church of England, the congregation's first building was erected in 1726. Richard Munday, master carpenter, incorporated into it important features of Sir Christopher Wren's London churches. It contains many treasures: a baptismal font of beautiful workmanship hammered from a single piece of silver; the first church bell sounded in New England; the second organ in America, installed in 1733; and an altarpiece dating from the same year. Eighty books received from England in 1701 formed the first parish library of Rhode Island.

As you leave the city, note the birthplace of Rev. William Ellery Channing, Unitarian leader, in a house built before 1785 at School and Mary streets.

NORTH KINGSTOWN

Old Saint Paul's Church

The trip across the bay via two bridges and historic Jamestown Island is a scenic interval. Turn north on Route 1 to Wickford, part of North Kingstown. Here you will find a two-story wooden church with arched windows, built in 1707, which originally stood at "The Platform" on Congdon Hill near the old church cemetery. Reputed to be the oldest Episcopal church in New England, it was moved in 1800 to Main Street in Wickford.

The silver communion service still in use was presented to the church by Queen Anne in 1710.

Before leaving the tiniest state in the country, you might also stop in Cumberland at Study Hill, Lonsdale, where the site of the home of Rhode Island's first settler (1635), Rev. William Blackstone, is marked.

NEW HAMPSHIRE

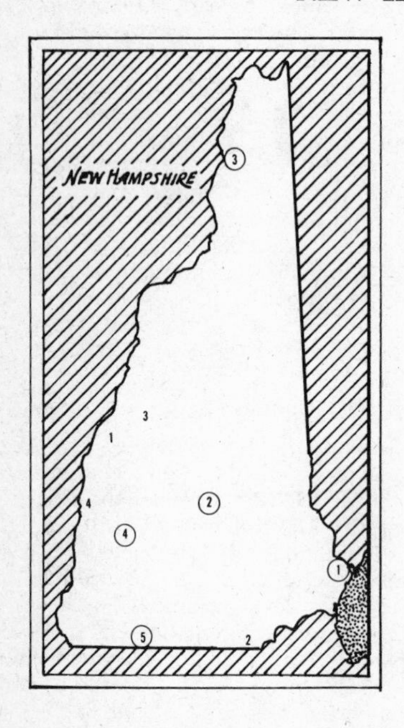

Several tiny seacoast fishing and trading settlements began New Hampshire's history only three years after the Pilgrims landed. In 1623 Strawbery Banke, later called Portsmouth, was begun along with Rye. Religious controversy in the Massachusetts Bay Colony also propelled settlers northward, for in 1638 Rev. John Wheeler, a sympathizer of the banished Anne Hutchinson, founded Exeter.

Congregationalism was in effect the established church in the state's early years, though there were a few other communions, such as Anglicans and Quakers. Gradually, as there was a large influx of ethnic groups and other denominations, religious tension grew between them and members of the unofficial state church. The controversies were ultimately settled by the 1819 Act of Toleration and the religious life of the state became diverse. Our tour begins in the southwest corner of the state, its oldest section.

PORTSMOUTH

Strawbery Banke

The fine old houses and narrow streets of this early colonial seafaring community remind us of its antiquity. Nowhere is this better seen than in this historic preservation project encompassing 10 acres and over 30 buildings in the Old South End. Excellent examples of Federal and Colonial architecture may be seen as well as demonstrations of early colonial skills like weaving, spinning, and pewter-, rug-, and cabinet-making.

Shaker Village, Canterbury

St. John's Church

On Chapel Street is St. John's Church, which is a successor to Queen's Chapel established in 1732. It houses the Brattle organ, reputedly the oldest pipe organ in the country. It also has one of the four copies of the "Vinegar Bible." Printed in 1717, this version has the word "vineyard" misspelled as "vinegar."

(2) CANTERBURY

Shaker Village

Going north on Route 106, turn west to view another of the amazing Shaker centers, one of the two remaining active. One is impressed by the simple grandeur of the small community. Just a handful remain of the colony that once numbered 400. Founded in 1792, it has left a legacy of crafts and dignified New Testament faith.

(3) COLEBROOK

Shrine of Our Lady of Grace

Close to the state's tip and just off Route 3 is a lovely garden with outdoor altar and beautifully landscaped Stations of the Cross. During warm months, it is open for services and is a reminder of the Catholic heritage which came late to this state by way of Roman Catholic settlements in Canada.

(4) WASHINGTON

Seventh-day Adventist Church

William Miller, a Baptist preacher who prophesied the Second Coming of Christ October 22, 1844, is credited with beginning the movement that led to the Seventh-day Adventist denomination. A group of his followers became the nucleus for the present church, after the fateful day passed uneventfully. The simple wooden structure built in 1843 is reputed to be the first Seventh-day Adventist church and is the scene of pilgrimages from around the globe.

(5) RINDGE

Cathedral of the Pines

This outdoor shrine for people of all faiths was created in memory of Sanderson Sloan, killed in World War

II, and is dedicated to all American war dead. The Congress of the United States voted recognition of this as the Altar of the Nation. It is an international shrine where 50 different faiths have held services.

Its Hilltop House has flags, relics, and art objects from around the world. The Memorial Bell Tower is a national memorial for American women war dead. This altar contains stones of historic and geological interest.

MAINE

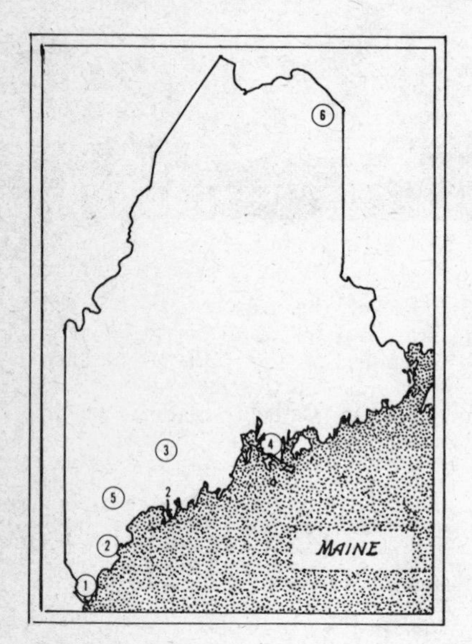

Traders were the first inhabitants of Maine, along with two aborted French mission communities. In 1603 to 1605, a fort was built at the mouth of the St. Croix River in the area then named Acadia by the French. Later Jesuits from France briefly established a fortified mission on Mount Desert Island.

It was the English who finally colonized most of the state, and brought their churches with them. The first was George Popham who settled at the mouth of the Kennebec River in 1607-1608. The first permanent settlement, however, was at York in 1624, followed by Scarborough and Portland in the early 1630s.

Separatists arrived in 1628 when Pilgrims John Alden and Miles Standish established a trading post at Augusta, for fur and pelt trading with the Indians.

Southern Maine

(1) KITTERY

First Congregational Church

Though records show that there was a church here as early as 1659, this Congregational parish was organized in 1714. The graceful center pulpit dates from then as do two old box pews. Sir William Pepperrell held one of these pews, and gave the silver christening bowl. A church founder, he had been made a baron for winning the siege of Louisburg on Cape Breton Island (Nova Scotia).

The parsonage of the church is Maine's oldest, dating from 1759.

(2) SOUTH PORTLAND

Church of the Exaltation of the Holy Cross

The original church in this area was Roman Catholic, near Eastport at St. Croix Island. It was dedicated in 1604, followed by missions at Mt. Desert in 1613 and at Pentagoet in 1633. The contemporary building dedicated in 1963 in this community is a reminder of those early dedicated missionaries. A memorial window commemorates the Indians and the missions.

The exterior has a breathtaking, slender tower of mosaics, which portrays the life of Christ from the Nativity to the Resurrection. It is formed of 350,000 pieces of Venetian glass.

3 AUGUSTA

Fort Western

The *Mayflower's* shallop sailed up the Kennebec River in 1625 and the Pilgrim party traded corn for furs and pelts. Recognizing the financial value of a trading post, the Pilgrims established one here in 1628. Governor Bradford recorded that "they now erected a house up above in ye river in ye most convenient place for trade." In 1634, John Alden and John Howland were in charge of the palisaded log structure. Trade continued here for about 30 more years, bringing financial success to the Pilgrims.

Fort Western, built on the shores of the river in 1775, is the only fort in Maine that predates the Revolution. It was erected as a stronghold and trading post. The main building still stands. The fenced area includes two blockhouses. Sixteen rooms of exhibits give a fine idea of the life in those days. In the early days all public meetings including religious services were held at the fort. It is a fine example of early fortifications.

4 CASTINE

Ancient Castine, located on a peninsula in Penobscot Bay farther north along the coast, dates to a French fishing station in 1556 and a French fort erected in 1613. The town was named for Baron de Castin who lived among the Indians in 1667 and married a sachem's daughter. He converted many natives to Catholicism. The first English settlement came in 1760. This is the only town in Maine to have existed under four flags: Dutch, French, British, and American.

First Parish Church Meeting House

The inhabitants had almost as many successive changes in religion as in flags. The lovely Unitarian church, with its white steeple and cupola, is similar to many built by the new colonists on their town greens. Native worship, Catholic missions, and Separatists or Congregational preaching took place here.

This meeting house was the scene of many civil and criminal trials. The most noted was the trial for murder of Peol Susup in 1817. The sachem made a successful plea, saying in part: "One God make us all. . . . The white man and the red man must always be friends. The Great Spirit is our Father."

5 POLAND SPRING

Shaker Village

At Sabbathday Lake on Route 26 is one of the last communities of the Shakers. Dating to 1783, four of the 17 buildings are open for tours, including the 1794 meeting house with original wood and the only remaining Shaker herb house. The Shakers are renowned for the elegant proportions, clean lines, and functional beauty of tools, furniture, and buildings they designed and made. Manuscripts and photographs are collected in a large library. A few Shakers still live in this austere community. They support themselves by selling herbs, weaving wool rugs, and leasing the orchards.

Northern Maine

NEW SWEDEN

Swedish Museum

Maine's William Thomas, Jr., consul to Sweden under Abraham Lincoln, arranged for a colony of Swedish immigrants to settle in the state. Fifty-one settlers came in 1870 and created a town out of heavily forested wilderness. The U.S. Board of Immigration had begun a road and some cabins. By late September, townspeople had raised a two-story capitol. Downstairs were offices and supply rooms. Upstairs was a room used as church, schoolhouse, and town hall.

A thunderbolt caused a fire that destroyed this landmark in 1971, though the priceless historical collection was saved. A replica was completed in 1974, and this historic museum stands again at the crossroads park where it was first erected.

Gustav Adolph Lutheran Church

The Swedish Evangelical Lutheran Congregation was formed in 1871 and a church building erected and dedicated by 1880. There were soon daughter churches at Stockholm and Caribou. The Swedish Midsummer Eve Festival has been celebrated regularly in this simple structure with Gothic touches and cross-tipped steeple.

CONNECTICUT

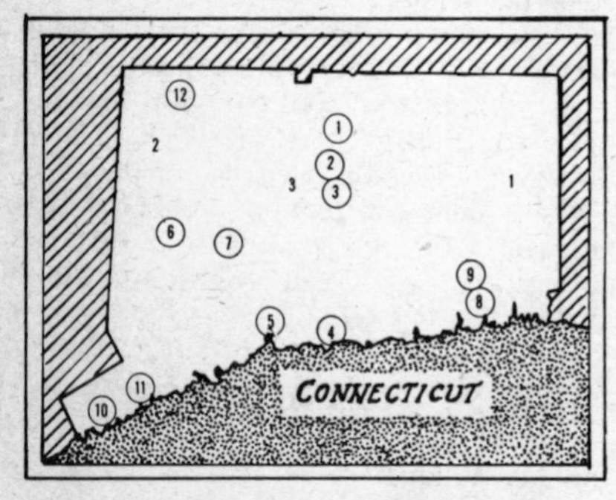

New England's second Bible Commonwealth was established principally by Massachusetts colonists unhappy with the Puritan's strict requirement that church membership was necessary for citizenship, though the desire for more land contributed, undoubtedly, to dissatisfaction. Rev. Thomas Hooker and incoming settlers split off from his congregation to found the other towns. Then he moved and "planted" Hartford and other towns split off.

Forerunners came to Windsor in 1633 and Wethersfield in 1635. At Hartford there was already a small Dutch Colony founded in 1633. The three new English towns banded together in 1639 under the "Fundamental Orders of Connecticut," often referred to as the grandfather of the U.S. Constitution. It contained no religious requirement for citizenship. As the English towns grew, Dutch influence waned.

Meanwhile, in 1638, Puritans settled southward in New Haven and declared the Scriptures to be the only supreme law in civil affairs. Religious tensions arose between the upper and lower colonies and continued for three decades. Finally a Royal Charter united the two in 1662 and eventually both colonies became as one, no doubt drawn together by the conflicts with England.

West Central Connecticut

WINDSOR

First Church

If we follow the path of those early religious pioneers, we will begin our pilgrimage to Connecticut going south through the central Connecticut River valley to Windsor, one of the oldest in the state. Settled by William Holmes and a small band of Pilgrims from Plymouth, it had at first only a fortified trading post beginning in 1633. The Congregational church on Palisade Avenue dates from the first settlers when it was gathered, but the present building was erected in 1794. Adjacent is an old burial ground which contains the state's oldest dated tombstone.

(2) HARTFORD

Center Church

Proceeding south, we come to Hartford, capital city and another of the state's earliest towns. At this Congregational historic church, founded in 1632 and now part of the United Church of Christ, is a monument to the city's founders. The cemetery, used from 1640 to 1803, is full of historic gravestones marking resting places of first settlers. Rev. Thomas Hooker "planted" this parish and town.

St. Joseph's Cathedral

On Farmington Avenue stands a monumental church of contemporary architecture which is the mother church of the Roman Catholic archdiocese. Replacing an earlier cathedral which burned in 1956, the structure is a building both in the past and in the present. There is a reminder of the traditional in the reredos, altar pieces, and mosaics. The present is symbolized by clean modern lines and telescoping tower. There are 26 huge stained-glass windows lining the nave. Stations of the Cross are cut into the piers which form the side aisles. Over the three bronze entrance doors is a statue of Christ reaching out His arms to all the world.

(3) WETHERSFIELD

First Church of Christ

Another of Connecticut's oldest towns is a few miles farther south where Route 91 leaves the river. Here in the old Congregational church are timbers from the first meeting house built in 1685. The cost of a brick church was high; so, when it was planned in 1761-1764, the town meeting voted "to accept in lieu of money, the red onions grown and shipped from this place." Consequently it has been referred to as the Onion Church.

A new clock and bell, ordered in 1784, were also paid for by onions. The bell was delivered from New Haven and was rung in each community through which it passed!

(4) GUILFORD

Henry Whitfield State Historical Museum

Built about 1639, this house is believed to be the oldest made of stone in New England. Rev. Henry Whitfield, Puritan leader and the town founder, built this from stone quarried nearby. The building is commodious and served the first residents as fort, church, and meeting hall. It is a fine example of the English architecture which the Puritans enjoyed in Surrey, England, before their pilgrimage for religious freedom. Restored in 1936, it contains 17th-century furniture and other colonial antiques and artifacts.

(5) NEW HAVEN

When the Puritans arrived in 1638, they laid out a town of nine equal squares, with the central one reserved as a green for the public. On it are three churches.

Center Church on the Green

First services were held in the open air but soon a Congregational meeting house was erected. The present building is the fourth on the site and was completed in 1814. It is built over part of the original burial ground, so in its crypt can be seen 137 historic gravestones beginning with the date 1687. The handsome brick structure was copied from a London church. Tiffany windows inside depict the colony's founding. It was then designated First Church of Christ in New Haven.

Trinity Church on the Green

The southernmost of the three churches on the Green, this was founded in

1752 on Church Street. The present Episcopal church was built here in 1816. The Gothic Revival stone church has Tiffany stained-glass windows, an Aeolian Skinner organ, and an impressive vaulted interior.

United Church on the Green

This Federal-style brick building with octagonal lantern tower was erected in 1815. It was the second Congregational church to be erected on the Green and contains the first Hilldebrand Tracker organ in the country. It is famous as the site of Henry Ward Beecher's address to 80 abolitionists before their departure for Kansas to join John Brown, whose raid on Harper's Ferry was one of the sparks that inflamed the Civil War. The men had been supplied with Bibles and rifles by the congregation.

Yale University

The second Puritan school to prepare an educated ministry was founded in 1701 as the Collegiate School. Branford, Killingworth, and Old Saybrook were its homes before New Haven became the permanent campus in 1716. In 1718 it was named for Elihu Yale, East India trader and generous donor.

Sterling Quadrangle, on Prospect Street, is the home of Yale Divinity School. Designed in rectangular fashion around a central green, it is headed by the lovely chapel. Of brick in colonial design, the various buildings are connected by arcades.

St. Thomas More House is the Roman Catholic Chapel and Center for the University. Named for the patron saint of lawyers, the center has many meetings, seminars, and social activities.

(6) WOODBURY

Glebe House

Drive west to Woodbury where on Hollow Road stands a house erected in 1690 and enlarged in 1745 to 1750. During a secret meeting here in 1783, Samuel Seabury was elected the first American Bishop of the Episcopal Church. Since this was after the Revolution, this former chaplain in a Loyalist regiment was denied consecration in England. Finally he sailed to Aberdeen, Scotland, where he was officially consecrated and returned to America and his bishop's duties. Shortly after, the Protestant Episcopal Church in the U.S.A. was organized. The English Prayer Book was revised, with civil authority substituted for the British sovereign.

(7) WATERBURY

Holy Land U.S.A.

On Fuller Street, this replica of Bethlehem and Jerusalem has been created in miniature on a terraced hilltop overlooking the city and the Naugatuck valley. A monumental work of personal devotion, this display, built slowly and by hand, also includes a chapel, Peace-through-Love Lending Library, and gift shop. A project of John Greco and begun 18 years ago, the exhibit endeavors to show the life of Christ. Probably the most impressive scene is the crucifixion.

Eastern Connecticut

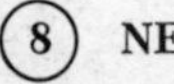

NEW LONDON

John Winthrop Monument

The tour of the eastern part of Connecticut should begin where a group of Puritan families under John Winthrop the younger settled in 1646. On Bulkeley Square is a statue of the founder done by Bela Lyon Pratt. Winthrop was governor of the colony from 1657 to 1676.

"Ye Ancientest Burial Grounds" are located nearby and date from 1653. At Main and Mill Streets is the old gristmill built by Winthrop and rebuilt in 1712. The old waterwheel can still be seen.

(9) UNCASVILLE

Tantaquidgeon Lodge Indian Museum

When the first English settlers arrived, they found the area inhabited by the Mohican Indian tribe. Uncas was one of their great chieftains. On Route 32 is this museum housing artifacts and objects made by the Mohicans. Behind the museum are replicas of the long and round houses typical of their early dwellings. An 1831 meeting house is still used.

Two miles north is the home of the Mohicans and of Samson Occum, the first Indian minister ordained in New England.

Western Connecticut

(10) STAMFORD

First Presbyterian Church

Spiritual descendants of Swiss John Calvin and Scots John Knox, the Presbyterians came to America in the 17th century to escape restrictions placed on their religious liberty. Scots and Irish came around 1700. By 1717 there were several congregations in New England and south to Virginia. Not many settled in New England because of an agreement with the clergy of the Puritan colonies which allotted different areas to each group.

One of the outstanding churches in the country is this Presbyterian structure on Bedford Street. A magnificent edifice of contemporary design, it is shaped like a fish, an early Christian symbol. The backbone stands six stories high. The elongated windows of stained glass are carved to give texture to the light. These depict the crucifixion, resurrection, and Christ's teachings. An outside wall of more than 100 stones tells the history of Christianity, while a walk leading to the sanctuary has names of Christian leaders inscribed.

(11) WESTPORT

The Unitarian Church in Westport

In 1949, the First Unitarian Society of Fairfield County was organized with 12 members. In 1960, it built the "new ship church" (as contrasted with the old one in Hingham, Massachusetts) and changed its name accordingly. The roof line is a breathtaking sweep upward which is reminiscent of sails. Light pours down a transparent strip between the two roof sections. (See next page.)

(12) NORFOLK

Evergreen Community

Nestled in the hills of the northwest corner of the state is a cluster of buildings belonging to the Society of Brothers, also called the Bruderhof. Other communities in this country are in Rifton, New York, and Farmington, Pennsylvania. Members live in these communities because they feel it is a way to true brotherhood. "Each individual has his place on the common tree of the community. . . . If Christ

Westport Unitarian Church

is the root, the fruit is good." Each Bruderhof has its own school through the eighth grade. In baby house tots are cared for while the mother helps with the communal tasks, though parents have the main responsibility. Like the other Bruderhofs, visitors seeking an alternative way of life are welcome; a week's notice for a stay is suggested.

VERMONT

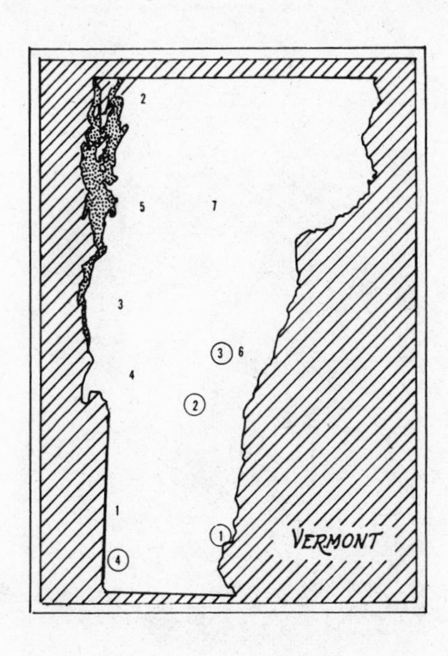

Though French Catholics had a tentative toehold for a brief while on the shores of Lake Champlain, it was the English coming in from the southeast who settled the green hills of Vermont. Fort Dummer, near Brattleboro, was the site of the first permanent settlement. With the new residents came the Congregational churches, followed in turn by Baptists, Methodists, and Catholics, along with the others in later years.

Eastern Vermont

(1) PUTNEY

On the Connecticut River is a 1753 community with several spiritual heritage routes. In 1932 the nonprofit Experiment in International Living was formed to foster international understanding. Each year about 5,000 people are enabled to live with families of differing culture through this socially oriented organization.

Here also may be seen the residence of John Humphrey Noyes, who as a divinity student in 1834, became a Perfectionist. He established a small colony where socialism through Christian love was to bring the Kingdom of God. In 1846 because of community pressure, he left to found New York's Oneida Community.

Our Lady of Mercy

The graceful brick colonial structure is a symbol of ecumenism, for it once housed a Methodist congregation. The two-sectioned steeple with cupola is typically New England yet is a reminder of the early Catholic heritage.

(2) PLYMOUTH

Union Christian Church

President Calvin Coolidge worshiped in this simple white frame meeting house. In the complex also is his restored birthplace.

(3) SHARON

Joseph Smith Birthplace Memorial

A memorial shaft to the Mormon prophet rises 38½ feet to commemorate the years of his life. The information center has exhibits and a movie telling the story of Smith and the Church of Jesus Christ Latter Day Saints.

Western Vermont

(4) BENNINGTON

Old First Church

The oldest church in the state, this parish dates from 1762 when 21 pioneers settled here. The surrounding graveyard is as old and contains graves of American and Hessian soldiers who fell in the Battle of Bennington in 1777. It was from this town that Ethan Allen led his Green Mountain Boys to resist New York staters who were trying to annex Vermont.

The present fine frame structure was designed by Lavius Fillmore. The interior, which has gone through several remodelings, was restored in 1937. High pulpit, box pews, and three-sided gallery make it an exceptionally beautiful church. Plaques honoring state figures hang in the church. Poet Robert Frost is buried in the graveyard.

II.
EASTERN GATEWAY

NEW YORK

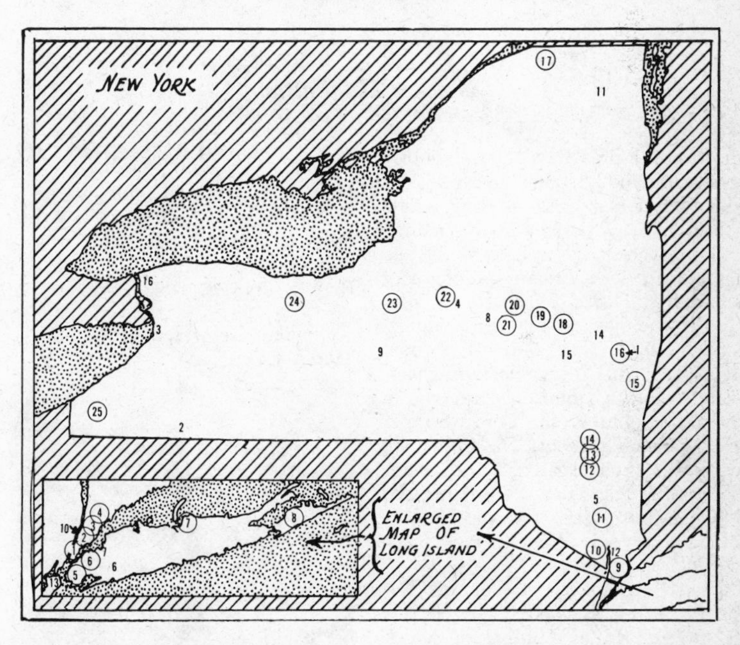

Religiously speaking New York began and has continued in diversity. Missionaries and their churches came along with the Dutch traders in the southern part of the state, and the French explorers in the northern section.

In 1609, Henry Hudson sailed his ship *Half Moon* up the majestic river that bears his name, claiming all the territory for the Dutch. By 1614, a permanent settlement was begun at Fort Orange (Albany), and there were several trading posts on Manhattan Island. The Dutch Reformed Church followed the traders, sent by the Dutch West India Company. Consistent with the government's tolerant policy in Holland, the Dutch Company opened its doors to colonists of other races and religious persuasions. America's melting pot soon began. In 1643, Father Isaac Joques, a Jesuit priest, reported that the 500 inhabitants of Manhattan spoke 18 different tongues. Then in 1664, the struggle between the Dutch and the English began for the strategic colony. It ended with an English victory in 1674. New Amsterdam was renamed New York and Anglicans began to establish churches.

Lutherans, Quakers, Jews, and Jesuits had already joined the Dutch Reformed denomination and had built small villages and churches, eventually fanning out from the waterfront in lower Manhattan as the population grew. When King's College (Columbia University) was chartered in 1754, the tradition of religious tolerance was continued, for no person was to be excluded from "equal liberty and advantage of education" because of his religious affiliations.

Religious diversity increased both in the Manhattan area and throughout the state with the immigration of people fleeing persecution and wars in Europe. German Protestants arrived from the Palatine, settling the Mohawk and Hudson valleys. Lutherans and German Reformed churches were established. Presbyterians, Quakers, and Congregationalists arrived from New England. The French Catholics continued their early settlements in the north and west.

Greater Manhattan

A spiritual pilgrimage to this religiously diverse state should begin in New York City, where the first trading posts began in 1619. Peter Minuit was named director of the fledgling colony in 1626 when he made his famous purchase of Manhattan for $24. Two lay "comforters of the sick" were sent to minister to the settlers of Dutch Reformed persuasion in 1626. Rev. Jonas Michaelius an ordained minister, arrived in 1628 and celebrated the Lord's Supper with 50 persons present. The Collegiate Church was then organized with Peter Minuit as the first elder. Michaelius also had separate services for the French-speaking Walloons. Worship took place in the loft of an old mill.

During the ministry of Dominie Evardus Bogardus, a wooden church was built on the tip of Manhattan which was replaced with a stone church in 1642. In 1664, British ships sailed up the Bay and took the town. In 1696, under an English edict, a Dutch Reformed church was allowed, followed the next year by the establishment of Trinity, the first Anglican church in New York City. Thus began the many hued religious scene which became as varied as the stained-glass windows that adorn the city's religious structures today.

(1) LOWER MANHATTAN

Since this area is so complex, the tourist should obtain a detailed city map in order to seek out the following spiritual heritage sites which are tucked amid the skyscrapers.

Collegiate Reformed Protestant Dutch Church

Marble Collegiate Church

Spiritual descendants of the first Dutch Reformed congregation gather in this church, one of the truly great spiritual heritage sites of the country. Daughter of the Reformed Church in Holland, it was organized in 1628, only nine years after the mother church was established by distinguished European church leaders who fled to Holland during the persecution period.

The daughter church in New Amsterdam continued the tradition of welcoming members of other denominations. It is considered to be the oldest Protestant church in America having a continuous organization. The Collegiate Church maintains four places of worship in Manhattan, each with its own distinctive program and ministry.

Middle Collegiate Church

Marble Church, at 29th Street and Fifth Avenue, was erected in 1854 and its ongoing program includes the Foundation for Christian Living, a global ministry by mail, and the Institute of Religion and Health.

Other places of worship are *Middle Congregation* at Second Avenue and Seventh Street, *West End Collegiate Church* at West End Avenue and Seventy-Seventh Street, and *Fort Washington Church* at Eighty-First Street and Fort Washington Avenue. *Bethany Memorial,* formerly connected, was separately incorporated in 1944. At the West End Church can be seen four 17th-century millstones formerly used in the mill over which the first congregation gathered.

Trinity Church

In the heart of the financial district at Broadway and Wall Street, dwarfed by surrounding skyscrapers, is the site occupied by Trinity Church (Episcopal) since 1697. The most valuable church property in the world, its tree-shaded yard surrounds a Gothic-style building dedicated in 1846. King's College, the forerunner of Columbia University, began here in an earlier structure. The present tower is a handsome spire holding three 18th-century bells. White marble altar, bronze doors, and graves of Alexander Hamilton and Robert Fulton are noteworthy. The first of the Anglican communions in the area to continue to this day, it was soon joined by others on Long Island and in Westchester County.

St. Paul's Chapel

At Broadway and Fulton Street is the oldest public building in Manhattan. Built in 1766 of stone and completed in Georgian style, it resembles St. Martin-in-the-Fields in London. It is noted for the handwrought woodwork, hardware, and 14 chandeliers of Waterford cut glass. George Washington attended this church regularly after his inauguration and his pew is so marked.

John Street Church

Many of the relics of Methodism are on display in this United Methodist Church, at 44 John Street, which was built in 1786. Philip Embury is credited with organizing the first Methodist Society in America when he began preaching the gospel of free grace in his own home in 1766. When the Society grew, a sail loft was rented; then a licensed preacher from England, Capt. Thomas Webb, began preaching. In 1767, the group erected this building, first called Wesley Chapel.

The Methodist movement began in 1729 in Oxford, England, when John and Charles Wesley, and their friend George Whitefield, organized societies dedicated to personal piety and social service, especially the needs of the underprivileged, on a democratic basis. They preached in barns, workshops, fields, and homes, in an effort to revitalize society, and have been credited with defusing the flammable industrial situation.

 MID-MANHATTAN

United Nations Chapel

The 39-story glass and marble Secretariat building rises dramatically at the 18-acre United Nations headquarters by the East River. Although the entire complex with its guided tours in many languages is well worth visiting, our religious heritage theme particularly highlights the meditation chapel. The plaque outside reads, "This chapel is devoted to peace and those who are giving their lives for peace. It is a room of quiet where only thoughts should speak." Though small, it is impressive and symbolic of the religious principles undergirding life on this globe.

St. Patrick's Cathedral

Just across from Rockefeller Center on Fifth Avenue is one of the largest churches in the country. St. Patrick's Catholic Church, begun in 1858 and consecrated in 1910, seats 2,500 and has 15 side altars. Gothic in design, its twin towers rise 330 feet. There are 70 magnificent stained-glass windows, with blue predominating in those over the high altar. Constantly filled with people, it is a mecca for people of all faiths.

Central Synagogue

Jews first came to New York, arriving in the Manhattan area, in 1654. They held services in their homes, though they purchased a cemetery as early as 1656. Their first synagogue was erected in 1729. By the 1850s there were 14 synagogues. So many ethnic groups arrived from Europe in the next 50 years, however, that over 300 separate congregations emerged.

Central Synagogue of Moorish and Gothic architecture, erected in 1872 at 123 E. 55th St. is of brownstone and has minarets and onion-shaped domes. It is the second oldest now remaining in the nation and American Judaism's oldest continuously used house of worship.

Temple Emanu-el

Synagogue life in America took three directions. Orthodox Jews maintained a strictness in their observance of laws, foods, Hebrew language, and communal society. Conservative Judaism became less rigid than orthodoxy but remained more traditional than Reform. Reform Judaism reinterpreted Jewish practice and doctrine in the light of the new era in America.

This Reform temple at Fifth Avenue and 65th Street, was dedicated in 1930. It is basilica style and over its three entrance doors is a beautiful rose window. The temple seats 2,500 and has side galleries with marble columns. The Ark and seven-branch menorahs are backed by beautiful mosaics.

Yoga Society of New York

The Society's New York headquarters at 100 West 72nd Street is open to visitors. Lectures and Hatha Yoga programs are given several times a week. Founded in 1957, it opened the Ananda Ashram in Monroe, New York, in July 1964; this also has many programs open to the public. The Society is a center for the investigation and practice of the science and philosophy of Yoga. It provides a place for the serious Yoga student to live and study.

Greek Orthodox Cathedral

A Byzantine Cathedral at 319 East 74th Street is spiritual center for the Greek Orthodox Diocese of North and South America. Offices are at 8-10 East 79th Street.

After World War I, there was a large influx of Greek immigrants, which continued into the 1920s. As the communities were established, priests were sent from Greece. Some Greeks came to New York earlier, however, and a Sunday school was organized by 1912. In 1922, the charter was granted for the organization of the archdiocese for this hemisphere, and thereafter priests have been assigned by the New York headquarters.

The cathedral is undergoing restoration and its beautiful mosaics are being given new life. Many of these are faithful replicas of iconography dating to the 7th to 10th centuries.

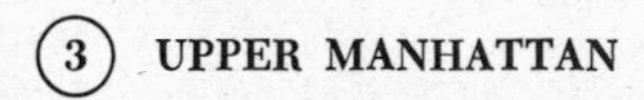

3 UPPER MANHATTAN

Jewish Museum

Proceeding northward, at 1109 Fifth Avenue, the religious pilgrim will enjoy a stop at Jewish Museum, once the home of Felix M. Warburg, built in 1908. In its permanent collection are artifacts, art works, photographs, textiles, and ceramics which illustrate the past history, the contemporary life, and the spirit of the Jewish people. There is a 1,600-year-old gold kiddush cup, an 18th-century silver menorah, and a spice container dating about 1550.

Cathedral of St. John the Divine

At Amsterdam Avenue and 112th Street is a Gothic cathedral which will be the largest in the world when completed. Begun in 1892, this Episcopal church is still in process of construction with front towers and central spire yet to be built. The nave is of breathtaking proportions and is surmounted by a tiled dome over the center crossing. The baptistry houses a 15-foot font carved of French marble. The seven chapels represent nationalities predominating in the city in 1892. Paintings and tapestries enhance the interior.

Riverside Church

At 490 Riverside Drive, overlooking the Hudson, stands Riverside Church, a monumental limestone structure of Gothic style. Of Baptist and Congregational origins, it is presently interdenominational. The main section of the church was opened in 1930, and the south wing was built in 1959. The tower, which rises 400 feet has a notable 74-bell carillon. Visitors are warned to make their tower tours between bell chimes or wear ear plugs! A special feature of the church is the collection of carved likenesses of famous persons in the chancel screen and in the west portal.

Interchurch Center

Headquarters for some denominations and for many church-related organizations, this stately structure rises 19 stories on Morningside Heights. The National Council of Churches' offices are here along with the American offices of the World Council of Churches. Rising on the western shore of Manhattan, it symbolizes ecumenicity among religious communions as the United Nations complex on the East River symbolizes unity among nations.

A chapel, manuscript exhibit, and art collection, along with meeting rooms, make the building useful for general meetings as well as administrative purposes. A Hall of Ministers, perpetuating the memory and Christian service of clergy, connects with Riverside Church where additional facilities are available.

The Cloisters

Situated in Fort Tryon Park at 190th Street and Fort Washington Avenue and commanding a magnificent view up the Hudson River is a special branch of the Metropolitan Museum of Art with exhibits based on a spiritual theme. Medieval man's devotion to God is highlighted in a monastery-like atmosphere throughout the authentic medieval rooms from France and Spain. Chapels, cloisters, chapter house, and halls are the setting for statuary, friezes, stained glass, tapestries, manuscripts, and altar pieces that trace medieval art and architecture from Romanesque to Gothic.

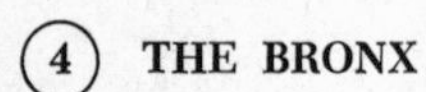

4 THE BRONX

Buddhist Association of the United States

At 3070 Albany Crescent and West 231st Street in the Bronx, is a Buddhist temple which presents the teachings of Ch'an (Zen) Buddhism in its meditation school. Sunday services include meditation, lecture, and discussion. The services and the library facilities are open to the public.

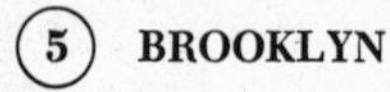

5 BROOKLYN

Plymouth Church of the Pilgrims

Henry Ward Beecher was first minister of Plymouth Church. A merger in 1934 brought together Plymouth Church, formed in 1847, and Church of the Pilgrims, established in 1844. Now a National Historic Landmark, the church is filled with reminders of Puritan influence on American Life.

Visitors should begin their tour at the Lincoln Pew, No. 89 on the left center aisle. The Colonial sanctuary has an unusual set of stained-glass windows with the broad theme of political, intellectual, and religious liberty. A memorial arcade from here to the Church House contains a fragment of Plymouth Rock. An oil painting of Henry Ward Beecher and Pinky, the little slave girl, commemorates the purchase of her freedom and Beecher's massive efforts to free the slaves.

Plymouth Church

Long Island

(6) FLUSHING

Long Island, like nearby Manhattan, was the site of early Dutch trading posts. The County of Queens, located at the western end, was organized in 1683, but was settled as early as 1645 by a company of Englishmen under the Dutch West India Company. First called Vlissingen, then later Flushing, this tiny outpost became famous for the Flushing Remonstrance in 1657, which protested persecution of Quakers and resulted in the first official proclamation of religious freedom in America.

Bowne House

Between 37th and 38th avenues, on Bowne Street, is the 1661 house built by John Bowne. It was used for 30 years as a meeting house by the Quakers. In 1657, Bowne was tried for harboring Quakers in this house—English settlers protested this persecution of Quakers and sent to Gov. Peter Stuyvesant a protest known as the Flushing Remonstrance. Fortunately this Protest was upheld by the Dutch West India Company and their Remonstrance became one of the great documents of American history.

In 1945, the house was dedicated as a shrine to religious freedom during the Flushing tercentenary. It contains half doors, tiny under-stair closets, and furnishings of the period.

In the garden visitors can see the Remonstrance Stone, a gift from Quakers of New York state. It contains the words of the Flushing Remonstrance: FOR THE GLORY OF THE TOWN THAT HAD SUCH MEN FOR FOUNDERS. Two famous Quakers visited here, George Fox in 1672 and William Penn in 1683. A boulder on the grounds marks the site of Fox Oaks, where Fox preached to a large gathering.

Quaker Meeting House

Behind a stone wall on the very busy modern Northern Boulevard is an ancient meeting house of the Society of Friends, built in 1694. The membership grew so rapidly, it was enlarged 23 years later and has remained practically unchanged since. The interior is a gem of early architecture, with ship's knees in the upper room, simple benches, raised facing benches, and clerk's table. There is also a screen of wooden panels which divided the room during business meetings.

For a time during the Revolutionary War, the meeting house was seized by the British and used as both prison and hospital. Today the interior has a quiet charm. Its simplicity allows no detraction from worship, which continues here in the present day.

(7) SETAUKET

Caroline Church of Brook-Haven

On Main Street at Setauket Green is the pre-Revolutionary Caroline Church, built in 1729 and restored in 1937. It was organized about 1671 just after the founding of the town, which was then called Brook-Haven. Both Presbyterian and Church of England pastors ministered in the town. There in 1729, this pleasing colonial structure was built and named for the English queen who gave the church a silver communion service and embroidered altar cloths. She was of German extraction but was Queen of George II of England.

The Revolutionary battle of Setauket was fought around the church August 22, 1777, and marks of the struggle can be seen. Wounded were cared for inside while the battle raged. Afterward many Loyalist families left for Canada, depleting the parish.

Visitors should look for bullet holes in the belfry, old ship's knees in the vestibule, slave gallery, and antique whale oil lamps.

(8) SAG HARBOR

Whalers Church

Surrounded by an old graveyard, the wood-frame Whalers Church, with its unusually ornamented steeple, stands as a reminder of whaling days. The church's slender telescoping steeple is adorned with Victorian framed clock faces and minute pilasters and carvings. The Suffolk County Whaling Museum nearby provides authentic relics of the era.

Hudson Valley

(9) NORTH TARRYTOWN

Old Dutch Church of Sleepy Hollow

Traveling north on the east side of the Hudson, stop off in Washington Irving country to see this gambrel-roofed church built by Dutch settler Frederick Philipse. Dating from 1685, the house walls are made of rubblestone and flat yellow brick imported from Holland. The original bell in the belfry also came from the Netherlands. The author of *The Legend of Sleepy Hollow* is buried in the old churchyard.

Irving's home, Sunnyside, is worth a side trip, as is Philipsburg Manor, an early trading complex. Included in it is an operating water-powered gristmill, oak and stone dam, and two-story stone manor house dating from 1683. This was once headquarters for the 90,000-acre Philipse estate. In the early barn there are craft demonstrations.

(10) HAVERSTRAW

Marian Shrine

On 300 acres on the west bank of the Hudson is "America's most beautiful Rosary Way and Pilgrim Center." It depicts the 15 Mysteries of the Rosary in life-sized statues by Arrighini. There is an outdoor altar of marble, mosaic, and bronze as well as fine Florentine religious art. Also here are replicas of the shrines at Fatima and Lourdes. A picnic area is available for visitors.

(11) WEST POINT

United States Military Academy

Overlooking the Hudson is this school founded in 1802 to train army officers. Three chapels are well worth a visit along with other points of interest on the campus. The daily parade held at varying times adds pleasure.

The Cadet Chapel is an outstanding Gothic structure with beautiful stained-glass windows. The unusually fine organ has more than 15,271 pipes ranging from one smaller than a lead pencil to one 32 feet long and weighing 500 pounds.

The Old Cadet Chapel is in the Post Cemetery. On the walls are battle flags and shields commemorating the Revolution. Benedict Arnold's is noted by rank (Major General) and date of birth, but no name.

The Catholic Chapel of the Most Holy Trinity is of Norman Gothic style and is designed similar to the St. Ethelreda Carthusian abbey church in England.

(12) NEW PALTZ

Huguenot Street

In 1677, 12 men united by religious and family ties purchased land from the five chiefs of the Esopus Indian tribe. Originally Protestant exiles from France, the purchasers had first found a haven in Germany, then fled to America. They named their new com-

French Church

munity New Paltz for their German home in the Rhine-Palatine.

Between 1692 and 1712 they replaced their log huts with the sturdy stone dwellings which now constitute the oldest street in the United States with its original houses. Five of the six houses remained virtually unchanged and until recently were occupied by the descendants of the original founders. Now under the ownership of the Huguenot Historical Society, the houses and their original furnishings are open to the public.

The only replica on the street is the French Church built in 1972 after ten years of careful research. It is square in design and of stone. From the cupola, a horn was sounded in lieu of a bell to summon worshipers to meeting. The French and the Dutch languages were used in services before the English prevailed. The brick Dutch Reformed Church of New Paltz, founded in 1683 by those early settlers, is still attended by descendants.

(13) RIFTON

The Society of Brothers

Proceeding up the west bank of the Hudson River, the traveler comes to Rifton, home of more recent religious pilgrims. The Society of Brothers (Bruderhof) began in Germany in the 1920s when, in the aftermath of World War I, Eberhard Arnold formed a community modeled after 1st century Christianity. Members held all property in common and attempted to live in harmony and brotherhood. The rise of Nazism forced a move to England, Paraguay, and eventually to the Hudson valley in the United States.

In 1954, with the establishment of the first community here, the Society began manufacturing children's play equipment under the name Community Playthings. Concern for children has always been a special interest. The Plough Publishing House at their Farmington, Pennsylvania, community disseminates the Christian faith through the printed word. Another community is in Norfolk, Connecticut. The Society is also connected with the Hutterite communities in this country.

The Society welcomes visitors who are interested in an alternative way of life but request a week's notice to make arrangements. Guests are not charged, but are expected to share in the community work while there.

(14) KINGSTON

Old Dutch Church

When a Dutch trading post was established in 1614, it was soon followed by the establishment of the third oldest settlement in New York. Religious services were held in homes until 1659, when Dominie Hermanus Blom arrived from the old country. A small wooden church, the first of several buildings, was erected in 1661 for this Reformed Protestant Dutch congregation.

The present bluestone building is of Renaissance Revival style and was built in 1852; Bethany Hall was added in 1951. Memorabilia in the vestibule represent four centuries: the first communion tablet, a silver beaker presented from Queen Anne of England in 1683, a letter from George Washington, Civil War battle flags, and the Book of Remembrance which contains signatures of visitors Queen Juliana and Princess Beatrix of the Netherlands. Outside is an ancient cemetery dating from 1661, where New York's first governor, George Clinton, is buried.

A self-guiding walking tour is available; the best time to visit is in early October during the Herfst (Harvest) Feast.

(15) OLD CHATHAM

The Shaker Museum

After crossing the Hudson and proceeding up Route 9, a side trip to Old Chatham (on the Berkshire spur between the Massachusetts Turnpike and the New York Thruway) brings one to the location of the largest and most significant of celibate Shaker colonies. It was the mother house of the order established in the late 18th century. Exhibits are housed in buildings containing 30 galleries and a museum store. Farm, household, and craft equipment are exhibited. The functional simplicity of design reflects Shaker beliefs and inventive genius. The museum library containing writings and documents is open during the season to visitors.

Shaker Festival Day is the first Saturday in August when the old Shaker trades of weaving, furniture making, and herb preparation are demonstrated. Often extra attractions like antique sales or autographing parties for authors of books on Shaker subjects add zest.

(16) ALBANY

The Dutch trading post of Fort Nassau was the first settlement here in 1614, followed ten years later by the establishment of Fort Orange by the English. The town was renamed Albany when the British finally took control in 1664. As a result, both Dutch Reformed and Anglican churches were here early.

First Church in Albany

This second oldest church in the state was organized in 1642 by Dominie Johannes Megapolensis, a Dutch missionary. The first "blockhouse church"

was built in 1654, then a stone church was erected round the blockhouse frame in 1715. The present sanctuary was built in 1799 and has recently been declared a National Historic Site.

Of its many treasured possessions, perhaps the most unusual is America's oldest pulpit, made in Holland and purchased with 25 beaver skins. The weathercock in its display case was first mounted over the church in 1656. The membership does not remain in the past, however. Its present "melting pot" congregation supports a Drive-in/Park-in Worship Service as well as radio and sidewalk ministries. The traveler will also enjoy the green oasis of its setting in Clee Memorial Park.

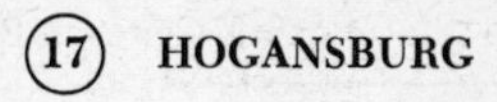

(17) HOGANSBURG

Akwesane Mohawk Indian Village

Either before or after the trip up the Mohawk Valley, the traveler will be rewarded by a visit to the St. Regis Reservation and Iroquois village on Route 81 at the Canadian border. Daily programs, tours, demonstrations and exhibits explain the life and worship of the first native Americans.

Mohawk Valley

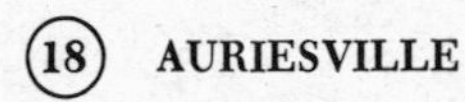

(18) AURIESVILLE

Shrine of Our Lady of Martyrs

Just west of Schenectady on the Thruway is the site of the martyrdom of Father Isaac Jogues, French Jesuit priest, and his companions René Goupil and John LaLande, who were killed by Mohawk Indians in the 1640s. These martyrs, along with five other Jesuit missionaries martyred in Canada, were canonized in 1930. Kateri Tekakwitha, Mohawk girl, who is a candidate for sainthood, was born here in 1656.

The shrine was begun in 1885 and includes outdoor chapels, an Indian museum, a coliseum seating 6,500 people, and a huge cross of evergreens.

(19) NELLISTON

Palatine Church

Evangelical Lutheran Palatines fled to America by way of England, building the limestone Palatine Church in 1770. It is one of the few structures in the Mohawk Valley that predate the Revolution. Several nearby communities were also founded by these refugees.

The church was used continuously until 1940, and summer services were held through 1959. It is presently the headquarters of the Palatine Society of New York and it has been restored to its original appearance.

(20) LITTLE FALLS

Indian Castle Church

Enroute from Nelliston to Little Falls is a simple white-frame mission church built in 1768 on land given by Joseph Brant and with materials contributed by Sir William Johnson. It is on the site of one of the last three castles (villages) of the Mohawk Indians. Though the building has been altered by a change inside and a new belfry, the structure is much the same as originally. It is the only surviving structure connected with the 16 Mohawk villages. In 1965, it was made the responsibility of the Indian Castle Restoration and Preservation Society. Behind it is a graveyard with Indian and English settler graves.

(21) JORDANVILLE

Holy Trinity Monastery

From Mohawk, turn southward to an unusual scene in an American valley. Rising from the plain is a turreted, onion-topped monastery operated by monks of the Orthodox Church. Founded in 1930 by Russian monks, the cathedral is of 12th-century Russian architecture. Consecrated in 1950, it has an incredibly elaborate inside with frescoes, ceiling paintings, icons, relics, and gold-ornamented furnishings. Most of the construction was done by the monks. Orthodox Easter services celebrated according to the Gregorian calendar here are memorable experiences.

 ONEIDA

Madison County Historical Society

Though now famous for silverware, Oneida was once known for a controversial religious experiment in communal living.

In 1848, John Humphrey Noyes brought a faithful group from Putney, Vermont, to carry out a "divine organization of society." In a system called "complex marriage," he endeavored to produce a higher order, rearing children as a community concern. People in the area rebelled at this tampering with traditional family life.

The center was abandoned in 1880 and a joint stock company was formed to carry on the various manufacturing enterprises begun by the community. William Rogers Community Plate silverware is made here, and the historical society at 435 Main Street display historical artifacts.

 SYRACUSE

Fort Ste. Marie du Gannentha

About 1570, Indian Chief Hiawatha chose this area for the capital of the Iroquois Confederacy. In the long house were the council fires of the Five Nations that dominated North America for 200 years. Then in 1656, the Jesuits founded a mission and a fort, abandoned two years later.

Off the Onondaga Lake Parkway, northwest of the city, is a reproduction of the fort as well as the original Jesuit well. There is also a salt spring and museum. Picnic sites and water activities make this a pleasant place to combine history and relaxation.

 PALMYRA

Hill Cumorah

In this area Joseph Smith, first prophet and president of the Church of Latter-Day Saints, lived his early years. Here he received the revelation of the Angel Moroni from which came the Book of Mormon. The church was

Hill Cumorah

organized April 6, 1830, and the Book of Mormon published that year. A 40-foot monument topped by a statue of Moroni stands on the hill. Each summer the Mormons portray their beliefs in a spectacular pageant called *America's Witness for Christ.* Over 600 young Mormons participate in the pageant which is held for a week in the midpoint of the summer and for which there is no charge. Adjacent is the attractive Visitors' Center with exhibits, movies, and guided tours.

Joseph Smith Home

On Stafford Road is the home where the Mormon founder lived as a boy and later returned with his bride. Completed in 1825 by his family, it was from this home the prophet kept his appointments with Angel Moroni at Hill Cumorah. Rooms contain period furnishings. Also on this property is the Sacred Grove where Smith had his first vision when he was 14 years old.

CHAUTAUQUA

Chautauqua Institution

A century ago, this community on Lake Chautauqua was begun as a summer center of religion, education, recreation, and the arts. Founded in 1874, it is nonsectarian, though many major denominations have special buildings and in summer cooperate in the programs which are for all ages and interests. Major programs are given in Norton Memorial Hall and the amphitheater. Outstanding religious programs are featured.

NEW JERSEY

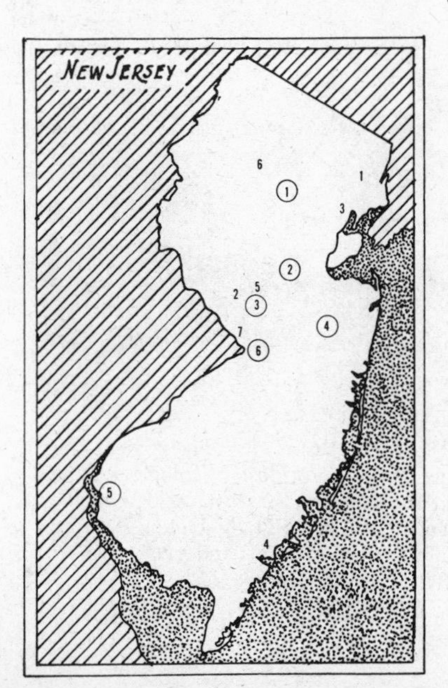

New Jersey began with a religious split personality in the 1600s. The eastern section was colonized by Dutch traders who brought along the Dutch Reformed Church. Then in the latter part of the 17th century, Presbyterians also arrived.

Meanwhile, beginning in 1675, the western section was being settled by Quakers. They moved over from Pennsylvania when William Penn and other prominent men received New Jersey land grants in the southern and western parts of the state after English takeover in 1664. It was not until 1702 that these two separate entities were finally united under a royal governor. These early pioneers had set an ecumenical tone for the state, however, and the diversity continues today.

Early Dutch settlements in eastern New Jersey were at Bergen, Hoboken, and Weehawken on the west bank of the Hudson. Even after English rule, churches in these settlements flourished, particularly in the 17th century under the vigorous preaching of reformer Rev. Theodore Frelinghuysen, who came to Raritan in 1719.

Rev. Gilbert Tennent introduced the revival movement to the Presbyterians in the area in 1726, when he was called to the New Brunswick church. Presbyterian colonies had been in that section in the late 17th century. Gilbert's brothers, John and William, Jr., labored in nearby Freehold.

Both Reformed and Presbyterian clergymen and laymen recognized the need for an educated ministry. In 1746, the College of New Jersey, later renamed Princeton University, was founded by Presbyterians. Its charter assured every denomination "free and equal liberty and advantage of education." Princeton's president during the Revolution, Rev. John Witherspoon, was the only clergyman to sign the Declaration of Independence.

The Dutch founded a college, too. Known as Queen's College, it was chartered in 1766 and was later called Rutgers University. Located in New Brunswick, it is near New Brunswick Theological Seminary, also Dutch Reformed.

Salem was the first Quaker colony settled in the western part of the state. It began in 1675 and two years later, 200 persons, mostly Quakers, sailed farther up the Delaware and established Burlington. These and later settlements were under the protection of the famous "Concessions and Agreements of Proprietors, Freeholders and Inhabitants of West New Jersey," a democratic constitution of 1676. Of it Penn wrote: "There we lay a foundation for after ages to understand their liberty as men and Christians."

Eastern New Jersey

It is well to begin our spiritual heritage tour in the eastern section, where the earliest settlements began, and travel in a semicircle.

(1) MORRISTOWN

St. Mary's Abbey

A modern Benedictine church, St. Mary's Abbey exhibits a dramatic arrangement of brick, concrete, and steel walls punctured by tall narrow windows. Designed by Victor Christ-Janer Associates, the church also has a Blessed Sacrament Chapel and a Lady Chapel. The Delbarton School is administered by Benedictine monks and laymen. The offices, in a home formerly owned by Stanford White, are on grounds beautifully landscaped with formal gardens.

(2) NEW BRUNSWICK

New Brunswick Theological Seminary

The New Brunswick Theological Seminary is the oldest theological school in the country. It was founded in New York City in 1784 by Dutch Reformed Church members and is close by Rutgers University.

Gardner A. Sage Library, dedicated in 1875, is the official depository of the denomination archives. Its Dutch Church Room has a priceless collection of colonial records. The 127,000 volumes and 354 periodicals contain the oldest and newest in all fields of theological study.

(3) PRINCETON

Princeton University

Originally founded in Elizabeth by royal charter as the College of New Jersey, the school moved to Princeton in 1756. Spread over 2,500 acres, it has many buildings worth visiting. The university chapel is one of the country's largest. The carved pulpit comes from France, and dates from the 16th century. Designed in 1925 by Ralph Adams Cram, the chapel is built in the shape of a cross. Choir stalls are carved from Sherwood Forest oak and stained-glass windows depict the life of Christ.

(4) FREEHOLD

Old Tennent Church

Known also as Freehold Meeting House, this imposing white structure was built in 1751 and replaces an earlier building. Chartered in 1749 by a Scotch Presbyterian congregation, it has also been called Old Scots Meeting House. During the Revolution, spectators gathered at this church to watch the Battle of Monmouth, and scars of the battlefield may still be seen.

The church is of two stories with steeply pitched roof. An octagonal steeple has an early Dutch weathercock atop the spire. Old-fashioned sounding board, narrow pews, and a slave gallery are inside. The active congregation maintains beautiful grounds around the peaceful cemetery.

The grave of Rev. William Tennent Jr. is marked in an aisle inside the church.

Western New Jersey

(5) SALEM

Friends Meeting House

Quakers established this first permanent English settlement on the Delaware River in 1675 as New Salem. In 1772, the historic Friends Meeting House on East Broadway was erected, replacing an earlier structure which had been built within the Friends Burial Ground on West Broadway. In the cemetery is the ancient Salem Oak where John Fenwick, leader of the settlers, bartered with the Indians for the land.

The present brick meeting house has two entrances, as was customary for Quaker meetings. The meeting house is still in use, and during the Revolution was also used as a court for the trial of Tories.

(6) CROSSWICKS

Chesterfield Meeting House

The old Quaker house of worship, built in 1773, was hit three times by American cannon during the course of the Revolution. A ball still remains lodged in the north wall. Scars on the floor are reputedly from British gun carriages. Then the little church was occupied by Patriots in 1776.

III.
GEORGE WASHINGTON COUNTRY

VIRGINIA

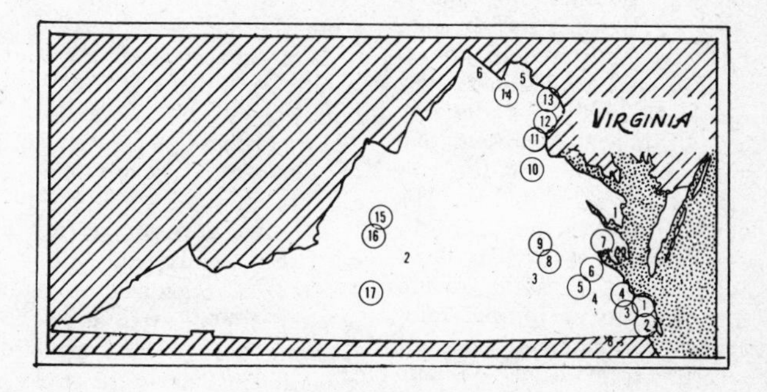

Thirteen years before the Pilgrims arrived in New England, a small band of hardy English pioneers had stepped ashore on the coast of Virginia. On April 26, 1607, these settlers, sent by the Virginia Company of London, disembarked from three ships—*Susan Constant, Godspeed,* and *Discovery*—and planted a cross at Cape Henry. This small band of 104 represented the established Church of England (Anglican) through the Virginia Company of London, whose leaders were convinced that Englishmen needed the church and that the gospel should be propagated in the New World.

Fifty miles upriver, their first town, Jamestown, was established. On the third Sunday after Trinity, Chaplain Robert Hunt celebrated the colony's first Holy Communion, thus beginning his lifelong ministry of 50 years.

Life was precarious, for the natives were not welcoming, the crops sparce, and the area plague-ridden. Nevertheless, the tiny colony managed to survive, and somewhere in those years built a wooden chapel.

When, in 1610, the sickly remnant was about to abandon the colony, reinforcements arrived, led by Governor DeLaWarr. His first act was to lead a service of worship in the dilapidated chapel. A year later a second clergyman, Alexander Whitaker, arrived. He ministered at Henrico, the second town established by the English 50 miles farther up the James River. He was the clergyman who converted and baptized Pocahontas and performed the celebrated wedding ceremony to Englishman John Rolfe.

Anglicans were well established in the state in the 17th century, partly because it banished competitors and partly because of the vigor of its "Holy Commonwealth." A guide for daily living was "The Lawes Divine, Morall and Martiall" which were drawn up by Gov. Thomas Gates and Sec'y William Strachey. Twice a day men and women were called to prayer by the tolling of a bell and army officers were commanded to see "that the Almightie God bee duly and daily served." Since the nearest bishop was in England and parishes were wide apart, the hierarchal control that existed in England was not possible here. Thus more religious rules were incorporated into daily life through civil authorities. Also, a more autonomous church structure developed, whereby the vestry (lay officials) became the governing body in the local churches. Rev. James Blair, who served Henrico parish from 1685 to 1694 and ministered in Jamestown until 1710 and in Williamsburg until his death in 1743, was the first "commissary" or official representative of the bishop of London and the colony's highest ecclesiastical officer. His greatest achievement was the establishment of the College of William and Mary at Williamsburg in 1693. Aware of the urgent need for a "proper ministry," he sailed for England and obtained a charter from King William, pleading the cause of education for the colony's youth. Blair was named president, a post he held for 50 years.

By 1700, there were about 50 Church of England parishes in the state. The tight Anglican control of the colony began to loosen after the 1689 Acts of Toleration passed in England. Though the Anglican churches continued to flourish (there were 100 parishes by 1750), other denominations which had been vigorously resisted earlier settled during the 18th century. Quakers, Puritans, Presbyterians, and Catholics arrived. Even a small group of German refugees were welcomed in 1713. Though 40 Baptist preachers were jailed for disturbing the peace between the years 1768 and 1776, this group, too, eventually found the state a haven. The Revolutionary period brought religious as well as political freedom to the citizenry when full liberty, not just toleration, was achieved.

Church life was somewhat modified by developments in Virginia: the early "Holy Commonwealth" emphasis on work was somewhat relaxed by the rise of the tobacco industry and the dependence upon African slave labor, both of which were introduced in 1619; likewise the early introduction of democratic government influenced church and political life. The first representative government in the colony and the county, the House of Burgesses, was organized in the choir loft at Jamestown after it was voted in London in 1619. This principle of self-government led to more local church control. This decentralization later led three Virginians—Patrick Henry, Thomas Jefferson, and George Washington—to influence the 13 colonies in the cause of independence.

Visitors to the state of Virginia (Old Dominion) will find a variety of faiths and shrines, though the Episcopal, American child of the Anglican Church of England, still predominates.

Southeastern Virginia

(1) CAPE HENRY

Cape Henry Memorial

Since the settlement of Virginia began on Cape Henry, which pushes outward into the Atlantic from the coast, we begin our spiritual heritage pilgrimage where those first English settlers landed on April 26, 1607, naming the spot for Henry, Prince of Wales. Stand by the stone cross on First Landing Dune, which is on the Fort Story Military Reservation, and picture the long-ago scene.

ARE Center

② VIRGINIA BEACH

Association for Research and Enlightenment

While in this area, the traveler might be interested in a modern spiritual pilgrimage center, the Association for Research and Enlightenment (ARE), which has resulted from the readings of Edgar Cayce, Kentucky-born mystic, who gave about 15,000 readings in his lifetime. The underlying principle is belief in Divine Creator and Plan. Man must seek to live in harmony with his Creator's plan, said Cayce, who was a Sunday school teacher and devout churchman during his lifetime.

National headquarters for the Association is a large building, erected originally as a hospital, now providing space for the educational programs, Braille Library, study groups, and public lectures. The ARE Press prints its booklets, books, and magazines. A striking new library houses a rooftop meditation room and open-air garden, as well as auditoriums, research areas, storage facilities, and offices.

③ NORFOLK

St. Paul's Church

The oldest building standing in Norfolk, St. Paul's Episcopal Church (erected in 1739) survived the burning of Norfolk in 1776. It stands on the site of an earlier building (1641), although the city was not officially founded until 1682. Located at St. Paul Boulevard and City Hall Avenue, the building still bears Revolutionary scars, for there is a British cannonball buried in its walls.

Continuously in use, the church was renovated in conformity with its original Colonial style in 1913. Ancient oaks shade the cemetery where there are headstones dated as early as 1673.

(4) HAMPTON

St. John's Church

Crossing to Hampton via the Hampton Roads Bridge Tunnel, the traveler comes to the oldest English settlement still in existence in the United States. The town was settled in 1610 simultaneously with this ancient Episcopal parish on Queen Street. In 1619, this was one of the original boroughs of the Virginia legislature.

The present building was erected in 1728. British troops were quartered there in 1812, and it was partially burned during the Civil War. It still has communion silver made in 1618. A window dedicated to Pocahontas was given by Indian students at Hampton Institute.

(5) JAMESTOWN

Old Church Tower

After landing at Cape Henry in 1607, the English colonists established their permanent settlement at Jamestown.

This site is now part of the Colonial National Historical Park. The ivy-covered tower ruin is the only structure still standing from the 17th century. It was the tower of the first brick church begun in 1639 and used until 1750. Foundations of the earliest church can be seen. Here Pocahontas was married and the state's first assembly met. A statue of the Indian princess, daughter of Chief Powhatan, is nearby.

Jamestown Festival Park

A re-creation of the Jamestown settlement is on Glasshouse Point adjacent to the Jamestown site. Here the religious pilgrim will find replicas of the three ships which carried the first settlers from England. *Susan Constant, Godspeed,* and *Discovery* carried 104 men and boys safely to Jamestown, after first stopping at Cape Henry. A visit aboard will show the cramped quarters they endured on the long trip. Pocahontas's father's lodge is here also. The long house is typical of those used for ceremonial occasions by Powhatan, chieftain of the Algonquin Nation. Made of saplings tied with rawhide and covered with cattails, it is reconstructed from a 1588 description.

(6) WILLIAMSBURG

Colonial Williamsburg

Originally the middle plantation and an outpost of Jamestown, this town was settled in 1633. In 1699, it became the capital city and was named in honor of King William III. Williamsburg was a social and cultural center for the next 80 years. When the capital was moved to Richmond, the town declined but was revived in 1926, when John D. Rockefeller, Jr., began to re-create the settlement of the 1770s. Eighty-eight original buildings which survived have been faithfully restored and replicas of others have been reconstructed in the period architecture.

Bruton Parish Church

This memorable Anglican church was built in 1711-1715, replacing an earlier one. To step inside the beautifully restored edifice is to move into the living past. The governor's chair is a reminder of colonial government.

College of William and Mary

At the head of Duke of Gloucester Street stands the country's second oldest college. It was chartered in 1693, when founder and first president Rev. James Blair sailed to England to request a school of a preparation of a "proper ministry." The 1695 Wren-style building still retains its original walls and is the oldest academic building of English origin still in use.

Visitors to the town and to the colonial restoration especially will enjoy a summer trip to see *The Common Glory*, Paul Green's drama of the American Revolution, presented nightly at Matoaka Lake Amphitheater.

(7) WHITE MARSH

Abingdon Episcopal Church

Long tradition and present-day vitality mix at this old colonial parish church. The queen of England traces her American ancestry through Robert Porteus who worshiped here. The date 1650 marks the beginning of the parish, with the first brick structure erected about 1660. The present church was built between 1751 and 1755 and is in the form of a maltese cross. The brick of Flemish bond was made nearby. After the Revolution, the

Glebe (parsonage) and lands were sold in accordance with legislative action, as were all such holdings of Church of England parishes. When the Protestant Episcopal Church was organized, in 1785, Col. John Page of this parish was the Virginia delegate. The communion service has been in regular use since 1702.

(8) HOPEWELL

Merchant's Hope Church

Built in 1657, Merchant's Hope Church is one of the oldest Protestant churches still standing in America. It is a gem of earliest Colonial architecture, with exceptionally fine brickwork. Though the exterior is original, the interior was destroyed by Union soldiers when they used the building for picket station and stables. Flagstones in the church are original, however, coming over from England as ship's ballast. Refurbished in 1870, the church continued as an active church until the 1930s and was reactivated in 1969. The beautiful memorial gardens surrounding the church will delight the gardener.

(9) RICHMOND

St. John's Church

Richmond originated in 1609 when Capt. John Smith bought a tract of land from Powhatan and founded a settlement called None Such. The name was later changed to Richmond and it became the capital in 1779. The Virginia Convention met in 1775 in this church with many delegates whose names would live on in Revolutionary history. Here Patrick Henry made his famous speech which ended "give me Liberty or give me death."

St. John's Church, situated on Church Hill, was erected in 1741. It is filled with historic mementos from both Revolutionary and Civil War days.

Northern Virginia

(10) FREDERICKSBURG

Masonic Lodge and Cemetery

One of the oldest Masonic burial grounds in America and portions of an old Lodge building are in this city. George Washington was a member of this Lodge, No. 4, and the Masonic Bible on which he took his oath as president is on display. The old Lodge building remnants are enclosed in the newer building which was built in 1815. The half-acre burying ground has an absorbing collection of ancient tombstones.

(11) ACCOTINK

Pohick Church

Continuing a northerly journey, travel next to the parish church for Mount Vernon, Gunston Hall, and Belvoir. Its site was chosen by George Washington; construction took place from 1769 to 1773 with first services held in 1774. Washington served as vestryman and owned Pews 28 and 29. The building was used as a stable during the Civil War, but was later restored. A side trip to Mount Vernon, Washington's home and tomb, would be natural here.

(12) ALEXANDRIA

National Masonic Memorial

This city, settled in 1670, has a reminder of a far more ancient monument towering over it. The ancient lighthouse at Alexandria, Egypt, is the model for the national Masonic memorial to George Washington. It rises 333 feet high over Alexandria. In the Replica Room one may gaze at the original furnishings of the first Lodge room where Washington was the first Worshipful Master. An observation tower gives one of the finest views of the city of Washington, D.C.

Old Presbyterian Meetinghouse

At 321 South Fairfax Street is a brick church built in 1774 by Scots sea captains and merchants. Its churchyard contains graves of many Masons and the Unknown Revolutionary Soldier. The church was a meeting place of Patriots.

The interior was renovated in 1837 after a fire, but outside walls and clock are original. The interior is Colonial and has old-fashioned gate pews.

Here Washington's memorial sermon was preached in December 1799 when the roads to Christ Church were impassable. The steeple bell began tolling as soon as news of his death reached the town.

Christ Church

Washington was among the worshipers at Christ Church (Episcopal) located at Columbus, Cameron and Washington Sts. The brick building of English country style was erected in 1767-1773 and is only slightly changed today. A gallery, tower, and steeple were added in 1818. A fine Palladian window and 18th-century brass and cut-glass chandeliers grace the interior.

Prior to the Revolution, the church was supported by taxes or tithes. After independence when support became voluntary, on April 25, 1785, Gen. George Washington and other parish laymen signed a contract to pay annually the sum of £5 a pew. Washington, who was a regular worshiper, purchased Pew 60 for the highest price paid. At this church he advocated independence, and to this church he returned when the peace was won nine years later.

(13) ARLINGTON

Arlington National Cemetery

Memorial Amphitheater in the largest of national cemeteries is the scene of Memorial Day services and other ceremonies. A graceful white marble structure, it is dedicated to those killed in service and seats 3,000 with an additional 1,008 places around the colonnade.

Though the entire area may be toured and is of spiritual heritage significance, the most notable scenes are the Tomb of the Unknown Soldier, with its 24-hour-a-day honor guard, and the grave of former president John F. Kennedy, with its Eternal Flame, and adjacent memorial to his brother, former senator Robert F. Kennedy.

(14) UPPERVILLE

Trinity Episcopal Church

Trinity Episcopal Church in a French country style, makes an unusual appearance in this town as the traveler turns southwest on Route 50. There were two earlier structures before this impressive church building was erected between 1651 and 1660. Designed by H. Page Cross, the building is similar to 12th- and 13th-century Norman structures. The materials, stone and wood, were handcrafted by local men, like medieval workers. The windows were imported from Amsterdam. Heinze Warneke's carvings of native plants, symbolic animals, and Christian preachers are justly famous.

Western Virginia

(15) LEXINGTON

Lee Chapel Museum

Southward on Route 29 along a lovely ride at the base of the Blue Ridge Mountains, the traveler comes to a gap at Route 60. On the other side of the mountains is Lexington, known as the Shrine of the South. Here on the campus of Washington and Lee University is a memorial to Robert E. Lee, Confederate general who was president of the school until his death in 1870. Edward Valentine's recumbent statue of General Lee is in the red brick limestone chapel. Family members also buried here include his father, "Light Horse Harry Lee."

(16) NATURAL BRIDGE

Natural Bridge

One of America's natural wonders is the phenomenon called by the native Monocans "The Bridge of God" off Route US 11. Owned by Thomas Jefferson, surveyed by George Washington, and visited by many famous early Americans, it is a mecca for modern tourists. Here in nature's cathedral, the "Drama of Creation" is presented in sound and light from March through September.

(17) ROCKY MOUNT

Booker T. Washington National Monument

Continuing southwest below Roanoke, the spiritual pilgrimage takes the traveler to the birthplace of Booker T. Washington (1856-1915), a black spiritual leader. Though not ordained, his work as a Christian layman advanced the cause of his race amazingly. A former slave, he became an educator, speaker, and founder of Tuskegee Institute in Alabama. He was honored in later years by degrees from Harvard and Dartmouth. In his lifetime he saw Tuskegee grow from three buildings and 30 students to a campus of 2,000 acres and 1,500 students. Acting on his philosophy of industrial education, he educated thousands of black leaders. Washington also wrote and spoke extensively on black history, industrial education, and the social and economic problems of his people. Probably the

most famous of his 11 volumes was *Up from Slavery*.

The Visitors' Center here contains exhibits on the life of Washington. A self-guiding tour winds through the old Burroughs plantation where, as a boy of 5, Washington watched as a man wrote on his slate, "One Negro boy (Booker) $400.", the price paid for him.

MARYLAND

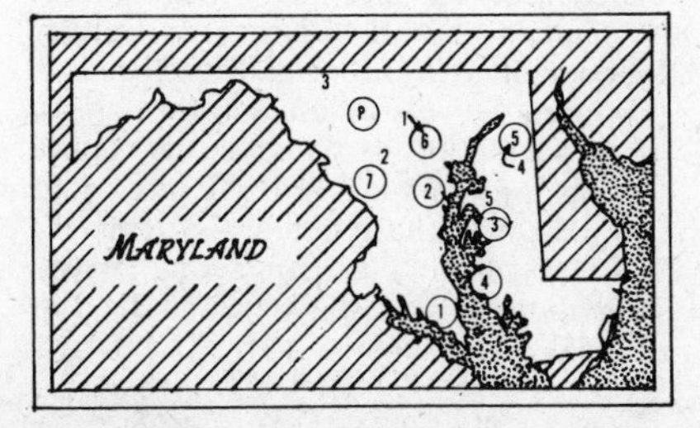

The Englishman George Calvert, Lord Baltimore, in 1632 chartered Maryland as a haven for his countrymen who were fleeing from religious persecution. While Europe was brutally torn by the struggle between Catholics and Protestants, Calvert, a Catholic, encouraged both to settle on his vast manoral estate in the New World.

In 1634, two ships *The Ark* and *The*

Dove sailed up the Chesapeake bringing settlers of both faiths to the virgin land. Father Andrew White, one of three Jesuits on board, celebrated mass Island. St. Mary's City was the first at their first stopping place, St. Clement permanent settlement and the early capital.

The second Lord Baltimore, Cecilius Calvert, continued his father's liberal religious policy, aware that there was some opposition to a Roman Catholic colony. Puritans were invited to settle there in addition to the Anglicans and Quakers. The Act of Toleration voted by the Colonial Assembly followed in 1649. This Act gave freedom to all trinitarian Christians, decreeing that "no persons professing to believe in Jesus Christ should be molested in respect of their religion, or in the free exercise thereof, or be compelled to the belief or exercise of any other religion against their consent." Thus in Maryland, as well as in Rhode Island and Pennsylvania, the beacon of religious liberty shone.

By 1675, when Charles Calvert became governor, Catholics and Quakers were well established but Anglicans were a minority. Then William III ascended the throne of England and made Maryland a royal province. The assembly, by vote in 1692, established the Church of England as the official church. The area was divided into parishes and vestries were appointed. In 1694, the capital was moved to Annapolis.

Though Roman Catholics appeared in many places in our country during the days of exploration and colonization, Maryland was the first stronghold. The first virtual see in America developed here.

Jesuits (Society of Jesus) were missionaries during the colonial period, working with natives as well as colonists. In addition to the church at St. Mary's, a rectory, chapel, and school were established at Bohemia Manor, close to the Pennsylvania border. Catholics comprised about one-eighth of the people then.

The first American-born bishop, Rev. John Carroll, a Jesuit, was appointed supervisor of the mission in the United States in 1784. In 1790, he was consecrated bishop of Baltimore, and held the first synod in 1791. That same year St. Mary's Seminary was founded and staffed by the Society of Saint Sulpice of Paris. The Roman Catholic Church in America spread from this foothold. In 1808, Bishop Carroll created four suffragan sees in Boston, Bardstown, Philadelphia, and New York.

Meanwhile Anglicans, Quakers, Presbyterians, Methodists—and later Jews and Unitarians—arrived and prospered. Maryland today reflects the same religious pattern of those earlier years, with a fascinating variety of religious heritage sites clustered around the Chesapeake Bay and westward into the Allegheny Mountains.

Southeastern Shores

(1) ST. MARYS CITY

Leonard Calvert Monument

At a peninsula where the waters of the Potomac and Chesapeake part, the first settlement in Maryland was established. The original town began in 1634 when Leonard Calvert, a younger son of the first Lord Baltimore, purchased the land from the Indian chief Yaocomico. The site of the negotiations is marked by the Leonard Calvert Monument to freedom of conscience. It portrays the liberation of the spirit, long bound by intolerance. A figure forcing aside a rock and emerging into the light, as others follow, is depicted. This was erected to commemorate the Toleration Act of 1649, passed by the colonial legislature.

Crypt of John Paul Jones

(2) ANNAPOLIS

U.S. Naval Academy Chapel

On the south side of the Severn River on 300 acres is the U.S. Military Academy with many places of interest, including Bancroft Hall, home of 4,300 midshipmen, the largest dormitory in the world. Of special interest to religious pilgrims is the chapel, which houses the crypt of John Paul Jones.

The present (and third) chapel building, sometimes called Cathedral of the Navy, is of white brick with granite trim. A towering copper-covered dome is placed above the cruciform church. Designer was Ernest Flagg, and Adm. George Dewey laid the cornerstone in 1904. The building was enlarged in 1940 to seat 2,500 people. Bronze bas-relief doors and anchors from the navy's first armored cruiser are special features.

St. Anne's Church

The first building on Church Circle was erected in 1699, though the Episcopal parish was organized in 1692. At first the support was by tobacco tax—40 pounds per taxpayer! Built in 1859, this is the third church house of worship. The building is particularly noted for the Sands Memorial Window, which won first prize at the Chicago World's Fair in 1893 for ecclesiastical art. The communion service still in use dates from 1695 and was a gift of King William III.

Manresa-on-Severn

Located on the Severn, with a breathtaking view of Annapolis and downriver, the palatial retreat house, Manresa-on-Severn, is operated by the Society of Jesus. Its impressive long structure, set in broad lawns and walkways, offers an ideal place for contemplation, as well as physical and spiritual renewal.

The dining room and sleeping areas can accommodate over 100 people. The chapel, a medieval Gothic-style addition, has been rearranged for more informality of worship. Though Manresa is a Catholic center, it is also catholic in the broad sense of being available to those of other faiths who wish to use the facilities.

(3) EASTON

Old Friends Meeting House

Continuing south on Route 50, we come to an early Quaker settlement and a meeting house dating to 1683. This Third Haven Meeting of the Society of Friends is reputed to be the oldest frame building for worship in America. William Penn was often among the worshipers.

(4) CHURCH CREEK

Trinity Episcopal Church

Traveling southwest on Route 16, the traveler comes to one of the nation's oldest churches in its original state and still in use. Constructed about 1675, the brick building has a semicircular sanctuary. A three-decker pulpit and high box pews were faithfully restored in 1953-1960. Situated on the banks of Church Creek, it is surrounded by an ancient cemetery which has many Revolutionary-period graves. Two huge millstones mark the grave of the last miller of the 18th-century gristmill.

Northern Maryland

(5) WARWICK

Old Bohemia Church

A shrine of colonial Catholicism was established in 1704 in the northwestern corner of Maryland by Rev. Thomas Mansell of the Society of Jesus. A plantation, covering 1,200 acres and supporting mission activities, was developed. An academy which educated many of Maryland's Catholic youth was begun about 1742. The first American Catholic bishop, John Carroll, studied here. Bohemia Academy, the immediate predecessor to Georgetown University in Washington, was founded by Carroll in 1789. A museum is in the rectory.

(6) BALTIMORE

Basilica of the Assumption of the Blessed Virgin Mary

The mother church of Catholicism in America stands at the corner of Cathedral and Mulberry streets. Built of brick and granite in Romanesque style,

the cruciform church was begun in 1806 and dedicated in 1821. Designed by Benjamin Latrobe, an important early architect, it has an impressive Greek Revival portico with fluted columns and two towers.

Lovely Lane Church Museum

A historical collection of the Baltimore Conference of United Methodists is exhibited at 2200 St. Paul St. in this museum: books, manuscripts, and other memorabilia of the development of Methodism in America. Here the religious pilgrim will find John Wesley's copy of *Imitation of Christ*, by Thomas à Kempis and a hand-hewn oak pulpit, called the Strawbridge Pulpit, first used by a Methodist preacher. The table and chair of Francis Asbury, the first Methodist bishop in this country, are on display, along with his portrait by Charles Polk.

Lovely Lane United Methodist Church

Adjacent to the museum is the fifth home of the congregation which was founded in 1772. The unique building of Etruscan style was designed by Stanford White and completed in 1887. When inside, one can look up and see a ceiling designed like the evening sky in the vaulted dome.

Mother Seton House

Elizabeth Bayley Seton, founder of the American Sisters of Charity, lived at 600 North Paca Street in 1808-1809. Mother Seton lived in this beautiful Federal-style house when she opened her Catholic school for girls and began her order. Visitors will see the mansion furnished in period furniture and can admire a stained-glass window of Mother Seton. She was canonized as America's first saint in 1975.

Old St. Mary's Chapel

A small brick chapel of Gothic Revival design on Paca St. is a Catholic shrine of great magnitude. Built in 1808, it was dedicated by Bishop John Carroll as the chapel for the first Catholic Seminary in the country. This latter was begun in 1791 by the French Society of St. Sulpice in the old One Mile Tavern.

The first U.S.-trained priest was ordained here in an earlier chapel building in 1793. Mother Seton took her vows in Old St. Mary's Chapel in 1809. The Oblate Sister of Providence, the first black community of nuns, began here in 1829. The Sister Servants of the Immaculate Heart of Mary also trace their history to this religious spot.

Mount Vernon Place United Methodist Church

The cathedral church of Methodism at North Charles St. and Vernon Place had its beginnings when John King, a lay preacher from England, formed a pioneer Methodist Society. The present structure, opposite the imposing Washington Monument, was dedicated in 1872. It is of green serpentine and gray stone, trimmed with brown sandstone and polished columns of granite. Gothic in style, both interior and exterior are lavishly decorated with symbolic carvings. The stone slab from Bishop Francis Asbury's tomb is in the narthex.

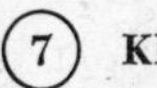 KENSINGTON

Temple of Church of Jesus Christ Latter-Day Saints

The 16th and largest temple of this church, whose headquarters are in Salt Lake City, this amazing edifice dominates the skyline just north of the Washington Beltway. The vast hexagon of white marble with six golden spires is a breathtaking sight. Atop the highest spire is an angel with a trumpet. Strips of stained glass run vertically the height of the building, creating an unusual lighting effect during the evening hours. When newly built, it was open to the public, but was closed to all but church members after November 1974.

Here as in all the temples, which are not for worship, marriages are sealed and essential sacraments take place. In the last decade, this indigenous American church has grown phenomenally, tripling its membership and spreading overseas.

(8) NEW WINDSOR

Brethren Service Center

A unique hub of cooperative activity is this facility for conferences and ecumenical world programs at Blue Ridge Ave. International gift shops, market handwork of overseas craftsmen in cooperation with denominational and ecumenical personnel. Fleets of trucks bring donations of clothing from churches. The used clothing plus new items made here are shipped to six continents. Medicines and medical supplies are collected for Interchurch Medical Assistance, a 23-denominational agency, for missions and disaster areas overseas. Zigler, Windsor, and Old Main halls have facilities for conferences and retreats. If the traveler can spare a day, he will find it rewarding to join the volunteer work force.

DELAWARE

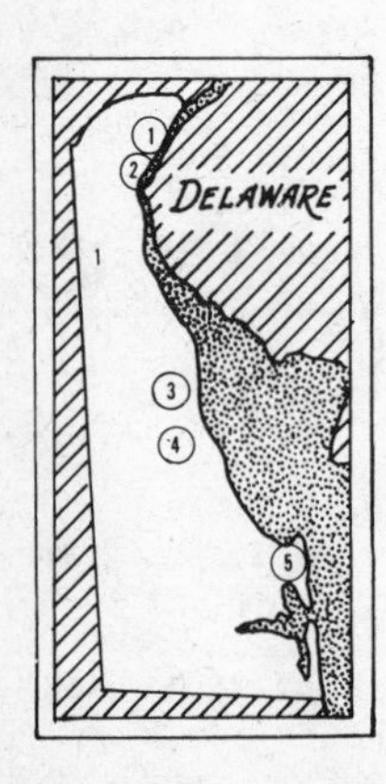

The Dutch, Swedes, and English all established colonies in Delaware, raising their country's flags in succession and bringing their country's churches. Henry Hudson came first, venturing up the Delaware River in 1609 and claiming all the land for the Dutch. Two early Dutch colonies were unsuccessful, however, and it was not until almost 20 years later that a permanent colony was established.

Peter Minuit led a combined Dutch and Swedish expedition in 1638 and began the state's first permanent settlement at Fort Christina, or New Sweden, on the banks of the Delaware River. Where the present Wilmington stands, there were both Dutch Reformed and Swedish colonists. A log chapel was one of the first structures erected. A Swedish clergyman arrived the next year (1639) with a second group of colonists. The noted missionary to the Indians, Swedish pastor John Campanius, landed in 1643.

Fort Casmir, a Dutch colony, was established in 1651 by Peter Stuyvesant, governor of New York. Its nearness to Fort Christina, rivalry over the fur trade, and a population explosion of 300 new Swedish settlers caused intense rivalry between the two nationalities. It culminated in the Swedish capture of the Dutch fort. The Dutch retaliated in 1634, and took over all of New Sweden.

The Dutch flag waved only ten years, however, for the English reasserted their claim to the eastern seaboard of the new territories in 1664.

Both Dutch and Swedish settlers feared the loss of their buildings and ecclesiastical privileges under the new regime. Fortunately the English permitted the other national churches to remain, while establishing their own Church of England parishes.

Rev. John Yee was appointed Anglican missionary to Delaware in 1677 and began his work at New Castle. Though appointed and encouraged by the governor, Yee found cultural differences made the populace unreceptive to Anglican worship. Gradually, as more English came, Anglican parishes were established, in some cases taking over from Swedish churches as the number of Swedish settlers declined.

Though the state was under Pennsylvania's government until 1704 when a separate legislature was established, it did not seem receptive to Quakerism. Other groups came, however, and the early attitude of tolerance continued. Though the religious spectrum of Delaware is varied, the three original strains are still evident.

(1) WILMINGTON

The northern gateway to Delaware, the route of the first explorers and settlers, Wilmington is the best place to start a spiritual heritage pilgrimage. Four flags, four nations, and three names characterize this flourishing port city at the juncture of the Brandywine, Christina, and Delaware rivers. Called Fort Christina by the Swedes, Altena by the Dutch, it was renamed Wilmington by the Pennsylvania Quakers.

Site of Fort Christina

At the shore near the foot of East 7th Street is the original landing spot of the Dutch-Swedish expedition in 1638. "The Rocks" is marked by a commemorative monument. Swedish sculptor Carl Milles designed the black granite monument in the park. A log cabin reminds visitors of early Swedish settlers who introduced this construction to the New World. Here in a forested wilderness founding fathers began this busy city of today. Leave the waterfront and tour the street market along King Street to get the flavor of the earlier days.

Old Swedes Church

Though preceded by a log chapel, this old church at 606 Church Street was erected in 1698 and is reputed to be the oldest Protestant church still serving as a place of worship in the northern part of America. It was simple and plain when it served a Swedish Lutheran congregation, but now Episcopal in affiliation it is more ornate, in keeping with Anglican worship.

The exterior is of both brick and stone and there is a six-sided white cupola. Inside is the original 1699 pulpit, also one of the country's oldest.

(2) NEW CASTLE

The Dutch, under Peter Stuyvesant, founded this city in 1651. The Green and the central area, laid out by Stuyvesant in 1655, is one of the best-preserved examples of colonial settlements. Brick houses line the narrow streets. A good time to visit is the third Saturday in May, when many historic homes are opened to the public.

Old Presbyterian Church

A fine old structure built in 1707 is on Second Street. The brownstone Victorian Gothic style church is believed to be the direct successor to the original Dutch Reformed Church organized by the first settlers in 1657. Now Presbyterian, it was one of the churches forming the first Presbytery in America. Unmarked gravestones in the churchyard date to the early 1700s.

Immanuel Church

At the corner of Market and Harmony streets is the home of the first Episcopal parish in Delaware. It was organized in 1689, 12 years after Delaware was given to Rev. John Yee as his parish. This mother church of the Episcopal diocese of Delaware was built in 1703 and is considered to be the oldest Episcopal church in continuous use in the country. In 1820, the building was renovated and repaired with "a grand spired tower and short transepts added to the west end." The altar was relocated, so that Bishop White had to reconsecrate the building. Communion silver was given to the parish in 1710 by General Gookin of Pennsylvania, a parishioner. In the tower are six "change ringing bells." At present there are only two of these in working order in the nation.

The rectory of Glebe House was given to the parish in 1719 and was the birthplace of George Ross, Jr., signer of the Declaration of Independence, who was son of the rector. His nephew was husband of Betsy Ross. Another interesting item from the Glebe House, which is now on the National Register, is that occupant Rev. Charles Wharton in 1787 was chairman of the committee which revised the Church of England's Book of Common Prayer for use of the newly independent Episcopal Church after the Revolution.

(3) DOVER

Delaware State Museum

At 316 South Governor's Avenue on the St. Jones River, several colonial buildings house exhibits pertaining to the early life and growth of the second smallest state in the Union. The four-building complex includes the Old Presbyterian Church, which was built in 1790. An outstanding feature is the spiral staircase leading to the gallery. It also has a fine collection of early silverware and furnishings, as well as a musical treat, a grand harmonicon, which is played daily.

The adjacent chapel has handcraft, Indian, farm, and firemen's exhibits. A log cabin dating from 1704 is a typical example of those built by early Swedish settlers in Delaware. These and the accompanying Johnson Memorial Building, which pays tribute to the founder of the Victor Talking Machine Company, give a fascinating glimpse of early days.

Farmers' Market

There are Amish residents in and around Dover. Each Friday they come to the city market. With their black garb and horse-drawn carriages, they lend an aura of another era. Visitors, angling their camera lenses down a street full of buggies, could well imagine they were back in the 1800s.

Jacob Amman, a Mennonite preacher of Berne, Switzerland, urged stricter observance of early Mennonite practices. After gaining adherents, the Amish began to immigrate to America about 1740. The plainest of the plain people, they oppose use of church buildings, use hooks and eyes rather than buttons, do not use motorized farm machinery, and insist on educating their own children. Farming represents the good life, they say, and an elementary education in the "3 R's" is sufficient.

(4) FREDERICA

Barratt's Chapel

Continuing southward on Route 9, the traveler will find 1 mile north of Frederica the cradle of Methodism in America. Barratt's Chapel was built in 1780 and the sacraments administered by Methodist preachers in 1784. Bishop Thomas Coke and Francis Asbury met here to organize the first Methodist church in the country. The same year Asbury was ordained as bishop of the Methodist Church in America.

Barratt's Chapel Museum, nearby, has exhibits devoted to early history of the Peninsula Methodist Conference. From here itinerant preachers carried the message of John and Charles Wesley. Classes were organized for discipline and religious nurture, many of which developed into today's Methodist churches.

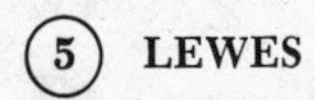 LEWES

Zwaanendael Museum

Driving southeast toward Delaware Bay, the traveler comes to Lewes, site of an unsuccessful attempt at Dutch colonization. Here, in 1631, Dutch from Hoorn, Holland, started the colony of Zwaanendael. It was a fledgling whaling and agricultural village when it was wiped out in 1632 by unfriendly Indians.

Later the community was reestablished and became in recent years the traditional home of pilots who guide the ships through Delaware Bay. In 1931, this unusual Dutch building housing the museum was erected to commemorate the 300th anniversary of the Dutch settlement. A strange sight for an American landscape, the museum is similar to the Town Hall of Hoorn. It houses exhibits of Indian, Dutch, colonial, and maritime relics. The exterior is a cameraman's dream. Its façade rises in pyramided gables to the peak, where there is a statue of Capt. David Pietersen de Vries, who dispatched the original expedition from Holland.

PENNSYLVANIA

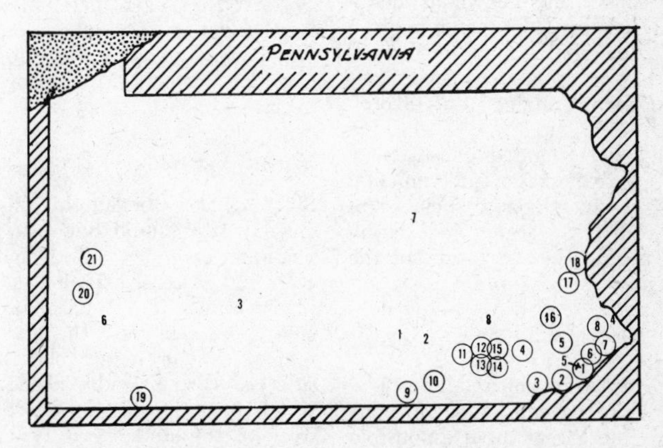

In the dome of the Pennsylvania state house at Harrisburg a lovely mural by Edwin Austin Abbey depicts three spirits—religious liberty, faith, and hope—guiding ships of the early settlers to the New World. Gov. William Penn's Quaker Colony, along with Rhode Island, was the haven to which many of the religiously persecuted of Europe came.

Though Gottenberg on Tinicum Island was settled in 1643 by Swedes and Finns, the major beginning of Pennsylvania came when Quaker William Penn asked the English Crown for land in the New World for his persecuted Quaker brethren. The charter was granted in 1681 and Penn immediately gave "unto all Freemen, Planters, Adventurers and other inhabitants" freedom of conscience.

"I hereby grant and declare that no Person . . . who shall confess and acknowledge ONE almighty God, the Creator, Upholder and Ruler of the World . . . shall be molested . . . nor be compelled to frequent or maintain any religious Worship, Place or Ministry contrary to his Mind or to do or suffer any Act or Thing contrary to his Religious persuasion." Soon after, accompanied by George Fox, founder of the Society of Friends, he traveled throughout Europe, proclaiming a haven to the persecuted of all faiths.

English Quakers came in large numbers, forming about one third of the colony, and overwhelming earlier Dutch and Swedish settlements. Then in response to Penn's invitation the Mennonites, Amish, Dunkards, and Moravians arrived from Germany. They formed another third of the population and were collectively known as Pennsylvania Deutsch—later colloquialized to Dutch. The final ethnic third were Scotch-Irish who gravitated toward the state's frontier, bringing the Scotch Presbyterian Church.

The religiously minded constituency pioneered in democratic governmental procedures, with religious, social, and political history converging in exciting form. Sharpening the conscience of the nation, Pennsylvania abolished slavery in 1780. Later, Quakers were key people in the underground railway, assisting slaves to freedom.

Although the freedom and liberty of this "Holy Experiment" of Penn's attracted to some extent an irresponsible element among the settlers, which Penn deplored, the Experiment did not fail. Because of it, America's richest mix of religious faith and practice developed in Pennsylvania. It was the launching pad for many denominations. In addition to those earlier mentioned, there came Welsh Presbyterians, Anglicans and Baptists, German Seventh-day Baptists, Lutherans, Catholics, and Jews. Here also the African Methodist Church, the first independent black denomination, originated.

It was no accident that Philadelphia, Quaker City of Brotherly Love and the first capital, was the birthplace of both the Declaration of Independence and the Constitution, both founded on religious premises. Thus Pennsylvania has long been known as the "Keystone State" of American religious history.

(1) PHILADELPHIA

William Penn chose a site overlooking the Schuylkill and Delaware rivers for the City of Brotherly Love, the governing seat of the new colony. America's first city planner, he laid out a "greene Countrie Towne" including five parks. The four in each corner section remain today, while the central park was eventually used for the City Hall.

Referred to as the Cradle of Liberty, the city is redolent with history. Whether one walks down the little street called Elfreth's Alley, a perfectly preserved Colonial gem, or steps into Independence Hall where our country was born, the visitor finds an authentic aura of history. Much has religious overtones.

Friends Center

Since Quakers began this city, a present-day trip should begin at their new headquarters and office building at 15th and Race streets. The edifice will place under one roof many Quaker enterprises including the Service Committee, its worldwide relief arm. Outside is the Friendly Talking Wall, which recently was decorated with art work of the students at Friends Select School. Cafeteria, offices, parking areas, and workrooms will make this an efficient arm of the Society of Friends, who are still following the example set by William Penn and putting religion into everyday life.

Friends Meeting House

A profusion of meeting houses exists in this Quaker area and most cannot be listed because of space. The meeting house at 4th and Arch streets, almost across from the quaint Betsy Ross house, is a must, however. It was built in 1804 on land given to the Quakers in 1693 by William Penn. In 1811, the west wing was added and in 1968 it was further enlarged. A historical exhibit includes six dioramas on the contributions of Penn and the Quakers.

Bishop White House

At 309 Walnut Street, also in the heart of the city's historic park, is the home built by the first Protestant Episcopal bishop of Pennsylvania. One of the imposing and elegant row houses, the home has been restored with many of the original furnishings. The visitor here can see the setting for the manner of life of the city's and country's early founders.

Bishop White was a founder of the Episcopal Church in America and was rector at the Christ Church. He was also a chaplain for both the Continental Congress and the Senate.

Christ Church

On Second Street stands Christ Church, where many Revolutionary War people worshiped, including George Washington. Though the parish was founded in 1695, the building was completed in 1744 and is a fine example of Georgian Colonial architecture. Stepping inside the worshipful interior, the visitor can note Palladian window, graceful brass chandelier, and 18th-century wineglass pulpit. Sitting in the dark pews, one can imagine the many great Americans who worshiped in the "nation's church," including Benjamin Franklin, whose tomb is in the nearby graveyard. One of the cherished possessions is a 1697 baptismal font used for William Penn's baptism in England.

St. George's Methodist Church

North of the Independence Square area is a historic Methodist church, considered to be the oldest in the world used continuously for worship. Adjoining is the Methodist Historical Center. It is well worth ringing the bell at the rectory for a guided tour.

Mother Bethel African Methodist Church

Bishop Richard Allen, black spiritual giant, founded this church at 419 South Sixth Street, which stands on the oldest parcel of real estate owned by black people in the United States. Allen, born a slave, purchased his freedom for $2,000. He belonged to the white congregation of St. George's Methodist Episcopal Church. In 1784, he was licensed to preach and held services early Sunday mornings in the church for black people. As the attendance of the blacks increased, friction arose in the congregation. In 1787, Allen, Absalom Jones, and other black people withdrew and formed the Free African Society. From this developed many social and educational movements and at least two churches.

Allen, who felt called to remain in the Methodist denomination, held services in his home, then purchased the present lot. A blacksmith shop was hauled to the site and remodeled for a church. Bishop Francis Asbury, assisted by the pastor of St. George's Church, dedicated the building in 1794. The independent corporation of the Mother Bethel Church began in 1796. It was here in April 1816 in the congregation's second structure, that the first conference of the African Methodist Episcopal Church, was formed and Allen elected its first bishop.

The fourth home of the congregation is an impressive stone Romanesque structure dedicated in 1890. Visitors are invited to browse in the museum, where Allen's pulpit, Bible, and prayerstool chair may be seen, along with other historical data. Allen's tomb may also be seen. The church, which in its beginning had financial support from Dr. Benjamin Rush, signer of the Declaration of Independence, has now been designated a National Shrine by the National Park Service. Schools, colleges, magazines, and other helpful organizations have roots here. Allen also was instrumental in the founding of the Prince Hall Masonic Lodge, in operating the Underground Railway, and in rendering great service to all Philadelphia citizens during the Black Plague of 1793.

St. Thomas Protestant Episcopal Church

When the black people withdrew from St. George's Methodist Church in 1787 (see preceding entry), the majority wished to unite with the Church of England. Rev. Absalom Jones became their minister and conducted the first service in 1791 at the home of Joseph Sharpless. The congregation, now located at 52nd and Parrish streets, was incorporated in 1796. Jones, ordained a priest in 1804 by the bishop of Pennsylvania, was the first Negro to enter the Episcopal ministry in America. The church became a great educational power in the early days of the republic.

After a disastrous fire in December 1951, the congregation moved into its present building on February 10, 1953. A very real help in rebuilding was the deluge of countrywide contributions resulting from the appearance of Louis Potter, Whiz Kid on the "Strike It Rich" television show, when the church's story became known.

Old St. Joseph's Church

Roman Catholics were welcomed into Penn's fledgling colony, and St. Joseph's (located at 321 Willings Alley, below Walnut Street) was the first church in the city. Founded in 1733, it was where the Marquis de Lafayette and Rochambeau worshiped in Revolutionary days.

Gloria Dei (Old Swedes') Church

On Delaware Avenue near Christian Street is a National Historic Site recognizing the first Swedish settlers, who came to the area as early as 1631. A small log blockhouse was the first house of worship for the parish, which was organized in 1643. The present red-brick structure was dedicated in 1700 and is reminiscent of early Swedish congregations. There is a steep gable roof, square belfry, and small spire. Inside are carved cherubim and a baptismal font dating from 1643, brought over by the settlers. Old Bibles and silver altar appointments are in the historical collection, which is worth seeing.

While examining the various treasures, imagine the wedding of Betsy Ross to her second husband here in 1777. Wander through the churchyard and find many famous names, including Daniel Boone's sister Margaret. Gloria Dei Church separated from the mother church in 1789 and in 1845 became Episcopal, which it remains today.

Ukranian Catholic Cathedral of the Immaculate Conception

In downtown Philadelphia is another Catholic church, the world's largest of the Ukranian Byzantine Rite. The massive gold dome is ringed with 32 stained-glass windows. Of Byzantine architecture, the material is reinforced concrete and limestone. Mosaics, icons, and paintings adorn the interior. In the crypt are buried the first two Ukranian Catholic bishops in the United States.

Cathedral of the Immaculate Conception

Mikveh Israel Cemetery

In 1738, the Jewish community secured this cemetery at Spruce and 9th streets. This oldest of Jewish burying grounds is included in the Independence National Historic Park, for it has graves of Jewish patriots. Nathan Levy, whose ship brought the Liberty Bell to America, is buried here. It is also the last resting place of Haym Solomon, a patriot who was imprisoned in British jails for subversive activity. He performed valuable service as financier of the Revolution.

Congregation Rodeph Shalom

Jewish migrants came in the 1790s to Philadelphia. Here at 615 North Broad Street is the Byzantine structure built in 1927. Bronze doors of the Ark, a marble altar, and hand-appliqued painted walls grace the interior. An earlier synagogue on this same location was erected in 1869. The extensive archives provide a splendid place to learn more of the early Philadelphia Jewish community.

Southeastern Corner

WALLINGFORD

Pendle Hill Study Center

In Wallingford, close to the Quaker Swarthmore College, is an educational community founded by the Society of Friends in 1930. It endeavors to provide a place for individuals to live apart and grow, becoming a community of seekers. Named for the hill in England where George Fox saw his first vision, it is open to all ages as a conference center or an individual retreat. It also accommodates about 45 students (beyond high school age), offering courses in faith and action as well as growth in Christian living.

The traveler will find a quiet, restful place where nature's acres soothe. A student volleyball game may be in progress, or diligent researchers may be using the Peace Collection and Friends Historical Library at Swarthmore. Office personnel are welcoming and may have time to show the traveler the house where noted Quakers have stayed, including Elizabeth Gray Vining, author of *Windows for the Crown Prince,* and Henry Cadbury.

CHADDS FORD

Birmingham Meeting House

Proceeding northwest, but following a semicircle around Philadelphia, the traveler can visit many unusual spiritual heritage sites such as this Friends Meeting House located in the middle of Brandywine Battlefield. While defending Philadelphia against the troops of General Howe, Gen. George Washington fought an unsuccessful engagement around the meeting house. The one-story simple building with interesting porticos over the doorways was used as a hospital for sick American soldiers. "While there was such confusion without," wrote an eyewitness, "all was quiet and peaceful within." The meeting had been transferred to a wheelwright shop three miles away because the meeting house was not available. Lafayette and Count Casimir Pulaski fought in this engagement and there is a memorial monument in the surrounding graveyard.

VALLEY FORGE

Washington Memorial Chapel

Set in a park of 2,000 acres, which honors the Revolutionary Patriot Army, is an outstanding Gothic stone church facing the meadow called Grand Parade. Here the troops were drilled and here the joyous news of the French alliance received. The chapel is a monument to the men who endured the bitter winter of 1777-1778. Glowing stained-glass windows picture historical and religious scenes, while the memorial carillon may chime from the adjacent bell tower. The Cloister of the Colonies, connecting the chapel with the bell tower, has relics and exhibits which vividly portray the hardships endured. Battle lines and entrenchments are still visible.

Washington's Headquarters

The two-story stone house used by General Washington at Valley Forge was owned by Isaac Potts, Quaker preacher. No doubt Washington appreciated its comforts after living in the field tent now preserved in the museum. Simple furnishings of the period and authentic atmosphere give the visitor the eerie feeling that Washington might appear around the corner! It was in this house that Potts was said to have discovered the commander in chief at prayer.

American Baptist Churches

Since 1962, all national boards of the American Baptist Churches work in the glistening, white, circular structure close to the Valley Forge exit, Pennsylvania Turnpike. Baptists had begun in 1638 in Rhode Island and spread prolifically as the country grew. Overseas mission work began in 1812 with support of Ann and Adoniram Judson in Burma. A publication society, forerunner of the Judson Press, began in 1824, while a home mission society began in 1832. These groups were coordinated under the Northern Baptist Convention in 1907, which changed to its present title of American Baptist Churches in the USA in 1950. There are now churches and missions in 45 states and overseas mission work around the globe.

Ariel View, National Offices, American Baptist Convention

The award-winning two-building headquarters, designed by Vincent Kling, sits on 50 acres. The structural composition of fabricated stone is created of quartz fragments set in concrete. The resulting bricks were broken and turned outside to give a pleasing, rough exterior finish, with quartz crystals reflecting the sunlight. The main building, which is somewhat like the Colosseum in Rome, has 247 rooms, while the Graphic Arts building has 14. The Judson Bookstore is open for browsing and visitors can also take a building tour, preferably by appointment.

(5) TRAPPE

Augustus Lutheran Church

The oldest Lutheran church building in America was built in 1743 by Heinrich Melchior Muhlenberg. The congregation dates to 1730, however, when German Lutherans arrived. When the patriarch Muhlenberg, called the father of American Lutheran churches, answered the call of three small Lutheran churches in Pennsylvania, he found congregations at Philadelphia, New Hanover, and New Providence (Trappe). He became a tremendous influence, and was a denominational founder equal to Methodist Francis Asbury and Roman Catholic Bishop John Carroll. In 1748, he called 30 Swedish and German delegates for the first Lutheran synod gathering.

The rustic building constructed in the style of a Pennsylvania barn was in continuous use until 1825, when the "new" church was built. Now a national Lutheran shrine, it is used occasionally for services. In the burial ground are graves of Muhlenberg, his wife, and their son, Gen. John Peter Muhlenberg, colonial soldier, clergyman, and statesman.

Beth Sholom Synagogue

(6) ELKINS PARK

Beth Sholom Synagogue

Frank Lloyd Wright designed this magnificent synagogue at Foxcroft and Old York Rd. In this spiritually meaningful structure, Mt. Sinai, source and base of religious law, rises symbolically to the sky, framed by menorahs and supported by the sacred law. Probably the most dramatic piece of architecture in the county, it is particularly striking when seen at night, so travelers should plan to stay in the area and drive back after dark.

(7) BRYN ATHYN

Swedenborgian Cathedral

This magnificent Gothic church is the headquarters of the Church of the New Jerusalem in America. The name of the denomination comes from the biblical Book of Revelation as interpreted by Swedish scientist-theologian and philosopher Emanuel Swedenborg. This versatile religious genius never came to America, but his followers formed the first New Church society in London in 1787. James Glen, a rich American planter, brought word across the ocean and soon societies were formed in Philadelphia, Baltimore, Boston, and New York, Swedenborg's writings influenced many, including Bronson Alcott and Ralph Waldo Emerson.

Dedicated in 1919, the beautifully proportioned cathedral has Romanesque and Gothic towers, stone carvings, wood and metal artistry, and colorful stained-glass windows.

The Academy of the New Church, an educational institution and a publishing house, are in this religious community which originated in 1898. Cathedral and general book rooms are open weekdays and tours are conducted.

(8) DOYLESTOWN

National Shrine of Our Lady of Czestochowa

On Ferry Road, the traveler will see rising out of the picturesque countryside a shrine dedicated to Polish Christianity consisting of a tall basilica and monastery. The modern church was dedicated in 1966, commemorating 1,000 years of Christianity in Poland. Probably the most outstanding feature of the church is the set of stained-glass windows, considered to be the largest installation in the country. The history of Christianity in Poland is the theme of the west window, and the contribution of Christians to American history is the subject of the east window. Also to be appreciated are the Holy Family sculpture over the altar and the copy of the painting of Our Lady of Czestochowa.

Mideastern Pennsylvania

(9) EDGEGROVE

Basilica of the Sacred Heart of Jesus

This shrine with beginnings dating to colonial times is in the oldest Catholic community west of the Susquehanna. The area, known as Conewago, has long been a center for missionary activity, with the first log chapel built here in 1741. The present fieldstone-and-brownstone church was built in 1787. In 1850, the transepts and apse were added. A spire was erected in 1873. The murals on the walls and ceiling, done by Franz Stecher, the Austrian painter, in 1851, are particularly beautiful.

(10) YORK

Farmers' Markets

At Central Market House, at the Farmers' Market, and at Eastern Market House, intriguing sights and scenes abound as Pennsylvania Dutch delicacies are sold in the hustle and bustle of a farming community. The center of a Mennonite area, the products of their agrarian way of life reach consumers here. The visitor can come away with a new taste treat if he purchases shoo-fly pie, with a choice of wet or dry bottom! Other delicacies are dandelion salad, fast nachercake, and vinegar pie.

Out of the Dutch Anabaptist movement, and related to Zwingli's influence in Switzerland, came a small group termed "Mennonites." Believing firmly in a church of believers, they were against infant baptism. They also believe in separation of church and state and in a true brotherhood with mutual aid and strength. The first Mennonites came to Germantown, Pennsylvania, in 1683, but spread to other areas as more adherents arrived from Europe. A plain and simple people, they have through the years divided into a variety of groups, which can be confusing to outsiders. They also have their own schools, with Pennsylvania having more Mennonite parochial schools than any other state.

(11) MANHEIM

Old Rose Church

Hopefully the traveler can arrange schedules so as to be in this town the second Sunday in June, for in Zion Lutheran Church, also known as Old Rose Church, the Feast of Roses ceremony is conducted.

Baron William Stiegel, of Stiegel glass fame, founded the city and rented the church property for an annual fee of one red rose. Payment to a Stiegel heir is made at the annual rose festival. Nearby on Main Street are the remains of Baron Stiegel's house.

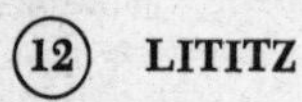

(12) LITITZ

Brothers House

Close to Manheim and north of Lancaster, is one of the communities settled by the Moravians, another of the Pietist sects who sought refuge in the New World. They were first known as United Brethren and were descended from 15th-century Hussites in Moravia and Bohemia.

Maintaining an underground existence, in the 18th century a few of the "hidden seed" found refuge on the Saxon estate of Count Nicholas Zinzendorf. Their colony of Herrenhut developed and Zinzendorf was made bishop. Wanting to minister to the American Indians, a party first went to Georgia in 1735. On a second voyage, their leader, Augustus Spangenberg, visited John Wesley. Later the Brethren went to Pennsylvania, settling Nazareth and Bethlehem. Though Bethlehem is the most complete settlement to visit, Lititz, founded by them in 1743, has remnants of the early town.

The Brothers House, erected in 1759, is one of several that can be toured. Visit the Sturgis Pretzel House first, then see Linden Hall—a girls' school founded in 1746. In Lititz Springs Park, if the traveler is here on July 4, the illumination of a thousand candles can be seen.

(13) LANCASTER

The Amish Homestead

Continuing south to Lancaster, the traveler can have a close look at Amish ways by stopping to see an Old Order Amish homestead. The 71 acre spread is still a working farm. Stop at the entrance with the orange milk cans, 3 miles east of Lancaster on Route 462. Be sure to arrive before mid-afternoon, so you can see the entire operation.

(14) BIRD-IN-HAND

Weavertown Church

Turning north, the traveler can view a church of the Church-Amish or Beachy-Amish seçt in Bird-in-Hand. Members broke away from the Old Order Amish in 1927 under the leadership of Bishop Moses Beachy, when he refused to pronounce the ban of avoidance on former members who left to join with Amish-Mennonites in Maryland.

Beachy-Amish, contrary to Old Amish, do have churches. They also use automobiles and allow use of electricity and tractors. The largest congregation meets in this plain, simple meeting house. They do, however, retain much of the unique Amish dress and use the German language and Pennsylvania Dutch dialect. Missionary-minded members aid the needy, and women sew clothing and other items.

(15) EPHRATA

Ephrata Cloister

Wending his or her way northward, the traveler comes upon one of the most unusual (and best preserved) complexes of the communal sects that ever arrived in the state. This medieval cloister of the pious and ascetic Seventh-day Baptists was founded in 1732 by Conrad Beissel, a German Pietist mystic. One of the many sects to find homes in Penn's tolerant colony, this community consisted of three orders—a brotherhood, a sisterhood, and a married order of householders. Household arts and other skills (bookmaking, carpentry, etc.) were developed as members worshiped God in the medieval manner through lives of austere self-denial and pious simplicity. At its height in 1750, the Society numbered about 300 persons and it continued until 1814. Then the remaining households incorporated as the Seventh-day Baptist Church, using the building as a congregation until 1934.

The visitor will be absorbed by the

Ephrata Cloister

log and stone buildings constructed in Rhenish style and by the austere style of life which included wooden pillows. The Stone Almonry, Saren (Sisters House), Academy, Saal (Chapel), and Householder's Cottage speak of a different way of life. Members nursed 500 soldiers here during the Revolution. They also established the Ephrata Press, which is still in operation. Magnificent hand-illuminated songbooks and inscriptions, as well as hymns, were produced here. Building tours are available by costumed guides, but the most dramatic way to hear the Ephrata story is via the music drama *Verspiel* on summer evenings.

Ephrata Clothing Center

Also in this community is the remarkable worldwide relief and service agency operated by the Mennonite Central Committee. Here volunteers at a recent Christmas season prepared 14,660 bundles for distribution to 30 countries. Central Committee headquarters is in Akron, Pennsylvania.

The first Mennonite Church for the Deaf, was established in Ephrata in 1946.

(16) PENNSBURG

Schwenkfelder Library

In 1734, 180 Schwenkfelders, exiled from Silesia, landed in Pennsylvania. Spiritual descendants of Caspar Schwenckfeld von Ossig, Silesian nobleman, scholar, reformer, and preacher, they were bitterly persecuted by the orthodox churches because they proposed "the Reformation by the Middle Way." On November 24, the Schwenkfelders held a service of Thanksgiving for the deliverance and for the safe arrival in the New World. Their five churches, which now form the General Conference of the Schwenkfelder Church, observe this Thanksgiving ser-

vice annually. Officially organized in 1782, the group now has an associate affiliation with the United Church of Christ.

This beautiful library set in the rustic Pennsylvania countryside has an unusually large collection of 18th- and 19th-century materials, and scholars find their way to it from afar. Nearby, in the library on the campus of Perkiomen School, is a museum which has the original hand-decorated wooden chests brought over on the first voyage as well as many other intriguing artifacts.

(17) BETHLEHEM

Moravian Museum

The oldest building in Bethlehem is the Gemeinhaus (Community House) at 66 W. Church St. built by the Moravians who arrived in 1741 from Bohemia and Saxony. David Zeisberger, leader, began the first building which was completed before Christmas when the second party under Count Zinzendorf arrived. A joyous Christmas Eve service has been repeated each year since. Many of the original stone buildings are still standing and form the nucleus of a remarkable city. Bell House, the girls' boarding school, First House, a replica of the first log cabin, and the Old Chapel are a few of the buildings to be seen on tour. Visitors should step into the old graveyard and see the simple equal stones. Here in God's Acre a black man, a bishop, a child are buried next to each other in order of death, for all people are equal before God. Though a visit here is fascinating at any time of year, Christmas Eve in Christmas City is a high point. Another special time is the annual Bach festival in May, which is usually sold out well in advance. This continuation of the Moravian service of song, begun by Zinzendorf in 1742, now includes the Philadelphia Philharmonic Orchestra, guest soloists, and a marvelous choir.

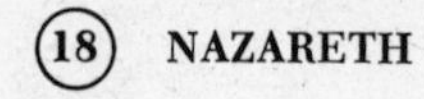

(18) NAZARETH

Whitefield House

Although Nazareth has long been known as a Moravian town, it was a Methodist, George Whitefield, who first purchased a 5,000-acre tract in 1740. He hired Peter Boehler and a few Moravians to erect a school for blacks. In 1742, the Moravians bought the property and two years later opened the first school on the "Barony of Nazareth."

At East Center and New streets is the museum and library of the Moravian Historical Society. First occupants were German emigrants in 1744. Now it contains extensive memorabilia of early days. Other unique possessions are the Revolutionary religious paintings of Rev. John Valentine Haidt, one of the country's first pipe organs, a viola made by an 8-year-old boy, and rare volumes of Bishop John Ames Comenius, Moravian clergyman and educator. His child's picture book written in Europe about 1654 is considered the first ever issued.

Nazareth Hall

This finest example of Moravian architecture in the country was intended for Count Zinzendorf, in 1755, but he never lived here. From 1785 to 1929, it housed a Moravian school for boys, and presently is part of the Will Beitel Children's Home.

Nearby, on Ephrata Place, is the oldest Moravian building in America, Gray Cottage. Built in 1740, it housed the first school in Nazareth. Now non-Moravians may own property in the town; but, until its incorporation in 1856, Nazareth was exclusively a Moravian settlement.

Southwestern Pennsylvania

(19) FARMINGTON

New Meadow Run Community

In the rolling hillside of southwest Pennsylvania, close to the West Virginia border, is one of the three Bruderhof communities in this country. Here in 1964 the print shop of the Society of Brothers was established where materials are produced for its Plough Publishing House. Its aim is to publish that which speaks of a new life for man—a life based not on "a man-made utopian dream, but on the reality experienced by the early Christians, the Quakers of George Fox's time, the Anabaptists, and others."

As in the communities at Rifton, New York, and Norfolk, Connecticut, visitors (not tourists) are welcome to stay for a while who are interested in an alternative way of life. Also, please write ahead, giving at least a week's notice.

(20) AMBRIDGE

Old Economy Village

Six hundred followers of German-born "Father" George Rapp established the Harmonie Society in Ambridge in 1805. Like the Shakers, the Rappites set upon the road to perfection by close personal discipline in order that a pure remnant could be ready for the Second Coming. The utopian experiment was devoted to communal living, brotherhood, celibacy, and pacifism. The new community was immediately successful

Old Economy Village

because of the labor-saving equipment and the willingness to work. There quickly developed occupations that produced textiles, wine, lumber, bricks, and flour.

Visitors will be entranced by the 18 well-preserved buildings, a formal garden with a meditation grotto and pavilion. There are craft shops and workrooms, as well as three other outstanding structures. The Feast Hall was arranged to seat 1,000 people when on ceremonial days all the inhabitants of Economy ate together. Twelve massive kettles repose in the Feast Kitchen. The Baker House is a typical dwelling of three to 11 men and women who made up a "family." The Great House of founder George Rapp, with its 25 well-furnished rooms, shows his life to have been less austere than that of his followers. The practice of celibacy eventually caused the Society's dissolution in 1905.

HARMONY

Harmony Museum

Surrounding the green diamond of picturesque Harmony are several original buildings of the Harmonists. The museum gives a historical record of the Harmonie Society founded by German Johann George Rapp and about 500 followers in 1805. Pledging their worldly possessions for the common good, the Society soon had 130 buildings erected and a flourishing society. In 1807, Father Rapp and his adopted son Frederick Reichert advocated celibacy, which ultimately led to extinction of the group.

Wanting to exclude luxuries and keep control, the Society moved to virgin land in Indiana, founding New Harmony in 1814. Another move was made in 1824 to Ohio and the Society disbanded there in 1905.

When the Harmonists departed for Indiana, the town was advertised for sale and purchased by the Mennonites. Many present-day residents are descendants of Abraham Ziegler and his five Mennonite associates.

The museum has the oldest tower clock in the Western hemisphere. It was brought from a German monastery by Frederick Rapp and dates to 1650. It was in operation for 300 years. The entrance to the Bentle Museum building has a figure of the Virgin Sophia carved by Frederick Rapp, which was used as a religious symbol by Harmonists.

Religious pilgrims will want to visit the Mennonite church and cemetery.

WEST VIRGINIA

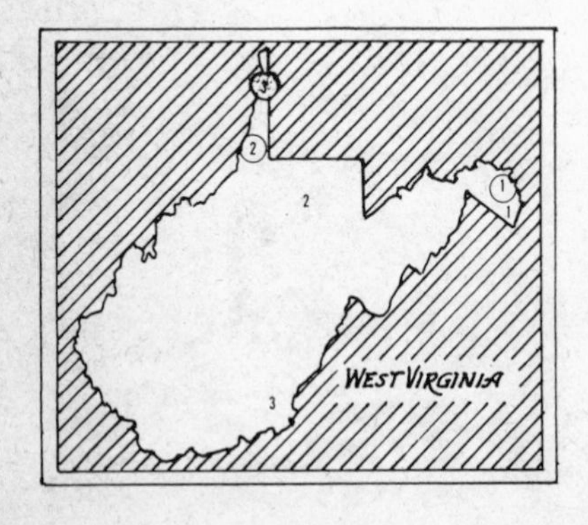

Ancient Mound Builders, then later native Americans, first occupied this territory in the heart of Appalachia. Broad plateaus, forested mountains, and deep valleys made for unusual beauty but hindered travel. The first settler is believed to be Morgan Morgan, who came to Bunker Hill, near today's Charlestown, in 1726. Shortly after, Scotch-Irish and German pioneers crossed over from Pennsylvania and Maryland (1730-1734) to begin the state's oldest town of Shepherdstown. Presbyterian and Lutheran churches resulted. Soon coal mining became the backbone of the region's economy.

Presbyterians were part of the east coast synod which was organized in 1717. Their parishes played an important part in the American Revolution, for they supported Jefferson's efforts to free dissenters from paying taxes to support the established Church of England. (In those days, West Virginia was part of Virginia and did not become a separate state until Civil War days.) The synod constitution included the statement, "God alone is Lord of the Conscience," so Presbyterians vigorously supported separation of church and state.

Lutherans were served by itinerant pastors as early as 1735, when Rev. Johannes Stoever traveled the area. Later the indefatigable missioner Rev. Henry Muhlenberg was in charge of the entire area.

In the early 1800s, Baptist and Methodist churches began when their missionaries traveled the area. With the increase of communication and travel through the isolated terrain, more religious groups have established congregations. Today there is an air of ecumenicity in this state on the Allegheny plateau.

(1) SHEPHERDSTOWN

St. Peter's Lutheran Church

A stone Gothic structure with corner tower entrance houses the spiritual descendants of the first German Lutherans who settled at Pack Horse Ford on the Potomac. The congregation dates from 1735 when itinerant pastor Stoever visited new settlements along the Potomac. First members worshiped in a church of "dressed logs," until a brick structure was built in 1695. The present notable building of native blue limestone is trimmed with Ohio granite. The tower door latch, "wrought" in 1795, has inscribed in German, "Guard your feet when you go into the House of the Lord."

The old Lutheran graveyard and its adjacent log school will take the traveler back to an earlier era. Built in 1774, the German school housed classes which began earlier in 1762. The town's founder, Thomas Shepherd, built a gristmill in 1739, which still stands. It is reputed to have the oldest and largest waterwheel anywhere, which can be seen on Town Run. On German Street, the main thoroughfare, a few original homes of the early German artisans—coppersmiths, clockmakers, gunsmiths, potters, and carpenters—still stand.

(2) MOUNDSVILLE

Mammoth Mound

On the northwestern boundary of West Virginia is the tallest prehistoric Indian burial ground of its type (69 feet) in the country. Dating between 1,000 and 2,000 years ago, it was originally surrounded by a moat and crossed by passageways. Built by the Mound Builder natives of the valley, it contains vaults, burial chambers, and tablets with hieroglyphics. It was excavated in 1838 and now is open, along with a museum, to visitors who wish to view something of the religious and ceremonial life of those first citizens.

(3) BETHANY

Bethany College

Continuing north on Route 88 into the West Virginia panhandle, the traveler comes to the birthplace of the Disciples of Christ denomination. The founder, Alexander Campbell, was a Presbyterian preacher's son from Ireland. Campbell came to America in 1808, moved to Bethany, and was ordained in 1812. Finding his ideas not accepted by Presbyterianism, he became Baptist. Finding the same difficulty, he and a few followers founded the Disciples of Christ. Campbell based the new congregation on primitive Christianity and stressed the unity of all Christian churches.

Alexander Campbell Mansion

In 1818, Campbell opened Buffalo Academy in his home to educate boys and girls. A print shop was established in 1823 and soon his prolific writings brought other adherents. Campbell fearlessly campaigned for free schools, public education, and the political recognition of West Virginia. When a college was needed, Bethany was founded in his home in 1840. Primarily for the youth of his church, it developed into one of the most influential centers west of the Alleghenies. By 1890, the denomination had grown to about 200,000 members.

Today, visitors to the campus may see Old Main and the Alexander Campbell Mansion, both of which are on the National Register.

DISTRICT OF COLUMBIA

The sites are so compacted here, it is best for the traveler to obtain a detailed street guide. Additional sites are in the Appendix.

The city of Washington, which is coextensive with the District of Columbia, became in 1800 the "Federal Town" of the young nation. The site had been selected by George Washington, who called on Pierre L'Enfant, French soldier and engineer, to design it. Though slow in developing, by 1850 the city of Washington had begun to resemble the beautiful, spacious metropolis of today, revealing how well L'Enfant had envisioned the capital.

Among the verdant parks, broad avenues, and elaborate buildings are a significant number of churches, as well as religious, medical, and educational institutions, indicating how religion was built into the fabric of American life. Here today is a microcosm of the religious life of the country at large. There are so many spiritual heritage sites that all cannot be mentioned in these few pages.

The religious pilgrim can begin, however, with the national shrines and headquarters of the various denominations and faiths. From these, other sites can be found. Such travels should start in the Capitol area, for here the city began when the cornerstone for the United States Capitol building was laid in 1793.

NORTHEAST WASHINGTON

National Shrine of the Immaculate Conception

The seventh largest church in the world and the largest Roman Catholic church in the United States, at Michigan Avenue and Fourth Street N.W., is still being completed. A large crypt was opened in 1926 and was used for over 30 years before the upper church was dedicated in 1959. Without a steel framework, it is made entirely of stone, brick, tile, and concrete. It combines Byzantine, Romanesque, and modern design in an interesting way.

The exterior has a blue-and-gold tiled dome, with mosaics and sculptures on the outside walls. A 320-foot high Knight's Tower holds a 56-bell carillon. The interior has rich tapestries, stained-glass windows, statues, and mosaic reproductions of famous paintings.

Though a day tour of the vast structure is recommended, the traveler may want to come back in the evening, for recitals on the carillon precede evening concerts.

Franciscan Monastery

If the traveler has not been able to visit the Holy Land, he should make every effort to visit Mount St. Sepulcher, Memorial Church to the Holy Land. Here at 14th and Quincy Sts. N.W. the Order of Friars Minor, guardians of the shrines of the Holy Land, founded and maintain a unique complex which re-creates many of the sites. Visitors can see replicas of the Holy Sepulcher, the Annunciation Grotto in Nazareth, and the Grotto of Bethlehem, as well as the Catacombs of Rome and the Grotto of Lourdes in France. There is a small museum of biblical arts and crafts, Holy Land artifacts, and Crusader relics. The Byzantine-style church and landscaped gardens provide a beautiful setting.

Howard University

The Reconstruction years were upon the young republic when Howard University opened its doors in 1867 on a tract of land at Georgia and Florida avenues, the site of a former slave plantation. The school was first conceived as a training school for colored preachers, then broadened to "prepare teachers for the colored population." Its first black president, Dr. Mordecai Johnson, underscored many years later, however, that the school continues as it began, educating all youth as well as the well-prepared and disadvantaged Negroes.

Normal, collegiate, medical, law, and theological departments opened first and in 1870 the first graduates headed a list of over 27,000 that have now received degrees and diplomas from the university's ten schools and colleges. Though many whites have attended, the majority of students have been blacks. A sizable number of graduates live in foreign countries, especially the British West Indies.

A walk around the extensive campus is an introduction to the stars of the emancipation movement, for many buildings are named for black leaders. Frederick Douglass Memorial Hall honors the great abolitionist; Tubman Court is a reminder of the black "Moses" of the Underground Railway; Baldwin Hall memorializes Maria Baldwin, the principal of noted Agassiz High School in Boston; Ira Aldridge Theater is a reminder of the famed Shakespearean actor.

Church of the Saviour

An unusual congregation is housed in a large mansion in the embassy area at 2025 Massachusetts Ave. N.W. When Rev. Gordon Cosby returned from the Pacific theater of World War II, he felt called to develop a new style of church for a rapidly changing age. That he has been instrumental in doing so is clear to a visitor who attends Sunday morning service, steps into the Potter's House coffee house, attends a conference at the retreat center Dayspring, or observes the many mission units in action. The inspiring books of staff member Elizabeth O'Connor detail the development of this ecumenical church and are heartily recommended. Winner of the 1970 national *Guideposts* Award, the church members, who go through a probationary period, pioneer in meeting needs of people. Visitors are welcome at Potter's House, 1658 Columbia Road N.W., which is open weekdays and evenings. Check for hours.

National Presbyterian Church and Center

A dual purpose is served by this impressive Neo-Gothic group of six buildings. Set on a 12-acre site and dominated by a 173-foot Tower of Faith, the center serves both as a national church for Presbyterians and as a conference center for people of all faiths. Opened in 1969, the center also presents musical programs and dramas.

The Chapel of the Presidents, dedicated to Dwight D. Eisenhower, has his pew marked as well as the prie-dieu

Tower of Faith,
National Presbyterian Church

on which he knelt at his baptism. Several presidents are shown in the stained-glass windows, and pews recall 17 presidents who worshiped with the congregation.

Islamic Center

An exotic touch awaits the traveler who visits the Muslim center (2551 Massachusetts Avenue N.W.) with its 160-foot minaret. The center contains a mosque, library, and lecture hall, as well as classrooms and offices of the Institute for Higher Study of Islamic Culture. It serves the Muslim community.

The walls and ceiling of the mosque are richly decorated with colorful patterns and contain gifts from Muslim countries. There are tiles from Turkey, rugs from Iran, and mosaic inscriptions in Arabic from the Holy Quran. Visitors remove their shoes and sit on luxurious carpets inside the mosque.

Islam, or Mohammedanism, was founded in the 7th century by Mohammed of Mecca. His teachings spread rapidly throughout lands to the south and east of the Mediterranean Sea. The Quran holds the body of his teaching. God is all-powerful, he said, and man's duty is submission to the will of God. Prayers, almsgiving, and abstinence from wine are among religious obligations taught the prophet.

Washington Cathedral

Another in this city of amazing structures is the Cathedral Church of St. Peter and St. Paul, reminiscent of the medieval cathedrals of Europe. At Massachusetts Ave. N.W. and Mt. St. Albans, it is a 14th-century Gothic-style building of the Episcopal church. Begun in 1907, it is still in the process of construction, with target date for completion in the 1980s. It will then be the sixth largest church in the world. A 310-foot-high Gloria-in-Excelsis Tower, the tallest point in Washington, contains a 53-bell carillon with a ten-bell peal for change ringing. On the grounds are a bishop's garden and Herb Cottage.

The vaulted interior gives a feeling of awe and wonder. The Jerusalem altar has 12 stones quarried from Solomon's mines in Jerusalem. Other features are the Children's Chapel, which is small in scale, and the Chapel of the Holy Spirit with N. C. Wyeth's wood reredos.

General Conference of Seventh-day Adventists

On the northwest border of the District at 6840 Eastern Ave. N.W. is the world headquarters of one of the denominations begun in America. Seventh-day Adventists around the world look to this central office for direction and coordination. Budgets, missionary appointments, and communications begin here. The building housing the offices of the major publication, *Review and Herald,* located next to the North Building, is home of one of the oldest continuously published religious journals in America. It is open for visitors. The three-building complex houses a staff of 300.

SOUTHWEST WASHINGTON

Georgetown University

Archbishop John Carroll was the founder of the nation's first Roman Catholic college, which later became a university. Originally a seminary, the Jesuit-managed complex now has ten schools, including many for the professions.

The Healy Building is particularly noteworthy, for it was commissioned by the son of a former slave. Father Healy had a sister who founded an order of nuns to teach black children. A brother was bishop of Portland, Maine. Healy was the 29th president of Georgetown University and the first black president. A statue of Carroll, by Jerome Connor, recalls the first American Catholic bishop and is a reminder of the illustrious Catholic Carroll family of Maryland.

IV.

THE SOUTH

FLORIDA

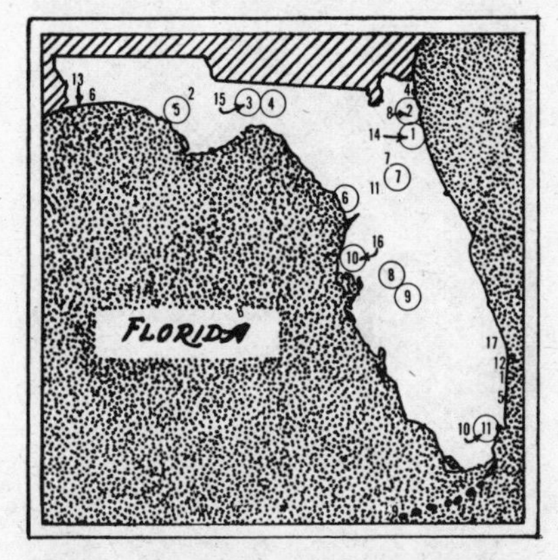

Spanish galleons brought white explorers to the southern part of America as early as 1513, when Ponce de Leon landed on Florida's east coast. Several later attempts at settlement were rebuffed by the sizable population of Seminoles. When French Huguenots established Fort Carolina near the present Jacksonville, however, King Philip of Spain sent an expedition both to eject the Protestants and to establish a permanent colony. After crushing the French, Spanish admiral Don Pedro Menendez de Aviles founded St. Augustine, America's oldest permanent white settlement.

Coming ashore with Menendez on September 8, 1565, was Father Francisco Lopez, carrying a cross. Here he established the first of many missions to whites and native Americans. So well did he and his colleagues transmit the message of their faith that a century later over 26,000 Christian Indians could be counted along the coast and as far inland as the present Tallahassee. Religious pilgrims should note that St. Augustine had 1,600 inhabitants before the Pilgrims were born!

Northeastern Florida

(1) ST. AUGUSTINE

Mission of Nombre De Dios

On a quiet point on Matanzas Bay is the ancient shrine of America's oldest mission, the site where Father Lopez de Mendoza offered the first mass in 1565. A marked walk through the peaceful grounds takes visitors to a statue of Father Lopez, the Prince of Peace Church, and the chapel and shrine of Our Lady of Leche. When the mission celebrated its 400th birthday in 1965, a 208-foot stainless steel cross was erected on the spot where the original cross was first planted. From the waterways and from the land, the cross, marking the first community of the Christian religion in the United States is an impressive site, especially when seen floodlit at night.

Cathedral of St. Augustine

St. Augustine City Gates

The fun way to see ancient St. Augustine is either by tram or by horse and carriage. Proceeding south from the mission, one can observe the old city gates, all that is now left of the 1704 Cubo Line of defense. Close by are old Protestant and Spanish cemeteries, reminders of the first two groups to settle here. Bypassing old St. George Street, which is beautifully restored and best seen walking, the tourist should next go to Cathedral Street.

This church, which is the oldest Christian parish in the United States, is custodian of church records dating back to 1594 when it was the headquarters of all Spanish missions in the southeast. The present building, erected in 1793, was made a cathedral in 1870. After a disastrous fire in 1887, the church was rebuilt. A transept and campanile were added to the original nave. A complete refurbishing was done in 1965. In the beautiful church are Spanish floor tiles, a baroque gold tabernacle from Ireland, and murals depicting the life of St. Augustine.

St. Francis Barracks

Across from the city's oldest house on St. Francis St., which is well worth visiting, is the site of a Franciscan Friary in operation from 1573 to 1763. Now the home of the St. Augustine Historical Society, its coquina (native shell) walls were once part of the Chapel and Convent of the Immaculate Conception established by Franciscan missionaries from Spain.

Flagler Memorial Presbyterian Church

This elegant Venetian Renaissance church was built in 1890 by Henry Flagler as a memorial to his daughter. Flagler, one of Florida's earliest developers, established the railroad systems of the state.

The 150-foot-high copper dome is inlaid with marble. The hand-carved mahogany woods came from Santo Domingo. The Aeolian-Skinner organ is considered one of the country's finest, having four manuals, 70 registers, 90 pipe ranks, and festival trumpets.

Summer is the best time to visit this fascinating city, when *The Cross and the Sword* can be seen. This reenactment of the city's founding combines acting, singing, dancing, lighting, and scenic design in an outdoor amphitheater. Tourists will find a visit to the information center and an introductory movie most helpful.

(2) JACKSONVILLE

Fort Caroline National Memorial

Proceeding north on A1A by the open ocean, one comes to a historic site by St. John's River. Here, east of the heart of Jacksonville, French Huguenots landed in 1564, beginning the first permanent European colony north of Mexico. Since the settlement was a threat to the Spanish territories, Menendez was sent north to crush the colony, which he did in 1565. Now Fort Caroline has been restored by the Park Service, using a sketch by Jaques de Moyne, member of the original company. The Visitors' Center has pictorial displays to highlight the history.

Western Florida

(3) TALLAHASSEE

The traveler following the path of the early Catholic missionaries and explorers will see western Florida next. The old Spanish Trail began in St. Augustine, where zero milepost can still be seen. It continued west to San Diego, becoming the first transcontinental highway. One of the first stops was this community, which was an early mission station. Now it serves as Florida's capital. In still earlier days, it was headquarters of the Micosukee tribe which, with white encroachment, moved south to the Everglades.

(4) CENTERVILLE

Pisgah Methodist Church

A little east of Tallahassee is the oldest Methodist church in the state. Men of the community hewed pine logs for walls and old casks for seats in 1825. Circuit riders preached here before this, however—as early as 1820. The fledgling church, named for the biblical mountain near the Dead Sea in the Holy Land, was officially organized in 1830. The log church was replaced with a frame building during territorial days. The present building, built in 1858, provided balconies for black members. It was dedicated in 1859, on the eve of the Civil War, and had a homecoming in 1971.

(5) VERNON

Moss Hill Methodist Church

Another of those Methodist churches planted by circuit riders is found 3 miles from Vernon. Established in 1823, it was first a mission and met in a blockhouse. Later the Methodists shared a combination log schoolhouse with Baptists and Presbyterians. The present building was erected in 1857, and the deed was signed by Abraham Lincoln. Planks came from virgin pines. The square nails and wooden pegs used can still be seen. A dividing line down the middle is a reminder of the days when women and men sat separately.

Central Florida

(6) CRYSTAL RIVER

Crystal River Historic Memorial

Turning south along the west coast, the traveler comes to a reminder of the first residents. The Mound Builders' culture, which originated in Mexico and spread northward, left many sites like this in our country. It is estimated that ceremonies at this area took place from about the 2nd century B.C. to the 15th century A.D. A walk around the trails reveals many interesting mounds, including a 40-foot-high temple mound and a burial crypt. Over 450 burial sites have been discovered. A museum has pottery and artifacts on display.

(7) SILVER SPRINGS

Prince of Peace Memorial

Sculptor Paul Cunningham is responsible for the art work in this series of ten chapel buildings. Each has fine handcarved scenes of the life of Christ from the nativity to the resurrection. Clothing, tools, landscape, and architecture are faithful to that period in the Holy Land.

This area is also noted for Silver River, a subterranean stream with water of such clarity that glass-bottom boats reveal remarkable details of underwater life.

(8) LAKELAND

Annie Pfeiffer Chapel

The Methodists established Florida Southern College. On the 100-acre campus is the largest collection of Frank Lloyd Wright buildings. For 20 years, beginning in 1936, the noted architect designed seven monumental buildings, of which this chapel is one of the most distinctive. Instead of a traditional steeple, there is a steel tower. Interesting light patterns play inside through the glass walls.

In the Garden of Meditation is a Hindu temple. Two ancient elephants made of stone stand guard.

(9) LAKE WALES

Masterpiece Gardens

Before turning toward the west coast, the traveler would do well to visit this town with its several attractions of religious interest. After driving by acres of citrus groves, one arrives at Lake Pierce and this amazing mosaic masterpiece. An intricate reproduction of Leonardo da Vinci's "Last Supper" is set beautifully in tropical gardens and jungle foliage. The mosaic, which is 12 by 24 feet, has more than 300,000 stones in 10,000 shades. It was made in Germany in 1930. Narrations of its story are given every half hour.

Black Hills Passion Play

Every winter, the whole cast, including the animals, travel from Spearfish, South Dakota, to Lake Wales to present the Passion Play. From February through April, an outdoor amphitheater is the scene of a dramatic presentation of the Passion. The staging, lights, and sound give the viewer the almost eerie feeling of being a participant.

(10) TARPON SPRINGS

Greek Orthodox Church of St. Nicholas

On the west coast, just above the St. Petersburg area, is a town settled by Greek sponge fishermen. At North Pinellas Avenue and Orange Street is the ornate church. Its altar, bishop's throne, and choir stations are of Greek marble and were donated by the royal Greek government.

Though the church retains many ancient ecclesiastical rites, one of the most colorful is the Epiphany (or Greek Cross) service on January 6. Before dawn candles glow and priests evoke chants commemorating the baptism of Jesus by John the Baptist, as well as the coming of the Wisemen. Then at noon a splendid procession moves through the streets. Church dignitaries are in front and acolytes swinging censers follow. At the bayou shore, a priest steps into a barge. Then he releases a dove which casts a shadow-cross on the water. A gold cross is cast into the water and olive-skinned divers leap into the water. One soon emerges with the cross and the blessing for the coming year. Feasting and a holiday follow.

Southern Florida

(11) MIAMI

Spanish Monastery Cloisters

An 800-year-old monastery in America? The traveler may wonder about this, until one hears that this wandering monastery, built in 1141 in Segovia, Spain, was purchased by William Randolph Hearst in 1920 and shipped over piece by piece. Its 37,784 stones were transported in 10,751 crates to Miami.

An incredible jigsaw puzzle resulted when the master plan of numbered pieces was lost. However, the building originally erected by King Alphonso VII was finally reassembled and looks as it did before except for a few modern touches required by the building code. It stands at 16711 West Dixie Highway in the North Miami section.

Visitors will want to stroll through cloister and patio, see the chapter house, and admire the inspiring stone figure of Christ sculpted by Cistercian monks long ago.

Today it is the home of an Episcopal congregation and the church is called St. Bernard de Clairvaux. The St. Bernard Foundation sponsors the tours and the gift shop.

GEORGIA

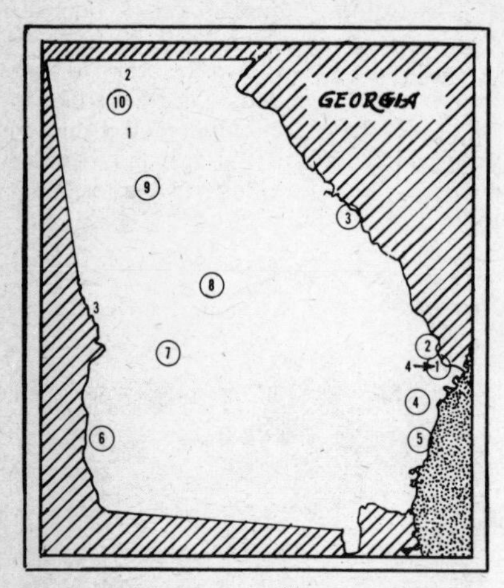

Though Spanish missions on St. Simons and Jekyll islands brought Catholicism to the area in 1566, Protestants established the first permanent settlement in the state. The British, watching warily the gradual encroachment of the Spanish in Florida, gave James Oglethorpe a charter for a colony just north of Savannah. Here, in 1733, Oglethorpe negotiated with Creek Indian chief Tomachichi for a tract of land. The purpose of the new colony was to welcome persecuted Protestants and debtors. German Protestants (Salzburgers), as well as English, Scotch, and Swiss Protestants, soon arrived, to be joined by Portuguese Jews.

Immediate prosperity brought an influx of more colonists from northern states to the inland Piedmont area and to St. John's coastal parish. Strict sanctions against rum and slavery of the earlier religious colonists were relaxed, problems arose between the groups, and Oglethorpe relinquished his colony to the Crown. The varied religious character of the colony which resulted from its early open policy continued, however. Here the Wesleys, John and Charles, found welcome in 1733, as did Moravians and others of differing religious persuasions. From the large slave population the indigenous black churches developed.

In recent times the civil rights movement developed its major thrust under the religious and political leadership of Atlanta's Rev. Martin Luther King, Jr. Here, too, whites took a stand for integration with the founding of Koinonia Community at Americus.

Eastern Georgia

(1) SAVANNAH

Congregation Mickve Israel

Spiritual descendants of the first Sephardic Jews who arrived from Portugal in 1733 worship in this oldest Reform temple in North America. Those arrivals brought with them the original Sofer Torah and copies of correspondence between Levi Sheftal to George Washington, which may be seen in the museum. The temple was consecrated in 1878 and still serves an active congregation at 20 East Gordon Street.

Christ Church

At 28 Bull Street, is this reminder of English early settlers. Christ Church

(Episcopal) was the home of the first parish organized in the colony as well as the first Protestant Sunday school in the country. To this congregation came John Wesley, where he spent the years 1736-1737 ministering in Savannah.

The present building, the third on this site, was built in 1838 and is of Greek Revival style. Six Ionic columns grace the entrance and an elaborate plaster ceiling, cast from molds made by Sir Christopher Wren, are special features. The only Paul Revere bell south of Washington calls people to worship. Several blocks away in Colonial Park is the old Christ Church Cemetery, the colony's first burying ground.

Wesley Monumental United Methodist Church

Methodists are very conscious that John and Charles Wesley, founders of Methodism, spent the years 1735-1738 preaching and teaching in the colony, most of the time in the Savannah area. In 1875, Methodists throughout the world contributed toward this Gothic-style memorial at 429 Abercorn St. to the brothers. It is modeled after Queen's Kirk in Amsterdam, Holland. In the large sanctuary are stained-glass windows by Tiffany, dedicated to the memory of famous Methodists.

Cathedral of St. John the Baptist

At first Savannah was a Protestant stronghold, but later, in accordance with the open policy toward religious groups, Catholics came to the city. This largest cathedral in the southeast, at 222 East Harris Street, was built in 1898, replacing an earlier building. It is of French Gothic design and has many stained-glass windows, most from the Austrian Tyrol. Other special features are the high altar made of Italian white marble which survived the burning of the previous church, hand-carved stations of the cross from Munich, and an Italian bronze bas-relief of St. John the Baptist, which is in the garden.

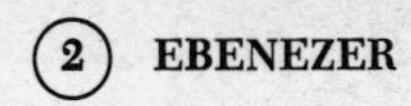

(2) EBENEZER

Jerusalem Lutheran Church

Two hundred Salzburg Lutherans arrived here northwest of Savannah in 1737, founding the town and building the first church in Georgia. The industrious settlers built a gristmill, sawmill, and rice mill as well as beginning the first silk culture. The site of New Ebenezer, as it was originally called, is now in ruins, but its church still remains standing on a bluff overlooking the Savannah River.

The present building was erected in 1769 and is a large brick edifice with frame belfry and interior balcony.

The Lutheran congregation added a parish house in 1958, which contains a museum and is connected to the original building with a covered porch. The Georgia Salzburger Society meets here March 12 and Labor Day each year.

(3) AUGUSTA

St. Paul's Episcopal Church

Continuing the path of Oglethorpe, Georgia's founder, northwest along the Savannah River, the traveler comes to Augusta, the town settled by Oglethorpe in 1735. Probably the best reminder of those first English settlers is St. Paul's Episcopal Church, which was officially founded in 1750 by members from the Church of England. The original building was on the same site at 605 Reynolds St. in the shelter of Fort Augusta and later Fort Cornwallis, and was the only church in the city for a number of years. The fort's site is marked by a large stone Celtic cross standing in the church garden.

The first church building was destroyed by gunfire during the Revolution.

The current brick Colonial-style church was built in 1919, the fourth for the congregation. A white portico and cupola enhance the exterior. Inside is the original baptismal font which Rev. Jonathan Copp, the first minister, brought from England in 1751.

(4) MIDWAY

Midway Congregation Meeting House and Museum

Returning south via Route 25, and west on Route 82, the traveler comes upon a scene reminiscent of New England. A white-frame church with steeple, a reconstructed-home museum, and historic markers record that Puritans originally from New England, but by way of South Carolina, settled here in 1754. They were accompanied by French Huguenots, Scots, and Carolinians. Together they organized the Midway Society, which was patterned after a New England town with selectmen to govern the church and community. In 1758 the Parish of St. Johns was formed. The church building was burned during a skirmish in the Revolution. It was rebuilt in 1792.

Midway Museum, which stands behind the church on Route 17 is made in the raised-cottage-style 18th-century architecture and contains a library and exhibits of the area. It is authentic in its furnishings, even having a detached kitchen in the rear. One remarkable feature of the community to be noted is its record of famous Americans. Eighty-six ministers, including the father of Oliver Wendell Holmes, seven foreign ministers, governors, congressmen, and cabinet members came from this small parish.

(5) ST. SIMONS ISLAND

Christ Church

John and Charles Wesley, busy travelers in early days, established Christ Church in 1736, when they were missionaries of the Church of England. A plaque marks the actual site, and on the wall of the present building is a cross made from the great oak log known as the tree where Wesley preached to 20 people, including Oglethorpe, on that first visit. The present building was erected in 1884 by Anson Green Phelps Dodge, Jr., as a memorial to his wife. Later Dodge became a rector and served this church.

Nearby is Fort Frederica National Monument with vestiges of Spanish missions and a museum.

Southwest Georgia

(6) BLAKELY

Kolomoki Mounds State Park

Turning away from the sea and crossing the state westward almost to the Alabama border, the traveler comes to a reminder that long before the white man arrived there was a large native American population here. The Kolomoki culture flourished during the 12th and 13th centuries, though archeologists think the earliest settlement here was A.D. 800. Large mounds that can still be seen were the foundations for the village temple. The Great Mound is 56½ feet high. A museum displays artifacts and dioramas of daily native life, to help the traveler reconstruct the culture of some of the state's first people.

(7) AMERICUS

Koinonia Farm

Northeast off Route 19 is the very modern Christian community of Koinonia Farm. Established in 1942 by Rev. Clarence Jordan, its purpose was twofold: to enable people to live together in community, witnessing to the Christian teachings on peace, sharing, and brotherhood; and second, to assist local farmers with scientific methods. Soon it became the object of mounting hostility because of its witness against racism. For years Koinonia withstood economic boycott, assisted by friends throughout the world.

In recent years the Koinonia Partners program was begun, providing a no-interest loan "Fund for Humanity," which allows black and white families to apply for new community-built homes with interest-free 20-year mortgages. Koinonia Village was developed and has a day-care center and recreational facilities. The community also has a mail-order business selling pecan products, fruit cakes, pottery, quilts, clothing, and the books of Clarence Jordan—particularly his popular colloquial Cotton Patch translations of the Scriptures.

(8) MACON

Ocmulgee National Monument

Continuing north, the traveler returns to another long-ago scene where six different Indian cultures existed between 8000 B.C. and A.D. 1717. Some were ancestors of the Creek Indians. The village of the Master Farmers, ancestors of the Creek Indians who met the English settlers, is especially notable. Of the several temple mounds, the most interesting is the Great Temple Mound at the southern end of the plateau. Here the well-being of the

Ocmulgee National Monument

tribe was ensured through religious observances. Nearby is a reconstructed large circular earth-covered lodge. Clay floor, wall benches, and eagle-shaped platform were built over 800 years ago. Also on the plateau is the site of a 1690 British colonial trading post. A Creek Indian craft shop, Visitors' Center, and museum are staffed by today's Creek Indians.

Northwest Georgia

(9) ATLANTA

Grave of Martin Luther King, Jr.

The Georgia capital, in the northern section of the state, is noted in recent years for the ministry of the late Rev. Martin Luther King, Jr., who with religious conviction led his people in the nonviolent civil rights movement. The traveler drives through the heart of Atlanta to Ebeneezer Baptist Church at 413 Auburn Avenue N.E. Here in the churchyard, not far from the busy street, is a simple tombstone which reads: FREE AT LAST, FREE AT LAST, THANK GOD ALMIGHTY, I'M FREE AT LAST.

(10) CALHOUN

New Echota

Still farther north on Route 41 is an amazing Indian development of recent times. When the encroaching English settlements pushed the natives farther inland, the Cherokee Indians sought to adopt the best of the white man's ways, yet retain a nation of their own. The capital of their nation was New Echota, founded in 1825 on their own lands. When gold was discovered there, the Indians were forced to leave for new land in Oklahoma, and their republican form of government patterned after young America was short-lived. A 200-acre historic site, which includes a portion of the original village and one surviving house, is a fascinating and little-known reminder of Indian democracy.

Sequoyah (or George Gist), a Cherokee who had long admired the books, or "talking leaves," of the white men, invented symbols for the sounds in the Cherokee language. This remarkable achievement enabled the native American to have a written language.

The reconstructed print shop produced the first Indian newspaper, the *Cherokee Phoenix*. It was printed in both English and Cherokee from 1828 to 1834. Publisher was Elias Boudinot, a three-quarter Cherokee, who was graduated from Andover-Newton Theological Seminary. Typecases, press, bookbinder, and March 13, 1828, copy of the *Phoenix* can be seen.

Supreme Court of the Cherokee Nation was held for two weeks each summer and again in the fall. Otherwise, the building, reconstructed in 1961 from the 1827 original, served as mission and school. Three men were judges, hearing appeals of decisions made in the Cherokees' eight district courts.

Worcester House, home of Samuel A. Worcester, Congregational missionary, is a two-story original New England-style house built in 1827. It contains period furnishings. Worcester, who loved his adopted people, traveled west to Oklahoma with them.

NORTH CAROLINA

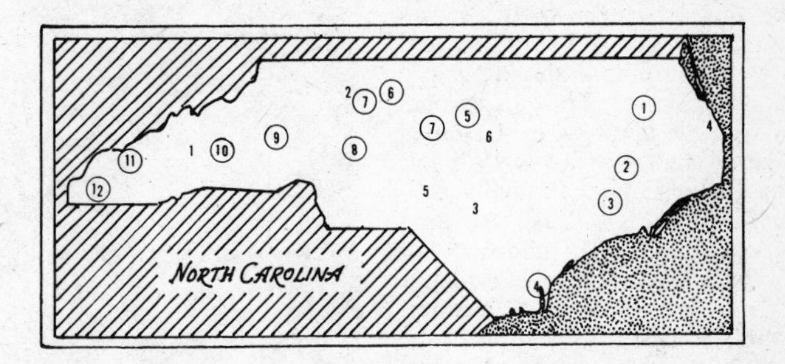

The symphonic drama *The Lost Colony,* at the Fort Raleigh National Historic Site, vividly portrays the attempt of the English to settle this area. Though French and Spanish explorers traveled the region in the early 1500s, it was the English who persisted in its settlement. Their first colony in 1585 was unsuccessful. Then came the second attempt in 1587, and this colony disappeared! The English persevered, however, and the first permanent white establishment was made on Albemarle Sound in 1660. Bath, on Pamlico Sound, is considered to be the oldest incorporated town in North Carolina.

Though the Church of England was represented by these colonists, folks of other faiths were allowed to find haven in the broad coastal plains, then the Piedmont plateau, and finally in the Appalachian highlands. Gradually the native Cherokees were pushed farther west as Scotch-Irish, Scotch Highlanders, Germans, Swiss, and French colonized. Waldensians, Moravians, and Quakers founded towns. A broad spectrum of religious faiths inhabited the land, later augmented by ecumenical movements and mission activities.

It is interesting to note that North Carolina was the last state to ratify the Constitution, holding out for a clause guaranteeing religious freedom.

Eastern North Carolina

EDENTON

St. Paul's Church

Proceeding north and west on Routes 158 and 17, the traveler comes to Albemarle Sound, site of the state's first permanent settlements in 1660. One of the state's oldest communities is this town named for Charles Eden, proprietary governor. Once it was the unofficial capital of the colony.

A walking tour, beginning with a slide presentation at the Barker House, will eventually lead to St. Paul's (Episcopal) Church, spiritual descendant of those first Church of England colonists. The second oldest church building in the state, it has been described as an ideal country church. It was built around 1736, was badly damaged by fire in 1949, and has since been restored. Its Georgian architecture is a good example of an early village church. The communion silver, still in use, dates from 1725.

(2) BATH

St. Thomas Church and Glebe House

Returning south via Route 17 to the coast, the traveler comes to the state's oldest town, incorporated in 1705, and the state's oldest church building still in continuous use. This Episcopal church was built of brick in a simple, rectangular design. Nearby is Williams House, or Glebe House, originally connected with the parish. When the Revolution was over, all Church of England buildings and glebe lands were taken over by the new country. Many were sold, like this Wilson Glebe House. Now the St. Thomas Restoration Committee is preserving these historic structures.

In this state historic area are also the Palmer-Marsh House and Bonner House. The film *A Town Called Bath,* at the Visitors' Center, tells of life in the area.

(3) NEW BERN

First Presbyterian Church

Swiss and German colonists settled New Bern, as one can deduce from the name. The 1710 settlement developed into an important seaport and the provincial capital. First Presbyterian Church, on New Street, houses spiritual descendants of the early residents. It was built in 1819-1822 of Greek Revival design. During the Civil War it served as a hospital. The original graceful center pulpit was restored in 1936 and an educational plant added in 1951.

(4) WILMINGTON

Brunswick Town

About 20 miles south of Wilmington via US 17 and state route 133 are the ruins of a colonial town which have been excavated for study and exhibit by the state. Once the leading town of the colony, this 1776 settlement was destroyed during the Revolution and abandoned. The picturesque and exceptionally interesting area has nature trails, Visitors Center, and excavations of many of the 60 dwellings. The 33-inch brick walls of St. Phillip's Church, built 1754-1768, still stand. This was one of the state's first churches and was probably burned during the Revolution.

Central North Carolina

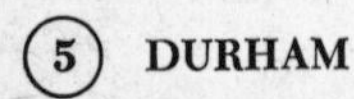

Duke University Chapel

A huge English Gothic church dominates the 7,000-acre campus of Duke University. The 210-foot bell tower resembles that of Canterbury Cathedral. The chapel, of native stone, was built in 1932 and is used for musical events as well as interdenominational services. It seats 2,000. The organ has over

7,000 pipes and a 50-bell carillon. Seventy-seven stained-glass windows, designed by G. Owen Bonawit, illustrate more than 800 Bible characters.

Duke University Museum of Art

On East Campus is a museum with the Brummer Collection, which is of religious interest. Medieval sculpture and decorative art have been collected. Pieces include the 13th-century "Head of the Virgin" from the rood screen of Chartres Cathedral and outstanding 12th-century stone carvings of the apostles.

(6) GUILFORD

New Garden Meeting House

North of Greensboro is the town of Guilford, which was begun by the Quakers. In 1757, they purchased a large tract of land and eventually built five meeting houses. They also established Guilford College, where New Garden Meeting House stands. During the Revolution, it was the site of a skirmish between Cornwallis's forces and those of Light Horse Harry Lee. The site of the original meeting house, marked by foundation stones, is about 200 yards off the campus.

(7) WINSTON-SALEM

Old Salem

Set in the middle of the bustling modern city of Winston-Salem is Old Salem, a complete Moravian town. Moravians were devout Germanic people who traced their faith to 15th-century Bohemian martyr John Hus. After his death, followers formed the Unity of the Brethren. For the next 300 years, their congregation was referred to as "the hidden seed" and was kept alive in Moravia, Bohemia, and Poland in spite of religious persecution. Finally, Count Nicholas Lewis of Zinzendorf gave them refuge on his great estate. Here the faith was reborn in the new town of Herrnhut, and many of the present-day traditions were developed.

First missionaries to the New World came to Georgia, but abandoned that settlement in favor of Pennsylvania where Bethlehem became the leading Moravian community. The town of Salem on the North Carolina piedmont was begun in 1766. Earlier a settlement had begun a temporary village at nearby Bethabara and Moravians from there began this permanent town.

Salem Square

Stroll along the brick walk through shady Salem Square, smell the herbs in the Miksch Tobacco Shop garden, hear the 180-year-old clock chime the hours from the spire of the Home Moravian Church. Then plan to spend at least a full day browsing in the seven restored buildings open for visitors. (Many more are restored and lived in as private homes.)

The Single Brothers House, where unmarried men 14 years and older lived and worked in trades, is an absorbing sight, for the trades are still being carried on by costumed craftsmen.

The Boys School, built in 1794, has a large collection of musical instruments and antiquities of the Wachovia Society. Winkler Bakery, with its mouth-watering smells, must be visited, as

The Single Brothers House

well as the Market Fire House, Salem Tavern, and Tavern Barn.

Home Moravian Church and God's Acre

On Church Street is the historic old church home of an active Moravian congregation. The brick structure is in keeping with the dignified style of the old town. Over the front entrance is an interesting half-circle protecting roof. Here the famous Easter sunrise service (over 200 consecutive) begins before dawn. Between 2 and 4 A.M., small groups from the Moravian Band assemble on street corners to awaken the city. Thousands of worshipers gather at the square, then march to God's Acre, the Moravian graveyard. The service is concluded at sunrise to the antiphonal playing of the more than 500 instrumentalists. Other services are held also in the churches in Moravian communities of Bethabara, Bethania, and Friedberg.

(8) SALISBURY

Thyatira Church

In the 1720s, Scotch-Irish settled in this town, which is south of Winston-Salem and reached via Route 85. Here on Moorseville Highway is a congregation of their spiritual descendants. Built in 1860 and restored in recent years, Thyatira Church has many Revolutionary graves in its churchyard. Three previous buildings stood on this land. The parish dates from 1753 and has historical materials on display in the memorial room.

Old Organ Church

Germans from the Palatine district on the Rhine River augmented Salisbury's inhabitants in the 1740s. The town was officially founded in 1753. Here in the Lutheran church descendants of the second ethnic group worship. The church was founded in 1791 and has the first organ in the state, noted because it was handmade by early craftsmen.

Western North Carolina

(9) VALDESE

Waldensian Presbyterian Church

Proceeding along Route 40, parallel to the Great Smoky Mountains, the traveler comes to another town settled by a persecuted overseas congregation, the Waldensians. The summer of 1974 saw Waldensians here and in their original country, Italy, celebrate their 800th anniversary. Peter Waldo (or Valdese), a wealthy merchant, was the spiritual leader who organized them. Hearing the story of St. Alexis, who gave all his property to the poor, Waldo did the same and soon attracted disciples. In seeking to purify the church, they incurred great persecution, but persisted by remaining isolated in the Alps. When the persecution ended in 1848 with the Edict of Emancipation, prosperity brought new growth and land was crowded. Hence a small party bought 15,000 acres in the foothills of the Blue Ridge Mountains and sailed by steamship steerage to their new home, arriving in May 1893.

This Romanesque-style church was built that same year, with stone cleared from the rocky soil of the farms. It has a museum containing artifacts, utensils, and records of the early years. To keep the heritage alive for the area, an outdoor amphitheater was constructed and annually the story is retold in the drama *From This Day Forward.* In the surrounding hills are some of the lovely old stone farmhouses reminiscent of those in the Alps. The church is part of the Presbyterian Church in America, though it still maintains contact with the Waldensian mother church in Italy.

(10) MONTREAT

Assembly Inn

Nestled in the foothills of the Blue Ridge Mountains is a year-round conference center of the General Assembly of the Presbyterian Church in the United States. A unique hotel, it is built of native rock, overlooking Lake Susan, and is the center of a small village. Though open year round, in summer it is thronged with church groups and individuals seeking rest and relaxation as well as inspiration. Its Convocation Hall and 100 modern rooms make it convenient and comfortable. A glimpse of Rev. Billy Graham's mountain home can be seen from the highway.

11 CHEROKEE

Museum of the Cherokee Indian

Cherokee is headquarters for the Qualla Indian Reservation, now home for over 8,000 Indians, descendants of those who met with the first white settlers. At the information center on U.S. 441, are displays that explain the lives and customs of the tribes.

At Mountainside Theater, in the magnificent drama *Unto These Hills,* each summer Indians portray their history from the time De Soto arrived in 1540 until the infamous Trail of Tears, when all but a remnant were removed to the west. How Tsalez gave his life so this remnant could remain is an inspiring part of the saga. Music is by Jack Kilpatrick, noted Cherokee Indian composer.

Oconaluftee Indian Village

In this re-created Cherokee Village of 200 years ago are homes built from notched logs and chinked with mud. Here the women pound corn, shape clay pottery, weave colorful strands of cord, and make beadwork decorations. Men make darts for blowguns, fashion dugout canoes, and carve ceremonial masks. Visitors can see the Council House, center of religious and political life for the tribe, and an Indian garden with its typical products. The Cherokee Historical Association, through the village, drama, and the museum, keeps alive the story of the Cherokee and reminds America of the real meaning of democracy for all men. It is fitting that both the English and native American heritages are celebrated with dramas in North Carolina.

12 MURPHY

Fields of the Woods

Almost at North Carolina's western border is a unique reminder of America's biblical heritage. A project of the Church of Prophecy Marker Association, the diplay features the world's largest Bible pages. The New Testament passage Matthew 22:37-39 is inscribed in pages standing 24 feet high, 60 feet long, and 13 feet wide. The purpose of the Association is to mark, locate, and beautify prominent places in the world that are of biblical interest to all Christians. Here are trees from Palestine, a gigantic Ten Commandments tablet, an all-nations cross, markers with other important verses, and large assembly facilities. Special celebrations are held at Easter and Thanksgiving. The Association is also responsible for markers in the Holy Land.

SOUTH CAROLINA

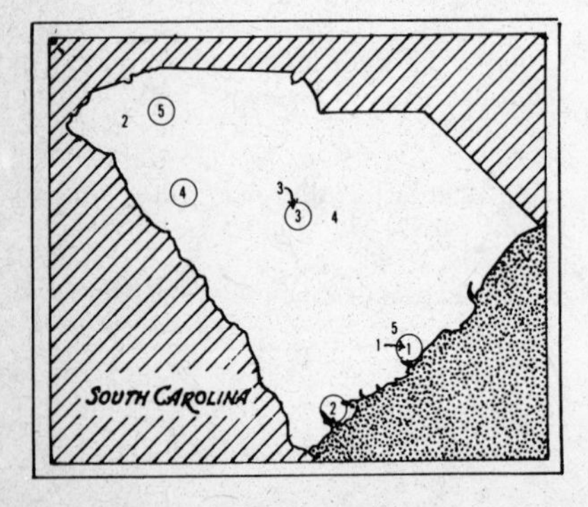

Spanish Catholics and French Huguenots (Protestants) landed on South Carolina shores in 1526 and 1562 respectively. It was the English, however, who permanently settled the coastal plain area in 1670, establishing Church of England parishes as villages developed. Eight Lord Proprietors had been given the Carolinian territory by England's King Charles II. The first colony, led by William Sayle and including 200 people, was founded on the Ashley River at Albemarle Point and called Charles Town. Ten years later, in 1680, the colony moved to a peninsula at the junction of the Cooper and Ashley rivers, the present site of Charleston.

A rapid immigration of Welsh, Swiss, and Scotch-Irish came after 1730. These settlers and others from northern colonies brought a variety of churches and settled the plateau region. They secured land from the Cherokee and gradually colonized the ten upper counties.

Though "upcountry" people from the Piedmont plateau and lowlanders from the coastal plains did not always mix well, they remained open-minded religiously. Charleston, in particular, was an early haven for religious pioneers, including Jews.

East Coast, South Carolina

1 CHARLESTON

Charles Town Landing

Here, in a 200-acre historic park created for the state's tricentennial, is the setting for the first colony in South Carolina, established in 1670. A palisade surrounds the original ten-acre site of the first settlement and an elegant pavilion has exhibits of South Carolina's first century. Visitors may view the 1670 Experimental Crop Garden to see the plantings arranged by the Lord Proprietors to ensure that the new land became productive. A theater shows a movie which introduces the surrounding lowland country.

Gateway Walk

In the city proper, across the Ashley River from the original landing site, is the bustling community of today that was established ten years after the first settlers arrived. Probably the best way to begin a tour is to stroll down this shaded walk which has been arranged by the Garden Club of Charleston. From St. Philip's Episcopal Church, it winds through the heart of the old city, by ancient cemeteries, over the yard of the Circular Congregational Church, and by the library and art gallery. Continuing across King Street, it touches the grounds of the Unitarian Church and ends at St. John's Lutheran Church.

Huguenot Church

South of Gateway Walk, on Church and Queen streets, is the only remaining Huguenot church in America. Though begun in 1680, when 45 Huguenots disembarked from the ship *Richmond* on April 30, 1680, the church had Huguenot parishioners here as early as 1677. The Gothic architecture of this French Protestant church is much admired. Inside, the panels and mural tablets, in memory of early Huguenots, have given it the name the Second Notre Dame des Victoires, after the church in Paris whose walls are covered with memorial tablets. The church is the third on this site. It was built in 1844 and had to be repaired after the damaging earthquake of 1886.

The liturgy now in use is adapted from that used in the churches of Neufchatel and Vallangin, with additions from the Protestant Episcopal. Until 1828, services were in French, but now are in English. The once-a-year service is usually on the last Sunday in March. Its rare 1845 Tracker organ was almost shipped to New York by Union soldiers during the Civil War, but was rescued by the organist. Recitals are given each spring.

St. Philip's Church

First settlers founded this Episcopal parish in 1670 when they arrived as communicants of the Church of England. The original church stood at

Broad and Meeting streets, the location of St. Michael's Episcopal Church. It was moved in 1723, then destroyed by fire. Today's building, erected in 1838, is an elegant structure with Doric porticoes and steeple. It has no chimes, for the original ones were cast into Confederate cannon in 1863. Among the church valuables are a 17th-century heart-shaped salver and 1710 communion service.

St. Michael's Episcopal Church

The second Episcopal parish church in the city, begun in 1751, is a splendid architectural achievement at Broad and Meeting Sts. Patterned after St. Martin-in-the-Fields in London, it has a Palladian portico and a 186-foot steeple. Dating from 1762, the building is the oldest church structure in the city, and most of its original features are intact though the city suffered wars and an earthquake. The interior has galleries on three sides, a 1772 wrought-iron chancel rail, and an 1803 chandelier. George Washington, Marquis de Lafayette, and Robert E. Lee have sat in its historic box pews.

Kahal Kadosh Beth Elohim

Immigrating Jews founded this second oldest congregation in the United States in 1750. The beautiful stone synagogue at 90 Hasell St. was built in 1841 to resemble a Greek Doric temple. It is the oldest Reform Jewish congregation and its Archives Room contains a wealth of historic documents. History buffs can examine the letter of thanks from George Washington in response to the congregation's congratulations on ascending to the presidency. Here also is the coat of arms and land deed of Francis Salvadore, first Jew to hold public office in the nation and the first one killed in the Revolution. The synagogue also holds the prayer book of Isaac Harby, the Jew who developed a liberal Judaism which led to the Reform movement. The Coming Street Cemetery is the oldest surviving Jewish cemetery in the south.

2 BEAUFORT

St. Helena's Episcopal Church

Driving south and returning to the coast, the traveler finds the picturesque

Beth Elohim Synagogue

old port town which has kept its early atmosphere. Established by the Lord Proprietors in 1711, Beaufort is the state's second-oldest town. Earlier abortive attempts at colonizing had been made by Spanish and French.

This church, built in 1724, houses a parish established by the Provincial government in 1712 by the Lord Proprietors. The large Colonial building with three-tiered steeple at King and North Sts., is framed by moss-hung trees, and surrounded by an ancient cemetery. On the north side, in the parish house grounds, are graves of persons not allowed to be buried inside the churchyard. Dueling and suicide were among the offenses which would keep a corpse outside the hallowed ground.

The ravages of war struck St. Helena when the building was used as a hospital by Federal troops. Graveyard slabs were used as operating tables.

This church also maintains the site of Sheldon Church, in Sheldon, where lie the ruins of the twice-built, twice-burned elegant church. Both times the burning was the result of war.

Central South Carolina

(3) COLUMBIA

First Baptist Church

Normally churches are not political landmarks. This church is, however, because it was the scene of the Secession Convention in 1860. Columbia was the place where delegates had come to decide the Secession question, and ended by leaving the Union.

The huge classical-style edifice at 1306 Hampton Street dates from 1859. Tremendous two-story brick columns are on the front portico. The interior seats 1,500 people. The communion table, which is still used, was the impromptu desk for the first draft of the Ordinance of Secession. The active congregation is one of the south's largest.

(4) GREENWOOD

Callie Self Memorial Carillon

Once this carillon containing 37 bells was part of the Netherlands exhibit at the 1939 New York World's Fair. James Self purchased the carillon, installing it in Greenwood in 1940 as a memorial to his mother, Callie Holloway Self. The carillon is electrically operated and can play folk music, popular songs, and patriotic melodies, as well as classical music and sacred songs. It is also equipped with an electronic keyboard and roll-player. The carillon stands in an 87-foot red brick tower on the grounds of the Callie Self Memorial Baptist Church, erected in 1940.

Western South Carolina

(5) GREENVILLE

Bob Jones University Museum and Gallery

About 3 miles north of town on a 200-acre tract of land in the foothills of the Great Smokies and the Blue Ridge Mountains is Bob Jones University, a Christian school established in 1927. The purpose of the school is to train Christian leaders for all walks of life. Its slogan is "Christianity with Culture." One result of this emphasis is the university's collection of sacred art, which is known worldwide as one of the important American collections. Excitingly displayed in 30 rooms, the 400-painting collection is rich in Flemish and Dutch paintings of the 16th cen-

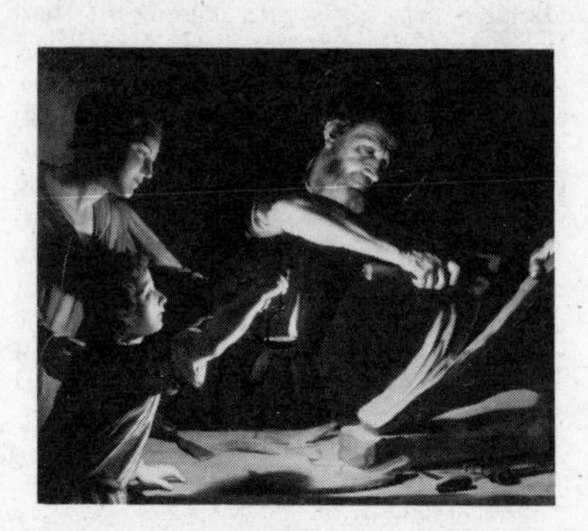

Art Treasures, Bob Jones University, Museum and Gallery

tury and in Baroque paintings of the 17th century. All major artists are represented, and the collection is enhanced by period furniture, statuary, and other art objects. Near East religious antiquities and icons also appear in the collection.

MISSISSIPPI

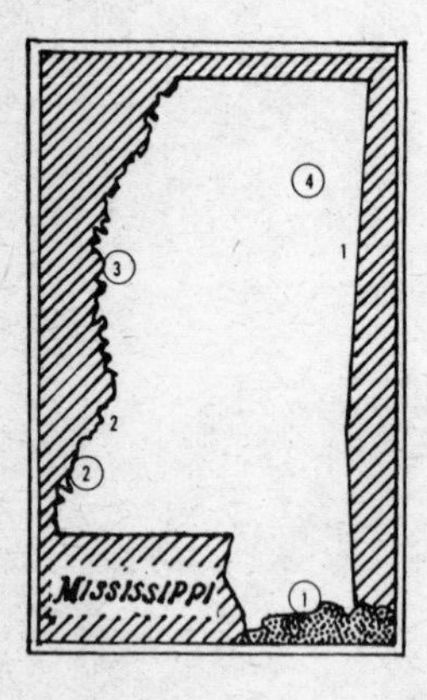

The Christian cross heralding Catholic settlements was planted early in the southern part of this state. Though the Spaniard DeSoto explored the area as early as 1541, it was the French who colonized it. LaSalle in 1682 planted a cross at the mouth of the Mississippi River, claiming the entire area for France. Pierre LeMoyne, Sieur d'Iberville, began the first settlement in 1699, when he brought 200 settlers to the present-day Ocean Springs and built Fort Maurepas on the east side of the bay.

Catholic settlements were later made at Biloxi and Natchez, though there was constant struggle with the Indians who already inhabited the area.

Two highways, reminiscent of the two cultures, cross the state. The Old Spanish Trail, now a modern highway, follows the westward path of Spanish explorers and priests. The Natchez Trace Parkway, extending from Natchez to Nashville, Tennessee, is a reminder of the state's earliest inhabitants.

Southern Mississippi

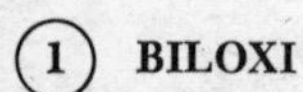

(1) BILOXI

Cross and Boulder

On the north end of the Back Bay Bridge, is a marker commemorating the landing of d'Iberville with 200 settlers in 1699. Here at Fort Maurepas, the white settlements began as did the Christian Catholic Church in the state. Until 1719, settlers remained at the first site (Ocean Springs), then moved to the present town of Biloxi, which became for a time the capital. A reminder of the early religious heritage is the Blessing of the Fleet, a colorful annual Catholic ceremony.

Church of the Redeemer

This old Episcopal church is a reminder that France ceded the region to the British in 1763 and the area was finally secured for the English-speaking people after Spanish dispute in 1795. The first Episcopal structure, where Jefferson Davis worshiped and was a vestryman, now is the parish house. The Davis pew, however, has been placed in the newer building. It

Blessing of the Fleet, Biloxi

is draped with a Confederate flag and marked with a silver plaque. Four memorial windows honor his family.

 NATCHEZ

St. Mary's Cathedral

Following the path of the early settlers, the traveler should drive northwest to the oldest city along the Mississippi River. Iberville and Bienville planted the French Catholic settlement here in 1716, calling it Fort Rosalie. Thirteen years later, the Natchez Indians decimated the town, leaving 200 dead and taking 500 prisoners. The town, which eventually was reestablished, bears their name. Spanish governors lived here until the late 1700s, when it became a territory. The town has lived under French, Spanish, British, Confederate, and United States flags.

This impressive cathedral is the first to be built in Mississippi, and continues the state's Catholic heritage.

Natchez is famous for its annual spring pilgrimages, and this is the best time to visit. Thirty-five antebellum homes are open to the public in March and a Confederate pageant is presented evenings.

Emerald Mound

Northeast of Natchez on the Natchez Trace Parkway is the third largest Indian mound in the United States. Covering almost 8 acres and measuring 770 by 435 feet at the base, the mound was built about 1300-1600 by the Mississippians, the Indian people living in this valley preceding the coming of the Europeans. Though of many tribes (Natchez, Choctaw, Creek, etc.), they shared a common way of life including religious ceremonials which took place in mounds, sometimes arranged around

Emerald Mound

a central plaza. More than a dozen such groups are located within 25 miles of Emerald Mound. On important occasions they were the scenes of civil processions, ceremonial dances, and solemn religious rites. Builders of Emerald Mound had a complex way of life with a high degree of social and political organization. DeSoto's men and later French pioneers reported that these ceremonials continued until about 1700.

Northern Mississippi

(3) GREENVILLE

Winterville Mounds State Park and Museum

Near the winding Mississippi is a historic spot where lower Mississippi valley Indians gathered for ceremonials in prewhite settlement days. Visitors can see the original ceremonial place which has been restored. A museum contains artifacts, jewelry, pottery, utensils, and art work that reach back into the mists of history.

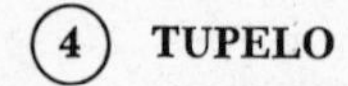

(4) TUPELO

Chickasaw Village Site

Northwest of Tupelo is the site of a fortified native village. A nature trail outlines the settlement and its foundation markers. Interpretive panels show the uses the Indians made of plants and the early environment of the Chickasaws, part of the Mississippian Indians. Skillful farmers and competent craftsmen, many of these Indians lived in strongly built homes with clay-plastered walls and thatched roofs. Nearby is Natchez Trace Parkway headquarters and its *Path of Empire* interpretive program.

ALABAMA

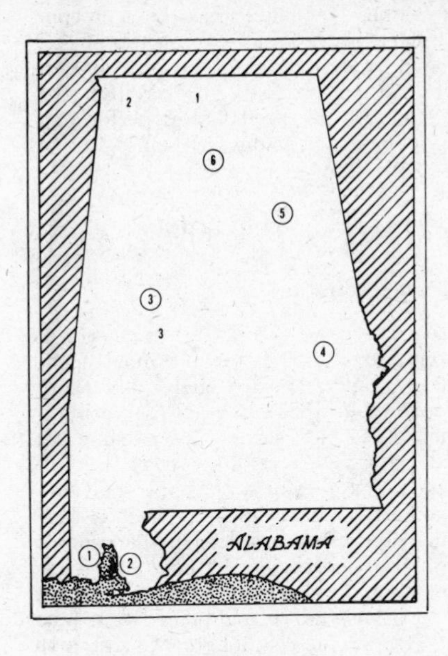

The coastal plains and higher plateaus of Alabama were fought for by Spanish, French, English, and native Indians for over 100 years. Finally ownership was resolved when it became a state in 1819 and when Choctaws in 1830 and Creeks in 1832 ceded their territory, leaving for lands in the west.

Dauphin Island on the southern coast was the setting for the first permanent colony, called Fort Louis. In 1711, inhabitants moved to the mainland and the present Mobile was established, becoming headquarters for the French on the Gulf coast. During the Revolution, this area was a refuge for Loyalists', base for Indian raids and the objective of Spanish expeditions. As a result, the spiritual heritage is mainly Catholic, with Protestant later comers.

Southern Alabama

(1) MOBILE

Bienville Square

The original settlement, founded in 1702 by the French, was at Twenty-seven Mile Bluff, north of the present city of Mobile. When Sieur de Bienville established the mainland location of the first permanent white settlement, he found the Mauvilla Indians already here. This rapidly growing city was the capital of the French colonial empire until . 1719. The later Spanish and English influx made for a distinctive atmosphere, which can be noted in this picturesque square in the business district. A French cannon from Fort Conde and British cannon from Fort Charlotte are in opposite corners. (When the Spanish held the same fort at the river shore, it was named Carlotta.) The entire Church Street Historic District is a pleasure to wander through at leisure.

Cathedral of the Immaculate Conception

One of the oldest churches in the city is found on Claiborne Street and is spiritual descendant of the earliest Catholic parish. It is built on the site of the burying ground used by the first settlers. This significant and beautiful building has enormous white columns and a turreted tower, surrounded by a cross. Not far away, at Bayou La Batre, the Catholic ceremony of the Blessing of the Shrimp Fleet takes place annually.

(2) MALBIS

Malbis Memorial Church

East of Mobile on U.S. 90, the traveler will find an outstanding Greek Orthodox church, a copy of a Byzantine church in Athens. The brick and marble structure commemorates the Greek Orthodox communal settlement founded in the early 1900s by an ex-monk at Malbis Plantation. Built in 1965, it has more than 100 wall and ceiling murals, mosaics, and hand-carved figures. Many-hued stained-glass windows give an unusually vivid effect. The elaborate altar and pulpit are of hand-carved white marble.

 MOUNDVILLE

Mound State Monument and Museum

Located farther north on Highway 69 is a recreational and educational park which includes, on its 300 acres, 40 mounds showing the site of an ancient native city. An Indian village contains five huts with life-sized figures shown performing the daily tasks of the Moundville Indians.

The tallest mound was built of earth, basket load by basket load, some 700 years ago and is 60 feet high. With temple ruins found by archeologists as a guide, a temple has been reconstructed to the exact size on top of this mound. Steps leading upward are of original log-type structure. Within the temple are life-sized figures performing a religious ceremony of some 400 to 700 years ago.

(4) TUSKEGEE

Tuskegee Institute

Continuing westward, the traveler will come to a noted coeducational technical and professional university founded in 1881. Booker T. Washington, a former slave who became an educator and a reformer, was the college's first president. His spiritual convictions enabled him to wrest a heritage for black people. On the campus are the Booker T. Washington Monument and his home, The Oaks, in which his study is maintained as it was.

The George Washington Carver Museum on the campus honors the black educator and scientist who developed 300 products from the peanut and 118 from the sweet potato, which gave a better economy to the south. Exhibits are authentic representations of his work. Twenty historic dioramas show the progress of the Negro race, and an art gallery contains African art.

Also on the campus is the Institute Chapel with its "singing windows."

Northern Alabama

 ANNISTON

Church of St. Michael and All Angels

The Episcopal church on 18th Street is considered one of America's most beautiful churches. A Norman Gothic structure built of Alabama sandstone, it was dedicated in 1890. The outstanding feature is an Italian marble altar with an alabaster reredos crowned by the figures of seven angels. The ceiling is hand-carved and made to resemble ribs of a ship. Ends are decorated with angel heads. The 95-foot tower holds

12 chime bells, each inscribed with a Scripture text.

(6) CULLMAN

Ave Maria Grotto

On the campus of St. Bernard College on U.S. 278 is an amazing "little Jerusalem" in miniature created by Benedictine monk Brother Joseph. A native of Bavaria, he came to study at St. Bernard College in 1892 and then entered the Benedictine order. When assigned to the abbey power plant in 1910, he began his hobby of creating miniature shrines in his spare time. Soon they attracted so many people, it was decided to move them to a more adequate site. The present location was officially dedicated May 17, 1934, and since then thousands have come each year to view the over 100 authentic shrines in the 4-acre park.

In addition to the cement replicas of the Holy City, Brother Joseph added internationally famous shrines like Our Lady of Fatima, Our Lady of Guadalupe, and the American missions. The accurate proportions of St. Peter's in Rome never cease to amaze visitors.

LOUISIANA

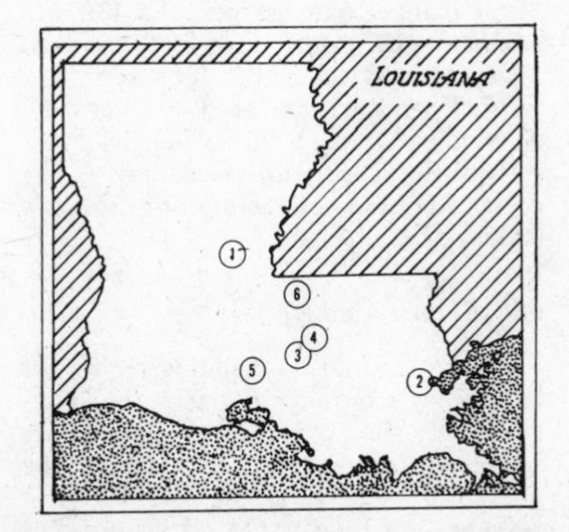

Louisiana was named by Robert Cavelier, Sieur de La Salle, in 1682, when he came down the Mississippi River and claimed all the land it drained for King Louis XIV of France. Later the French brothers d'Iberville and de Bienville solidified the claim in the early 1700s by bringing French colonists and their faith to the present state. The oldest settlement is considered to be the 1714 town of Natchitoches.

When French Acadians were driven from their homes in Canada in 1765, they found refuge here, bringing their Catholic heritage.

Brief Spanish rule in the late 1700s brought more Catholics and added to the delightful blend of Creole culture found in this state today.

Protestants arrived much later when the territory came under American control in 1803 and the westward drive brought settlers from the coastal states.

Western Louisiana

MARKSVILLE

Marksville Prehistoric Indian Park State Monument

Our Louisiana spiritual heritage tour begins where the oldest inhabitants held their religious ceremonies. In the 40-acre park are earthen embankments of an early Indian fort and burial mounds. Temple and refuse mounds date back to 400 B.C. A Spanish mission-style museum has archeological and geological exhibits of the area. Pictures illustrate life in the valley from early man until today.

Eastern Louisiana

NEW ORLEANS

St. Louis Cathedral

One of the most exciting cities in America is this sprawling metropolis known for the Mardi Gras, iron grillwork, Creole cooking, and jazz. It is also known as an early Catholic stronghold since its foundation by the Frenchman de Bienville in 1718.

The combination Spanish-style and Greek Revival St. Louis Cathedral is a reminder of that first Catholic congregation, as it is the third building to stand on the site where since 1727 a parish church has served French, Spanish, Swiss, German, and American colonists.

The present imposing structure, which fronts on Jackson Square in the heart of the charming French Quarter, was built in 1794 and was extensively rebuilt in 1851. The church is reminiscent of a turreted castle, with its large steeple flanked by smaller ones.

The interior has an enormous mural over the altar that shows St. Louis announcing the Seventh Crusade. Stained-glass windows of the saint's life, statues, and paintings add richness.

Ursuline Convent

At 1114 Chartres Street is the first nunnery in Louisiana and the oldest building in the Mississippi River valley. Six Ursuline nuns arrived in 1727 to educate girls and care for the sick. Seven years later the convent was finished and it was used until a new convent was ready in 1824. Briefly it served the legislature and now is incorporated into the rectory of St. Mary's Italian Church.

Old French Cemeteries

Some of the most intriguing sights for Americans who have not seen this overseas are the old French cemeteries scattered through the city. Since the city has such wet soil, burials must be above ground and coffins are interred in tiers within walled plots. Old Creole family names and elaborately decorated tombs with interesting epitaphs may be seen.

(3) PLAQUEMINE

Chapel of the Madonna

One of the country's tiniest churches is the Chapel of the Madonna on Route 168. Measuring 6 feet wide and 8 feet long, it has room for an altar, five chairs, a priest, and an acolyte. During Mass, the worshipers stay outside. An Italian immigrant, Anthony Gullo, promised to build the chapel if his desperately ill child survived. The child did live and Gullo built the church in 1901 all by himself as a labor of love. Since 1904, services for the Feast of Assumption have been held here.

(4) BATON ROUGE

St. Joseph's Cathedral

In this picturesque state capital is a cathedral at Main and Fourth streets, which has been serving Catholic parishioners since 1853. It has been restored three times and is an interesting blend of old and new, reflecting the state's culture. Delicate stained-glass windows, stations of the cross in mosaics, and a mahogany crucifix by sculptor Ivan Mestrovic are special features.

(5) ST. MARTINVILLE

St. Martin Catholic Church

Established with the town in 1765, St. Martin Catholic Church is one of the state's oldest. The famous painting of St. Martin of Tours, by Mouchet, is part of the main altar. The church also has a replica of the Grotto of Lourdes built in 1883 from a small sketch. The Evangeline of Longfellow's poem is immortalized by a statue in the courtyard, and her grave—marked EMMELINE LABICEH—is at the rear of the church. The Longfellow-Evangeline Memorial State Park off Route 90 highlights her Acadian story. An Acadian House Museum, built of hand hewn beams is furnished in the period.

(6) ST. FRANCISVILLE

Grace Episcopal Church

This second oldest Episcopal church in Lousiana is a reminder of the later Protestant heritage. Formed by the legislature in 1829, Grace Episcopal Church is unique in that, for a short time between Spanish and American control, it stood in an independent country called "The Republic of the West Florida Parishes."

The present building follows an earlier one built in 1828 and destroyed in 1858. The pleasing brick structure sits amid tall moss-hung oaks, surrounded by a simple graveyard. During the annual pilgrimage in March is the best time to view the church, local museum, and graceful homes of the area which are open to the public.

TENNESSEE

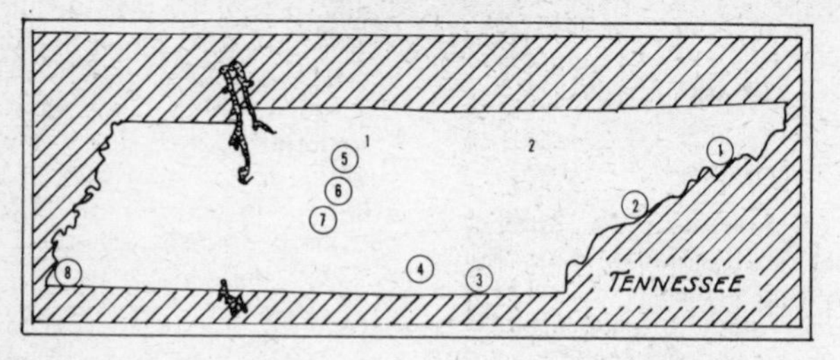

Amazing Tennessee had several sovereign nations within its bounds prior to becoming part of the United States of America. Long before DeSoto visited in 1540—and garrison outposts were built there later by French and English—the Cherokees had a vast, civilized nation with the capital at Echota, Georgia.

Cherokee domination and the terrain kept settlers out until 1769, when William Bean built a cabin by the Watauga River. Settlers, including Daniel Boone, soon poured through the Cumberland Gap. Purchasing 20 million acres from the Cherokees, they formed the Watauga Association in 1772, which was the first white independent government west of the Alleghenies. This lasted until 1776 when the inhabitants joined North Carolina.

Incensed by North Carolina's joining the United States without consulting them, the inhabitants withdrew and created their own independent state of Franklin. John Sevier was governor and Jonesboro the first capital of this sovereign territory, which lasted four years. After a brief time, as part of the territory south of Ohio, Tennessee became a state in 1796.

Though religion was not the prime cause of settlement, it was an integral part of native Indian life and also of the life of the white settlers. Churches were organized almost simultaneously with the settlers' arrival. Protestants (Baptists, Methodists, and Presbyterians) came early, with Catholics and Anglican congregations established later in the 1820s.

Our visit to spiritual heritage sites should begin in the northeastern part of the state.

Eastern Tennessee

JONESBORO

Historic District of Jonesboro

The oldest town in Tennessee is on Route 411. While there are numerous old buildings throughout the state's first historic district, main points of interest are concentrated in five blocks on Jonesboro's Main Street. The Chester Inn is the oldest remaining structure, built in 1797. Presidents Polk, Jackson, and Johnson along with other important figures stayed here. The huge long porch extending over the sidewalk attracts attention.

The Methodist, Baptist, and Presbyterian churches date from the mid-1800s and are excellent examples of Greek Revival architecture. The old cemetery beyond the Baptist church has stones dating from 1800. Beside it is the large two-story brick house built in 1850 as the Holston Female Institute. After the Civil War it became the Holston Male Institute. Later it was renamed Warner Academy and became a school for recently freed slaves and their children.

The Washington County Courthouse Square is especially significant for on this site in an earlier courthouse built around 1779 was the headquarters of the short-lived state of Franklin. Here John Sevier was made governor in 1784, and citizens continued the independent state until 1788. The first convention, the constitutional convention, and the first two meetings of the General Assembly were held here. The present impressive Greek Revival courthouse, fifth on this site, was built in 1913.

An especially good time to wander around this amazing collection of well-preserved buildings is during the Jonesboro Days Celebration held annually during the week of July 4th. It is an old-fashioned celebration of family fun, games, and displays.

(2) GATLINBURG

Christus Gardens

Southwest on Route 441, amid the grandeur of the Great Smokies, is a nondenominational re-creation of scenes from the life of Jesus Christ. Established in 1960 by Ronald Ligon as a unique memorial to Christ, it is well worth visiting. In a stately, cloistered structure of unpolished marble, are a series of still-life dioramas depicting authentically the biblical scenes. Choral music, dramatic lighting, and a moving narrative convey an atmosphere of realism and of spiritual serenity. Probably the most photographed object is the sculpture of the face of Christ in the Patio Garden. Carved in a 6-ton block of Carrara marble, the face has eyes that seem to follow the viewer no matter where he stands.

(3) CHATTANOOGA

Museum of Religious and Ceremonial Art

A collection of rare volumes and art objects of all religions was assembled here by the chief rabbi of the British Forces during World War II, Rabbi Harris Swift. There are 3,500 books which include 42 volumes of Voltaire. Some of the many works are in original bindings and a few date to the 16th century. The art work includes the ivory carving of "Jacob's Dream" by a Flemish artist of the 18th century.

The museum is operated by the Siskin Memorial Foundation and has a nondenominational chapel, rehabilitation center, and facilities in its three buildings for civil, religious, and educational groups.

Western Tennessee

(4) SEWANEE

All Saints Chapel

Continuing northwest on Route 24, the traveler comes to the University of the South, founded in 1857 by the Episcopal Church in the South. The campus has 10,000 scenic acres on the Cumberland plateau. Ralph Adams Cram was the architect for this striking Gothic chapel, All Saints, which seats 1,000 and was begun in 1904. This replaced an earlier wooden Chapel of

St. Augustine built in 1868. Cram used the Church of St. Mary the Virgin at Oxford University, England, as the model. The history of the university's first 100 years is told in the stained-glass windows. The tower has the 23-ton, 56-bell, 5-octave Leonidas Polk Memorial Carillon.

Another unusual building on the campus is the Breslin Tower, modeled after Magdalen College tower at Oxford University, which forms the entrance to Convocation Hall.

(5) NASHVILLE

Downtown Presbyterian Church

An architecturally unique church stands at the corner of Church Street and Fifth Avenue, Nashville. Founded in 1814, it is the third building, the two previous ones having burned. Begun in 1849, the Egyptian Revival church was completed in 1851. Designed by William Strickland, it is probably the largest and best preserved of this type in America. The auditorium is a replica of an Egyptian temple, with its symbolic colors and decorations. In the ancient, mystical meaning, red represents Divine Love; blue, Divine Intelligence; and yellow, the Mercy of God. Lilies symbolize Innocence and Purity, and the triangle the Trinity. The cluster of seeds held together with gold represents the membership held together with a band of love.

During the Civil War the church was used as a hospital by Federal troops. Pews were stored to make room for hospital beds and horses were stabled in the dining room. The church was later restored with payment of war damages.

Holy Trinity Episcopal Church

At 615 Sixth Avenue South is Holy Trinity Church, an outstanding example of early Gothic Revival style. The church, established in 1830, was designed by Wills and Dudley and modeled after an English village church. The present building of native blue limestone was built in 1853 but not consecrated until 1888. In the meantime, it had been used by Federal troops as a powder magazine and stable.

First used by black worshipers in 1895, the church was given to the black congregation in 1907. The interior has a vaulted ceiling where the rafters are joined with carved emblems of the Trinity.

The Upper Room Chapel

United Methodist Publishing House Headquarters are in Nashville. Begun in 1789, its first headquarters was in Philadelphia. Book publishing through

Abingdon Press, the issuing of many periodicals, and printing under Parthenon Press imprint means an average of two railroad cars full of paper are used every working day. Tours of the publishing house are available, though groups should give two weeks' notice.

At 1908 Grand Avenue is the Upper Room Building in which the Methodist devotional booklet is published. On the second floor is a lovely chapel of Georgian design, which expresses prayer and devotion. The chancel contains an extraordinary wood carving of "The Last Supper," which took 14 months and 50 workers to complete. The chancel ceiling and tapestries reflect those in the wood carving by Ernest Pellegrini of Leonardo da Vinci's "Last Supper." The stained-glass window in the rear depicts the work of the Holy Spirit at Pentecost and in the growth of the church.

At the left of the pulpit is a small prayer room seating only eight people. It is dedicated to the memory of Grover C. Emmons, founder of the *Upper Room.*

St. Mary's Church

Catholics came to this state early when French explorers and trappers passed through. A permanent Catholic church began in 1834 when spiritual ancestors of this congregation built a small church on Cedar Knoll, later renamed Capitol Hill. Priests from Kentucky attended the few members until 1837 when a resident bishop was appointed.

The present church at 328 Fifth Avenue North, was designed by William Strickland, who also built the majestic capitol building. The church, which was dedicated in 1847, is of Grecian architectural design. The front portico is supported by Ionic columns and the whole effect is one of grandeur. The church served as a cathedral until 1914, when the new cathedral was built and St. Mary's reverted to its status as a parish church. This well-kept, historic shrine is noted for its choir and is on the National Register of Historic Places.

(6) FRANKLIN

St. Paul's Episcopal Church

A few miles south on Route 65 is the oldest Episcopal church and congregation in the state, organized in 1827. The "Mother Church of the Diocese," St. Paul's was built in 1831 and its rector, Rev. James Otey, was made the first bishop of Tennessee. It was damaged extensively after its use as a barracks and hospital in the Civil War, so was rebuilt in 1869. It is considered the oldest Episcopal church building in continual use west of the Appalachians.

(7) COLUMBIA

St. John's Episcopal Church

What is probably the last of the plantation churches of Tennessee is located farther south and west of Columbia. Just off Route 43, the traveler comes on a 6-acre plot surrounded by a stone fence. Leonidas Polk, an Episcopal minister, gave the land, drew plans, and supervised construction. His brothers contributed to the building fund and the church, free of debt, was given to the people in 1842 with the understanding it would be used for public worship. Most of the congregation, both blacks and whites, were from the Polk Plantations, including Leonidas's Ashwood Hall. The church was of "chaste and simple Gothic architecture . . . capable of seating with a small gallery about five hundred persons." The brick structure remains little changed today. Polk's mother gave the silver communion service and his sister contributed the baptismal font. In the surrounding graveyard many of the Polk family and their slaves are buried. Browsers among the graves can read, "Mammy Sue, tender loving nurse of the eleven children of George W. and Sally L. Polk," or "Calvin Polk, a slave faithful and devoted through five generations." Every Whitsunday, the Episcopal diocese holds services in this memorial to the Christian faith of the Polk brothers and this symbol of the vanished plantation society.

(8) MEMPHIS

Chucalissa Indian Town

South of Memphis in Fuller State Park is a reminder of the ancient Indian culture that flourished here from about A.D. 900 to the late 1500s. Around 1,500 inhabitants were in the thriving settlement which had permanent, thatch-roofed homes, great earthworks, and a temple mound honoring the sun.

The Department of Anthropology at Memphis State University has developed the facility, which begins at the C. H. Nash Museum building. A slide show and exhibits portray the early civilization. Arts, crafts, tools, and other artifacts are exhibited. Then the village tour leads to the central plaza with its ten reconstructed homes and temple mound. Here Choctow Indians guide the visitors and illustrate the crafts. During the summer, people may also observe work in progress on archeological "digs."

KENTUCKY

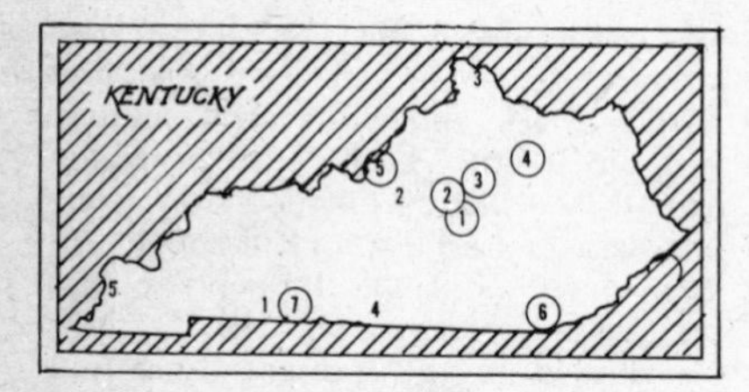

The raw frontier quality of this state attracted settlers soon after the pioneering Loyal Land Company of Virginia passed through the Cumberland Gap in 1750. Shawnee and Cherokee hunters as well as skirmishes of the French and Indian Wars deterred permanency, but meanwhile Daniel Boone and other adventurers were scouting the territory.

Soon the Wilderness Road, or Boone's Trace, developed from the Gap northwest to the Ohio River. Settlements began along this path almost simultaneously. Captain James Harrod began the first English settlement at Harrodsburg in 1774. Then Boone established Boonesboro in 1775 under sponsorship of the Transylvania Company.

Protestants (Presbyterians, Disciples of Christ, etc.) and Catholics organized churches as settlements developed. In the early 1800s an American religious phenomenon, the Shakers, established two communities in the wilderness frontier. This varied background, plus the fact that the region included the birthplace of Abraham Lincoln, has given the state an interesting spiritual heritage, to which one may add the present-day establishment of religious drama, biblical collections, and a shrine devoted to the life of Jesus Christ.

Northern Kentucky

DANVILLE

Constitution Square State Shrine

Here in the central part of Kentucky is the first capital of the district and later the state. A restored village commemorating those days is in the town center. The first post office west of the Allegheny Mountains stands here with original building intact. Here also, where the first constitutional convention was held, are the courthouse and jail. Religion played a prominent part

in those early settlements, for we note in the square the first Presbyterian church. Browsers may follow self-guiding tours through the buildings and to the McDowell House and Apothecary Shop, authentic restorations of one of the country's early leading surgeons, Dr. Ephraim McDowell.

(2) HARRODSBURG

Old Mud Meeting House

About 5 miles south of Harrodsburg on Dry Branch Road is one of the first Dutch Reformed churches built west of the Alleghenies. Constructed in 1800, it was made of mud thatch. Though the exterior has been covered with wood now, visitors may see, through a glass panel, a portion of the over-a-century-and-a-half-old original walls.

Nearby is old Fort Harrod State Park, with a replica of the first settlement and where the outdoor drama *The Legend of Daniel Boone* is presented nightly in summer.

(3) PLEASANT HILL

Shaker Village

This community, also known as Shakertown, came into existence in 1806 when the United Society of Believers in Christ's Second Appearing established a colony. Three Believer Missionaries from the Shaker Colony in New York, attracted by the great Kentucky religious revival in the late 18th century, came to establish two colonies in Kentucky and one in Ohio.

Because of the trembling in their devotional dancing, they were commonly called Shakers. They believed in celibacy, common ownership of property, confession of sins, and separation from the world. Their ideals of simplicity, industry, and maximum utility gave impetus to their communal farm, which rapidly developed into economic success. Celibacy, the Civil War, and the industrial revolution, however, decimated their ranks and all but two of the 19 communities in the United States have dissolved. The last survivor of the Pleasant Hill colony, Sister Mary Settles, died in 1923.

Now the pastoral scene has been restored as a memorial to the gentle people who sought to establish God's own Kingdom in the Kentucky Blue Grass region. Visitors may stay at the two-story brick Trustees' House, where guests were housed during the Shaker period. Center Family House has an extensive museum of Shaker life. A weaver will be at work in the Sisters' House and a cabinetmaker will probably be reproducing the chaste Shaker designs in the Brethren's Shop.

A lively religious center still exists at Shakertown with the establishment of the Quaker-oriented "Yokefellows at Shakertown Retreat Center." The West Family Wash House of the Shakers is the conference building, while the office and bookstore are in the adjacent restored Preserved Shop. People attending retreats or just visiting the Shaker Center should be prepared for mouthwatering delicacies, like Shaker Lemon Pie, that are served by costumed workers.

(4) PARIS

Cane Ridge Meeting House

Travelers enroute to this settlement, which is northeast on Route 68, might want to stop at Fort Boonesborough State Park, where the site of Boone's

1775 settlement is marked. The first sermon was preached that same year within its palisaded walls.

Pressing on 8 miles east of Paris, the traveler finds a meeting house nestled for protection within a native limestone superstructure. Here in 1791 Presbyterians from North Carolina established a church. Then on August 6, 1801, a great revival called by the pastor, Rev. Barton Stone, began a powerful camp meeting attracting thousands. This "greatest outpouring of the Spirit since Pentecost" marked a watershed in American church history, revitalizing religious life. A great revival swept across Tennessee, Ohio, and Kentucky during the next three years, affecting Presbyterians, Baptists, and Methodists and forming other groups. Thus this log meeting house has become a historic shrine.

(5) LOUISVILLE

Near Eastern and Biblical Antiquities

Continuing the circular swing around the northern section of the state, the traveler next journeys to the campus of the Southern Baptist Theological Seminary at 2825 Lexington Road. Here in the Nichols Museum of Biblical Archeology and the Eisenberg Museum of Egyptian and Near East Antiquities, the traveler will find a fabulous wealth of material including statuary dating to 2500 B.C. Ordinarily it would be necessary to travel around the Mediterranean to see similar objects. Now, in a single trip to Louisville, one can see coins; tools; utensils; replicas of tombs, synagogues, temples; and excavated materials from biblical sites including Caesarea.

Southern Kentucky

(6) PINEVILLE

Book of Job

Our southern tour begins at the eastern border where a relatively recent addition to the religious scene is found each summer. The Everyman Players have presented a religious drama based on the King James Bible version of Job for more than 16 summers in the outdoor amphitheater at Pine Mountain State Park. Using an intricate arrangement of singing and chanting, and striking harlequin-style make-up, the poem and the personality of Job emerges as does his search into the meaning of life. "There is spirit in man . . . . Man in his very soul, wiser than his head, knows this. Hope like Job's survives," says the adapter, Orlin Corey. The play has been presented at the Brussels and New York world fairs and tours on the off season.

(7) SOUTH UNION

Shakertown

Still farther west is the second Shaker community established in 1807 on the rich farmland. There were 26 initial converts to the Gasper Society, as it was first called. By 1827, however, there were 349 members and 60 buildings on the 6,000-acre holding. Known and respected for their inventiveness, honesty, and hard work, the Shakers became leading agriculturalists, with crop rotation and specialized cattle breeding. They also were industrialists, having gristmills, sawmills, a whiskey distillery, a broom factory, and a large textile operation. The sisters were famous for their silks, preserved fruit, and wines. Inventions and improvements on clothespins, apple peelers, revolving ovens, tilting chairs, washing machines, and condensed milk were made.

From the 1860s on, Shakers declined, finally disbanding in 1922 with a public sale of land, buildings, and furnishings. Friends of South Union determined to preserve this heritage and in 1960 opened a Shaker museum near Auburn. They also purchased original Shaker land with two buildings. The massive Center Family House is a 40-room Georgian-designed structure with a sweeping double stairway up to the fourth floor. The meeting room has the original cherry speaker's stand. Visitors can find a variety of books and reproductions in the gift shop. In the summer, they can also enjoy in mid-July the annual Shaker festival and the outdoor drama *Shakertown Revisited.*

ARKANSAS

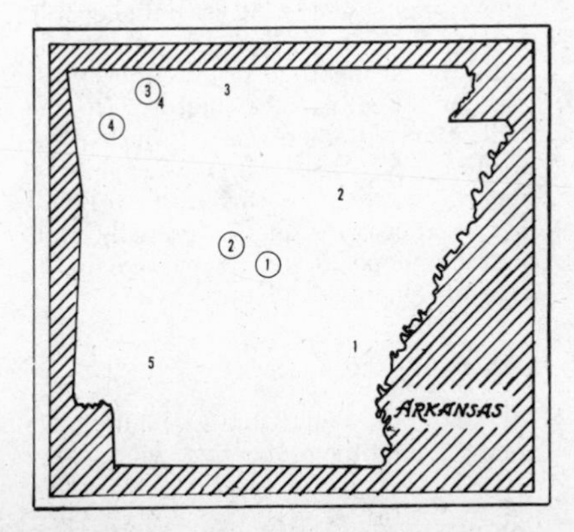

Religiously significant sites in Arkansas seem to be either very old or contemporary.

White explorers penetrated this ancient Moundbuilder stronghold as early as the DeSoto expedition in 1541. A permanent settlement, the first in the Mississippi valley, was made by Henri de Tonti in 1686. He brought the flag of France and the Jesuits who established a mission. The little settlement persisted through a seemingly continuous change of ownership, which undoubtedly hindered more colonization.

France, Spain, the United States, the

Confederacy, and the states of Louisiana and Missouri all successively claimed Arkansas until 1819 when it became a United States territory, and 1836 when it was made a full state.

White pioneers began arriving about 1803, but full development was difficult because of unceasing activity through the state due to the Mexican War, the Civil War, the border dispute with Texas, and the launching of covered-wagon trains and expeditions searching for gold.

Thus it was only in the last century that Protestant and Catholic churches developed and spiritually significant activities arose like the Mt. Sequoyah Methodist Assembly, the Christ-centered art collection at Eureka Springs, and the International Heifer Projects Fourche River Ranch.

Central Arkansas

(1) LITTLE ROCK

St. Andrew's Cathedral

In the capital, which as at the center of Arkansas, is a Roman Catholic church symbolizing the Catholic population which began in the now extinct Jesuit mission at Arkanas Post. The granite Gothic cathedral at 623 Louisiana Street, is a copy of a German church and far more elaborate than the early mission.

While in the city, the traveler might well visit the Arkansas Territorial Capitol Restoration, which is a museum containing 13 original buildings at East Third and Cumberland streets. The homes, capitol, and print shop give a revealing picture of early days. It is considered by authorities to be one of the nation's finest small restorations.

(2) PERRYVILLE

Fourche River Ranch

"Gifts of life" are born at this World Livestock Center and home of Heifer Project International about 40 miles west of Little Rock and 1½ miles south of Perryville. The nonsectarian charitable organization, organized in 1944, sends animals to needy families in the states and abroad. The purpose is to help the families produce food and income for themselves and pass this on to others, for the first animal offspring must go to a needy neighbor.

At the 1,200-acre area, visitors are welcome to view the donated animals, the foundation herd, and the personnel training program. Many churches of all denominations support the Heifer Project (which also includes goats, chickens, rabbits, and other livestock). "Cowboys" deliver the animals directly to recipients in the United States and abroad.

(3) EUREKA SPRINGS

Christ of the Ozarks

Probably the most unusual of the Christ-centered establishments in the spa city of Eureka Springs, oldest resort of the Ozarks, is the seven-story-high statue of Christ atop Magnetic Mountain. A project of the Elna M. Smith Foundation, the figure was constructed by Emmet Sullivan and dedicated in 1966. Built to withstand 500-mile-an-hour winds, it is unbelievably strong. It is said that an automobile could be suspended from either wrist without affecting the statue. In the dedication statement, Mrs. Smith commented, "We are not image worshipers, but we do believe this portrayal will inspire thousands and eventually millions of people to reflect on the teachings and character of our Savior."

Christ Only Art Gallery

Mr. and Mrs. Gerald L. K. Smith have spent a lifetime collecting more than

400 portrayals of Christ in every known art form. Now they can be seen in a gallery of Mediterranean architectural design which stands on Mt. Oberammergau, a short distance from Christ of the Ozarks. Crown Dresden figurines, carvings in wood and ivory, as well as portraits on copper and in glass, are but a few of the items contained in the varied exhibit. Here are great masterpieces as well as provincial manifestations of the Christian faith. One of the rarest pieces is a bronze, silver, and copper figure of Christ journeying into Jerusalem on a donkey. The gallery pleases all because it satisfies the amateur as well as the professional eye. From its windows four states may be seen: Arkansas, Missouri, Kansas, and Oklahoma.

The Great Passion Play

Across from the art gallery, the traveler will see a duplicate of the streets of Jerusalem, for here each summer is staged the events of Christ's last week on earth. In a beautiful outdoor amphitheater the Palm Sunday procession, the scenes leading to the crucifixion, burial, resurrection, and ascension are reenacted with a cast of thousands.

On a nearby slope, a replica of the Holy Land is under construction which will have a location for baptisms on the banks of the new River Jordan.

Church in the Wildwood Museum

Between the Alpine-looking resort town of Eureka Springs and the Passion Play setting stands a white-frame church which was abandoned. Purchased by the Smith Foundation and restored, it now houses their collection of 10,000 rare Bibles and related manuscripts. After entering through the tiny Victorian porch, visitors can see a Gutenberg facsimile Bible, translations of the Bible into the Cherokee language, a 16th-century hymnal, the famous Breeches Bible of Geneva, Switzerland, and the Polyglot Bible of 1657 that contains 12 languages.

Passion Play, Eureka Springs

 FAYETTEVILLE

Mt. Sequoyah Assembly

On a hill overlooking the city is a large cross, illuminated at night, which marks the grounds of the United Methodist Church. Opening in 1923, the conference center now operates year round, and continues a long history of service to the churches. The large Clapp Auditorium, cafeteria seating 400, and other modern, comfortable buildings make almost a complete village in itself. Sequoyah is an honored name in history, for it belonged to the chieftain who created the Cherokee alphabet of 85 symbols and helped make his nation the most literate of all Indian tribes. Fayetteville was the seat of administration for Cherokee affairs and near the "Trail of Tears" that displaced Cherokees followed to reservations in the west. Assembly grounds on Skyline Drive are especially fine to view in fall, when the abundance of maple trees show their multicolored splendor.

V.

GREAT LAKES COUNTRY

WISCONSIN

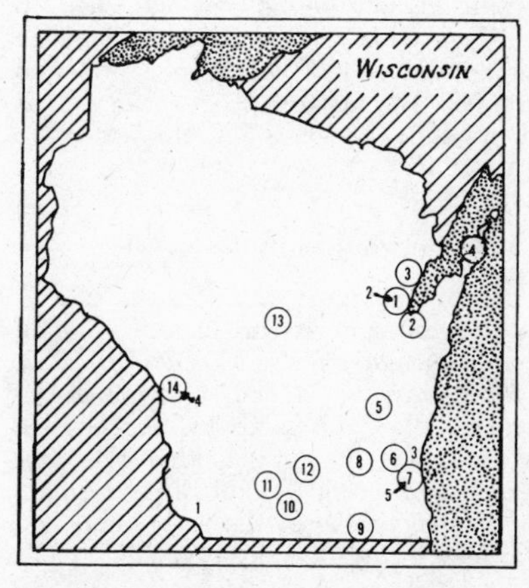

The Great Lakes were the first gateways to the states in America's northeast. Jacques Cartier arrived in Canada, claiming the land in 1534 for Francis I, king of France. Then almost seven decades later, in 1608, Samuel de Champlain founded Quebec. When De Mont established a permanent agricultural settlement at Port Royal (Annapolis Royal), France claimed control of the region west to Lake Superior and down the Mississippi to the Gulf of Mexico.

Soon pressure to build an empire and to unlock the wealth in furs and other hidden riches sent explorers, the military, and the accompanying Catholic missionary priests down the inland seas to the northern shores of Wisconsin, Michigan, Indiana, Ohio, and Minnesota. Similar French parties were journeying up the internal waterway of the Mississippi to penetrate the lands in southern Illinois and Iowa.

Wisconsin's 500 miles of shoreline on lakes Michigan and Superior, as well as its some 7,000 lakes and many negotiable rivers, made traveling comparatively easy.

It was in 1634 that Jean Nicolet, a representative of Champlain, governor of New France, stepped ashore in the Green Bay area, expecting to find indications of the northwest passage to China. Instead, he met the Winnebago Indians and started a lucrative fur trade.

Jesuit priests began misisonary work among the Indians almost immediately, following trappers and hunters to new forts at La Baye (Green Bay), La Pointe, and Prairie du Chine.

The next two centuries were unsettled in Wisconsin as the British took over after the French and Indian Wars and then the Americans sought to oust the British. After a period of hostilities with the natives, climaxing in the Black Hawk War, Wisconsin became a territory of the United States in 1836 and a state in 1848.

An influx of settlers came, drawn by the profitable fur trade in the north and lead mining in the south. With them came their churches, and Protestants joined earlier Catholics. Another kind of settler appeared, drawn by the unspoiled acreage. Here Norwegians,

Swiss, Swedish, and German colonists could carve out communities to their own liking. Thus Lutheran, Swiss Reform, and Moravian churches were organized.

Recent years have seen the advent of Catholic shrines and churches of contemporary art form. Our tour begins at Green Bay and in general follows the coast, pathway of the early pioneers.

East Coast Wisconsin

(1) GREEN BAY

Robinsonville Chapel

Father Claude Allouez established a mission in the Green Bay area in 1669. Called by a succession of names, depending on which country was in possession, the little community was the earliest white settlement west of Lake Michigan. In this early Catholic settlement is a Belgian shrine established in the 1860s by Sister Adele Brice, who is buried in the nearby cemetery. While in this thriving city, the traveler should make his or her way to the waterfront and imagine that long-ago scene when whites and Indians had their historic confrontation.

(2) DE PERE

National Shrine of St. Joseph

South of Green Bay is the site of the first mission mentioned above. The historic community was known as the "Rapides Des Peres," because of those early Jesuits. This 1669 post was in a strategic spot, a crossroads for travelers. It was the departure point for the expedition of Marquette and Joliet.

St. Norbert Abbey and the National Shrine of St. Joseph are here and both can be toured by visitors.

(3) OCONTO

Oconto County Historical Museum

Before leaving the bay area, journey up the west side to this ancient community, home of the prehistoric Copper Culture people whose settlement flourished about 5556 B.C. These were the first known Americans to use copper for tools. Archeological finds of that era and of the later fur-trading and Jesuit-mission peroid can be seen in this museum. The old Beyer Home, a mansion of the Civil War period and the county's first brick house, as well as a modern annex, hold the extensive collection.

First Church of Christ, Scientist

One of the later additions to church life in the state is this church at Main and Chicago streets. Erected in 1886, it is known as the first structure in the world to be built as a Christian Science church. The pleasing Gothic-style edifice has its original Kimball reed organ, and memorabilia of the early years can be seen in the Reading Room.

(4) EPHRAIM

The Anderson Store

Moravians from Norway founded Ephraim in 1853. Andrew Iverson, leader of a little society of Norwegian

Christians, met Moravian missionary John Frederick Fett in Milwaukee in 1849. Together they planned the location of a new community of the Norwegian immigrants. Choosing virgin land on the Green Bay peninsula, they chose the name "Ephraim" and reorganized as a Moravian congregation. The first church was built in 1857 and was a "commodious log cabin" crowned by a 20-foot steeple built by Iverson. Now the community is a thriving resort that still reflects proudly on its heritage.

The Anderson Store is an excellent place to relive the history. Aslag Anderson established it in 1858 on his arrival from Norway. Continuing in the same family until 1960, it is now a project of Anderson Restoration. Here, amid calico prints, lemon drops, and sapolio soap, are relics of the early pioneer days in a lively setting.

(5) FOND DU LAC

Cathedral Church of St. Paul the Apostle

Continuing south, the traveler will find at the lower edge of Lake Winnebago another of the early communities. At 51 West Division Street stands the Gothic Cathedral Church of St. Paul the Apostle, set amid broad lawns. Lifesized wood carvings of the apostles were created in Oberammergau, Germany. Choir stalls and sanctuary have especially fine wood carvings. Stained-glass windows, made both in America and abroad, adorn this impressive Episcopal church. A stone from Westminster Abbey, sent as a gesture of friendship in 1887, may be seen in the chancel.

(6) DELAFIELD

Church of St. John Chrysostom

In Delafield, close to Milwaukee, is a fine example of a frontier parish church. Built in the early 1850s, its construction began with the stone altar, which was fixed firmly in the ground first. Then a Neo-Gothic building was constructed around it. Hinges, latches, and nails were made by local people. This Episcopal church in its simplicity has a strangely new and contemporary effect.

(7) MILWAUKEE

St. Joan of Arc Chapel

On the campus of Marquette University is a much traveled 15th-century French chapel, which was originally brought to Long Island, New York, then rebuilt here. This outstanding stone building of medieval Gothic architecture is most appropriate in the area where French priests worked among the Indians three centuries ago. (Jacques Marquette came in 1674 and the Sulpician missionary, Father Saint-Cosme, in 1699.)

The interior of St. Joan of Arc Chapel is authentically furnished and contains relics dating from the 11th to the 15th centuries. Charles Connick designed the four stained-glass windows in recent years.

Annunciation Greek Orthodox Church

This awe-inspiring church at 9400 West Congress Street is the last major building to come from the drawing board of famed architect Frank Lloyd Wright. It was opened July 2, 1961, and serves one of the ten oldest Greek Orthodox congregations in the country.

Wright referred to the church as "my little jewel . . . a miniature Santa Sophia." The Greek cross with circular components provides the architectural theme. The great dome, of blue tile, is 104 feet in diameter and 45 feet high. It rests on some 700,000 "ball-bearings," and 325 hollow glass spheres form a necklace below. Gold anodized aluminum forms inside and outside trim. The interior is elaborately adorned with icons and rich sanctuary appointments.

Central Wisconsin

(8) WATERTOWN

Moravian Church

Moravians from Frankfort, Germany, decided to go to America and chose Watertown in southern Wisconsin. After an eleven-week freighter passage, they arrived in Milwaukee then walked the 60 miles to Watertown, with their possessions on ox wagons. While felling trees for their houses, they burned the branches, selling ashes for lye-making at 7 cents per bushel. Missionary John Kaltenbrunn arrived in 1853 and 17 families were organized into the Ebeneezer congregation. At first a log building was church, school, and parsonage. In 1856, a substantial brick building was erected, and the congregation now has a modern church plant.

(9) JEFFERSON PRAIRIE

Augustana Lutheran Commemorative Monument

While traveling south, close to the Illinois border, the visitor should stop in this historic community, where the Augustana Lutheran Church was born in 1860. A commemorative granite monument in the church cemetery was placed here in 1930 to "commemorate the goodness of God to the early fathers and their descendents . . . and to pledge unto the Lord our faithfulness."

Earlier, in 1836, Ansten and Numedal (Ole) Nattestad heard of America while still living in their native Norway and came for a visit. Austen returned to Norway in the spring of 1838 to organize the migration of over 100 immigrants. Numedal, meanwhile, explored the area and located in Jefferson Prairie. Some of the immigrants settled here and others at Rock Prairie (Luther Valley). Two separate Lutheran congregations were organized. These are believed to be the first Norwegian settlements in Wisconsin and the fourth in the country.

In Muskego is the oldest Norwegian Lutheran church and a museum, with church and pioneer memorabilia. The Norwegian Lutheran Synod, now part of the American Lutheran Church, was founded in this area in 1853.

(10) NEW GLARUS

New Glarus Historical Society

Another of the ethnic settlements in Wisconsin is farther west from Jefferson Prairie in this community settled by Swiss in 1845. Often called "Little Switzerland," New Glarus is rich in atmosphere as well as Swiss attributes of industry and steadfastness.

The first church was a log one constructed in 1849 for their first Swiss Reformed minister. In 1858, a stone building was erected, and in 1900 the present brick structure to house the congregation.

The historical society maintains the Swiss Museum Village, which includes in its ten buildings and pioneer exhibits a replica of that first log church.

At the 6th Avenue location, visitors may also see a reconstructed blacksmith shop, cabin, schoolhouse, store, and cheese factory. Nearby also is a Swiss Miss Lace Factory which produces Swiss embroidery with German machinery of the 1900s. Many descendants of those first colonists tend the various enterprises.

(11) BLUE MOUNDS

Little Norway

Ethnic interest will continue to be heightened at this 1856 homestead of a Norwegian settler northwest of New Glarus. Here, by a quiet stream in the Valley of the Elves, are a dozen log buildings constructed as if they were in Norway. The most unusual is probably the Norway Building, which is an 1885 model of a 12th-century Norwegian stave church. Fire-breathing dragon heads adorn the tiered gable roof to ward off evil spirits. Made of oak and beautifully hand-carved throughout, the building houses a museum of Norwegian culture ranging from household objects to manuscripts of Edvard Grieg. The church was originally built for exhibition at several world expositions, and now this and the remaining compound give a glimpse of how pioneer immigrants lived.

(12) MADISON

First Unitarian Society

Circling northeast and driving to 900 University Bay Drive, the traveler comes to another of the dramatic Frank Lloyd Wright buildings. The meeting house, built in 1949-1950, is triangular. A dramatic, thrusting roof expresses aspiration and worship. The inspiring interior has layers of rugged stone and glass. Facing the pulpit, one sees it as a prow. When facing in the opposite direction, toward the hearth room, the warm colors and simple design bring the congregation close together.

(13) RUDOLPH

Grotto Shrine

Our last stop in the central section of the state is north of Madison on Route 34. As the result of a visit to Lourdes, France, and a physical healing, Father Philip J. Wagner began constructing this grotto shrine in 1928. Though pastor in the village of Rudolph, he found time to create painstakingly the religious scenes beginning with the Lourdes grouping of Mary and St. Bernadette. Inside the man-made Wonder Cave, the traveler can follow the Path of Faith where commandments, sacraments, prayer, virtues, and good works are noted in scenes along the way. Extensive floral gardens and woodland paths cover more than four acres, all dedicated to the peace, majesty, and wonder of God.

West Wisconsin

 LA CROSSE

Maria Angelorum Chapel

At St. Rose Convent on Market Street in La Crosse, farther north from Dickeyville on the Mississippi, is the elaborate Romanesque Catholic chapel, Maria Angelorum. It was built in 1906 by the Franciscan Sisters of Perpetual Adoration. Scenes from the history of the three orders founded by St. Francis are depicted in a series of paintings. They are the Friars Minor, Poor Clares, and Third Order Secular. Windows of Bavarian stained-glass and rich mosaics, marble, and bronzes further adorn the interior.

St. Joseph the Workman Cathedral

The old and the new mesh well together in this Roman Catholic church at 530 Main Street. The design is contemporary, but it is inspired by Gothic churches. Built in 1962, it has a tower that rises 216 feet, and especially beautiful stained-glass windows. The Blessed Sacrament Chapel has black marble walls and an altar of gold mosaic glass. Probably it is symbolic that we end our tour of Wisconsin with Catholic places of worship, in honor of those early Jesuits who spread the faith amid pioneer hardships.

MICHIGAN

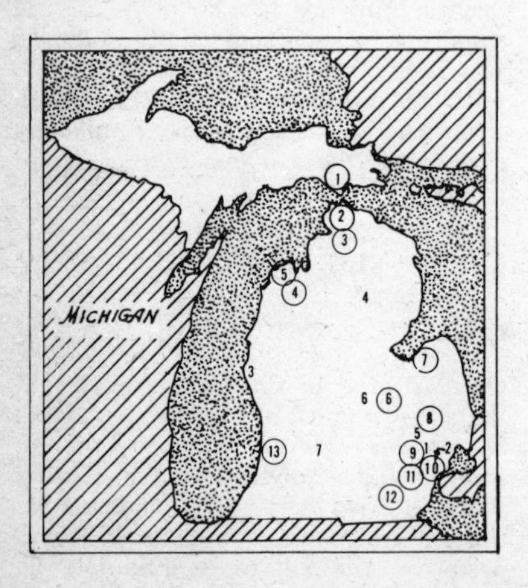

Exploring parties sent out by the French government at Quebec, Canada, passed through the swirling rapids above St. Joseph Island into the Great North Sea (Lake Superior) as early as 1621, when Etienne Brule searched for the northwest passage. Jean Nicolet followed in 1634. They were forerunners of a large number of explorers, trappers, and priests who were in contact with the natives. Fathers Charles Raymbault and Isaac Joques preached at the site of Sault Ste. Marie in 1641. Father Jacques Marquette founded the first permanent mission there in 1668. Settlements soon followed at St. Ignatius in 1671 and at Detroit in 1701.

The gigantic amount of shoreline on

four of the Great Lakes and the over 10,000 ponds and lakes made this water world available early to French travelers and kept the fur trade profitable even through the ensuing two centuries of struggle for control of the region. Michigan became a state in 1837. It had developed into two geographical entities, the Upper and Lower Peninsula, joined at the Straits of Mackinac. Over the swirling 4½-mile waterway today stretches one of the world's longest suspension bridges.

Spiritual heritage sites seem confined to the more easily traveled Lower Peninsula. Our tour begins at the Straits, where the white and Indian cultures first met.

Upper Straits, Michigan

(1) ST. IGNACE

Marquette Park

The second oldest Michigan settlement is St. Ignace. At Marquette and State streets is the grave of Father Jacques Marquette with accompanying statue. Originally a military post, St. Ignace was established in 1671. After viewing the French and Indian Museum in the park, the traveler might drive 4 miles north to Castle Rock, an ancient lookout of the Algonquin Indians.

(2) MACKINAW CITY

Fort Michilimackinac Historic Park

The French built this fort in 1715 to protect the Straits. In 1761, British troops occupied it until it was abandoned in 1780 for the island fortress of Fort Mackinac. Jesuit missionaries erected the Church of Ste. Anne de Michilimackinac in 1743 to replace an earlier structure. The simple but pleasing little wooden French church has an ancient French-style cemetery at its rear wall and the church is topped with a tiny cupola and cross. Every hour on the hour at the sound of the church bell, there is a sound-and-light show inside the vaulted, wood-paneled church. Afterward, visitors may wander through a priest's house, blacksmith shop, barracks, storehouse, and trader's home in the authentically restored palisade-enclosed fort.

Mackinac Island State Park

On a strategically located island connected to the city by ferry during the warm months is Fort Mackinac, constructed in 1780. A trip by carriage is recommended up the impressive "Avenue of Flags" to the fort. Dioramas, murals, and lifelike period settings depict the highlights of history in the blockhouse and rooms where the events actually occurred.

Bark Chapel and Mission Church

A short way from Fort Makinac, but still on Mackinac Island, is a missionary rustic bark chapel with a huge wooden cross alongside. A reminder of the first houses of worship, it is constructed Indian-fashion in the style preferred by the first Indian congregation.

Also on the island is the Mission Church, a white clapboard edifice with central tower and cupola. It was built in 1830 by Rev. William Ferry for the first Protestant congregation north of Detroit. Admission is by combination ticket to the fort, Mission Church, an Indian dormitory, and a blacksmith shop.

(3) INDIAN RIVER

Catholic Shrine

In the peaceful wooded setting of Burt Lake State Park farther south of Mackinaw City on Route 75, is the world's largest crucifix. On a landscaped knoll overlooking Lake Burt a 55-foot, 14-ton redwood cross supports a 7-ton statue of Christ. The monument to Christ was begun in 1948 and now includes an outdoor church at the foot of the crucifix, Long House Chapel, and nine miniature shrines to saints.

On the grounds is an arresting statue of Kateri Tekakwitha, "Lily of the Mohawks," who was born in 1656 near Auriesville, New York, where St. Isaac Jogues and his companions were martyred earlier. She is a candidate for sainthood and the shrine is dedicated to her. A holy staircase has relics of different saints including the six who died on American soil.

Thousands of pilgrims visit the shrine constantly, though more come in summer. There are daily masses, and every Friday and Saturday evening a candlelight procession led by the Statue of Our Lady is held as part of the pilgrimage program.

(4) TRAVERSE CITY

Old Indian Mission

Westward on the Old Mission peninsula, which extends into Grand Traverse Bay, is the site of the oldest Indian mission of the first settlement

established in 1839 by Rev. Peter Dougherty. In 1842, he erected the tiny frame mission house which still stands on the west side of Mission Road, just north of the store and post office.

When he first arrived, representing Presbyterian missions to the Chippewa Indians, Dougherty taught school in a little bark wigwam vacated for the purpose. In 1840, a log house was built for use as both school and church. A replica of that first log church now stands on Mission Road south of the village. It was officially opened in 1974 and has exhibits of Indian and settler days.

In 1852, peninsula lands were opened to whites and the Indians were forced to move across to Omena and a new mission. The name Old Mission still persists here, however, even to the original lighthouse built at the tip of land in 1870.

(5) MAPLE CITY

Lund's Scenic Garden

Northeast of Traverse City and just north of Maple City is a nondenominational shrine begun in 1944 by artists Mr. and Mrs. E. K. Lund, on land donated by Mr. and Mrs. James Swanson. This most beautiful religious spot has a footpath winding over 16 acres that leads among 36 life-sized scenes of the life of Christ done with oil paints. A self-guided tour is available during the day. At night, there is a conducted walk with special lighting effects.

Central Michigan

(6) FRANKENMUTH

Log Church and Franconian Museum

According to an old marker on Main Street, Frankenmuth, a small town southeast of Saginaw: FIFTEEN GERMAN IMMIGRANTS FROM FRANCONIA, BAVARIA, LED BY REV. AUGUST CRAEMER FOUNDED FRANENMUTH IN 1845. From this came three other mission outposts to the Chippewa Indians at Frankentrost, Frankenlust, and Frankenhilf. Each community has a church school and cemetery, and travelers, particularly of the Lutheran heritage, may want to seek them out. At Frankenmuth, across from St. Lorenz Lutheran Church, there is a log-cabin replica of the place where Missionary Craemer taught the Indians (using their own language), the Franconian Museum, and Church Bells in the Forest display. A modern Christian day school has eight grades and 24 teachers.

(7) SEBEWAING

Indian Mission House

Northeast of Frankenmuth in the "thumb" area of Michigan is another of the early mission houses, probably the oldest extant, in which Lutheran missionaries conducted services for American Indians. The plain, two-story frame house originally stood a few miles farther northeast at the mouth of the Shebahyonk River and was moved to a site across from the contemporary Immanuel Lutheran Church in 1949. The authentically furnished mission was headquarters for all work with the Chippewa Indian population under administration of Rev. J. J. F. Auch.

Southern Michigan

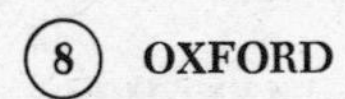

(8) OXFORD

St. Augustine's House

On a hilltop about 3 miles from Route 24 above Pontiac, is a place for quiet, meditation, reflection, liturgical celebration, and community sharing sponsored by the Congregation of the Servants of Christ. The ecumenical retreat center, dedicated to the understanding of religious life in community, is connected with the Church of Sweden. Bishop Olaf Herrlin of Sweden dedicated the retreat house in September 1966, when the congregation became a community within the Brotherhood of the Holy Cross in Sweden. Professing the faith of the ecumenical creeds of the undivided church of Christian antiquity and connected with the Lutheran World Federation, the Swedish church is in a unique position to work toward the healing of Christian schisms. The present retreat leader was ordained in Sweden for ecumenical work in the United States.

In addition to the comfortable and functional main house, there are a pleasing Chapel of the Visitation of the Blessed Virgin Mary and Saint Monica's Retreat House for women.

(9) SOUTHFIELD

St. John's Armenian Apostolic Church

On Northwestern Highway in the Detroit area is an octagonal church with a striking sawtooth conical dome crowned by a gold cross. The church was built in 1966, but is reminiscent of early Byzantine architecture. There are eight gabled bays decorated with arches and columns in this limestone structure. The stained-glass windows were made in Chartres, France, and portray saints and Armenian motifs.

(10) DETROIT

Old Mariner's Church

Continuing south into Detroit, the traveler will find this Episcopal parish church, an integral part of the Civic Center. Founded in 1842 as a haven for the sailors traveling the Great Lakes, Old Mariner's Church resulted from bequests from Charlotte Taylor and her sister Julia Anderson. Built originally 880 feet away, it was moved in 1955 to its present site, which was the location of the Indian Council House where Episcopal services in Michigan were first held. The "perpendicular Gothic" church is on the National and State Historic Registers and is rich with memorials, including the Helen Calder organ, the Rands Tower, and the Brotherhood Bell.

(11) DEARBORN

Greenfield Village

During his lifetime Henry Ford assembled on a 60-acre setting a full-scale panorama of American life as our forefathers knew it. He moved homes and shrines from all parts of America and re-erected them in a typical setting around a village green. In a prominent place at its head is the graceful Mary-Martha Chapel. Designed along Colonial lines, the chapel was built in 1929. The spire is patterned after the church at Bradford, Massachusetts. Corinthian columns flank the portico. An electro-pneumatic organ was developed at the suggestion of Ford. It has 1,484 pipes ranging in size from a pencil to a telephone pole! The bell was cast by the son of Paul Reverve in 1834.

(12) ANN ARBOR

The Word of God

In the university community just west of Dearborn, on Route 94, is an ecumenical Christian community. Though Catholic in origin, the charismatic community, which began in 1967 with four people, has grown to include about 1,000 people who belong to some 40 different churches (about 61 percent Catholic and 39 percent Protestant). At first university-centered, the community now serves older single people and families and has expanded to neighboring towns. There are 42 residential households and 26 nonresidential and dorm households which meet regularly for prayer and meals. Most members are involved in a variety of services to the community, including a mercy team to sick, aged, and imprisoned.

The only building owned by the community is Harris Hall, which contains the *New Covenant* international magazine serving charismatic renewal; the Word of Life, a publishing and cassette-tape editing office; the International Communication Office and the Ecumenical Relations Office, both of which are service arms for Catholic charismatic renewal; and a conference office which sponsors conferences throughout the country. Guests are welcome to tour the facilities.

Visitors are also invited to prayer and praise services held on Thursday nights at two school facilities, and to spend a few days visiting, if contact is made in advance (write Guestmaster, P.O. Box 87, Ann Arbor, Michigan 48107). Visitors will find a people whose main purpose is to be open to the Holy Spirit and to witness by living in a Christian community.

(13) HOLLAND

Religious, political, and economic conditions caused 53 Dutch people under the leadership of Rev. A. C. Van Raalte to sail to America. Wishing to be free from the restrictions of a state church, they continued up the Hudson River to the Dutch in Albany, New York, then traveled to Michigan to find virgin land for their "Kolonie." Arriving in February 1847 on the site chosen, which was close to Lake Michigan on the western edge of the state, they immediately held services to thank God and started erecting log cabins.

In spite of disease and lack of food caused by the arrival of close to 800 more settlers that year, the colony grew. Pilgrim Home cemetery is a reminder of those who died that first hard year. A log church was built, which served

for school classes as well as church services. Holland Academy, later Hope College, began in 1857 to prepare youth for the Dutch Reformed Rutgers College. The Dutch Reformed White Pillar Church on Ninth Street was erected in 1856. The modern community still has an Old World flavor as typical Dutch-style buildings stand by modern architecture. The community sponsors Tulip Time in mid-May when the town becomes a place of festival. Windmill Island, Netherlands Museum, the wooden shoe factory and Dutch Village re-create early atmosphere.

ILLINOIS

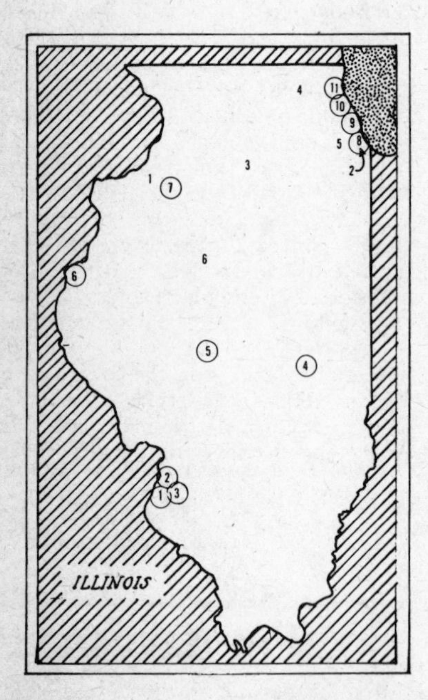

The La Salle expedition came over the Great Lakes from the north as the Marquette-Joliet party traveled up the Mississippi River from the south to bring the flag of France to Illinois in the 1670s. On Good Friday 1675, Father Marquette returned and opened a mission at the great village of the Illinois Indians near the present Starved Rock State Park in the state's midsection. Ill health led to his abandoning the mission.

La Salle returned to the area in 1680 and established Fort Creve Coeur near the present Peoria. A later outpost, Fort St. Louis, was erected at Starved Rock in 1683. Catholic missions which had been successful in the area were moved to a new headquarters near the mouth of the Kaskaskia River about 1700. Permanent French settlements grew here along the Mississippi River with Cohokia and Kaskaskia as principal villages. Historic Fort Kaskaskia was built in 1736 on a site preserved by Fort Kaskaskia State Park.

The little communities spent the next century and a half under different governments which included the countries of Spain, England, and France, as well as the states of Louisiana and Virginia. No doubt the Catholic fathers labored among the native and early pioneer population whatever flag was currently flying.

At the conclusion of the War of 1812, settlers came with a rush and statehood soon followed in 1818. The last of the Indian hostilities ceased with the Black Hawk War of 1832, when the tribes were relocated to allow for more white expansion. With the whites came their churches. In most cases these were organized when the settlers arrived. The Mormons, however, arrived en masse to settle Nauvoo in 1839-1840, after being forced to leave Missouri. Conflict with those not appreciating their beliefs led to their expulsion and they left for Utah in 1844.

Recent days have brought a wide variety of religious activity from the Black Muslims to the Vedanta Society, from the Baha'is to the Reba Place Fellowship, a Christian community of the Anabaptist tradition.

Southern Illinois

(1) CAHOKIA

Church of the Holy Family

Three missionaries from the Seminary of Foreign Missions of Quebec, Canada, founded Cahokia in March 1699. By May, Father St. Cosme had completed a house and a chapel here, the first roughly constructed church in Illinois country. The priests ministered to the Cahokia Indians, part of the Illinois Federation. A century later, in 1799, Rev. Gabriel Richard built the church of walnut logs that can be seen today. It is believed to be the oldest church west of the Alleghenies. Close by is the oldest occidental cemetery in the western United States. Here bones of Spanish cavaliers and grand dames of France decay along with those of Indians and Negroes.

At the tourist center in City Hall, the traveler can find directions to a frontier courthouse built in 1737 and the Jarrot House, the oldest brick home in the Mississippi valley. Nicholas and Madame Jarrot, a devout couple, always led the family procession to Mass on Sundays and holy days. Though becoming somewhat of a feudal lord, Jarrot always was most generous and hospitable and the beautiful home is a treat to see.

(2) EAST ST. LOUIS

Cahokia Mounds State Park

From about A.D. 800 to 1500, a prehistoric city of first Woodland and later Mississippian culture existed at this site northeast of East St. Louis. These preceded the Illinois Indians of the French pioneer days. Of the many mound communities in the United States, this is the most extensive and includes the third largest man-made temple mound in North America, whose enormous base covers nearly 14 acres. Its sides are broken into four terraces rising 100 feet above the floodplain. On the fourth terrace there was once a large ceremonial building, probably used as a religious structure and residence of head priest or ruler.

This mound has been known in recent years as Monks Mound because Trappist Monks secured permission from Nicholas Jarrot to establish a monastery here. They built their settlements on a mound west of the main mound and gardened on the first terrace of the largest mound. The site was abandoned and land deeded back to Jarrot in 1813.

The 650-acre site with 40 Indian mounds is open to visitors year round and its museum displays archeological discoveries of prehistoric Indian life.

(3) BELLEVILLE

Shrine of Our Lady of the Snows

We return to the present-day world at this national shrine of the Oblates of Mary Immaculate. Placed at first in a small chapel at St. Henry's Seminary in Bellville, the shrine attracted so many people for prayer and devotion it was necessary to relocate. The Oblate fathers purchased 80 acres (later increased to 200) in the rolling hills and on historic bluffs overlooking the Mississippi River. The shrine with its striking outdoor altar housing several chapels, rosary courts, and the amphitheater seating 20,000 was completed for use in 1962. The unique edifice is a skillful and harmonious blend of art and architecture.

The Annunciation Garden, with its triangular bell pool, German angelus bells, fountain, and sculpture of the Virgin Mary and the Angel Gabriel, is a quiet place for meditation.

St. Joseph's Hall and Pilgrims' Inn, serving needs of tourists, and a retirement community are also part of this beautifully landscaped complex. Masses are said daily with many more held in warm months of the year. An especially fine time to visit is directly after Thanksgiving through Christmas when thousands of lights cover trees and bushes, transforming the shrine and life-sized figures of the nativity into a fairyland.

Central Illinois

ARCOLA

Rockome Gardens

In the heart of the quaint Amish country off Route 57 in southeast central Illinois, is Rockome Gardens, begun as a hobby in 1939, which developed into a fascinating reminder of the religious sect that has inhabited the region for over 100 years. An authentic Amish house, furnished like the homes in the area, and Amish buggy rides are available to see and ride. On the grounds also is a stone Spanish mission house and many lovely gardens and rock formations, as well as an Amish gift shop.

SPRINGFIELD

First Presbyterian Church

Springfield city has a wealth of memories of Abraham Lincoln, the president who said "that this nation under God shall have a new birth of freedom" upon the occasion of the dedication of the Gettysburg soldiers' cemetery. In First Presbyterian Church at Seventh Street and Capitol Avenue is a draped pew, No. 20. This was the seat occupied by the Lincolns when they attended services in an earlier church building. When the present structure was built in 1868, the old bell and the Lincoln pew were moved to the new sanctuary. The congregation was organized in 1828 and its records have receipts of the bills for the pew rental. These were given to the church by Lincoln's son Robert.

A section of Eighth Street has been made into a Pedestrian Mall, enabling the traveler to walk to several other Lincoln attractions, among them the Abraham Lincoln Museum, the Lincoln and Mary Museum and Lincoln Home, and Lincoln's offices.

(6) NAUVOO

Joseph Smith Historic Center

When Joseph Smith, Jr., and the Latter-Day Saints fled from Missouri in 1839, they relocated on the Mississippi River in Nauvoo (Beautiful Place), once the site of the Indian village of Quashquema. Church and settlement flourished and a magnificent temple was begun in 1841. Friction within the community and from surrounding neighbors resulted in the arrest of Joseph Smith, Jr., and his brother, Hyrum. When the brothers went to Carthage to answer charges, they were arrested and placed in the Carthage jail. A mob stormed the jail and the two men were assassinated.

In the ensuing confusion arising from the loss of leadership, splinter groups arose. Many followed Brigham Young to Utah and some, including Joseph Smith III and his mother, remained in Nauvou. In 1860, he was ordained president of the Reorganized Church of Jesus Christ Latter-Day Saints with headquarters at Independence, Missouri.

At the Joseph Smith Historic Center, which was established in 1918, visitors may see an audiovisual historic presentation and may then tour the grave site, Homestead, and Mansion House.

Nauvoo Restoration, Inc.

French Icarians, a socialistic sect that occupied Nauvoo from 1849 to 1858, built this old house, using stone from the demolished Nauvoo Temple. It was used as a schoolhouse, then adapted by the Church of Jesus Christ Latter-Day Saints as an information center. These represent the followers of Brigham Young, who made the long trek to Salt Lake City, Utah.

Visitors should allow plenty of time to view the Brigham Young House; Times and Seasons Building, which housed the Mormon Church Printing Office and post office; and the Jonathan Browning House and Workshop, to name a few. The traveler can have guide service or use tape cassettes and move at his own pace through the old town, situated in a bend of the river and a little distance from the modern community. Over 38 buildings are either still standing or being rebuilt, which gives an idea of the size of the restoration.

 BISHOP HILL

Bishop Hill Colony

Among the ethnic groups that contributed to the spiritual heritage of Illinois was a colony founded by dissenters from the state church of Sweden in 1846. Pooling their resources, they emigrated to Chicago and walked the 160 miles to this land which they purchased. Inadequate food and shelter caused the deaths of 96 that winter, but more Swedes soon arrived. Bishop Hill was a major center of commerce. The 20 communal buildings (including several apartment residences) housed the people until dissension arose over religious and social doctrine. The colony was dissolved in 1862 and property was divided among the members.

Colony Church was the first permanent building. The basement and first floor housed 20 families who took meals in the communal dining room. The second floor served as the Sanctuary and it reflects their simplicity of worship. White walls contrast with black walnut pews. A center divider separates men's and women's pews. Wrought-iron chandeliers show the Swedish influence. The collection of artifacts includes a few items brought from Sweden and furniture made by the excellent craftsmen at Bishop Hill.

An interesting walking tour takes the travelers to the church, blacksmith shop (now a center for the Bishop Hill Crafts Program), and the steeple building (now a museum and gift shop).

(8) CHICAGO

Basilica of Our Lady of Sorrows

At 3121 West Jackson Boulevard is the Basilica of Our Lady of Sorrows, an Italian Renaissance church which reminds us of the state's Catholic heritage. We know Catholics were here much earlier, however, for Joliet and Marquette came as early as 1673 and the first cabin was built around 1779. Fort Dearborn blockhouse was built in 1804 but abandoned in 1812 and burned in 1816. The town was laid out in 1830, but the disastrous fire of 1871 destroyed most of what was built, except for the unique old water tower on Michigan Avenue.

This beautiful cathedral church was built in 1902. It has many reminders of other Catholic shrines. Balconies are modeled after the one in the Sistine Chapel in Rome. In the lower shrine is a copy of a Michelangelo "Pieta." Many fine altars and wood carvings are in the side chapels. The main sanctuary has a dominating altar as well as decorative pilasters, arches, and an ornamented ceiling.

Rockefeller Memorial Chapel

Protestants followed Catholics to Illinois to add their contribution to its spiritual heritage. Representative of these is Rockefeller Memorial Chapel on the grounds of the University of Chicago, which was founded by John D. Rockefeller in 1890. The campus sprawls both sides of Midway. Older buildings are Gothic, as is this beautiful chapel at Woodlawn Avenue and 59th Street named for Rockefeller. The 72-bell carillon in the 207-foot tower was given to the university by John D. Rockefeller, Jr., in memory of his mother, Laura Spelman Rockefeller. The chapel, designed by Bertram G. Goodhue, was dedicated in 1928 and is built in the form of an irregular cross with vaulted ceilings. A series of life-sized figures, representing the March of Religion from Abraham to the Reformation, extends across the gable of the south front.

Vivekananda Vedanta Society

A large brick building at 5423 South Hyde Park Boulevard is the headquarters of the Chicago Vedanta Society which, though independent and self-supporting, is connected with the Ramakrisha Order of Belue Math, India. When Swami Vivekananda addressed the World Parliament of Religions in 1893 held at the Art Institute in Chicago, he made an instant impression on the nation and soon Vedanta societies were forming in America.

The Chicago Temple was organized in 1930 and members moved into the present quarters in 1966. The complex contains a temple, monastery, and guest house as well as a library, reading room, and bookshop. Sunday services and Sunday school are held regularly and the temple is open daily for meditation. There are 14 such centers in the country. This center also has a monastery and retreat house in Fennville, Michigan.

Vedanta (or Hinduism) is the philosophy which evolved from the teachings of the Vedas, ancient Indian scriptures. It holds that man's real nature is divine, that each person must unfold and manifest the Godhead within, and that truth is universal. Of the many saints and teachers, Ramakrishna, who lived 1836-1886, was among the greatest. After his death his disciples formed a monastic community which grew into the Ramakrishna Order. In the West, the emphasis is on teaching universal principles, but in the East activities include schools, libraries, hospitals, orphanages, social service, and relief work.

(9) EVANSTON

Reba Place Fellowship

Dr. John Miller, a Mennonite minister and New Testament scholar, began Reba Place Fellowship, a Christian community, in 1957. It numbers about 100 people who live in nine community houses. It is a local church fellowship with an ecumenical outlook. Most members work in society but give their earnings to the community, using surplus money for needs outside the community. Reba Place members try to be disciples in the modern world, uniting worship, fellowship, and social action. Members are active in confronting social ills.

(10) WILMETTE

Baha'i House of Worship

One of the country's most beautiful and most photographed structures is located at Sheridan Road and Linden Avenue, Wilmette. The Baha'i House of Worship, a white nine-sided temple, rises from a circular platform into a hemispherical dome. Nine entrance doors each with special spiritual significance open into the auditorium which seats 1,200. Exterior and interior surfaces are a mixture of white cement and ground quartz. Intricate lacy designs both inside and out will intrigue the visitor. The landscape design is similar to the temple and has nine gardens complete with fountains and circular walks.

This house of worship was dedicated May 2, 1953. Meetings are held for worship each Sunday afternoon at 3 P.M. and are open to the public. A discussion on the faith is held afterward in Foundation Hall. The Wilmette temple is designed to illustrate the basic beliefs of the faith and is open to all people of any race or creed.

Baha'i was founded by Bahaullah who was born in Persia in 1817. He announced in 1863 that only in one common faith and order could the world find enduring peace. Worship means more than prayer and meditation for he said any work done in the spirit of service is a form of prayer. Educational, humanitarian, and scientific institutions complete the dedication of the individual to God. The main Temple is in Israel and there are other houses of worship in various countries with spiritual assemblies in over 300 countries.

(11) GLENCOE

North Shore Congregation Israel

At 1185 Sheridan Road, Glencoe, is a white concrete synagogue designed by Minoru Yamasaki. The structure seems like an enormous exotic plant, with vaults unfolding like leaves to enclose the sanctuary. Amber glass skylights and leaded-glass windows soften the light. A raised marble platform holds sacred objects connected with Jewish worship. It is a reminder that many Jewish people came early to this country and contributed to its heritage.

INDIANA

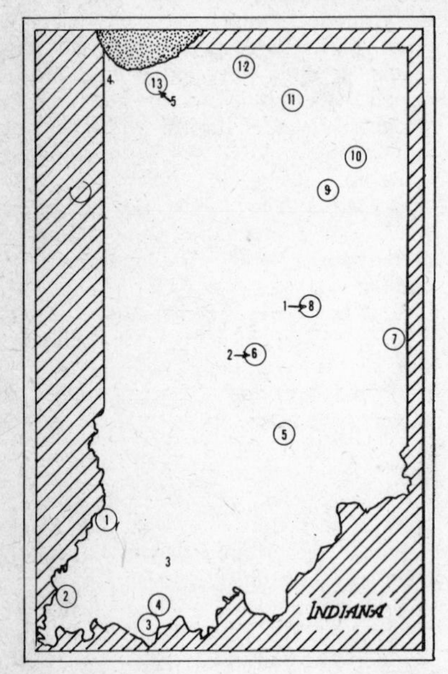

French soldiers of fortune, explorers, and Jesuit missionaries traversed this state beginning about 1679, but they were not the first inhabitants. Mound-building Indians preceded them and their extensive earthworks can be seen especially at Anderson and Evansville. After they declined, the Miami Confederation of Indians roamed the woodlands. These natives were in league with the Algonquins, an alliance opposed to the Iroquois.

The first white settlement was at Vincennes in 1735, beginning with eight French families. Earlier, in 1731, François Margane, Sieur de Vincennes, had put up a military outpost. Another early fort had been established as Fort Miami at the present Fort Wayne.

Part of the Northwest Territory, it was fought over by French, English, Americans, and natives for a century. American settlements began also in the southern section at Clarksville about 1784. The rush of settlers did not come till after the War of 1812. Statehood followed in 1816.

Like its near neighbors, Illinois and Wisconsin, there are reminders of early Catholics, later Protestants, Utopian groups, ethnic pioneers, and the later variety of denominations that have contributed to America's religious heritage. Our tour begins in the south where the early settlers lived, near the Wabash and the Ohio rivers.

Southwest Indiana

VINCENNES

Old Cathedral

The white-spired red-brick basilica of St. Francis Xavier stands at Second and Church streets, where the first log church was built in 1749 by the Jesuit missionaries. The present building was erected in 1826 and has a bell from the original chapel, later recast, hanging in its tower. The church is one of 20 in the country accorded Basilica status.

A remarkable library, begun in 1849 and kept in an adjacent building built in 1968, has a wealth of rare manuscripts, including letters from Sts. Isaac Joques and Vincent de Paul as well as a 1619 letter from Pope John XXII. There is also a 1619 copy of the *Voyages of Champlain*. The 11,000 rare books and manuscripts were part of the collection of Rev. Simon Brute, first bishop of Vincennes, and many pieces came from France.

In the complex are a French and Indian cemetery, the George Rogers Clark Memorial, St. Gabriel's College, St. Rose Chapel, and the Christian Life Center.

(2) NEW HARMONY

New Harmony Historic District

George Rapp founded the Harmonie Society, an offshoot of the German Lutheran Church, in Pennsylvania in 1805. He and the community moved to Indiana in 1814, settling the village of Harmonie. Rapp, a German, along with other German artisans of the sect believed in community ownership of goods, that celibacy was most pleasing to the Almighty, and that the Second Coming would be soon. After 11 years here, they moved back to Pennsylvania.

Robert Owen, a Welsh philanthropist, purchased the site, renaming it New Harmony. He established a colony dedicated to building a perfect society seeing "universal happiness through universal education." For 50 years, the Owenites exerted a scientific and cultural influence on the state, though the colony itself dissolved in 1927. Owen had brought in scholars and artists by keelboat, but they did not meld into a community. By 1830 several Owenite groups had come and gone. Many firsts are credited to them, however, including public school kindergarten, nursery school, trade school, free library, civic drama club, women's club, and first office of the U.S. Geological Survey.

Restorations by the state and other groups began in 1939 and nine buildings are open to the public. No. 2 Dormitory housed single men of the Harmonist Society and a print shop under Owen. The Harmonist House is a typical frame one-family home, now housing a museum. The Old Fauntleroy Home was built by Harmonists in 1815. Owen made it the headquarters of the Minerva Society, first women's club with a formal, written constitution. Fourth Dormitory, erected by Harmonists, became an opera house under the Rappites and now accommodates summer theater.

Roofless Church

This church inspired by the words of George Sand is of special interest. "Only one roof, the sky, was vast enough to embrace all worshiping humanity," said the author. Architect Philip Johnson designed the dome of the 1960 building like an inverted rosebud. It casts the shadow of a full rose. Bronze gate medallions and the statue "Descent of the Holy Spirit" are by Jacques Lipchitz.

Before leaving New Harmony, visit the Labyrinth, a garden maze patterned on the original Harmonist one. It represents various choices in life and the reward to those who choose wisely.

ROCKPORT

Lincoln Pioneer Village

Rockport is Lincoln country—14 of his youthful years were spent here. Replicas of Lincoln Homestead, Old Pigeon Baptist Church, 16 other log structures, and a pioneer museum and a transportation museum give the flavor of the days of Lincoln.

Lincoln was the only member of the family who did not belong to this old church, which is a replica of the original. He did help build it, however. A stairway to the loft gave space for the men to sleep overnight when they came long distances to service. Women and children were accommodated in homes. At nearby Lincoln City is the Lincoln Boyhood National Memorial.

(4) ST. MEINRAD

St. Meinrad Archabbey and Seminary

Over a hundred years ago (1854), the need for German-speaking priests in Indiana caused the abbot of a Benedictine community in Switzerland to send monks to establish this community on 2,400 acres in the wilderness. The principal work of the 180 monks still continues to be the operation of a seminary to educate young men for Roman Catholic priesthood. Today it is the largest such in the country, with 230 collegians and 170 theologians. They represent 58 dioceses and archdioceses and 16 religious communities. Mass has been said daily since the monks' arrival, even on the day of a disastrous fire in 1887.

The beautiful complex of buildings is made from native limestone and includes the monastery, the abbey church which is a center for Gregorian chant; the guest house for retreats; Abbey Press, gift shop, as well as offices; an arts and crafts center; Scholar Shop; and a meat-packing plant. There is also a large mail-order and printing house. Tours are scheduled by appointment.

Central Indiana

(5) COLUMBUS

North Christian Church

We begin our central Indiana tour in a city noted for imaginative, modern architecture. The Cummins Engine Foundation pays design fees for public buildings done by firms selected by two disinterested and distinguished architects. The result is a collection of outstanding buildings by such noted men as I. M. Pel, Eero Saarinen, John Carl Warnecke, etc.

Since church architecture is one of our spiritual heritages, it is well to pause here and see, along with the unusual schools, library, etc., three churches.

The hexagonal-shaped church on Tipton Lane reminds us that Christianity came from Judaism, for it is built in the form of the star of David. Eero Saarinen was designer and he created the sanctuary in the shape of a bowl, symbolizing the congregation in the hand of God. The upsweeping effect of the roof leads the eyes to a 192-foot spire, topped with a gold cross. In the chapel is a unique baptismal ledge.

The congregation of this church was organized in 1955 but the church was not erected until 1964. Membership is with the Christian Churches of Indiana (Disciples of Christ), but the congregation is ecumenical in outlook and belongs to the National and World councils of churches.

First Baptist Church

At Fairlawn Drive is a brick church built in 1969, designed by Harry Weese. The steeply-pitched roof reminds one of Gothic lines. A low section connects the two tall end units. Interior finish is of natural wood.

First Christian Church

Eliel Saarinen, father of Eero, designed First Christian Church at Fifth Street and Lafayette Avenue. It is a simple rectangle with adjacent high bell tower extending upwards 166 feet. Designed "as simple and fundamental architecturally as the gospel it proclaims," it was built in 1942, the first of the modern buildings.

(6) INDIANAPOLIS

Scottish Rite Cathedral

The traveler now is in about the exact center of the state and in its capital. The imposing Scottish Rite Cathedral at 650 North Meridan Street is a reminder of the many religiously oriented fraternal organizations in American society. It is one of the largest and most elaborate. The 212-foot-high Gothic carillon tower has a set of bells weighing from 19 to 11,000 pounds. Travertine marble decorates the interior, which is adorned with Masonic symbols. The oak-paneled auditorium seats 1,100.

(7) RICHMOND

Wayne County Historical Museum

Quakers founded this town, which is due east from Indianapolis almost to the state's border, in 1806. The museum at 1150 North A Street was originally the meeting house of the Whitewater Society of Friends. It was built in 1865 and now contains historical material, including a pioneer kitchen, farm equipment, and Indian artifacts. The lower floor is arranged like an early village street with cobbler, print, and apothecary shops and a general store. Auxiliary buildings include a two-story pioneer cabin and an early log schoolhouse.

The Historical Society came into being in 1929 when Julia Meek Gaar gave her extensive personal collection and the Meeting of Friends, known as Hicksites, contributed their meeting house. This outstanding record of the past is particularly appropriate here, since Richmond was the gateway to the west.

Yokefellow International

Other Quaker institutions in Richmond include Earlham College and Earlham School of Religion, whose buildings surround a central green. Here Yokefellow International, a small prayer-study group movement introduced by Dr. D. Elton Trueblood, had its beginnings. The book distribution center and general offices are on Earlham Drive. Yokefellow Institute, a nondenominational center for the renewal of church and society, is adjacent to the campus. Founded in 1957, its modern, spacious facility was constructed in 1964. Library, book store, and meeting rooms are open to the public. Especially noteworthy is the circular Yoke Room with its high vertical lines. Yokefellows now have prayer-study fellowships around the world.

Northern Indiana

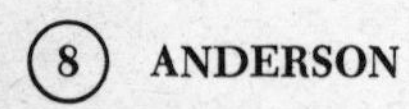

8 ANDERSON

Warner Auditorium

The past and present merge here, for Anderson is not only an Indian area but also world headquarters for the Church of God. This fellowship, born in the 1880s, now has over 2,300 autonomous congregations in 49 states and 40 other countries. The movement disregards barriers of creedal statements and church membership rolls.

One of its four educational institutions is Anderson College. On the campus is the ultra-modern Warner Auditorium, scene of the annual International Convention of the Church of God. A milestone in architecture and engineering occurred in 1961 with the lifting of its mammoth dome. According to technical journals, it is the largest thin-shelled concrete dome in the world, exceeding even St. Peter's in Rome. The dome was molded on the grounds and a "lift slab" took five days to hoist it in place.

9 HUNTINGTON

Sunday Visitor Publishing House

This town, too, has a mixture of old and new, for along with its Indian heritage is the Catholic influence. The publishing house which produces the most Catholic publications in the United States is here.

In May 1912, Father John Noll saw the need of a low-priced weekly newspaper to combat anti-Catholic sentiment in the nation. Purchasing a well-equipped print shop, he embarked on a venture that today employs over 350 people and publishes eight magazines as well as a quantity of general books and textbooks. It also includes a collection-envelope division.

10 FORT WAYNE

Concordia Senior College

Here where Miami Indians gathered and French and English trading posts were established stands the community named for Gen. "Mad Anthony" Wayne.

The beautiful campus of this pre-theological college for Lutheran ministers lies along Clinton Avenue and the 31 buildings designed by Eero Saarinen create a northern European-type village. International recognition has been given to the plan which even includes a man-made lake.

The chapel and its free-standing tapered tower is in the center of the campus. The main altar is a 6-ton slab of Vermont granite. A unifying theme of thanksgiving to God is seen in the decorative motifs, bas reliefs, linen tapestries, and bronze shields.

Cathedral of the Immaculate Conception

The Miami Indians were buried long ago where now the twin towers of this masterpiece of Gothic architecture pierce the skies. The Cathedral of the Immaculate Conception (Roman Catholic) was built in 1859-1860 for a congregation dating prior to 1830.

The magnificent, intricate carvings in the sanctuary depict the redemption of mankind and stations of the cross. They are among the finest wood carvings in the country. Bavarian stained-glass windows superbly portray scenes in the life of Christ.

NAPANEE

Amish Acres

In north-central Indiana the traveler can visit an 80-acre farm and forest which faithfully recreate the Amish way of life. The farm is operated as it was in the 19th century, thus is an important part of Indiana's historic cultural and religious heritage. In the surrounding countryside, Amish folk hold to the religious beliefs, dress, and language of their forefathers.

Church of the Brethren Center

Here at 201 South Main Street, is another international gift shop and clothing collection center. Stop here for around-the-world articles, and know that the money goes directly back to the artisans via church workers. Clothing collected here for Church World Service and Lutheran World Relief goes to the New Windsor, Maryland, Church of the Brethren center for processing.

SOUTH BEND

Sacred Heart Church

On the 1,250-acre campus of Notre Dame University, just north of South Bend, is Sacred Heart Church. Its congregation began in 1842, when a young priest of the French missionary order Congregation of the Holy Cross started his school in the wilderness with $300 and three dilapidated log buildings. A replica of the first log chapel stands on the campus. It was used by Father Stephen Badin, first Catholic priest ordained in this country, who is buried here. Masses are still said in the rustic building.

The magnificent Gothic building now serving as the university church is on the central green. The intricate tower, whose lower and higher points are topped with crosses, has smaller side towers. The interior is richly adorned with art work including the Mestrovic sculpture the "Pieta."

Also on the campus and part of a self-guiding tour, are Abbey Press, Grotto of Our Lady of Lourdes, Fatima Retreat House, Moreau Seminary, and Fatima Shrine.

(13) VALPARAISO

Chapel of the Resurrection

On the Valparaiso University campus stands the striking, contemporary Chapel of the Resurrection. With a seating capacity of 3,000, it is said to be the largest house of worship on any educational campus. This largest Lutheran university in the nation was founded in 1895, but the chapel was not dedicated until 1959. Towering over the campus, the Brandt Campanile rises 140 feet and plays morning and evening hymns, as well as the change in classes. The chapel itself resembles the Church of the Nativity in Bethlehem. Immense Munderloh stained-glass windows behind the altar culminate in a roof shaped like a nine-pointed star. A baptistry, designed as a series of concentric circles, has a Rockville granite font in the center. The Gloria Christi Chapel below the chancel is available for smaller worship services, weddings, etc. Evening prayers are conducted here daily.

IOWA

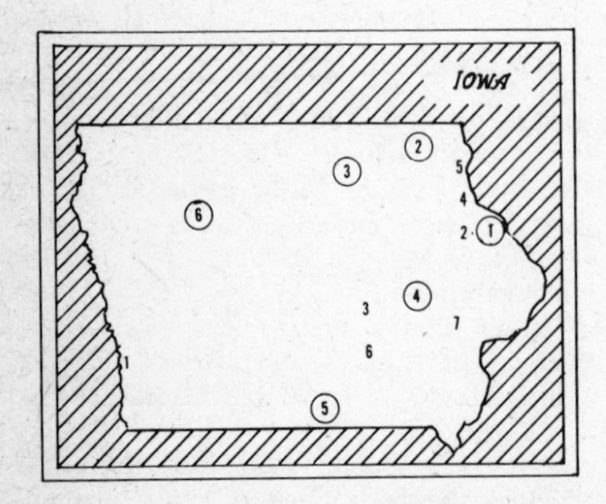

A tribe of Sioux Indians named Iowa (Sleepy Ones) gave this state its name. The natives occupied the area when Marquette and Joliet in 1673, and Hennepin in 1680, explored the lands along the Mississippi. French Canadian Julien Dubuque made the first settlement at the site of the city that bears his name in the year 1788. He came to trade with the Indians, who had been augmented by more tribes moving west after their defeat in Michigan. Soon Dubuque discovered lead deposits and added mining to his fur trade.

Further white settlement was slow because the territory was being passed around from country to country and state to state as treaties were made and renegotiated. Also, when Dubuque died in 1810, the Indians protested further development of their lead and zinc mines. They were supported and protected against white encroachment by government troops.

Black Hawk War, which ended disastrously for the Indians in 1832, opened the door to the whites, however, and settlers arrived in droves to mine and farm. Statehood came in 1846.

Catholics came early. Protestant pioneers were later arrivals, and included Mormons and Quakers. Ethnic colonies like the Amana communities and more recent shrines have created a diverse religious heritage across the broad tableland.

Our pilgrimage begins on Iowa's eastern Mississippi shores where the first white settlements were planted.

Eastern Iowa

(1) DUBUQUE

Church of the Nativity

Catholics arrived here in 1788, when French Canadian Julien Dubuque founded his fur-trading post, then added mining operations. Spiritual descendants worship in this contemporary church at 1225 Alta Vista St. The 42 stained-glass windows were created in Chartres, cathedral city of France, by the artist Gabriel Loire. The sanctuary has a polished limestone floor and a brick wall picturing nine angels.

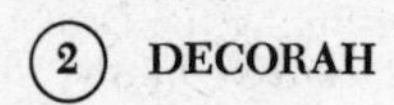

(2) DECORAH

Vesterheim Center

West on Route 52 is Decorah, a Norwegian Lutheran community that is the home of Luther College. In three buildings are housed a comprehensive collection from early pioneer days with particular emphasis on the Norwegian influence in the midwest. In addition, there are displays of the arts, culture, and crafts of the mother country.

Vesterheim, which means "western home," is a complex of historic buildings relating to Norwegian Americans. It includes a large hotel, three-story stone mill, four log cabins, a log school, and an early immigrant stone church. All buildings are authentic originals or restored structures.

The old Washington Prairie Methodist Church was the early home of the congregation. The minister returned to Norway in 1853 to found the first Methodist church in that country. In the old hotel, which serves as the main museum building, is a Church Gallery,

devoted to spiritual life of the immigrants and its reflection in art and architecture.

The best time to visit is the last weekend in July during the Nordic festival. The center of the complex is in downtown Decorah, not on the campus. The pioneer church is located 9 miles outside town.

(3) NASHUA

Little Brown Church in the Vale

A short way south and west is the inspiration for the hymn "The Church in the Wildwood." Just northwest of the town on Route 346 is the rustic brown church, built in 1860-1864 for a congregation formed in 1855 as the First Congregational Church. Members contributed land, labor, and lumber. The bell, first in Chickasaw County, was cast in Troy, New York, and given by Thomas and Catherine Cole. Its arrival was so wondrous that the bell was rung continuously as it was transported from Dubuque.

The story of the hymn is even more unusual. In 1857, Rev. William S. Pitts

got out of the stagecoach at a noon stopover in Dubuque and walked up Cedar Street. He was inspired by the wooded glen, where no church stood, to write the hymn. Imagine his surprise when he came this way again in 1863 and found a church on the spot. He first sang the hymn in 1864, and it was later published. The Weatherwax Brothers, America's popular male quartette in 1910-1920, made this their theme, since this was near their boyhood home. Darlings of the Lyceum and Chautauqua circuit, they made the hymn a household refrain in America and overseas. Now hundreds of couples come each year to be married in the church, and visitors stop at all seasons to see the "church in the vale."

4 AMANA

Amana Colonies

Conveniently located in east-central Iowa just north of Route 80 are seven villages which comprise one of the largest national historic landmarks. In 1854, God-fearing people of West German, Swiss, and Alsatian ancestry left New York state (where they first settled in America) and founded villages on these fertile fields. Families acquired homestead lands, but deeded them to the Society of the True Inspirationalists, in keeping with their communal way of life. They established woolen mills, a furniture factory, meat-smoking plants, and other industries which provided the necessities. Amana was the first planned village, followed by East, Middle, High, West, and South Amana, as well as Homestead. In 1932, by vote of the people, the Amanas dropped the communal way for free enterprise and the elders of the church no longer direct all the affairs of the people. The century-old flavor of the villages continues, as well as their many enterprises. The best time to visit is during the summer when the lotus lily is in bloom in Amana Lily Lake or during the October festivities at *Oktoberfest*. In the village of Homestead, a century-old Amana house, Amana Heim Museum, re-creates the past.

Museum of Amana History

The Amana Heritage Society operates this museum next to the pharmacy in Amana. It pictures the history of the colonies from the 1700s to the present and includes Old Country beginnings. The Church Exhibit Room tells of Amana's basis, the church. Here is a *saal bank* (church bench), books and items pertaining to the *Liebesmaal* (communion service), as well as the foot-washing tub and the apron used in the foot-washing service. A Germany and Ebenezer Room tells of the Germany and Ebenezer, New York, days and the Movement to Amana Room recalls the ten-year migration to Iowa. Bygone industries like basket-making, pottery, broom-making, and calico manufacture are included.

Western Iowa

(5) CORYDON

Wayne County Historical Museum

Over 20,000 artifacts of early Iowa are gathered in Wayne County Historical Museum east of the town. Small stores, a shop, and household rooms can be seen. The Mormons are immortalized in the exhibit entitled "The Hymn That Went around the World," based on the famous Mormon hymn, "Come, Come Ye Saints."

A historic marker at nearby Garden Grove indicates the place where many Mormon pioneers are buried. Thousands made the trek across these lands to Utah. Many settled temporarily at Council Bluffs, starting that community on the Missouri River. Final enrollment of the Mormon Battalion took place there in 1846. The Mormon Pioneer Memorial Bridge across the Missouri at Council Bluffs is a reminder of that difficult trek.

(6) WEST BEND

Grotto of the Redemption

West Bend has the largest grotto in the world. It covers a city block and represents an immense collection of minerals, fossils, shells, and gems set into concrete. Begun in 1912, it contains nine grottos and 14 stations of the cross. St. Peter and Paul's Church is adjacent, with its Christmas Chapel created by Father Paul Dobbersteirn, the grotto's late builder. The historical altar in the sanctuary won first place at the Chicago World's Fair in 1893, and is handcarved from bird's-eye maple. Geological value of the grotto is estimated at over $2 million.

OHIO

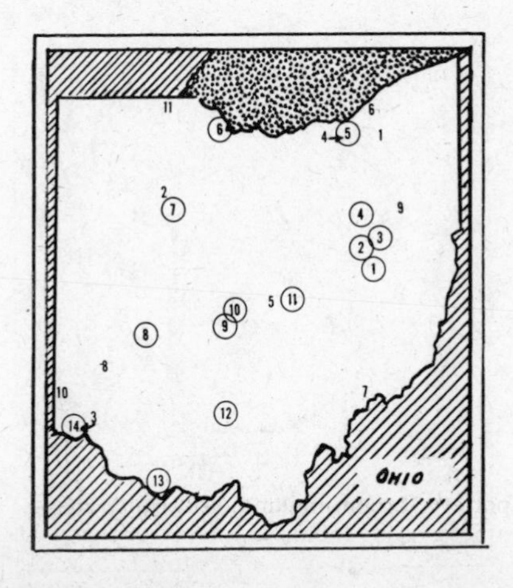

A flourishing civilization covered Ohio from 800 B.C. to A.D. 1500, long before the white influx. Mound Builders, whose earthworks are still scattered across the state, preceded the Shawnees, Miamis, Wyandots, and Delawares who were pushed in from the eastern shores as white settlers arrived.

French explorers and trappers traversed the rivers and Jesuit priests attempted work with the natives, a fact recalled by the marked site of a 1650 French Mission in Kingsbury Park at Defiance. The struggle of nations and races for the land, however, made permanent settlement impossible.

It was the Americans who finally planted Ohio towns. In 1788, the Ohio

Company of Associates, mostly New Englanders, bought a tract along the Ohio River and established Marietta. About the same time, many Virginians migrated into the southern section, though the grant to the Ohio Company of Virginia was received earlier in 1749. Since the Ohio territory was just beyond the Alleghenies, it received the first wave of settlers. Statehood came in 1803.

A variety of churches came with the new Ohioans. Ethnic religious pilgrims like the Germans who settled Zoar and American religious communities like Mormons and Shakers arrived. Moravians were among the first as they ministered to the natives, even helping them form Christian Indian towns. Catholic shrines, Jewish synagogues, conference centers, and even a replica of a Japanese Shinto shrine added many facets to the religious heritage.

We will begin our tour in the east where the first white people settled, noting however the many places where Indian religious ceremonials took place at a much earlier date.

Eastern Ohio

(1) GNADENHUTTEN

Gnadenhutten Historical Society

Northwest, off Route 77, is a 9-acre memorial which is the site of the blackest page in the history of the Northwest Territory. That energetic and committed Moravian missionary, David Zeisberger, who worked with the Indians for 60 years, assisted Joshua, a Mohican, in establishing here a Christian Indian town in 1772. This followed the similar Moravian settlement at Schoenbrunn by five months. Soon there were over 50 cabins, and the standard of living was high. Glass windows, pewter utensils, crafts, and music were part of Indian life. One member played a spinet piano and another led singing. Gardens were fenced, and natives had droves of cattle, hogs, and horses.

Ohio's first white child was born here to resident missionaries John Roth and his wife. Joshua's burial place (1775) is the oldest marked grave in the state.

The Revolutionary War brought trouble, when the Indians refused to fight. The English forcibly moved the community to Lichteneau and later Captives Town, near Upper Sandusky. Moravian missionaries were arrested by the British. Since supplies were meager, 90 men, women, and children went back to Gnadenhutten to get food.

While there, renegade militiamen accused them of raiding Americans and

herded them into two cabins. After a night of prayer and hymn singing, 88 were massacred on March 8, 1782. Only two boys escaped to tell the infamous news.

Years later, missionary John Heckewelder returned, buried the bones of the martyred Indians, and set about rebuilding the town. The Moravian church organization here dates from 1799.

Visitors can browse in a museum, see the Indian cemetery, stand in tribute before a slender monument memorializing the massacre, and see the excavations of cabins in that Christian Indian town.

NEW PHILADELPHIA

Schoenbrunn Village State Memorial

A few miles north of Gnadenhutten is the Christian Indian town founded by Moravian missionary David Zeisberger in 1772, at the invitation of the Delaware chief White Eyes. Here stood Ohio's first church and school, along with over 60 cabins, teepees, and sheds. When the town was abandoned in 1777 because of British and Indian hostility, Zeisberger and his converts razed the church to prevent desecration. Later the entire village was destroyed.

The schoolhouse, church, and cabins have been rebuilt. A museum depicts the life of the Indian residents and original textbooks used by the missionaries. Costumed attendants demonstrate crafts.

Ohio's Bicentennial contribution is the historical *Trumpet in the Land* by Paul Green, which tells the true story of Ohio's first settlement. The best time to visit is during the summer when the travelers can see this moving, beautifully performed play.

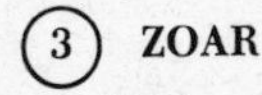

ZOAR

Zoar Village State Memorial

Over 300 Separatists from Württemberg, Germany, fled from persecution to this 5,500-acre tract just north of New Philadelphia. They upheld mystical beliefs when rationalism arose in the Lutheran Church. Joseph Baumeler led a few members here that fall to erect the first homes. All property and wealth were pooled and held by the Society of Separatists of Zoar. An economically sound, happy, religion-centered community resulted, which continued to 1898 when property and cash were divided among permanent members. Their decline was attributed to lack of strong leadership after Baumeler's death and failure to keep pace with changes in agriculture and industry.

The Ohio Historical Society has acquired and restored several buildings. No. 1 house, the handsome, two-story brick home of Baumeler, is maintained as a museum, portraying the manner in which Zoarites lived and worked. The garden house, bakery, and the blacksmith, tinsmith, sewing, and wagon shops can be seen, as well as the cow barn and store. The meeting house, built in 1853, is of brick and stands at the north edge of town. It was divided down the middle for separate seating of men and women.

(4) MASSILLON

National Shrine of St. Dymphna

Returning to the present era, we continue north to the grounds of Massillon State Hospital and this shrine to St. Dymphna, patroness of those afflicted with mental and nervous disorders. This Irish saint was born in the 7th century and fled to Gheel, Belgium, where she was martyred at age 15. Healing miracles were attributed to her. The first American shrine was dedicated in May 1939, and masses and novenas are held here continuously. League members are from all parts of the country. The Out-Door Votive Shrine is a dramatic glass structure which arches over a statue of St. Dymphna, with a brick chapel nearby in the parklike setting.

(5) CLEVELAND

Shaker Historical Society Museum

At 16740 South Park Boulevard, Cleveland, the Shaker museum commemorates the North Union community of Shakers who occupied most of what is now Shaker Heights. From 1821 to 1889, the community prospered and its relics and historical materials are preserved in this Tudor building. Furniture, tools, inventions, and clothing portray the life of this communal sect.

Park Synagogue

Probably the world's largest Conservative Jewish congregation is served by this complex of interconnected brick buildings designed by Eric Mendelsohn and completed in 1950. An immense copper-covered dome rests on a band of clear windows and rises 65 feet. The unusual structure is set on 33 wooded acres and has a unique Gallery of Contemporary Art.

Temple Museum

Also highlighting the Jewish heritage is this Byzantine temple at University Circle. The limestone edifice has tiled domes and graceful arches. Inside is a museum of religious and ceremonial art and music. Exhibits feature biblical antiquities, tapestries, and silver. There are more than 500 items that concern Jewish religious ceremonies.

St. Michael the Archangel Church

At 3114 Scranton Road is a church recalling the Roman Catholic heritage. The stone Gothic Revival building was dedicated in 1892. It has been cited for outstanding beauty in architecture. The interior has vaulted arches and hand-carved statues and other decorations from Germany.

Central Ohio

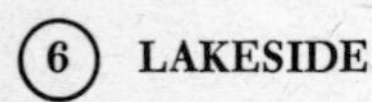

(6) LAKESIDE

Lakeside Association

On the shores of Lake Erie is a United Methodist conference center established in 1873. Called Ohio's Chautauqua of the Great Lakes, its beginnings were an old-time camp meeting. Sunday school encampments and normal institutes were held here; Chautauqua lecturers and performers, as well as the great preachers of all denominations, held forth. Wesley Lodge, the auditorium, Fountain Inn, and other accommodations are available year round for religious meetings and vacations-with-a-purpose. This "place like the whole world ought to be" is perhaps the largest of such facilities in America. Century-old camp-meeting architecture brings the past to mind.

(7) UPPER SANDUSKY

Wyandott Indian Mission Church

South of Carey, and not to be confused with Sandusky, is a United Methodist Shrine. Set in an old Indian cemetery, it is the first Methodist mission in the country. John Stewart, a mulatto, was converted to Christianity in 1816, and responded to a call to preach to the

Wyandott (native spelling) Indians. He was licensed in 1819 and built this mission church in 1824 with government funds. The Indians worshiped here until they were removed to Kansas in 1843. An earlier mission building became the first Manual Training Institute in 1922. Stewart and the chiefs are buried in the cemetery. The mission, neglected after 1843, was restored in 1889. A paperback book, *Moccasin Trails to the Cross,* by Thelma Marsh, archivist of the mission, tells the dramatic story of how black, white, and red men worshiped in the old mission.

(8) SPRINGFIELD

Weaver Chapel

On the grounds of the Wittenberg University, founded by Lutherans in 1845, is Weaver Chapel. The brick-and-stone structure has a free standing, 212-foot tower with huge limestone statues of Protestant personages. Narrow stained-glass windows are heavy with lead and light with glass, almost stencil fashion. The three-story library has a fine collection of materials on Martin Luther, which includes some letters and manuscripts in his handwriting. Cranach etchings and original editions of Lutheran tracts make the collection unique.

(9) COLUMBUS

German Village

Continuing south to the center of Ohio, the traveler comes to a section of Columbus settled by Germans. About 450 of the 19th-century buildings with their thick walls and lintels are found a mile south of the city center. Brick sidewalks and cobblestone streets framed with wrought-iron fences, together the restored buildings, create a century-old aura. St. Mary Church, built in 1866, stands on Third Street. Most of the homes were built earlier, between 1840 and 1860. Sausage houses, bazaars, and handcraft shops are interesting places to browse. A good time to visit is during Oktoberfest, at Christmas, or during the annual Haus and Garten Tours the last Sunday in June.

(10) WESTERVILLE

Usa Janja-Kyoto Tea House

Though this community northeast of Columbus was settled by Virginia pioneers and Pennsylvania Quakers, it is also noted as the location of an authentic Shinto shrine. Originally built in Okinawa, it was erected here and is open by appointment. It is a reminder of pioneers from the East who came to our country over western paths through California.

(11) NEWARK

Mound Builders Earthworks and Octagon House

East of Columbus are several of the most elaborate Indian mounds in the midwest. Mound Builders Earthworks on Route 79 is the site of a giant circular earthen wall, 1,200 feet in diameter. Prehistoric Hopewell Indians held elaborate ceremonies within the 18-foot-high walls as part of their "cult of the dead." The first center in America for prehistoric Indian art work may be seen at the opening in Great Circle Mound.

Octagon Mound, on North 33rd Street, once joined Great Circle Mound with a set of parallel connecting walls. A 1,900-year-old circle of earth remains. Though it is now part of a country club, visitors are welcome to see the earthworks.

(12) CHILLICOTHE

Mound City Group National Monument

On a 67-acre tract south of Columbus is a restoration of one of the finest examples of Hopewell Indian culture. The Visitors' Center contains exhibits of ornaments by prehistoric artisans. An observation deck gives an outstanding view of the score or more of burial mounds. Marked trails and trail-side exhibits assist the traveler in understanding Mound City.

Western Ohio

RIPLEY

Rankin House State Memorial

Our way continues southwest to the Ohio River and the home once owned by Rev. John Rankin, one of the first and most active of the conductors of the Underground Railway. From 1825 to 1865 more than 2,000 slaves were sheltered here and guided north to freedom by the Presbyterian clergyman and other residents. Rankin had preached against slavery since 1815 and his *Letters on American Slavery,* published in 1826, helped spread antislavery sentiment. Among Rankin's many friends was Harriet Beecher Stowe, who heard here the incident of Eliza's escape over the Ohio River, which she incorporated into *Uncle Tom's Cabin.* The modest brick home was restored and dedicated as a state memorial in 1948. It contains original woodwork and many Rankin items, including the family Bible. Visitors can follow the route of escaping slaves by climbing the newly rebuilt "stairway to liberty."

CINCINNATI

St. Peter in Chains

In downtown Cincinnati at Plum and Eighth streets is a gleaming white Grecian-style cathedral often referred to as the "white angel." It was built in 1845 as the headquarters of the vast diocese of Ohio. Catholic roots go farther back, however, to a few resident families in 1790 when the city received its name. Several buildings preceded the present one, including an earlier brick Gothic cathedral. The new cathedral had a great square tower and was surrounded with a Corinthian colonnade similar to the Tower of the Winds in Athens, Greece. Interior support is also given by massive Greek columns. The building was remodeled

and expanded, beginning in 1952, with rededication in November 1957. The interior is richly decorated with symbols of Christianity in murals, windows, and paintings. A few of the treasures are an ancient Spanish missal stand, a crucifix by Benvenuto Cellini, replicas of the Rheims chalice, and embroidered chasubles made in Belgium.

MINNESOTA

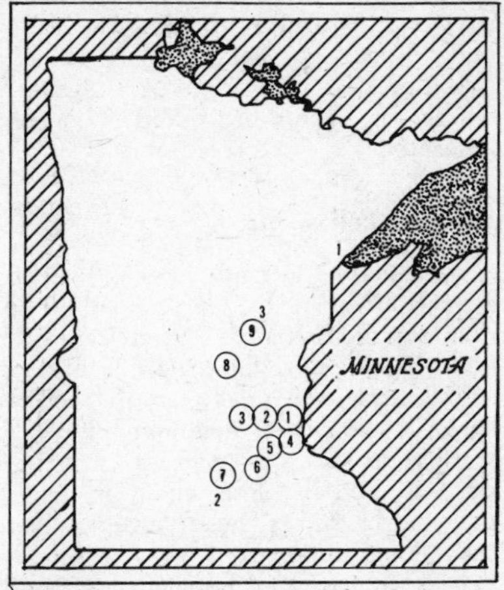

Chippewas in the north and Sioux in the south populated this area in the 17th and early 18th centuries. The first whites to visit were Frenchmen, who came by way of the Greak Lakes in 1659-1660. They were forerunners of other explorers, trappers, and missionary priests. One of the latter was Father Louis Hennepin, energetic Belgian diarist, who ascended the Mississippi to St. Anthony Falls, future site of Minneapolis.

An American, Lt. Zebulon Pike, prepared the way for a settlement when in 1805 he bought land at the junction of the Mississippi and Minnesota rivers for a government outpost. Fort St. Anthony, later renamed Snelling, was built in 1819. Father Galtier built a missionary chapel below the fort in 1841 and the state's oldest continuous settlement of St. Paul was begun. Stillwater was founded in 1843 and Minneapolis in 1847.

Between 1838 and 1855, both Chippewas and Sioux were forced to release most of their territory as white settlers arrived. The stream of settlers gradually increased and statehood came in 1858.

Resentful Sioux warriors angrily attacked residents in Minnesota Valley in 1864. After their defeat at Wood Lake, the Indians fled to the Dakotas. Now the floodgates were open and there was room for Europe's immigrants as well as for American pioneers. Swedes, Germans, and Norwegians flowed in to farm.

Thus the religious heritage swings from Indian ceremonials and Catholic missions to Protestants and latter-day movements like the Bethany Fellowship with its emphasis on missions. Lutheranism, brought early by European immigrants, seems to predominate.

Our tour begins in the south at the confluence of the Minnesota and Mississippi rivers, where the settlers of old first came.

Southern Minnesota

ST. PAUL

Fort Snelling

The first permanent outpost of whites was at Fort Snelling in 1819-1820. A 1,500-foot stone enclosure was constructed around 13 stone buildings. A memorial chapel, towers, guardhouse, magazine, shops, and barracks are being reconstructed to show how it looked when several hundred soldiers and their dependents lived here. There are military drills as well as crafts of the frontier for the visitor to watch. Round Tower, built in 1820, may be the state's oldest structure.

Cathedral of St. Paul

At 225 Summit Avenue in the city's heart is a tremendous church adapted from St. Peter's Basilica in Rome, Italy. Custodian of the early Catholic heritage, the church is the seat of the archdiocese of St. Paul and Minneapolis. First services were held here in 1915.

A green dome 306 feet high and 96 feet across rises over this Classical Renaissance building. The interior of the ornate sanctuary is Neo-Baroque, decorated with bronze, marble carvings, stained-glass, and paintings. The Shrine of Nations surrounding the sanctuary depicts national patron saints of people who colonized the state. A library and historical museum are interesting features.

Log Cabin Church

On the grounds of Luther Theological Seminary at 2375 Como Avenue is a log cabin church originally built at Muskego, Wisconsin, in 1844 and moved to St. Paul in 1924. A shrine of Norwegian Lutheranism, it has an interesting exhibit of hymnals, Bibles, communion plate, and paintings. The pulpit is placed above the altar, and the chancel has tiny boxlike pews.

Several other Lutheran educational institutions, coming from the various ethnic groups, are also here, including Concordia College.

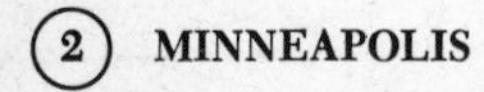

(2) MINNEAPOLIS

Augsburg College

Minneapolis, twin city of St. Paul, also abounds with Lutherans. Augsburg College, founded originally in Marshall, Wisconsin, in 1869, moved to 731 21st Avenue South, Minneapolis, in 1872. A Norwegian Lutheran institution, it served the Free Lutheran Church and now is American Lutheran. The Augsburg Room on campus has exhibits from the German city of Augsburg, where the Augsburg Confession was presented.

Bethany Fellowship

A missionary training center is featured at the 6820 Auto Club Road headquarters of Bethany Church and Fellowship. Organized in 1943 as a result of home prayer meetings, the fellowship developed a common vision of worldwide missions. Selling their possessions and pooling their resources, they purchased a headquarters where they could unite in work and service. Others joined and now in a campus setting there is, in addition to the training school, a publishing house, industrial plant, and missionary society. Evangelical and interdenominational, it now has more than 100 missionaries in 27 countries. Visitors are welcome to the 60-acre complex southwest of the city limits.

(3) HOPKINS

Church of St. John the Evangelist

Directly west of Minneapolis is the Church of St. John the Evangelist, whose contemporary architecture has won many awards. A wonderful blending of natural materials, space, and light give a powerful worship feeling. A Roman Catholic church, it was completed in 1969 and has high-paneled ceilings, curving brick walls, and oak furnishings.

(4) HASTINGS

Guardian Angels Church

Architecture in this 1850 community to the southeast of Minneapolis reflects the countries from which its settlers came. Guardian Angels Church, dedicated in 1869, resembles a small French church. The first pastor came from Alsace-Lorraine. The brick courthouse has German touches with its square shape and corner towers. It is pleasant to walk down the central streets. Visitors will be amazed by the fabric shop which has no walls, but hangs between two buildings.

5 NORTHFIELD

St. Olaf College

Norwegian Lutheran immigrants founded St. Olaf in 1874 to provide higher education and preserve the best in the Norwegian heritage. In 1899, it associated with the American Lutheran Church. The famous St. Olaf Choir, begun here in 1912, still continues along with global seminars and a Paracollege wherein students design their own majors.

Rolvaag Memorial Library, named for St. Olaf's best-known man of letters (*Giants in the Earth,* etc.) is home of the Norwegian-American Historical Association, an independent organization which preserves manuscripts, photographs, and other historical data of Norwegian immigrants.

6 FARIBAULT

Episcopal Cathedral of Our Merciful Saviour

The first Episcopal church built in the country to serve as a cathedral was completed in 1869, though the parish began much earlier. One of the first Episcopal clergyman arrived as chaplain to the troops at Fort Snelling. A thriving parish developed as settlers arrived.

The stately Gothic building is noted for its stained-glass windows and bishop's throne. Anton Lang of Oberammergau did some of the carving on the throne. Christian Indians gave the Agnus Dei and pipe-of-peace windows in appreciation for the help of the first bishop, Right Rev. Henry Whipple. His trip to see President Lincoln after the Sioux massacre at New Ulm reprieved many innocent braves under sentence of execution. Indians called him "straight tongue." When the bishop died in 1901, Sioux and Chippewa choirs sang requiem hymns in their native tongues.

The memorial tower was dedicated in 1902 in his memory.

7 ST. PETER

Christ Chapel

The central building and focal point on the campus of Gustavus Adolphus College is Christ Chapel, a glorious structure which suggests the ancient symbol of cross and crown. The college, privately founded in 1862, is affiliated with the Lutheran Church in America.

The chapel was begun in 1959 and dedicated in 1962, with Clement Attlee, England's former prime minister, in attendance. Walls are of precast concrete panels, and lower stained-glass sections contain contemporary forms of historic symbols: fish, anchor, flame, star, dove, uniting chain, ship, sacramental cup and wafer, serpent, and cup of incense. In the 1,500-seat chapel the central altar is the base of the spire and light floods in over the large black cross. The four-manual, 58-rank organ has 3,811 pipes.

Northern Minnesota

8 COLLEGEVILLE

St. John's Abbey and University

On Route 32, east of St. Cloud, is the world's largest Benedictine monastery, which was founded in 1856. On the 2,400-acre campus are a university, seminary, and college preparatory school conducted by the monks.

At the center of the campus is the famed abbey church designed by renowned architect Marcel Breuer, who did several other of the dramatic buildings also. The outstanding, contemporary chapel is made of reinforced concrete and honeycomb glass. A 112-foot bell banner in front of the church can be seen from great distances. The purpose is threefold: to give a dramatic entry, to hold cross and bells, and to reflect sunlight into the church. Visitors are always welcome and will find much to see, including the Alcuin Library which has huge concrete "trees" supporting the interior ceiling.

9 ONAMIA

Mille Lacs Indian Museum

About 10 miles north of Collegeville on Route 169, the traveler can immerse himself in local Indian history. From prehistoric times until the white man came, Chippewa and Sioux lived peacefully. When land became scarce and guns became available, the two tribes fought, with the Chippewas defeating the Sioux in 1745. Thus the Sioux were cast out of their great village here, which was visited by Sieur de Luht in 1673.

This history, plus the culture and crafts of the Chippewas, is presented in exhibits and dioramas. Canoe-building, weaving, hide preparation, and toy-making are explained. At nearby Mille Lacs Kathio State Park is the centuries-old site of Sioux encampments called *kathio*.

VI.

FRONTIER WEST

NEW MEXICO

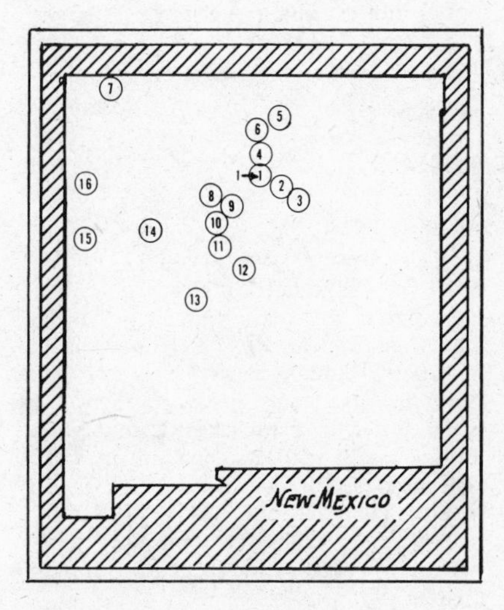

The southwest has a profusion of spiritual heritage sites. The first culture was of the prehistoric man who left traces in New Mexico long before recorded history. By A.D. 1000 the social, ceremonial, economic, and religious life of these early peoples had drawn them into villages in the north and pueblos in the south. This was their Golden Age, when the Sacred Triad—maize, squash, and beans—provided a staple food supply, allowing crafts, architecture, and ceremonials to become more complex.

Then Navajo and Apache raids in the north caused many natives to move into pueblos in the Rio Grande Valley near Acoma and Zuni. Acoma vies with the Hopi pueblo of Oraibi for the distinction of being "the oldest continuously inhabited community in the United States."

The search for Cibola, a mythical province containing seven cities of silver and gold, brought Spanish conquerors up the Rio Grande from Mexico. In 1598, Don Juan de Onate claimed the colony for Spain. In return for tribute (food, labor, buckskin, textiles) each pueblo was given a Spanish name, religious instruction, and military protection from marauding tribes.

Franciscan fathers provided the religious instruction, bringing Christianity and a new religious heritage. As shepherds of their new flocks, they provided iron tools, fruit trees, new plants, and herds of animals, establishing large mission towns. There were 50 in New Mexico and Arizona by 1630.

Some Spanish were oppressive, however, and in 1680 the tribes united and drove out all Spaniards. But in 1693, Diego de Vargas reconquered the Indians and reestablished Spanish authority. A few of the early mission towns remain the earliest white settlements. Santa Fe, established in 1610, is the oldest continuously inhabited settlement and, in fact, claims to be the oldest seat of government in the United States. This provincial Spanish capital was connected to Mexico City by a long arduous road called Camino Real (Royal Road).

Mexico claimed the area in 1821 when it secured independence from Spain. Then New Mexico was deeded to the United States in 1848 after the Mexican War. Statehood finally came in 1912.

Although the Catholic Church has had converts among the Indians of the southwest for over 300 years, the importance of native ceremonials persists. Many Indians have found nothing inconsistent in observing both native rituals and Catholic practices.

Further diversity came when Protestants arrived including some ethnic groups that settled complete towns. After the bitter years, when pioneers and Indians fought over the land, a pleasing mosaic of spiritual tradition developed. Some of the most fascinating aspects are found in New Mexico, where the blend of native and Catholic influences has produced a unique art form. Holy images (or santos) of wood gypsum and tempera can be seen in the native-built churches which dominate the towns.

There are many such villages and pueblos here, but not all welcome visitors. Therefore only a representative grouping are in this travel guide. The traveler may discover many others of equal interest along the way.

Northern New Mexico

SANTA FE

Museum of Navaho Ceremonial Art

At 704 Camino Lejo, in this ancient city of Santa Fe at the foot of the Sangre de Cristo, is a recently founded museum (1937) that honors Indian religious heritage. Hosteen Klah, famous singer or "medicine man" of the Navaho and descendant of Chief Norbona, was the first of his people to collect their holy stories, ritual objects, and sand paintings. He assisted Mary Cabot Wheelwright in establishing this museum to preserve for posterity Navaho ceremonialism. These are not regarded as curiosities, but are in a form which conveys their vital significance. The visitor can enter the beautifully proportioned hogan and examine hundreds of sand-painting reproductions and other art work as well as browse in the very complete gift and book shop.

Mission of San Miguel of Santa Fe

The nation's oldest thick-walled mission church is at 401 Santa Fe Trail in this picturesque capital city, built in 1610 by Tlaxcalan Indians from Mexico, with Franciscan friars supervising. The thick walls withstood the uprising of 1680, though early records were burned. Buttresses to strengthen the walls and a new tower and front were added, but it still looks ancient. A 1312 bell used in Spain and Mexico is on display. The interior has a 1798 altar backdrop, portraits, two picture charts dating to 1630, and excavated Indian artifacts.

Cathedral of St. Francis of Assisi

America's oldest madonna, Our Lady of Conquest, is in the Conquistador Chapel of the Cathedral of St. Francis of Assisi. Fray Alonso Benavides, Franciscan mission supervisor brought it here in 1625. The small wooden statue is covered with gold leaf and rests on the altar.

The French Romanesque building, made of brown sandstone, seems elaborate for the Spanish setting. It was constructed between 1870 and 1889 and is the sixth church on the site.

(2) GLORIETA

Glorieta Baptist Assembly

East of Santa Fe on Route 25, are the western assembly grounds of the Southern Baptist Convention. In a superb 2,500-acre setting in Glorieta Pass, at the foot of Glorieta Baldy Mountain, the elaborate complex of buildings can accommodate over 2,000 people for meals and meetings. Apartments, lodges, cottages, camp shelters, and Chaparral Inn provide a variety of accommodations. A tremendous dining hall, Holcomb Auditorium, and 30 conference rooms attract all denominations for inspirational conferences, retreats, and vacations in this Christian resort. The dramatic, triple-tiered 160-foot lighted tower of Holcomb stands out as a central beacon.

(3) PECOS

Benedictine Abbey

In the pleasant hill country a bit farther east of Glorieta is a former Trappist monastery which is now a Benedictine abbey. It is a center for Catholic Pentecostal renewal. The low Spanish-style adobe buildings contain chapel, meeting rooms, dining area, and sleeping facilities for the thousands who come for men's, women's, family, and marriage encounter weeks, as well as to clergy retreats. General Pentecostal weekends are regularly interspersed to make room for the many who inquire about the charismatic movement. A wide-ranging collection of religious paperbacks and gifts are for sale in the book store, a former Trappist porter's lodge.

(4) CHIMAYO

El Santuario de Chimayo

One of the most picturesque, worshipful, and beautifully decorated churches in America can be found in Chimayo, north of Santa Fe. It was built between 1813 and 1816 at the east end of town. Legend says the chuch was built at a site directed by a vision. A healing well in a small room off the sancristy attracts many health-seeking pilgrims. A beautiful Bulto, "Our Lord of Esquipulas," can be seen in one of the small rooms back of the altar. It was brought from the town of Esquipulas in Guatemala. The many intricate carvings, prints, and hangings have been labors of love, as was the intricately carved door. Masses are said daily.

(5) TAOS

Pueblo de Taos

Taos is one of the most interesting of the pueblos. The traveler gazing at North and South Houses, one on either side of the creek, is reminded of sprawling apartment houses. Adobe brown "boxes" spread sideways and upward with ladder leading from one level to another. Inside they are comfortably furnished with Indian rugs and handcrafts. Gaily dressed Indians are on hand to show their handwork and sell their wares. Taos pueblo has been inhabited for 800 years.

Ownership of the nearby sacred blue lake in the Sangre de Cristo Mountains has been returned to the pueblo by the United States government. It is a reminder that strong religious and ceremonial ties hold the tribal members together. Many ceremonial dances are held throughout the year, to which visitors are invited. There is a camera fee and no pictures are allowed during sacred dances.

Ruins of a mission church built around 1598 may be seen inside the pueblo walls. The church was burned during the 1680 revolt, rebuilt, and destroyed in a revolt in 1847. The newer church, Mission of San Geronimo de Taos, was built in 1847.

(6) RANCHOS DE TAOS

Mission of St. Francis of Assisi

A splendid Spanish church lies south of Ranchos de Taos on Route 64. Twin belfries with crosses and a fan decoration over the door give an elaborate impression almost overwhelming the simple surroundings. One pastor refers to it lovingly as "a symphony in mud"! It was built in 1710 by the Franciscans and is cruciform shape.

The interior has an old reredos, images of saints, a statute of Christ, and a 17th-century silver cross. On display also is the mysterious painting by Henry Ault called "The Shadow of the Cross." In certain light, Christ appears to carry a cross. In other light, the cross cannot be seen. Masses are said daily. In summer, visitors can hear a lecture and can view Henri Ault's painting "The Shadow of the Cross." On October 4, the Fiesta of St. Francis heralds homecoming day for the parish.

(7) AZTEC

Aztec Ruins National Monument

The state's northwest corner contains one of the best-preserved pueblo ruins. Particularly outstanding is the Great Kiva, or place of worship, which is centrally located in the plaza. (Great kivas were used by whole villages while small kivas were used by indi-

vidual clans.) This large one consists of a circular chamber 48 feet in diameter and sunk 8 feet into the ground. It is surrounded by 14 arc-shaped rooms, with doorways and ladders leading into the main chamber. A large square room on the north probably contained an altar. The roof was supported by four large masonry columns.

The large U-shaped complex of rooms surrounding the kiva originally had about 500 rooms. Many remain intact today, including some ascending three stories. This pueblo dates to the 1100s. In the museum are pottery, baskets, and other objects made by the inhabitants. A self-guiding trail leads through the monument and into the Great Kiva, which was restored in 1934.

(8) JEMEZ

Jemez State Monument

Turning south again, via Route 44, the traveler comes back to the Santa Fe area and this memorial, which preserves the San José de los Jemez Mission and Guisewa Pueblo ruins. The natives, under the direction of Franciscans, built the mission in 1622. The massive sandstone walls are 8 feet thick. A large octagonal tower gives a fortress effect.

The Guisewa Pueblo ruins go back to 1300. There are three kivas and a few houses to be seen. In the museum are memorabilia relating to both church and pueblo as well as a reproduction of some very fine murals that were painted on the church walls early in its existence.

SANTO DOMINGO

Church of the Pueblo of Santo Domingo

The traveler will enjoy a visit to live pueblo life again, leaving the ruins behind. Hundreds of Indians live in the country around this church and gather for Green Corn Dance on August 4. All couples wed by Indian ceremonies during the year are married in the church at this festival time. At Christmas they gather again for ceremonial dances. The church, erected in 1886, is flat-roofed, of mission style and with a bell tower. The front of the white-walled church is elaborately decorated in blue and shades of brown. The villagers are best known for their shell and turquoise beads. Religious leaders exert strong control over village government.

Central New Mexico

ALBUQUERQUE

Church of San Felipe de Neri

On a corner of Old Town Plaza in Albuquerque is the Church of San Felipe de Neri, built along with the town in 1706. When larger quarters were needed, the original walls were built into the ensuing remodeled church. Renovations were in 1895 and resulted in abode, pueblo architecture being surmounted with Victorian decor. Two large bell towers with Gothic arches are late additions. Choir members reach their posts by climbing a stairway that winds around a spruce tree.

The little square is a gem and the traveler will want to wander into the shops, rest on the benches, and taste sopaipilla at the inn.

ISLETA

St. Augustine Church

The heavy, buttressed mission church is believed to be the oldest mission church still in regular use in the country. It was built about 1613 to 1621 and was partly destroyed in the 1680 revolt. The adobe (mud brick) walls were rebuilt over the original ones and roof timbers replaced. The church was rededicated in 1710 and, until 1720, was named for St. Anthony, then changed to St. Augustine. Franciscan friars were in charge until 1846, when diocesan priests took over. In front of the church, within the enclosing walls, is an ancient cemetery.

Isleta pueblo is adjacent. Agriculture is the community enterprise, though work in nearby Albuquerque also provides income. Pottery is made here by the Laguna colony which settled here in 1880. There is an active ceremonial life. In addition the Fiesta of St. Augustine is celebrated August 28.

12 MOUNTAINAIR

Quarai State Monument

Northwest of Mountainair are ruins of the Mission Church of the Immaculate Conception (La Purisima Concepcion). It was built about 1620 by the Indians under the direction of their architect-friar. A later priest, Fray Estevan de Perea, served here while holding the powerful post of head of the Holy Office of the Inquisition. This is the only time the dread Inquisition seems to have touched America. Apache raids and famine led to the abandonment of the pueblo and church about 1677.

The Visitors Center and Museum has a pictured display of mission and church architecture, which is especially helpful to the traveler in the southwest. The large church and 17 friar-house- or convento-room ruins have been shored

Gran Quivira National Monument, Air View 1

Gran Quivira National Monument, Air View 2

up. The dry atmosphere has kept the remains remarkably well.

Abo State Monument

About ten miles west of Mountainair are the red sandstone walls of another Franciscan mission and friar house, along with remains of an extensive Indian pueblo. The church walls rise 30 feet high and dominate the site. Archeologists think the pueblo was occupied continuously from A.D. 1300 to 1672. In Spanish days it housed many people. The church and friar house were probably built around 1630. In 1641, a report said Abo had a church, convento (friar house), organ, and choir, with 1,580 souls in its care. A combination of drought, famine, and Apache raids led to its destruction and abandonment in the late seventeenth century.

Gran Quivira National Monument

Completing the triumvirate of mission ruin monuments in this area is Gran Quivira, established in 1909. Recording a civilization of a thousand years, the ruins show that two churches were built here during Spanish days and ceremonial kivas were used in the pueblo. Indian religion permeated all facets of life. Forces of nature could be controlled by the proper performances of rites. Hence, katchina (clown) dances were held to secure good fortune. A stone face and a ceremonial candlestick were found in this kiva.

The first Spanish church, San Isidro, was built in 1629, along with priests' living quarters and classrooms. The larger San Buenaventura and attached convento was built in 1659. Pueblo and mission were abandoned in the 1670s. A 30-minute walking tour begins at the Visitors Center, where there are archeological and historical displays.

SOCORRO

Old San Miguel Mission

North of the plaza, at 403 Camino Real, is the ancient mission church of San Miguel, which sits in the center of the original Spanish land grant of 17,002 acres. The main church was built between 1615 and 1626. Of pueblo style with thick adobe walls, massive supporting beams came from the mountains many miles away. The rich silver deposits of the area were used to create a solid silver communion rail, tabernacle, and sacred vessels. When the 1680 rebellion was brewing, the priests and Indians disassembled these treasures and buried them. The map was lost—and for two centuries people have been looking for this lost treasure.

Restored several times, the church has deviated somewhat from pueblo architecture. Its hand-carved pews, old paintings, and sacred vessels may be seen at or between regular masses, for it is a parish church.

ACOMA

Mission San Esteban Rey

High above the Enchanted Mesa sits Acoma pueblo, the "Sky City." With history stretching back 1,000 years before the arrival of the Spaniards, this is said to be the oldest continuously inhabited site in the country. When the first European arrived in 1540, there were 5,000 people occupying this site and the many villages. After much bloodshed, the Acomas were subdued by the Spaniards in 1599, and again in 1696.

The immense Church of San Esteban Rey was built in 1629, using Indian labor. Every bit of material had to be carried to the mesa top or hoisted with grass ropes. Log beams came from mountains 30 miles away. The twin-towered structure has 9-foot-thick walls and 40-foot-long roof logs. The hand-carved altar, images of saints, and paintings are particularly interesting. The best-known craft in Acoma, however, is the carefully decorated, thin-walled pottery. Visitors will find this and other wares, as well as Indian guides, at "Sky City."

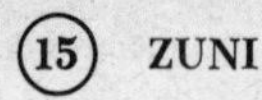

ZUNI

Zuni Pueblo

The Zuni people, who are located close to New Mexico's western border, are unique. Because of their isolation, both geographically and linguistically, they have perpetuated many of their ancient ways. Native religious activities transcend all others and are controlled by priests, or caciques, who hold office for life and direct ceremonial work through 12 medicine societies and six fraternal kiva organizations. The basis of their belief is that everything in nature has a soul and man must live in harmony with nature. Individual, community, art, craft, and workday activities are integrated with religion. Thus, masked dances are moving, colorful, and held most frequently at the winter and summer solstice. Most famous is the Shalako ceremony and the blessing of new homes in December, which draws many visitors and friends. Huge birdlike kachina figures, couriers of rainmakers, dance in Shalako houses.

In the pueblo village, with headquarters at the modern Zuni Tribal Administration Building, visitors may secure maps and information about the pueblo and its coming events. In addition to Indian religious activity, there is a Baptist mission, St. Anthony's Mission, and ruins of an early mission. The tribe is famous for its jewelry. An estimated 900 silversmiths and stone cutters produce inlay, nugget, channel, overlay, and cast items of turquoise, black jet, red coral, and shells.

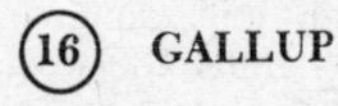

GALLUP

Museum of Indian Arts and Crafts

The last stop on our tour in this predominately Indian state is at Gallup, where each August the Intertribal Indian Ceremonials are held. For four days, members of about 20 tribes perform dance rituals and chants. They also display arts and handcrafts. Parades and a variety of other programs can be seen.

Since much of the art has a religious base, it is well to spend time in the Museum of Indian Arts and Crafts at 103 East 66th Avenue. Exhibits explain the culture and handwork. Each evening there is an audiovisual program giving additional background of the Indian religious heritage.

TEXAS

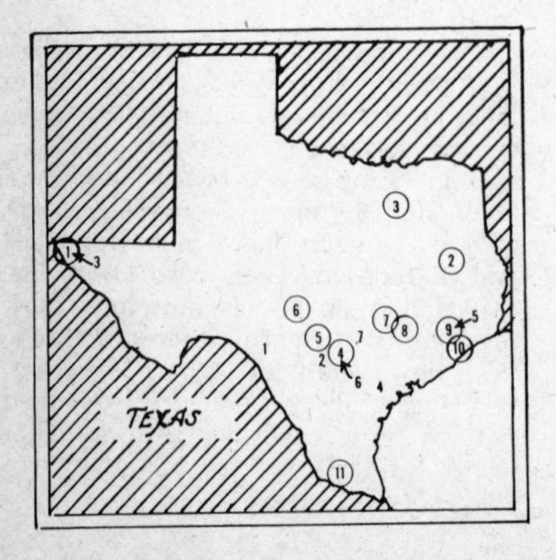

Many Spanish conquistadors crisscrossed this land from 1519 through the 1600s in their search for the Northwest Passage. When French explorers began claiming land along the Gulf of Mexico, however, the Spaniards decided to colonize. Ysleta (now El Paso) was founded in 1662 with the establishment of the Mission Nuestra Senora del Carmen. This state's oldest settlement on its western border was joined by another on the eastern edge in 1690. Spurred by reports of an aborted French colony on Lavaca Bay, a Spanish expedition established Mission San

Francisco de los Tejas near the present-day town of Weches. By 1721, there were six missions and two forts planted between. San Antonio, one of the forts (or presidios) founded in 1718, became the principal Spanish settlement in Texas.

The state was named for its first inhabitants, the Tejas (or Texas) Indians, who became the congregations of the first Catholic missionaries. Some of the early mission churches, which were made of stone, survive; but many, constructed of wood, have not.

The first Anglo-American settlement was at Austin in 1823. With American pioneers arriving from the east, a struggle ensued between Mexico (which had become independent of Spain) and the United States for control. At first Texas was a federal state of Mexico. The famous Battle of the Alamo was part of the military struggle that freed Texas to become a republic in 1836. This lasted until 1845 when the state was annexed to the United States.

The religious heritage is thus originally Catholic, with Protestants arriving later. Ethnic groups, who settled towns in the central section, plus recent conference centers and college chapels, give a wide range of diversity, both architecturally and theologically.

Our tour begins in the western part of Texas in the state's oldest town.

Western Texas

(1) EL PASO

Nuestra Senora del Carmen

Descendants of the Tigua Indians still live in the ancient community of Ysleta, now part of El Paso. Age-old, white-washed adobe buildings blend with modern structures in a picturesque setting in the state's oldest town. Blue-painted doors and window trim ward off evil and ensure good luck.

This oldest mission was built in 1681 as Corpus Christi de la Isleta. It has survived floods and fires to be restored into its original style. Franciscans founded it to Christianize the Tigua Indians. Today Indian crafts are demonstrated on the grounds and dances are performed at a museum run by the Indians.

Sierra de Christo Rey

A few feet from the boundary between Mexico and the United States the traveler will find a statue of Christ. The huge figure looms on the horizon at the top of Mount Cristo Rey, overlooking both El Paso and Mexican towns. Fourteen stations of the cross lead up the winding trail to the shrine which was created by the artist Urbici Soler. The figure stands 33.5 feet high and is built of Cordova cream limestone. Thousands make this climb the last Sunday of October, which is the Feast of Christ the King.

Temple Mount Sinai

In the foothills of the dramatic mountains that surround the city is a building that also comes to a dramatic peak. Thin-shelled concrete pierces the sky in unusual angles. Architect Sidney Eisenshtat has designed the arches and windows to put the worshiper in touch with the sky, desert, and surrounding hills. The congregation represents the newer element in the state's religious heritage.

Northeast Texas

(2) WECHES

Mission San Francisco de Los Tejas State Historic Park

Our tour of eastern Texas begins in the second oldest of the state's communities. Set within a 118-acre park is a replica of the first Spanish mission in East Texas. It was established in 1690 to ensure no French encroachment. It was then near a very large Tejas Indian village. A white settlement came later and in 1847 the town was named Weches. The log replica is rustic and simple. A small square tower surmounts the roof and a tiny porch extends over the front door.

(3) DALLAS

Biblical Arts Center

Continuing northwest from Weches to Dallas, the traveler should drive through Hillcrest Memorial Park to this Center. The Miracle at Pentecost presented here is a 30-minute sound-and-light show. America's largest original religious painting comes to life as the second chapter of Acts is narrated. Tiny spotlights illumine the various characters and a symphony orchestra in stereophonic sound adds drama. The 124-foot-wide by 20-foot-high mural was painted by Torger Thompson and took eight years to complete. Over 200 figures are represented. There are about eight presentations daily and four on Sunday afternoons. The nondenominational, nonsectarian presentation follows the biblical account closely.

Central Texas

(4) SAN ANTONIO

The Alamo

An absolutely wonderful way to get acquainted with the 1718 city of San Antonio is by water taxi or the river walk. The San Antonio River winds in and around, but mostly underneath, the city; its sidewalks are lined with shops, dining rooms, art exhibits, and even an open-air theater. The night lighting is exotic. The river is also close to the Hemisfair Plaza of 1968, where the Tower of the Americas gives a commanding view of the city.

Then step from a central square directly into the Alamo. Established along with the town in 1718, it was called Mission San Antonio de Valero. The historic old structure was built in 1755 as a combination church and fortress. The Franciscans used it as a house of worship and an Indian school. On occasion it was a welcome shelter for settlers during times of unrest. The Alamo, as it was later called, became a symbol of patriotism when in 1836 it was defended for two weeks from the Mexican army by 187 men. When Santa Anna's troops prevailed, all defenders were killed.

One can sense the poignancy of the event in the main hall. Flags, swords, manuscripts, and letters, as well as a diorama depicting the final seige hours are in this museum. Behind the Alamo is the Texas Research Library with a comprehensive collection on Texas history.

Mission San Jose

In addition to the Alamo, four other missions were established here by Franciscan friars. A Day of Missions on August 6 is an annual salute. This "Queen of Missions," San Jose, at 6539 San Jose Drive was founded in 1720 and is both a state and a national landmark. The church, which was built between 1768 and 1782, is now restored and is surrounded by the mission compound. Indian homes, a granary, workshop, and clergy quarters may be seen. The rose window is especially beautiful and is said to be one of the finest pieces of Spanish colonial sculpture in America.

Mission Concepcion

Another of the old churches on Mission Road is this massive edifice with twin towers and a cupola. It is the oldest unrestored church in the United States standing as it was completed in 1755. Work on it began in 1731. Records show that 792 Indians were baptized and 249 Indian marriages were celebrated here during the first 30 years. Indian population declined in 1794 and it became a sub-mission. Then in 1855 the Brothers of Mary at St. Mary's College had charge. St. John's Seminary building was begun next to the mission in 1919. Masses are said on Sundays and Holy Days.

Mission Espada

Known as the "gem of missions," San Francisco de la Espada on Espada St. is a successor to that first East Texas mission to the Tejas Indians. When the site was abandoned, it was reestablished here in 1731. The building, which is a photographer's favorite, was begun in 1745 and has been restored many times. After the Indian population declined, visiting priests said Mass. In 1956 it became a diocesan church and serves the community. Visitors may walk through the cloisters, museum, convento, and Indian quarters as well as step into the lovely old chapel.

Mission San Juan Capistrano

The Capistrano mission was also founded in East Texas and moved west during the troubles with France. In 1731, it was reestablished here near the Payaya Indian Village. By 1956, a long narrow church of stone, as well as a stone friary and granary, were completed. Ruins of a larger church, begun in 1760 and never completed, may still be seen. Various church orders have cared for the mission. Now Franciscans are in charge and there are services for the people of Berg's Mill community.

Trinity Baptist Church

One of the largest and most progressive of the Southern Baptist churches is found in San Antonio. Trinity Baptist's brick colonial plant has an enormous sanctuary that seats several thousand. Others of its well-appointed buildings spread over a wide area. One complete house stands filled with clothing, furnishings, and food, ready to meet any need immediately. The worshiping congregation generates an electric atmosphere on a Sunday morning. Comprising all ages, the fellowship overflows to strangers.

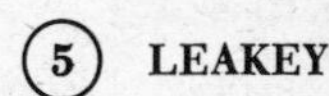

5 LEAKEY

Laity Lodge

Returning east, the traveler should arrange ahead for a look at an outstanding conference center. Hidden away in a canyon in the Texas hill country is Laity Lodge operated by the Howard E. Butt Foundation. The ecumenical facility is dedicated to Christian renewal. Retreats for adults are held at the lodge, which is dramatically cantilevered over a mountain stream and is luxuriously furnished.

Young people find high-quality activities and challenge at separate camps like Linnet's Wings, Echo Valley, Commanche Outpost, Wind Song, Singing Hills, and North Wind. It's a total facility much in demand by Texas area churches. It's fun to walk around the grounds and see approprate quotations from the poets and the Scriptures on signposts.

(6) FREDERICKSBURG

Vereins Kirche

In the center of town, travelers will find and exclaim over Vereins Kirche, replica of the very first community building in town. When German families from New Brauneels staked out the town, they built an eight-sided church. Erected in 1847, it became known as the "Coffee Mill Church" because of its shape. It served both as a town house and as a worship center. The replica was built in the 1930s and houses a small museum and offices. In front of the unconventional building with its eight-sided cupola is a bust of John Meusebach, leader of the colony. At Kammlah House is the Pioneer Museum and one of the first stores.

Southeastern Texas

(7) GIDDINGS

Old Wendish Church

Wendish Lutherans, a small German sect, settled Giddings in 1872. Its newspaper, the Giddings Star, has the only type available in this country to print copy in the Wendish language.

At the nearby Serbin community, 6 miles south, is the Old Wendish Church. The unusual seating arrangement called for men to occupy the balcony and women and children the main floor.

(8) ROUND TOP

Bethlehem Lutheran Church

Another of the state's charming ethnic communities is Round Top, southeast of Giddings on Route 237. Judge Henkel Square contains eight historic homes of early German pioneers enclosed by split-rail fences. These have been restored by the Texas Pioneer Arts Foundation. Established about 1840, it was a center for Lutherans for miles around.

The German-style church, of stone, was dedicated in 1866. Fayette County Lutheran residents form its active parish. The unique pipe organ is made of hand-shaped cedar wood.

(9) HOUSTON

Rothko Chapel

A modern religious shrine is found in this space-age city. On the grounds of the Texas Medical Center can be seen Rothko Chapel, a simply designed octagonal sanctuary dedicated in 1971 to all religions. Within is created a spiritual environment for the paintings without images by the artist Mark Rothko. His 14 panels are among the world's most famed 20th-century art. Outside is a remarkable obelisk dedicated to Dr. Martin Luther King, Jr. Called the Broken Obelisk, the 26-foot steel memorial rises beside a reflecting pool.

(10) GALVESTON

Bishop's Palace

In the former stronghold of pirate Jean Lafitte and on the shores where La Salle's men explored in the 1600s lies this city on an island in the Gulf of Mexico. St. Mary's Church, the state's first Catholic cathedral, and the magnificent old Bishop's Palace are reminders of the early Catholic heritage.

The palace is the state's only edifice on the American Institute of Architects' list of 100 outstanding buildings. It was built originally by Col. Walter Gresham in 1886 and purchased for the Galveston-Houston diocese in 1923. Turrets and towers on the stone building give a medieval aura. Furnishings come from around the world.

(11) MISSION

La Lomita Chapel

Hidden away in the Texas brush is a tiny chapel close to the Mexican border. The doll-like white La Lomita Chapel measures 15 by 25 feet and is topped by a miniature cupola and cross. It was built by the Oblate fathers in 1849. They established the town earlier in 1824. For 25 years visitors have enjoyed the annual "tropical Christmas" all-poinsettia show, largest in the country. Travelers to this southernmost point in the country are well rewarded by the amazing display of the Christmas plants in homes, banks, and public buildings at Christmastime.

ARIZONA

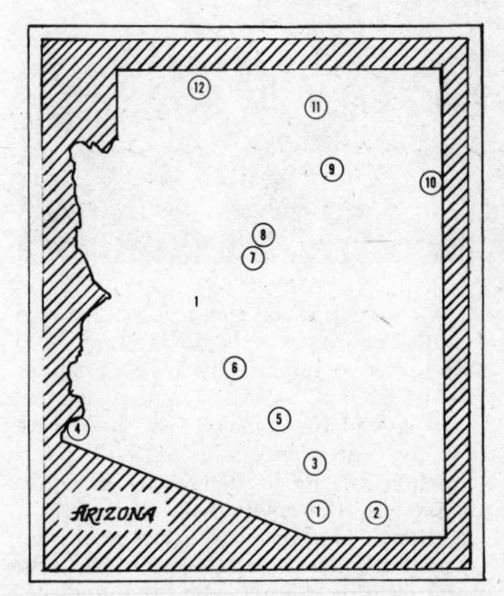

Arizona, like New Mexico, was once the home of a highly civilized race of Pueblo Indians. When Spanish explorers came around 1539 looking for the fabled Seven Cities of Cibola, drought, famine, and northern Indian raids had caused a decline in population. Instead of mythical wealth, they found a people rich in ceremonials but poor in material possessions. Jesuit Father Eusebio Francisco Kino is credited with the first successful misison work, beginning in 1692. Tumacacori, built in 1696 near the southern border, is one of the oldest missions, followed by the other handsome remaining structure, San Xavier Del Bac, at Tucson. Though Father Kino begain the missions, it was the Franciscans who later erected the buildings.

The fundamental religious conviction that man must live in harmony with the natural world meant that Pueblo Indians did not separate religion from everyday activities. Societies headed by priests in each pueblo are responsible for maintaining harmony with the supernatural world. Properly conducted ceremonies will control the weather, effect cures, bring rain, mature crops, and ensure hunting success, the Indians believe. Therefore, the pueblos have many ceremonial events that have continued through the Christian era. Along with the attendance at mission services and churches, promotion of native religious ceremonies has continued. In recent years, as interest in tribal heritage has increased, old ceremonies have been revived. As in New Mexico, only a representative few of the many current and ancient sites have been chosen for inclusion here.

Latecomers, again, have been the Protestants. Mormon and Moravian missionaries came next, then Episcopalians and Congregationalists. Other denominations have flourished too, along with the shrines and present-day ministries on campuses and in flourishing retirement colonies.

Our tour begins in the steps of Father Kino, in the southeast corner of the territory which became a state in 1912.

Southern Arizona

(1) TUBAC

Tumacacori National Monument

Energetic Jesuit missionary Father Kino is credited with beginning this mission and others in the Sonora chain, which extended into Mexico. When he first visited the nearby Pima village, he said Mass under a brush shelter built by the Indians. By 1698, there was an "earth-roofed house of adobe." After the Pima Rebellion of 1751, the mission was moved to Tubac and a small chapel erected. A protective presidio was built at Tubac. When the Jesuits were expelled from New Spain, the Franciscans took over.

Construction of the present massive adobe church was begun around 1800 and was in full use by 1822. Troubles with Indians, Mexican independence, and lack of funds meant that there were no resident priests after 1827. The old mission began to decay. It was preserved by the government in 1908 as a National Monument. Visitors will step first into the museum, which has several exciting dioramas portraying events in the mission's past. A self-guided tour leads through the tremendous sanctuary, to the excavations of the Indian town, and into the cemetery where an unusual mortuary chapel stands. It is a simple abode circle with fired-brick cornice and molding. An arched door provides entrance and two high round holes give ventilation. It was apparently used to lay out the dead before burial.

Two special annual events in December are a fiesta and a Christmas eve luminarias.

(2) TOMBSTONE

Tombstone National Historical Site

One of the state's old mining camps is immortalized east on Route 80. Though mining lasted only seven years, millions in silver and gold came from the rich ground. The thriving health resort of today is mining wealth of another sort.

The oldest Protestant church in Arizona is found at Third and Safford streets, Tombstone. St. Paul's Episcopal Church was built in 1882 of adobe brick, handmade from desert earth. The original structure still stands, though a protective covering of stucco has been placed over the "dobes." The hand-hewn lumber was brought from the Chiricahua Mountains by ox team. The two nave lighting fixtures are from a sailing vessel which came around the Horn. The church, like the town, is "too tough to die" and is one of the designated historic sites within the historic district.

(3) TUCSON

Mission San Xavier Del Bac

Picking up the trail of Father Kino (see Arizona introductory material), we travel to the Papago Indian Reservation, 9 miles south of Tucson. Here is probably the most beautiful of the Spanish missions. Called "White Dove of the Desert," its domes, arches, and carvings make it by far the most ornate. A striking feature is the reddish façade flanked by two white towers. Franciscans and Indians built the church from 1782 to 1797. Missionaries were forced to leave in 1828 but returned in 1911. Since that time the mission has served as the Papagos' main church and school. Fiestas are held in October and December. To the west of the church is a mortuary chapel where two pioneer missionaries are buried. On the hill to the east is a replica of Lourdes Grotto in France. The baroque interior is elaborately

Mission San Xavier del Bac

decorated. Original paintings, mural decorations, and a richly adorned altar give an air of tranquil antiquity. The well-worn floors show how numerous the worshipers have been.

(4) YUMA

Fort Yuma Quechan Museum

Before continuing north, the traveler should take a trip to the state's western border and another Indian headquarters. On the grounds of the interesting old Spanish Catholic mission is a statue of Father Garces. The original mission stood on this site when the massacre of 1781 took place. After founding the mission in 1779, Garces and all the colonists were killed in the massacre. The Fort Yuma Indian School and Agency are here along with the museum, which is filled with authentic Indian lore and artifacts. The Spanish mission era and the time of military occupancy are also covered. Yuman Indians live across the river in California.

(5) COOLIDGE

Casa Grande Ruins National Monument

Leaving the west and present-day Indians, we travel east through Gila Bend to a memorial to the ancient Hohokam Indians. When Father Kino came upon the ruins in 1694, they had already been abandoned over two centuries. The Hohokams lived as early as 400 B.C. and were noted for their remarkable irrigation canals, which enabled them to farm the arid desert.

Casa Grande, or Big House, shows amazing construction ability. Even though it is partially in ruins, the four-story earthen building has withstood the ravages of 600 years. Probably used as a ceremonial building, the main room is surrounded by remnants of 60 to 90 individual rooms enclosed in a wall. Traces of other villages are seen in the monument's boundaries. The Visitors' Center has exhibits and provides a self-guiding tour.

(6) PHOENIX

Mormon Temple

Mormons founded Mesa, a suburb of Phoenix, in 1878. The early settlers must have been grateful to their Hohokam forerunners, for they used the Indian irrigation ditches to good advantage.

The beautiful temple is used exclusively for marriages, baptisms, and other sacred ordinances. Only conforming members of the Church of Jesus Christ Latter-Day Saints, who hold "temple recommends," are admitted. The Visitors' Center is open for guided tours of the garden and for information about the Arizona temple.

Canaan in the Desert

Tucked away in the quiet desert under Camelback Mountain, at 9849 North 40th Street, is a retreat house of the Evangelical Sisterhood of Mary, a Protestant order with headquarters in Germany. A chapel, conversation room, and 12 lodging rooms await retreatants and quiet prayer-day participants all year long. The traveler might be lucky and have Sister Dikla with her simple habit and shining face as tour guide. Joyful plaques and banners hang in every conceivable place and a book-room invites the browser. One of the worldwide projects of this sisterhood is the placing of Scripture plaques in national parks. Grand Canyon and Lake Mead now have these inspiring words placed by appropriate vistas. A schedule of retreats is available and the sisters are most welcoming.

Franciscan Renewal Center

Over three centuries after the first Franciscans found their way to this land of mesquite and sage, the same order is still ministering. At 5802 East Lincoln Road, in Scottsdale suburb, is an exhilarating center of Christian renewal. Youth, adults, clergy, couples, students all gather here for spiritual growth under the resident retreat master. The buildings are set around a pleasant green courtyard. A chapel, dining room, motel-type rooms, and a dynamic program create a vigorous, ongoing center.

Northern Arizona

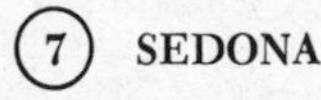

7 SEDONA

Chapel of the Holy Spirit

One of the most spectacular drives in the country begins here and proceeds north through the towering red cliffs of Oak Creek Canyon, the setting for Zane Gray's *Call of the Canyon.* First, though, visit this red-hued Chapel of the Holy Spirit, which seems to rise out of the rocks and blend with the towering cliffs behind it. With government approval, the chapel was erected in park grounds as a memorial to parents of sculptor Marguerite Brunsing Stoude. Though Catholic in background, the chapel is of universal appeal and has a steady stream of visitors.

Entrance is through two extremely high aluminum doors. Ahead is the lofty chancel of glass with a 90-foot cross standing against the panoramic view. On the way out, glance up at the Shrine of the Red Rocks. Here a hand-hewn wooden cross stands by a permanent outside altar, scene of annual Easter sunrise services.

Church of the Red Rocks

Not far down the canyon is Church of the Red Rocks (United Church of Christ), a modern structure whose sanctuary thrusts forward to a peak where a cross is placed. A remarkable backdrop of high cliffs in various shades of red rising above the green valley floor is seen from within the all-glass chancel. The interior design is extremely simple, for God's handiwork is the focal point.

8 FLAGSTAFF

United Church of Christ, Congregational

After an incredible trip up Oak Creek Canyon and a climb of 5,000 feet, the traveler comes to another center for modern-day life and Indian culture. On the outskirts, close to Northern Arizona University, at 740 North Turquoise Drive, is a United Church of Christ congregation attempting to meet needs in unique ways. In addition to working with the Navajo Tribal Council to augment red power, help with a local guidance clinic and crisis intervention needs, the congregation also made available space for a much needed youth hostel.

In the angular, cedar-shake building among the pines in Switzer Canyon, a wing off the sanctuary leads to kitchen, dormitory, and house-parents' room. Here members of Arizona Youth Hostel, and any International Youth Hosteler, may stay for a minimum fee. By-products have been twofold. The church folk often drop in to "rap" with visiting youth. Also, if any juvenile is in trouble, local officials can bring him to this 24-hour center for help. Hostel fees help with the building upkeep.

(9) ORAIBI

Oraibi Pueblo

The Hopi "place of the rock called Orai" claims to be, along with Acoma in New Mexico, the oldest inhabited town in the United States. It dates from A.D. 1150 and sits high atop a rocky mesa. The mission of San Francisco was established here in 1629. Its ruins are now north of the village. An abandoned Mennonite church is at the mesa edge. Tiny springs at the mesa edge fed by drainage from Black Mesa have sustained the Hopis for hundreds of years as they have become experts at dry farming.

Hopi religious activities are still some of the most complex and beautiful of all the tribes. They still maintain an elaborate religious calendar. The most famous ceremonial, the Snake Dance, is held in late August. Hopi dances, open to the public, concern prayers for rain, growth of crops, and health and well-being of all people. Hopi crafts include basketry, pottery, kachina dolls, silverwork, and weaving. The tribal headquarters, Indian school, and trading post are at New Oraibi, where permission to visit should be requested of the chief.

(10) WINDOW ROCK

Navaho Tribal Museum

The largest tribal area in Arizona belongs to the Navajos, whose headquarters are in Window Rock on the state's eastern border. Tribal Government, Bureau of Indian Affairs, and Navajo Arts and Crafts Guild all have offices here. The 74 members of the Tribal Council gather in the octagonal Council House.

Buildings are constructed according to ancient Indian techniques. The museum on the Navajo Tribal Fairgrounds tells of Indian cultural development beginning with prehistoric cliff dwellers. Artifacts of southwestern Indians are on display. A research library, picture displays, and a zoo and herbarium emphasizing products of the area are illuminating.

(11) TONALEA

Navajo National Monuments

Set in some of the most rugged mountains in the southwest is the largest and most complex of Arizona's ancient cliff dwellings. Each of the three areas in Navajo National Monument has a 13th-century pueblo ruin. The most easily reached is the Betatakin, or Ledge House. The rough and rugged trails lead to a 135-room apartment house. Living quarters, granaries, and one kiva can be seen in a natural declivity under sheer rock walls. The kiva, used for ceremonials, is a round room made like a well. Plenty of time and energy must be saved for the trip. Keet Seel Area, or Broken Pottery, is 8 miles beyond over a trail for foot or horseback. The Visitors' Center display is on the archeology and history of these "ancient ones." The Navajo Arts and Crafts Center is close by.

(12) MOCCASIN

Pipe Spring National Monument

Our last stop in Arizona is close to the Utah border and contains a stone fort built in 1870 by the Mormons. Water flowing from the Sevier fault in the Arizona Strip was discovered by Mormon missionaries to the Indians led by Jacob Hamlin in 1858. A claim was

made in 1863 and a livestock ranch begun. Because of growing Navajo raids due to army campaigns from the south, several settlers were killed in 1866 and the claim was abandoned. After hostilities ceased, Brigham Young reestablished the cattle ranch in 1870. A fort, originally called Windsom Castle, was built to protect Mormon families and workers. It was never attacked and served as a ranch house till it became Pipe Spring National Monument in 1923.

The stone fort encloses the spring and two facing rows of two-story houses. Huge doors could be swung open at the entrance. That first settlement was a success, soon including a cheese factory and the first telegraph station in Arizona Territory. Visitors can see the original settlers' dugout, the old fort, with its double porches and other outbuildings. Furnishings are authentic to the 1770 period. In the well-appointed kitchen with its old wood stove, it's not hard to imagine the aroma of fresh bread and the scent of herb spices. It is also easier to understand how the west was won as advancing settlements like this took root, many under the impetus of the church.

MISSOURI

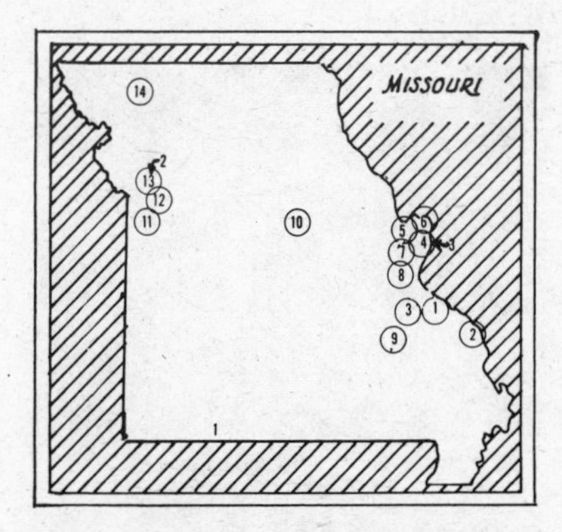

The midsection of America was colonized from the south and the east, finally becoming a crossroads for western pioneers. Ste. Genevieve on the Mississippi was the earliest community, settled as French traders and miners searched for riches in the virgin country, and Catholic missionaries sought the natives' souls.

It was around the year 1732 that French Catholics planted Ste. Genevieve in "Upper Louisiana," bringing the Creole atmosphere of the Gulf towns. Then St. Louis sprouted a few crude structures in 1764, with St. Charles following suit in 1769. The rich Catholic heritage descending from those first missions, convents, and schools is still much in evidence.

Protestants came with the eastern pioneers. Saxon Lutherans found a haven in the gently rolling fields below Ste. Genevieve. Mormons settled at Independence in 1831. The Evangelical Synod, Reorganized Church of Latter-Day Saints, and Unity called Missouri home.

Later comers are the Vedanta Society, ecumenical centers, and shrines.

Thus the rainbow hues of many spiritual searchers have blossomed from one stalk into many flowers. Like those of early Creoles, our trip will begin by the Mississippi River gateway, south of the symbolic and stupendous Gateway Arch.

Eastern Missouri

(1) STE. GENEVIEVE

Ste. Genevieve Catholic Church

The oldest permanent settlement west of the Mississippi began when French miners struck lead in the ground around 1732-1735. The broad Mississippi carried settlers up from the French Gulf towns and soon Ste. Genevieve Catholic Church was there. Today's building is the third on this site and is far more elaborate than the first one, which was built in 1752. The present, 1880 church has religious paintings, however, that date from 1663, carried here by the French Catholics. The adjacent museum contains old documents, Indian relics, and Spanish land-grant documents.

Stepping outside, the traveler can walk down Market Street by Price Brick House, oldest brick building once used as a courthouse. On Second Street is the one-time Fur Trading Post, made of stone and containing displays and conveying atmosphere of days when furs were used as money. A block away are the Bolduc Houses, examples of early architecture. French costumes and cooking abound during *Jour de Fête* in August.

(2) ALTENBURG

Saxon Lutheran Memorial

Saxon immigrants, searching for opportunity in a new land, found the Mississippi valley below Ste. Genevieve ideal, and founded Frohana, Altenburg, and Wittenberg in 1839. With them came the Lutheran Church. The Saxon Lutheran Memorial, a museum that houses artifacts of the early era, is the oldest building known to be used as a parochial school. An old Spanish bell is a prized possession.

(3) DESOTO

Washington State Park

Missouri was well-populated with Indians when the French arrived and the concern of the religious was to help them with education and spiritual insight. Part of their own heritage is preserved in this 1,101-acre park, which was the site of prehistoric Indian ceremonials. Symbolic rock carvings called petroglyphs made between A.D. 1000 and 1600 can be seen in two locations. Pictures of birds, footprints, claws, humans, and arrows were used by chiefs as cues for ceremonial activities. Indian culture is explained and pictured in the museum.

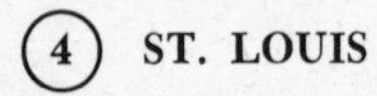

(4) ST. LOUIS

Old Cathedral

When this area was all wilderness, three missionary priests celebrated Mass under the trees in 1689. Explorers and traders tamed the forests and sailed the rivers until 1764, when St. Louis was settled. Even then the resident priest performed the first baptism "in a tent for want of a church." In 1770, at the insistence of townsfolk, a small chapel of vertical logs was set in Church Square. In 1835, the nun Philippine Duchesne opened an academy and free school.

The chapel's successor is the Basilica of St. Louis the King, originally a cathedral, which stands in the Jefferson National Expansion Memorial, under the famed Gateway Arch. Dedicated in 1834, the Old Cathedral was the first west of the Mississippi and was designated a Minor Basilica in 1961. The handsome Greek Revival building, restored in 1963, still ministers near the river front and has, downstairs, a museum of early history. Treasures include the original 1772 church bell, an 800-year-old Spanish crucifix, and paintings dating to the late 1700s.

Christ Church Cathedral

One of the first Protestant churches founded west of the Mississippi is to be seen at 13th and Locust streets. The Episcopal congregation with a long heritage does not look backward but has a new outlook. In the interior of the stone Gothic church recent renovation has provided a flexible arrangement of furniture to accommodate many forms of worship, including music and drama.

St. Louis Cathedral

Today Catholics worship in this magnificent Cathedral at 4439 Lindell Boulevard. The huge green dome, flanked by twin towers and two half-domes, is as much a landmark as Ero Saarinen's soaring stainless steel Gateway Arch. Begun in 1908 and consecrated in 1926, the church has the world's largest collection of Byzantine-style mosaics. Half the churches in the country could fit under its dome! Decorations are on Biblical themes and Catholicism's development in mid-America.

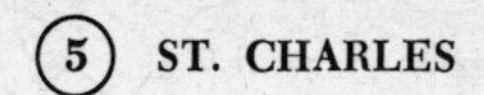

(5) ST. CHARLES

Shrine of Blessed Rose Philippine Duchesne

When the hunter Louis Blanchette built a log hut here in 1769, he probably didn't realize he was starting a town. A log church dedicated to St. Charles Borromeo was erected in 1791. The Duquette "mansion" was a log house on a stone foundation. The roof was of pegged shingles and construction did not give much insulation from the cold. A later brick addition created today's Sacred Heart Academy on Highway 94.

Mother Duchesne arrived 27 years later to open the first free day school west of the Mississippi. A dedicated, tireless worker, she was transferred to Florissant in 1819, and to St. Louis in 1827. She finally achieved her lifelong ambition to work with the Indians when at the age of 72 she helped establish an Indian Mission at Sugar Creek, Kansas. After her death in 1852, Mother Duchesne's body was interred in the cemetery. After she was made a saint in 1940, the Duchesne Memorial

Shrine was built nearby and her casket was placed in a handsome marble sarcophagus above ground level. A steady stream of pilgrims comes to the shrine of the Blessed Philippine.

(6) FLORISSANT

Old St. Ferdinand's Shrine

Florissant was an early French community on the Missouri River, east of St. Charles. Begun in 1786, it soon had a chapel and large house more suitable than convent quarters in St. Charles. A larger, permanent convent was immediately planned and Mother Duchesne's school in St. Charles moved en masse (chickens and cattle included) to Florissant. From these primitive beginnings developed a free school, small orphanage, short-lived academy for Indians, and a boarding academy. Here, too, was the first American novitiate of the Sacred Heart.

The brick St. Ferdinand's Church was built in 1821. The original 1819 convent is still standing, too, though with more additions. A historical museum unfolds many facets of the work which included ordination of world-famous missionary Father Pierre de Smet and the Indian Seminary begun by Jesuits in 1824.

(7) CREVE COEUR

Priory of St. Mary and St. Louis

A delicate flowerlike chapel stands off Route 244 east of St. Louis. The Benedictine abbey church is a white, circular structure made of thin-shelled concrete arches which rise like a triple-tiered fountain. The 40 lower-level arches have fiberglass windows which let in a soft light. The top tier creates a bell tower and a skylight over the central altar. Seating is circular with baptistry, confessionals, and side altars along the walls. This stunning building, winner of many awards, was dedicated in 1962. The entire campus, which includes a preparatory school, is set deftly into rolling wooded surroundings.

(8) EUREKA

Black Madonna Shrine

Southwest of St. Louis, off Route 44, is the Franciscan-maintained Black Madonna Shrine containing a galaxy of magnificent multicolored rock grottos, which took 22 years to construct. Local rocks, glass fragments, and costume jewelry are the materials used for the grottos and the outdoor Chapel of the Hills. It is named for Our Lady of Czestochowa, who is known as the Black Madonna.

(9) IRONTON

St. Paul's Episcopal Church

Episcopalians came late to the area, following Methodists and Presbyterians. In 1869, a handful of communicants organized St. Paul's Episcopal Church and began building plans. A Missouri guidebook described the 1870 structure as "sheathed in vertical boards to create the illusion of added height and whose pointed gables and tiny casement sashes represent the ultimate development of Gothic architecture in Missouri." The resultant gem with its many tiny towers and square steeple is a picture-book structure.

(10) FULTON

St. Mary Aldermanbury Church

On the Churchill Quadrangle on the Westminster College campus south of Interstate 70 is a much traveled church. One of London's war-ravaged buildings, it was chosen as a typical Christopher Wren church and moved to Fulton piece by piece. The enormous jigsaw puzzle was put together, rehallowed, and dedicated in 1966 as part of the Winston Churchill Memorial in the United States. In 1972, the memorial became the first foreign building to be placed on the National Historic Site Register. The church, which was designed by Wren in 1666, serves as a college chapel and ecumenical center. A museum filled with Churchill memorabilia and housing a research library devoted to Sir Winston's life and era is in a lower level. It was at Westminster in 1946 that Churchill delivered his "Sinews of Peace" speech in which he said, "If we adhere faithfully to the Charter of the United Nations and walk forward in sedate and sober strength seeking no one's land or treasure, seeking to lay no arbitrary control upon the thoughts of men . . . the high roads of the future will be clear, not only for us but for all, not only for our time, but for a century to come."

Western Missouri

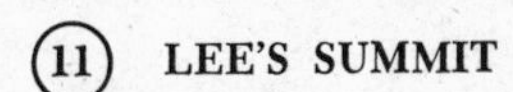

(11) LEE'S SUMMIT

Unity Village

A prayer tower dominates the landscape at this charming center of the Unity School of Christianity founded in 1889 in nearby Kansas City. According to the founder, Charles Fillmore, Unity is a religious philosophy with an "open end," seeking to "find God's truth in all of life." At the movement's heart is prayer. So for 80 years a prayer vigil has been kept. Now Silent Unity receives thousands of letters and calls for prayer. These are remembered in the vigils but especially at times in the day when Unity workers gather in the prayer room. Radio messages, a correspondence school, and about 500 local Unity centers reach out to the nation. Publications include *Unity* for adults and *Wee Wisdom* for children.

(12) INDEPENDENCE

Saints Auditorium

World Center of the Restoration is found at River and Walnut streets, where the Reorganized Church of Latter-Day Saints has its headquarters. Mormons came here from Kirtland, Ohio, in 1831, hoping to make this their permanent home. The printed word was always of great importance and soon the earliest printing press in western Missouri turned out *The Evening Star* and *The Morning Star*. An editorial on slavery inflamed others in the community and eventually the Saints were officially expelled and their leader, Joseph Smith, Jr., held in the Liberty jail. Finally a new settlement was made at Nauvoo, Illinois. After a similar hostile reception there, the congregation fragmented. Under the leadership of Joseph Smith III, the Reorganized Church of Jesus Christ Latter-Day Saints was formed at Independence.

This amazing auditorium, which covers a city block, has a conference chamber seating 6,000 and a splendid Aeolian-Skinner organ with 109 ranks and 6,000 pipes. Organ recitals are given daily in the summer. In other sections of the mammoth structure are the Laurel Club dining room, chapel, assembly room, museum, and offices. Here all phases of church work from religious education to world missions are planned. Though begun in 1926, the auditorium was not completed until

Saints Auditorium, Independence

1962. It is the first unit of a planned temple complex.

(13) LIBERTY

Historic Liberty Jail

Though *liberty* and *jail* do not seem synonymous, it was here that Joseph Smith, Jr., Mormon prophet, lost his liberty for four months. He and five others were held here during a bitter winter while controversy stormed around his church members in nearby Independence. Finally freed, he led his people to Nauvoo, Illinois. The jail, built in 1833, is now housed in a museum north of the city square. While Smith was jailed in 1838-1839, he is said to have received further prophetic revelations of divine doctrine.

(14) CONCEPTION

Conception Abbey

A Benedictine monastery founded in 1873 stands in the northwest corner of the state. The central feature is the Romanesque Basilica of the Immaculate Conception, with its murals of Beurinese art style. In 1940, it was made a Major Basilica in recognition of the monastery's efforts in furthering liturgical worship and Gregorian chant in the United States. A farm, a four-year college, the Printery House, and its hospitality for retreats form part of the many projects. The basilica was dedicated in 1891. The archives contain an unusual collection of records on mission work among the Sioux Indians.

KANSAS

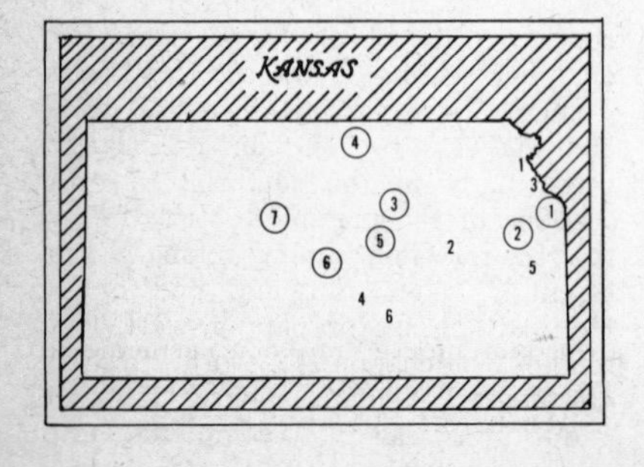

An Indian empire flourished in Kansas Territory until the early 1800s. It was occasionally visited by whites, beginning with Coronado in 1541 when he sought the "rumored wealth of Quivera." Not finding a treasure, Coronado never returned, but his accompanying Franciscan friar, Father Juan de Padilla, did. Touched by the vast numbers who had not heard the gospel, he returned in 1542 with a white man, a black, and two Mexican Indians to found a church. Later that year he was killed, becoming one of the country's earliest Christian martyrs.

French fur traders and Spanish explorers occasionally passed through until 1803, when the Louisiana Purchase gave ownership to the United States. Army personnel Capt. Zebulon Pike and Maj. Stephen Long, explored for the government but reported the area part of the "Great American Desert." In 1830, Congress set it aside as Indian land and moved many tribes here from the east. By that same year there were several trading posts.

Fort Leavenworth, established in 1827 for frontier defense, was the first community, followed by Fort Scott (1842) and Fort Riley (1853). Missionaries arrived to assist the burgeoning and harassed Indian population. Protestants and Catholics sent teaching clergy.

The land also harbored ethnic groups from Europe in the late 1800s. Swedish Lutherans settled in the Smoky Valley in 1881. Volga Germans came from Russia to plant six towns in 1876. Also, the Santa Fe and Oregon Trail led many "prairie schooners" through to the west.

Thus ancient and modern spiritual heritage sites can be seen on this prairie expanse, with the erection in recent years of the Meditation Chapel at Abilene as a memorial to the late president and general Dwight D. Eisenhower. Our tour begins on the eastern frontier, where so many of the residents entered.

Eastern Kansas

(1) KANSAS CITY

Shawnee Methodist Mission

Shawnee Methodist Mission was founded by Rev. Thomas Johnson in 1830. By agreement with the Methodist Church and the U.S. government, it was also the setting for a central manual-labor school, and construction began here on Shawnee land in 1939. Indian children of many tribes studied English, manual arts, and agriculture. At its height, the school had an enrollment of 200 boys and girls and had 2,000 acres with 16 buildings, including the three large brick structures that can be visited now. Among the many guests in this stopping point on the Santa Fe and Oregon Trail was Dr. Marcus Whitman, missionary to Oregon. The first Territorial Legislature met here in the East Building in 1855. The school was discontinued in 1862 and the 12 acres remaining were acquired by the state in 1927.

Sixty Indian children were in that first (1840) class. Spinning and weaving were taught the girls. A teacher of 1850 wrote she was much pleased with the accomplishments. "For many miles around you see neat farms and good dwelling occupied by red men." East Building was added in 1841 and North Building in 1845. Original furnishings and authentic reproductions bring back the flavor of those early years. Also on exhibit are historical items of the mission's early history.

(2) BALDWIN CITY

Baker University Library

On the grounds of Baker University (founded 1858) is a rare collection of Bibles. Bishop William A. Quale, once the president of the school, bequeathed his extensive collection which includes exquisite Bibles artistically illuminated by monks, two first editions of the King James version and several books printed before A.D. 1500. Also featured are a Nuremberg Chronicle, a medieval synagogue scroll, and cuneiform tablets written before the Christian era.

Central Kansas

(3) ABILENE

Eisenhower Center

The newest and most distinctive building in the Eisenhower Center at Abilene is the Place of Meditation, which is the former president's final resting place. It was designed to harmonize with the museum and library. A slender tower rises over the entrance of the limestone chapel. Inside are richly colored windows, Travertine wall panels, and walnut woodwork. Memorial pylons stand dramatically in front of the chapel.

REPUBLIC

Pawnee Indian Village Museum

The traveler leaves the present for the past as he journeys northwest almost to the state's border. A large round museum is built over the excavated base of a circular Pawnee earth lodge of the 1800s. Once 30 similar lodges comprised this village. The homes were dome-shaped and about 50 feet in diameter. They had timber framework, covered with saplings, thatch, grass, and sod. A central fire pit provided cooking facilities and warmth. Whetstones, knives, scrapers, and other artifacts lie where they were unearthed. A self-guiding tour explains the extensive village site. Artifacts explaining the tribe's culture and ceremonials are on view in the museum.

(5) LINDSBORG

Bethany College

Swedish immigrants from Varmland Province settled Lindsborg in 1869. Bethany Lutheran Church was immediately organized. In 1881, 60 singers from the community responded to a call to present *Messiah* by George Frederick Handel. For nine decades since, this glorious oratorio has been performed, and the town has been called "Oberammergau of the Plains." The college buildings have provided the setting, after a few years of performance in the Lutheran church.

Now about 400 singers present the annual Good Friday performance in the auditorium built in 1929 just for *Messiah*. On stage and in the audience 2,700 people can be seated in the acoustically perfect Presser Hall facility. Galli-Curci, Elman, Pablo Casals, and Lillian Nordica are some of the musical greats who have performed in the productions. The choir and noted singers like Marion Talley and Ernestine Schumann-Heink gave benefit performances to pay for the auditorium.

On the college campus is recently built Burnett Center for Religion and the Performing Arts, which contains Swenson Chapel, named for the Oratorio Society's founder. In the McPherson County Museum are a water-driven flour mill, an early schoolhouse, the first classroom of Bethany College used in 1881, and "Sweadal," the first U.S. Post Office. On odd-numbered years, in October, travelers can enjoy the *Hyllningsfest,* a celebration of Old World happenings.

6 LYONS

Padilla Cross

Northwest on Route 56 and 4 miles west of Lyons, is a huge stone cross honoring Father Juan de Padilla, the Franciscan friar who accompanied Coronado to Kansas in 1541. Together, they erected the first Christian cross in this land. Afterward, Father Padilla returned with four companions to found a church. Later he was killed, becoming one of the first Christian martyrs in the United States. It is not clear whether he was killed by enemies of the Indians to whom he ministered, or

whether he was killed because he was about to leave. In any event, his followers buried his body and returned to Mexico. He was the forerunner of many who came to preach to the Indians.

The stone cross was erected in 1950 and "denotes the four corners of the world brought to Christian unity" when Father Padilla carried the cross of Christianity into the center of the New World.

7 VICTORIA

St. Fidelis Church

Northwest of Lyons on Route 70 is one of the communities begun in 1860 by the Volga Germans who came here from Russia. One has an eerie feeling, riding along the super-highway over the great plains, on seeing on the horizon an enormous twin-towered cathedral. One is irresistibly drawn to turn a few blocks south and investigate the "Cathedral of the Plains." When the Germans fled Russian oppression and migrated here, they lived in sod huts and built a crude church.

From the beginning, however, they wanted a monument to God. Plans were drawn in 1905 and construction began in 1907. In the formidable process, each family hauled some of the 4,000 wagon-loads of stone from quarries 8 miles away. Day after day for four years there was a steady procession of wagons from the quarries. Then the people contributed their time and effort to hauling 4,000 loads of sand, donated by the farmer who owned the pit. Stone was hauled up the walls by wheelbarrows on sloping earth-ramps, and later by horse-operated hoist.

The interior was to be as beautiful as the exterior, so stained-glass windows and ornamental archway stone were imported. The Lutheran bishop of Concordia diocese officiated at the dedication in 1811. It is an amazing memorial to early pioneer zeal. Other towns founded by the Volga Germans are Catherine, Liebenthal, Munjor, Preifer, and Schoenchen.

The traveler is now not only in the center of Kansas, but also of North America. At Osborne is the official marker noting the geodetic center of the continent, on which all geodetic surveys are based.

OKLAHOMA

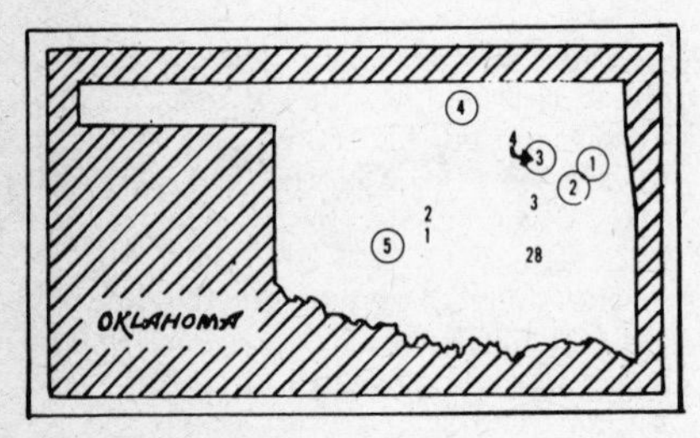

Nearly 100,000 Indians belonging to 65 tribes dwell in Oklahoma. This was the land of the red men by inheritance and also by adoption as the eastern tribes were relocated here, victims of white expansion. Though whites explored and hunted, the land remained Indian, even so confirmed by Act of Congress. Whites were kept out until 1889 when Congress opened negotiations with the Creek and Seminole nations. The resulting Oklahoma Territory was set aside from the Indian Territory and the two were separate and autonomous. The latter contained tribal nations within its bounds. In order to receive statehood in 1907, however, the Indian and Oklahoma governments came together. Today, of course, rich and poor, ballerinas and businessmen, as well as scholars and professional people, are found in the Indian population. The basic spiritual heritage, therefore, is Indian and is portrayed in its ceremonies. Most ancient is the 2,000-year-old Sacred Fire ritual of the Cherokees.

By contrast, the white man's religious institutions (more Protestant than Catholic) came late and are startlingly symbolic of tomorrow. The futuristic prayer tower at Oral Roberts University and the glowing chancel in St. Patrick Catholic Church in Oklahoma City are examples. The same contrast is on the land, where agriculture and oil wells exist together.

The journey across Oklahoma is an absorbing one because nowhere is the blend of ancient and modern more vivid. The four-story-high Ten Commandments of Tulsa's Temple Israel, joined to a sleek low contemporary wing, reflects the fact that these two worlds can live in harmony.

Our trip begins in the eastern part of the state with the ancients.

Eastern Oklahoma

(1) TAHLEQUAH

Tsa-La-Gi

Once this town in the Ozark foothills was the capital city of the Cherokee Indian Nation. Government buildings still standing are the supreme court buildings, erected in 1844; the capitol building, erected in 1867; and the 1879 national prison. The Cherokee Female Seminary now serves as the administration building of Northeastern State College. In the museum and library on campus are Indian artifacts and memorabilia.

The Cherokee Cultural Center (Tsa-La-Gi) is a re-creation of an early Cherokee settlement. It is authentically portrayed by today's Indians, who faithfully show what an Indian village in their first Georgia homeland was like before the whites came. Here too each summer *Trail of Tears,* the poignant tale of the forced march of the Cherokees from their homeland to the Oklahoma wilderness, is performed in an outdoor amphitheater.

The Cherokee National Museum records the high standard of civilization that existed among the Indians a century ago.

(2) MUSKOGEE

Five Civilized Tribes Museum

In the Federal Building is the agency of the Five Civilized Indian Tribes. It represents 60,000 Indians of the Cherokee, Chickasaw, Choctaw, Creek, and Seminole tribes who were forcibly moved from America's southern states in 1817 and 1840. A museum of Indian arts and crafts is on the campus of Bacone College.

At 1012 Honor Heights Drive, in the old 1875 Union Agency Building, is the Five Civilized Tribes Museum relating the culture and history of the tribes. Paintings and sculptures are outstanding, and there is a fine collection of jewelry, utensils, dress, instruments, and photographs. Newspapers, treaties, and documents reveal the negotiations with the government and the general historical picture.

(3) TULSA

Prayer Tower

On the campus of Oral Roberts University, a 200-foot glass-and-steel tower pierces the sky in the campus center. It symbolizes a 20th-century cross. The "crown of thorns" observation deck reaches out to a needy world.

The cross portrays the loving and healing hand of God reaching down to touch man's outstretched hand of need. The flame at the peak symbolizes man's dependence on the Holy Spirit for power to witness to Christ's redeeming love. An abundant-life mural, blending light, color, sculpture, and sound, may be seen on the ground floor. Two meditation rooms are on observation-deck level.

Tours begin at the Prayer Tower and lead to the academic hub of the 500-acre campus—the six-story triangular Learning Resource Center as well as other futuristic buildings. The unusual Mabee Center is an elliptical arena for indoor sports seating 10,000. The nonsectarian university, begun in 1962 by evangelist Oral Roberts, now has 2,400 full-time students representing over 40 denominations.

Central Oklahoma

(4) PONCA CITY

Ponca City Indian Museum

Here at the entrance of the Cherokee Strip, which was opened for white settlement in 1893, is a museum capturing the flavor of many tribes. Peyote ritual pieces, an Osage wedding costume, Kaw ceremonial dress, and kachina dolls are found in this wide-ranging collection. Special exhibits of present-day Indian arts and crafts are held regularly. The setting is a former governor's very elaborate home.

(5) ANADARKO

Indian City

A short distance east of Norman on Route 281, the traveler comes to Indian City. Once designated an Indian reservation, it still serves natives of the tristate area. In the Federal Building headquarters are artistic Kiowa murals. The American Indian Exposition is staged annually here in mid-August.

South on Route 8 is a re-creation of seven villages common to the Plains Indians. The Anthropology Department of the University of Oklahoma has supervised construction of teepees, grass homes, earth houses, and mud huts, showing the culture of the Kiowa, Caddo, Comanche, Wichita, Pawnee, Navaho, and Apache people. Ceremonials and crafts are featured as well as dances of the different tribes. Indians serve as guides. Designed as a vast outdoor museum, it is a reliable information source.

The national Hall of Fame for American Indians, Southern Plains Indian Museum and a Mormon information center are nearby.

VII.
THE OLD WEST

NORTH DAKOTA

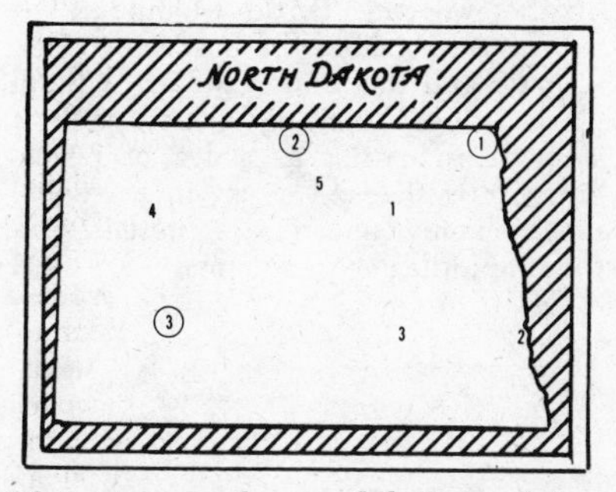

Glistening peaks, undulating plains, fertile prairies, rocky gorges, and arid desert can be found in the last frontier of America to be tamed. The Pilgrim village at Plymouth, Massachusetts, had celebrated its 200th anniversary by the time white men had planted settlements along these western trails and Indians were disturbed in their paradise.

Native sun dances, which reached back into prehistory, were the first religious observances. Then missionary "black robes" accompanying traders and Protestant homesteaders brought the Christian message.

French Canadians from the north were the first white men to penetrate the virgin forests, when Pierre Gaultier de Varennes reached a Hidatsa Indian town near the present Minot in 1738. Later he and his sons searched unsuccessfully for the Western Sea. Next comers were fur traders, also from the north, who traveled down the Red River valley in 1793. For the next 20 years, trappers wandered through the wilderness establishing short-lived trading posts and visiting with the natives.

Mandans, Chippewas, Hidatsas, Arikara, and Sioux are a few of the tribes they found. Many of their descendants still call this state home.

First home seekers were Scots Highlanders, also from the north. Thomas Douglas, the fifth Earl of Selkirk, had been given a large land grant by the Hudson's Bay Company, and the Highlanders settled at the present-day Winnipeg in 1812. Part of the company moved south and colonized on what they thought was British land. Instead, they began the North Dakota's oldest town, joining fur traders who put up a few buildings in 1797.

Thus the religious heritage is a mixture of Indian ceremonials, Protestant services, and Catholic rituals, with a strong Mormon influence. As in other states, the recent years have brought a religious melting pot, with ecumenicity more pronounced than in the earlier era.

We start in the northeast corner of the state, the gateway for trappers, explorers, and Highlanders.

Northern North Dakota

(1) PEMBINA

Pembina State Park

Bagpipes must have whined and kilts swirled as Scots Highlanders settled down in this border town, calling it Fort Daer. Charles Chaboillez of the North West Company already had built a few cabins for fur traders earlier in 1797. The town was considered a British territory until 1818, when the international boundary placed it in the United States.

The section of Pembina State Park which marks the site of the first homes is at the confluence of the Red and Pembina rivers and has a historical museum with exhibits on the explorations and pioneer days. Farther north on Route 129 is a marker noting the site of the first church and the school opened in 1818.

(2) BOTTINEAU

International Peace Gardens

Just north of Rugby on the international border are the beautiful International Peace Gardens commemorating the friendship between two countries and the longest unfortified border in the world. Since peace is a wish of religious people everywhere, the pilgrim will enjoy a visit to this over-2,000-acre tract in the wooded Turtle Mountains. A formal garden lines the border between Canada and the United States. A floral clock brings admiring glances and a stone cairn carries a pledge of peace. Since it is the site of an international music camp, concerts are presented in the amphitheater in summer.

Southern North Dakota

(3) RICHARDTON

Assumption Abbey

In the southwestern section of North Dakota, on Route 94, is a splendid old Gothic-Romanesque church called the Cathedral of the Prairies. It is part of the Benedictine monastery complex and has twin steeples with gray slate roofs and high burnished crosses. The early buildings, which were constructed by the monks between 1899 and 1909, form a quadrangle. The basic material is local clay, shaped into bricks and baked in a kiln. The complex includes high school, junior college, and a library which was built in 1942.

SOUTH DAKOTA

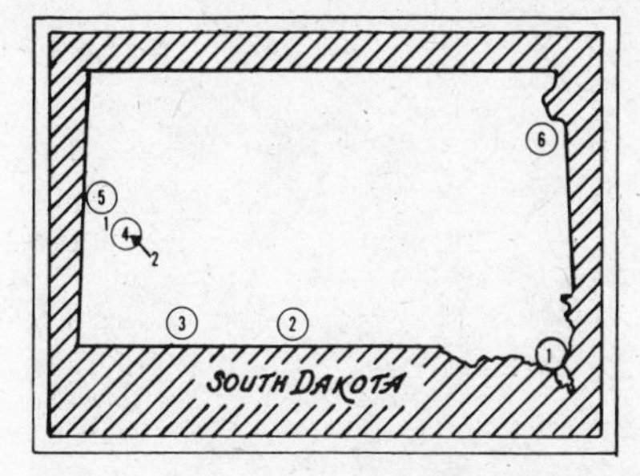

Children playing in a Pierre, South Dakota, schoolyard unexpectedly found evidence that the French Verendrye party traveled down the Missouri River in 1743. Historians had long looked for the marker described in the Verendrye's diary and which now may be seen at the South Dakota State Historical Museum.

The Missouri, which wanders diagonally north to south through the state, was the pathway for many early explorers, trappers, and missionaries through the land of the red men. Brula and Ogala Sioux, who migrated from the east, predominated with a smaller number of Arikaras occupying the northern section. Earliest missionary was probably Jesuit Father Pierre de Smet, who traveled to many Indian encampments.

The first settlement was at the present capital of Pierre, which began as Fort Teton in 1817 and was renamed Fort Pierre. Yankton followed in 1859 and Sioux Falls about 1857.

Spiritual heritage sites recall Indian ceremonials of long ago and today, as well as the amazing phenomena of the Messiah War and its Ghost Dance rites that precipitated the massacre at Wounded Knee. Catholics, with their missions, abbeys, and shrines, came with the white man, followed by Protestants with their churches and educational institutions.

Our tour begins in the south by the Missouri, that broad road of exploration.

Southern South Dakota

 VERMILLION

W. H. Over Dakota Museum

Sioux history and culture are featured in the museum of the University of South Dakota. Oscar Howe, well-known Sioux artist, has both his studio and his gallery here. Abstract paintings are based on Sioux life and culture. Here, too, is a replica of a Sioux Indian encampment. The pilgrim will be particularly interested, however, in the exhibit pertaining to the Sioux Ghost Dance, for here are visible reminders of a religion that swept Indian tribes around 1889.

Rumors of an Indian Messiah, who prophesied the obliteration of the non-Indians and the restoration of the old way of life, had trickled up to the Sioux. A delegation from Rosebud, Cheyenne River and Pine Ridge reservations journeyed to Pyramid Lake, Nevada, to hear details from Messiah Wovoka himself. Soon three disciples of the Messiah craze, or Wanagi Wacipi (Ghost Dance), vigorously spread the gospel and ceremonies taught by Wovoka. By October 1890, Sioux Indians here were openly dancing the Ghost Dance. Ceremonial objects of clothing and accouterments have been collected in the W. H. Over Dakota Museum.

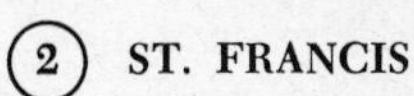 ST. FRANCIS

Buechel Memorial Sioux Indian Mission

Farther east of Vermillion, in the heart of the Rosebud Reservation, is a superior collection of Indian artifacts collected by Father Eugene Buechel,

Jesuit priest who served here for 50 years. The St. Francis Mission and School was begun in 1885 at the request of Spotted Tail, great chief of Brule Sioux. At the close of hostilities in 1890, the government had assigned a specific denomination to each reservation. Though Episcopalians had been assigned to Rosebud, Spotted Tail requested the "Great White Father in Washington" (Pres. Ulysses S. Grant) to send the Black Robes (Jesuits). So in December 1885, the first Jesuits arrived on the outskirts of the Indian Village of Owl Feather War Bonnet, which eventually became the Indian community of St. Francis. A school was immediately begun and by 1900 had a vast complex of buildings and more than 500 Indian boarding students. Father Buechel served here from 1902 until 1954, save for three intervening years.

St. Francis Jesuit Mission is still serving the Indians, realizing that each individual should best develop his God-given talents within his cultural heritage. Native language (Lakota), history, arts and crafts are offered, along with academic subjects, and Indian parents from the school board. At present 480 Sioux attend school, ranging from Head Start to high school. An impressive chapel is on the grounds.

In the museum are many items collected by Father Buechel (Black Eagle) as he traveled by horse and wagon to the Indian camps. He catalogued a woman's ghost shirt worn in the Ghost Dance by Mrs. "Crow Eagle" and other Ghost shirts with decorations for males and females. Also here is a ceremonial rattle of the Peyote Indian church which has the inscription: "The devil is my enemy but I trust in Jesus." Copies of his four books may be secured at the museum. They include a Lakota Bible history, a prayer book and hymnal, Lakota grammar, and Lakota dictionary.

(3) WOUNDED KNEE

Wounded Knee National Historical Massacre Site

Still farther east of St. Francis on the Pine Ridge Indian Reservation, is a memorial to the 129 Sioux Indians who fell victim to the U.S. Seventh Cavalry in December 1890. Chief Big Foot and about 400 Sioux were apprehended 5 miles northwest and escorted to Wounded Knee for the night. The military and settlers were quite apprehensive over the Ghost Dance craze, which included chanting a frenzied vision of deliverance from the yoke of the white man (which the whites thought was a war dance). At Wounded Knee, after a night of apprehension, a search for weapons was made and a shot rang out. A storm of gunfire followed that killed the defenseless Indian men, women, and children, including Chief Big Foot, and red power was broken.

(4) RAPID CITY

Chapel in the Hills

About the year 1948, Rev. Harry Gregerson began Lutheran Vespers, a program broadcast from his basement, which was eventually carried by more than 68 stations in 22 states. Then money was given for a meditation chapel and broadcast home in memory of Rev. and Mrs. Anton Dahl. A faithful reproduction was built on Route 40 of a Scandinavian *stavekirke* in Borgund, Norway, which dates to A.D. 1150. The Borgund church offered to furnish plans if an exact replica were built. The wooden chapel is accurate.

It even has the duplicate of a crack which has developed through the years in one of the columns of the original church. Much of the carving was actually done in Norway.

The traveler can stop for meditation and to see the amazing structure set in the Black Hills. Simulated prows of Viking longboats with dragonheads extend from the roof, and serpents and animals are depicted in interior carvings. St. Andrew's crosses form part of the roof structure.

(5) SPEARFISH

Black Hills Passion Play

West of Spearfish and almost to the state's border is the setting for portrayal of the last seven days of Christ's earthly life. Each summer the dramatic story is reenacted in 22 scenes, with Lookout Mountain as a backdrop for the open-air amphitheater. Oldest of the known Passion plays were by monks of Cappenberg Monastery in Germany in

1241. The annual Black Hills portrayal has followed the German tradition of families taking parts and training their children to succeed them. Joseph Meier, of the Black Hills production, is from Westphalia and his ancestors for generations have participated in the biblical drama.

In 1932, Meier, world-famous Christus player, presented the Passion in America, and in 1938 established its permanent home in Spearfish. He and the cast travel to Lake Wales, Florida, for performances each winter. The three-block-long, intricate stage is in keeping with the architecture of 2,000 years ago. Travelers will be well rewarded by stopping here long enough to see the Passion of Christ vividly and grippingly portrayed.

Northern South Dakota

6 MARVIN

Blue Cloud Abbey

Journeying east to the South Dakota border, the traveler comes to a Benedictine abbey named for a prominent Christian Sioux Indian. Dedicated in 1967, it is of contemporary design and built of sandstone. A granite mural of the Virgin is an unusual exterior decoration. The visitors' lounge has an abstract mural whose theme is the arrival of Benedictines to work with the Indians a century ago.

Monks have recently founded the American Indian Culture Research Center, which has an advisory service, library, and displays of Indian items that illustrate the culture.

MONTANA

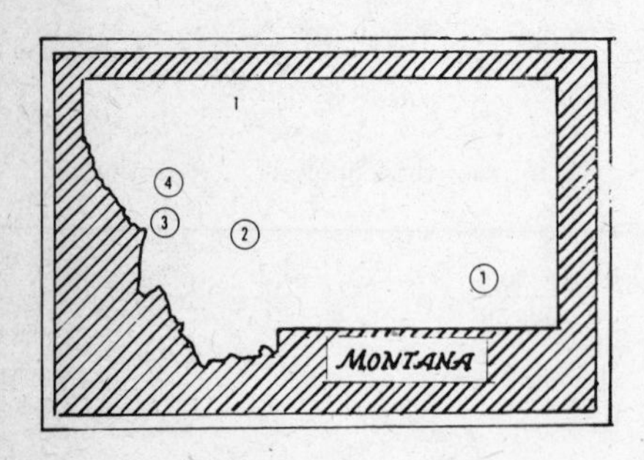

The persistent requests of the Salish (Flathead) Indians for "Black Robes" for their people and the committed response of a Belgian Jesuit missionary resulted in Montana's first town and an amicable meeting of the cultures.

Through Iroquois Indians who had wandered west, the Flatheads had heard of the Black Robes and the Great Spirit about whom they preached. Four times, beginning in 1831, the Flatheads sent delegates to St. Louis to request help. In 1839, they pleaded so well that Bishop Rosati, who had no missionaries to spare, sent a special request to Rome. Father Pierre de Smet offered himself to spread the word of God to the Indians and left on April 5, 1840.

Imagine his surprise on reaching Green River (Wyoming) June 30 to find a special guard of ten men sent by the Great Chief to welcome him. When de Smet and the young warriors reached the main body of the Flatheads, men, women, and children rushed to give him a triumphant reception. Old men openly wept and young men danced and shouted.

Instruction began immediately as the tribe moved slowly north to home ground. All showed eagerness to learn the prayers and please the Great Spirit.

Father de Smet established St. Mary's

Mission in 1841 near Stevensville in the Bitterroot valley, which was the first mission in the northwest and the state's first church. It also began the first permanent settlement, with Fort Benton following soon after (1846).

Thus Catholicism came to vast numbers of Indians who inhabited the state. These included Flathead, North Cheyenne, Crow Pigeon, and Sioux. The new prayers existed along with other ceremonials of the Indians, including the Sun Dance as well as the Sacred Hat and Arrow Renewal ceremonies.

Protestants came later and, by 1900, Methodists, Presbyterians, Episcopalians, and Baptists had arrived. Several established colleges.

Colonies of Hutterites, Plain People of the West, dot the Montana plains. Though the traveler probably won't see anything but their rolling rangeland and substantial buildings, it is well to know of their presence.

Three original colonies, founded in the 1870s in South Dakota, have now grown to 200 in several states, having a total population of 20,000. Thus they are the largest true communal group in the western world. Colonies are now farming in North and South Dakota and Canada, as well as in Montana.

Like the Mennonites and Old Order Amish, the Hutterites came from the Anabaptist tradition that originated in Europe in the 16th-century Protestant Reformation. Their name comes from Jacob Huter, a leader who died at the stake in 1536. Much persecuted for their pacifism and communal way, they drifted toward Russia and finally found a haven in America.

Hutterites believe their practice of Christian communism is in true harmony with the spirit and teachings of early Christianity. Each colony has a number of self-sufficient families who work the mammoth ranches. Children are educated in their own schools with a state-licensed teacher. Pastors are chosen from the members. Strict religious practices are observed.

A few of the colonies have contacts with other religious communities and share resources and food. When residents of Koinonia Farm were under siege in Americus, Georgia, in 1956 the Hutterites provided a restful respite for their frazzled nerves.

The German dialect and the Old World clothing will identify these Plain People, who are reported to be excellent and helpful neighbors.

We begin our trip in the land of the Big Sky in the east.

Eastern Montana

1 ASHLAND

St. Labre Indian School

On the Northern Cheyenne Indian Reservation, which is traversed by Route 212, is a Jesuit school ranging from a primary and day-care center to a high school and college. Many volunteers assist through the Jesuit Volunteer Corporation. Elders of the tribe act as resource people in the bilingual program which instructs in the Cheyenne language and culture.

The school paper reports that the council of 44 chiefs among the Cheyenne people is now active in preserving Indian ways and in assisting in meeting today's complex society. The annual Sun Dance is held in August at Lame Deer, North Cheyenne Tourist Center.

Western Montana

(2) HELENA

Cathedral of St. Helena

The traveler will find on Warren Street an impressive Gothic church which is modeled after the famous Votive Church of Vienna, Austria. The twin-spired limestone Cathedral of St. Helena was built by Roman Catholics in 1908. Over two dozen statues in niches outside and 56 Bavarian stained-glass windows create a marvelous effect. Massive pillars, decorated arches, and hand-forged bronze lights adorn the rich interior.

(3) STEVENSVILLE

St. Mary's Mission

Father Pierre de Smet built this log church, St. Mary's Mission, in 1841 with the help of Indian natives. The oldest section was the first mission in the northwest. Enlarged through the years, it now houses historical exhibits. A museum is nearby along with the original tiny mission cabin that held the first pharmacy and hospital in Montana. Now it, too, has pioneer artifacts of the region. The elongated building, with its white façade and tower, stands in the foothills of the spectacular Bitterroot Mountains.

(4) RONAN

St. Ignatius Mission

First home of St. Ignatius Mission was in Cusick, Washington, in 1844, when Father Pierre de Smet located it on the Pond d'Oreille River. Finally the Indians requested this location and the first log cabin, which still stands across from Holy Family Hospital, was begun here in 1854. Mass was said first in the open air, but soon a chapel, blacksmith shop, and carpenter shop were built and wigwams surrounded them. By the feast of Easter 1855, over 1,000 Indians of different tribes had arrived to make permanent homes. A boarding school began in 1863.

Fullest development was in the 1890s when 320 Indian children were in residence and Sisters of Providence and Ursuline nuns were assisting.

One of the most outstanding church buildings in the valley (and the third for the mission) was begun in 1891. The upper walls and ceiling of the brick church are decorated with magnificent murals by Jesuit J. Carignano, a self-taught artist. The original log church and many historical artifacts may be seen.

UTAH

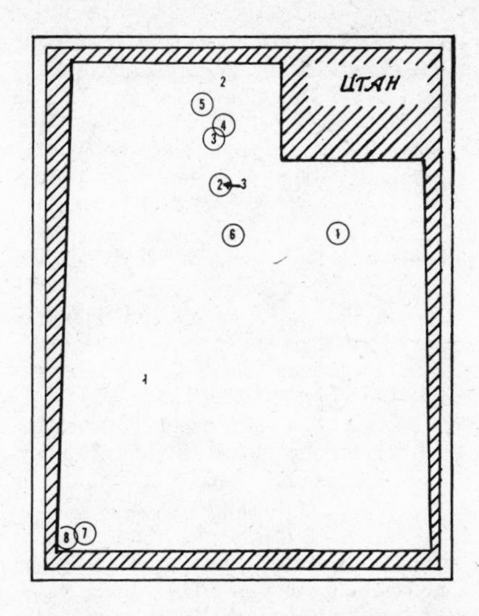

Mormons and Utah are almost synonymous in religious history, for it was here that members of the Church of Jesus Christ Latter-Day Saints fled after being driven from their homes in Nauvoo, Illinois. Brigham Young and 150 Saints reached what is now Salt Lake City in July 1847, seeking a new commonwealth outside the jurisdiction of the United States, where they could worship as they pleased. That September, 580 wagons brought 1,533 more religious refugees. Many had perished along the way.

Utah, Mexican territory then, was virgin land, inhabited by the Ute Indians and other tribes. The natives called their home Utah, "high in the mountains," because of its towering peaks and multicolored canyons. Explorers had been in the region since 1540. Two Franciscan Friars had traveled through in 1775-1776 and James Bridger had discovered the Great Salt Lake in 1825.

By 1849, citizens of the "State of Deseret," with Young as governor, had built a town and, through irrigation, had made "the desert bloom as a rose." Soon the Saints spread out to Ogden, Brigham City, and Provo. When Mormon explorers brought word of mineral wealth and semitropical sunshine in the south, 300 families founded St. George in the state's southwest corner in 1861.

At first, Indians and Mormons were the exclusive inhabitants. Then the United States secured the territory after the Mexican War, and the coming of the railroad and gold rush brought a constant stream of pioneers from the east. Statehood came in 1896; earlier applications had been denied, until the church took a stand against plural marriages.

Not long after the turn of the century, adherents of all major denominations had arrived. Today Protestant, Catholic, and Jewish citizens exist in a climate of tolerance. About two thirds of the present-day population are Mormons. Our visit begins in northeastern Utah with the very first inhabitants.

Northern Utah

 FORT DUCHESNE

Ute Indian Reservation

The Uintah, White River, and Uncompaghre tribes totaling about 1,600 natives call this million-acre Ute Indian Reservation their home. A large complex including a culture center, arts and crafts center, and tourist facilities is located at a 450-acre lake. The Ceremonial Bear Dance and the famous Sun Dances are performed. Many of the Indians are members of the Native American Church. Nearby Nine-Mile Canyon has Indian hieroglyphics and Uintah Canyon is the gateway to the High Uintah Primitive Area.

(2) SALT LAKE CITY

Temple Square

World headquarters for the Church of Jesus Christ Latter-Day Saints are found in this mammoth and striking 10-acre square in the heart of the city. With the Great Salt Lake on the northwest and the Wasatch Mountains and desert on other sides, the setting is outstanding. The traveler will find in the new Visitors' Center displays, murals, statues, and narrative exhibits of the history and doctrine of the church. Tours begin at the museum, which contains pioneer relics as well as artifacts of Indians, church history, and life in 19th-century America. Information can be secured here on the vast genealogical program with its cavern in the mountains for safe record-keeping.

Mormon Temple

The monumental Mormon Temple dominates Temple Square with its six spires and ornamented towers. The center tower on the east rises 210 feet and is capped by a gold-leaf statue of Angel Moroni, from the Book of Mormon. The temple is of granite and took 40 years to build. Completed in 1893, it is used for baptisms, marriages, and other sacred ordinances by church members and is not open to the public.

Tabernacle

The interesting dome-shaped Tabernacle is noted as home of the 375-member Tabernacle Choir, famed throughout the world. It is so acoustically perfect that a pin dropped near the pulpit can be heard 200 feet away. The Tabernacle seats 8,000 and the organ with its 11,000 pipes is one of the finest in the world. The dome is 250 by 150 feet, supported only by interlocking wooden arches. Since 1867, the building has sheltered semiannual conferences of the church. Visitors are welcome to the daily organ recitals and the choir rehearsals and broadcasts.

Temple Square, Salt Lake City, Air View

Beehive House

A Colonial-style house at 67 East Temple Street was completed in 1854 by Brigham Young and was his official residence as president of the church from 1855 to 1918. A carved wooden beehive atop the cupola is a symbol of both the state and the Mormon emphasis on work. Many of Young's family possessions are here along with his offices, sitting room, and the ceremonial long hall.

Cathedral of the Madeleine

Also on East Temple Street one can find a representative of one of the religious minorities in Utah. The elegant Roman Catholic Cathedral is filled with works of art. The cornerstone was laid in 1900 and completion date was 1909. Over the main entrance are carvings of Christ and the 12 apostles. German stained-glass windows are intricate in detail. Over the altar are murals of the Holy Trinity and saints of both the Old and New Testaments. Other carvings and fine paintings adorn the large edifice.

(3) OGDEN

Tabernacle Square

A few miles north of Salt Lake City, on Route 81, is the second largest city in Utah, settled by Mormons soon after they began in Salt Lake City. In the central square is the Miles Goodyear cabin built in 1846. It contains, in the pioneer relic hall, costumes, pictures, furnishings, and handcrafts of the early era.

The white-steepled Tabernacle is in the square, too. Also in the downtown area is the Ogden Temple, one of 16 throughout the world. It has a strikingly modern design. The gleaming white cast-stone structure, its slender spire rising 185 feet, is a picturesque landmark. It was dedicated in 1972.

(4) HUNTSVILLE

Abbey of the Holy Trinity

Northwest of Ogden on a peaceful plain surrounded by rugged mountains is a Roman Catholic abbey founded in 1947. Its appearance is unusual, for it is constructed of interconnected Quonset-type buildings. The monks are of the Cistercian Order, which was a 12th-century reform movement within the Benedictine family. From the beginning Cistercian monasteries have been ordered in solitude, oriented toward contemplative prayer and manual labor. The loving search for God through a life of prayer is the heart of a monk's daily life and the bond that fuses the men into a single community of brothers. The monastic day includes communal and private prayer, spiritual reading, courses in the sacred sciences, and productive labor on the farm or in small industries. The monks remain in loving solidarity to the world, sensitive to all its pains and problems.

Some of the results of their labors on the farm may be purchased by visitors. Inquire at the gatehouse for honey, cheese, and stone-ground flour. The chapel may be seen also, but women are not allowed on the grounds beyond it.

(5) BRIGHAM CITY

Box Elder Tabernacle

Continuing northwest, the traveler comes to another-Mormon-settled community, begun in 1851. One of their more unusual looking tabernacles is found at Second and Main streets. Gray-flecked stone, red vertical buttresses topped with white spires, and a central white tower make an interesting blend of Gothic and Neo-Classical design. The first church, built in 1890, was destroyed by fire in 1896. Because of the sturdy construction by the early pioneers the walls still stood. Before the fateful day was over, pledges and donations were pouring in and plans were begun to rebuild. The present

building resulted, with dedication in 1897.

The interior has a majestic Reuter organ and "acoustics like a violin box." Music is a medium of worship, prayer, adoration, praise, and thanksgiving in the Latter-Day Saints church services, so it is always a major concern in building plans. Tours are scheduled daily each summer, for tabernacles, unlike temples, are open for viewing.

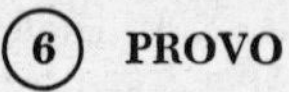

6 PROVO

Provo Stakes Tabernacle

Our way next leads south again below Salt Lake City to a community on Utah Lake. Mormons came to this fertile valley by the Provo River in 1849 to establish a farming and industrial community. Provo Canyon and 12,000-foot Mt. Timpanogos are lovely enough to take people's minds from their work! Here on a beautifully landscaped campus is Brigham Young University, founded in 1875 by the Mormon Church. Three of its museums as well as the art center can be viewed.

At 90 South University Avenue is one of the largest of the Mormon churches. The red-brick building with twin octagonal towers was finished in 1898. As in all of the tabernacles, music is an important element and it was built to provide excellent concert facilities. Many musical greats including Sergei Rachmaninoff and Fritz Kreisler have performed there.

Southern Utah

7 ST. GEORGE

St. George Temple

The Mormons needed cotton and word came that it could be grown in the very southern part of Utah. So Brigham Young called for 28 families in 1857 to establish a "cotton mission." Soon the first crop was harvested, raised from one jar of seed. The successful Saints were joined by 300 more in 1861 and St. George came into existence. Since wood was scarce, they built their town of stone.

In addition to a tabernacle and a courthouse, they raised the gleaming-white St. George Temple. As it stands high above the town, it is reminiscent of an elaborate wedding cake. It was completed in 1877, thus becoming the oldest temple west of the Mississippi. A renovation in 1937–1938 of grounds and building was in keeping with the slogan, "Our Church Buildings Shall be Beautiful." Though the building itself is open only to Mormons, the Visitors' Center has a movie of the interior and the ceremonies that are performed.

8 SANTA CLARA

Jacob Hamlin Home State Historic Site

Probably the best known of the Mormon missionaries was Jacob Hamlin, who spent most of his life preaching among the Piute, Navajo, and Hopi

nations of southern Utah and Arizona. No doubt it was because of him that peace was kept between them and the Mormons. The commodious two-story stone home northwest of St. George was built by Hamlin for his family in 1864. Though he worked along with 22 other Mormon missionaries, he especially was known as the white man whom the Indians could trust. His home is maintained by the state as a reminder of his dedicated life.

COLORADO

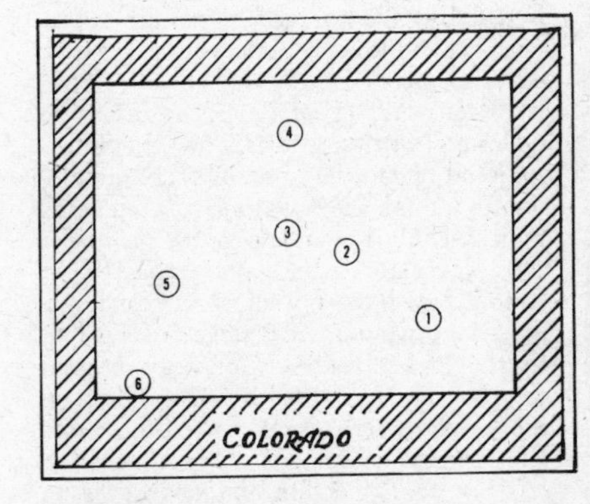

The gold bonanza discovered in 1898 in the front range of the Rockies brought a great stampede of men and wagons to "Pike's Peak" country. In one year (1859), Denver, Golden, Central City, Black Hawk, Mount Vernon, and Nevada City were founded. Word of fabulous lodes enticed thousands more in the 1860s to this rich, rough territory of peaks and plains.

Spanish and American explorers had traveled through earlier. Trappers and hunters had carved out transient trading posts in the forests. Only the natives in the southern section were true inhabitants in the pregold days. Ruined pueblos and cliff dwellings were abodes of the vanished Anasazi. Ouray, Great Chief of the Utes, held sway in the south.

In 1876, the year of the United States Centennial, Colorado became a state. In the century since, a complex society has developed. Most of the populace (80%) resides in the eastern plains at the foot of the Rockies.

Spiritual heritage sites begin with the ancient Anasazi kivas and later native Ute ceremonials. Protestant and Catholic congregations were formed with the stampede west. The Colorado Council of Churches in Denver now has nine major Protestant denominations cooperating. Recent pilgrimage sites include the newly developed forms of mission like Young Life and the Navigators, as well as conference centers of the Young Men's Christian Association and the United Church of Christ. These many religious organisms blend into a harmonious whole in this state of amazing physical contrasts, where white-blanketed mountains 2½ miles high and sky piercing red rocks in the Garden of the Gods point to the awesome power of the Creator.

Eastern Colorado

1 LA JUNTA

Koshare Indian Kiva

Near Colorado's south-central border on Route 50 may be found a present-day tribute to the ancient Indian civilizations. The Koshare Indian Museum is staffed by Boy Scouts, who each summer give exhibitions of authentic American Indian dances. The museum was built in 1933, designed after Indian ceremonial kivas of the southwest. Dances are performed within the facsimile of the Great Kiva, with the audience seated in tiers around the edge. Since the Koshares have dedicated their museum to the Indian as an artist, they have acquired a vast collection of baskets, pottery, jewelry, blankets, and paintings, as well as bead and quill work.

COLORADO SPRINGS

Garden of the Gods

One of the greatest thrills in traveling over the western plains is suddenly to see the snow-capped Rockies ringing the far horizon. But this thrill is further compounded when the traveler finds his way to the wonderland of red rocks of every conceivable shape. Helen Hunt Jackson said they were "all motionless and silent, with a strange look of having been stopped . . . in the very climax of some supernatural catastrophe."

In ancient days this area was a tribal meeting place of Indians, who called it the Old Red Land. Today it is one of the more spectacular settings of an annual Easter sunrise service. Begun in 1921, the service includes the *Resurrection Pantomime,* choral selections, and a featured message. The ruddy stone amphitheater has magnificent snow-capped Pike's Peak as a backdrop.

Other sights on the Ridge Road are Cathedral Rocks, Montezuma's Temple, and the observation deck where a 360-mile panoramic view of red rocks and snowy mountains may be seen through a giant camera.

Glen Eyrie Castle

Set in the Garden of the Gods terrain is a 1,100-acre rugged mountain estate with 21 buildings, including a massive 67-room castle. Built in the late 1800s by Gen. W. J. Palmer, founder of Colorado Springs, it is now the international headquarters of the nondenominational Navigators. Influencing men for Christ in the navy has been the Navigators' goal since the 1930s. Later they have branched out to reach men and women in colleges as well as in the armed forces. Countries around the world ask for Navigator-trained men, who work on a one-to-one relationship. When one catches the vision of the Christian life, he or she is to win another. Converts are urged to join local churches but to be faithful to prayer and Bible study. Thus the Glen Eyrie estate was needed for training, for conferences, as well as for offices. Thousands are enrolled each year in the Scripture Memory Correspondence Course. Bible study materials are sent from here to all 50 states and to over 30 foreign countries. An office staff of 68 and a castle staff of 37 regulars and trainees oversee this vital Christian program.

The spectacular drive up the canyon through towering red cliffs leads to the castle, perched at the narrow end. Visitors are taken on tour through the medieval-type rooms and rest in the mammoth audience hall with its huge fireplace to hear the Navigators' story. Pamphlets and books are available and a friendly welcome awaits all who stop by. It is well to call ahead for the tour schedule.

Young Life

At 720 West Monument Street is the international headquarters of Young Life, one of the fast-growing nondenominational missions to youth. It began in 1938 when a Presbyterian minister in Texas challenged his seminary assistant to reach disinterested high-schoolers. In the following weeks, James Rayburn learned that club meetings were the format, and that week nights and home locations were best. He reached out with genuine friendliness and the message of Jesus Christ. In 1941, the resulting organization was incorporated as Young Life.

From this contemporary office structure assistance goes to over 600 regional directors and local staff members in 200 cities and four overseas locations. They seek to penetrate the teenage culture and communicate the Christian faith by word and example. Workers cooperate with local churches and seek the unchurched youth. In addition to clubs, there are youth summer programs at Star, Silver Cliff, and Frontier Ranches in Colorado as well as at Malibu Club, Castaway Club, Woodleaf, Saranac Village, and Windy Gap in other parts of the country. Visitors to the home office will find a warm welcome and much information.

Air Force Academy Cadet Chapel

About 10 miles north of Colorado Springs is the newest of the country's service schools. It is located on 18,000 acres with a breathtaking backdrop of the Rocky's Rampart Range. From South Overlook on Pine Drive, one sees the spectacular Cadet Chapel, completed in 1963. "It is at once old and new, physical and spiritual, solid and

Cadet Chapel, U.S. Air Force Academy

Protestant Altar, USAF

Jewish Synagogue, USAF

Catholic Nave, USAF

soaring, of the earth and of outer space," commented a magazine of the structure whose 17 silvery spires soar 150 feet toward the Colorado skies. It is the crowning architectural feature of the campus and it symbolizes the religious aspect of life as well as providing chapels for the major faiths.

As the traveler enters, he is overwhelmed by the multicolored shafts of light flooding in from the stained-glass windows which are placed between silvery tetrahedrons. A 46-foot silver cross hangs suspended from the roof peak over the Holy Table, which is a marble slab 15 feet long. The Catholic Chapel has a sculpture of Our Lady of the Skies and the Guardian Angel on an 18- by 45-foot reredos, in the chancel. Background is an abstract portrayal of the firmament constructed of Venetian glass tessera in varying shades of blue, turquoise, rose, and gray. Above the figures hovers a spread-winged dove, symbol of the Holy Spirit. Stations of the cross are of white marble set in side panels of amber glass.

The Jewish Chapel is circular, enclosed in cyprus stanchions separated by translucent pebble glass. The focal point is the Holy Ark which shelters the Torah. The foyer is paved with Jerusalem brownstone, a donation from the Israeli Defense Forces.

If the visitor is here at noontime during the school year, he can see the Noon Meal Formation from the Court of Honor. On Saturdays there are cadet parades. The Air Force Museum is an intriguing place to browse.

(3) FAIR PLAY

Sheldon Jackson Memorial Chapel

A small frame Gothic chapel was built at Sixth and Hathaway streets in 1874

YMCA of the Rockies

by Dr. Sheldon Jackson, noted Presbyterian missionary. Only 5 feet high, Dr. Jackson was possessed of indomitable energy, tremendous faith, and exceptional ability as an organizer. He worked in home missionary activities between the Mississippi and the Rockies, then spent 25 years in Alaska. The missionary worked here for a time with the gold miners. Though not architecturally designed, it is a gem and a favorite subject for artists and photographers.

(4) ESTES PARK

YMCA of the Rockies

Northwest of Denver on U.S. 24 is a conference center and family vacation spot in Christian atmosphere. The Colorado Young Men's Christian Association acquired Wind River Lodge in Glacier Basin near Longs Peak and established the Estes Park Center. About 100 rustic structures have been built through the years to accommodate families and conferences for religious, educational, and recreational activities. Corral Camp, Pioneer Camp, Buckaroos, and Rangers accommodate the young fry, while Alpen Inn, Mt. Ypsilon Lodge, and Friendship Lodge house others. Hyde Memorial Chapel, known as "The Church of the Rockies," provides worship services each summer. Underneath is Dannen Chapel for smaller functions. A book store has ample browsing material. Miles of pleasant drives produce outstanding views. Winter holidays bring guests, too, at this year-round facility in the heart of the Rockies.

Southwestern Colorado

(5) MONTROSE

Ute Indian Museum

Our trip takes us into the southwest to visit the land of the Utes. There are now about 1,800 living on two reservations. At this museum on U.S. 550 are exhibits, dioramas, and information about the tribal history. A monument marks the burial place of Great Chief Ouray and his wife Chipeta, who endeavored to keep the peace between the white man and their people.

(6) CORTEZ

Mesa Verde Sun Temple

East of town on Route 160 are the incredible remains of an Indian civilization that existed from about A.D. 400 to 1276. During the later two centuries, hundreds of pueblo homes were clustered on mesa tops and in the caves. Discovered in the 1800s, the ruins are now preserved in the 52,073-acre national park established in 1906.

As travelers follow the entrance road, they see ahead a high mesa "green table" rising over the surrounding country. After stopping at the overlooks, travelers will reach the Visitors' Center where maps may be secured and tours arranged. The very fine museum, explaining the area, is probably the next stop.

It is an experience to climb through the intricate cliff dwellings, noting especially the kivas, ceremonial chambers entered by ladder through the ceilings. Visitors must be sure to see the Sun Temple near Cliff Palace on the mesa top. The Indians were apparently working on this large ceremonial building when the drought struck in 1276, and they abandoned the work before it was finished. Climb on top of the low walls, which have been reinforced, to see the building plan. The 131- by 64-foot ruin has 3-foot thick walls and is "D"-shaped. The three larger circular rooms are kivas, we are assured by modern-day Pueblo Indians who confirm its ceremonial use.

When darkness falls, travel down a

Mesa Verde Sun Temple

nature path from the campground to the outdoor amphitheater. Each night a ranger tells of the long ago and sometimes Navajo Indians perform authentic dances. It is not hard, as one sits by the firelight, with the moon overhead and the forest sighing, to lose eight centuries.

NEBRASKA

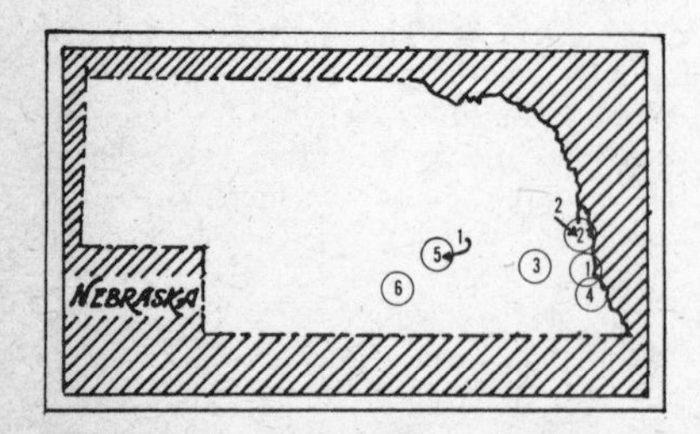

When Maj. Stephen Long followed the Platte and North Platte rivers across the state in 1819, his despairing report of the semiarid buffalo plain led to the myth of the Great American Desert. Hence, a few traders living in lonely trading posts continued to be the only inhabitants along with the many subtribes of the Sioux, Pawnee, and Cheyenne Indians.

Bellevue, a Missouri River town, is considered to be the oldest continuously inhabited white settlement in Nebraska. John Jacob Astor's American Fur Company established it about 1820.

When pioneers' wagons began rumbling through to the west, Nebraska became a corridor, with an ever increasing tide of humanity traversing the Oregon, Mormon, and Overland trails. Missionaries followed to start new white churches and Christianize the Indians. Some estimate that over 350,000 people had passed through the state by 1866.

At first Indians and whites dwelt peaceably together. When it became obvious that some pioneers had realized the potential of the undulating prairie and were going to remain, the Indians were alarmed. The Pawnees had a bloodless confrontation in 1859. Sioux and Cheyenne, however, waged endless war. After the death of Chief Crazy Horse in 1877, bloodshed ceased and most natives left for reservations in other states.

Spiritual heritage sites, then, are mostly recent and are Protestant and Catholic, since both were here in force by the late 1800s.

Eastern Nebraska

(1) BELLEVUE

Old Presbyterian Church

First church in Nebraska territory was built in 1855–1856 and can be seen at 20th and Franklin streets. The edifice was constructed of rubble stone and grout mixture and is of Greek style with Italian influences. Original pews, handmade by an elder, may still be seen along with valuable stained-glass windows. The piano, built in 1850, was brought by steam ferry by a wealthy fur trader. A tornado took the steeple in 1908, and it was replaced when the edifice was restored in 1974. Until recently it housed a Presbyterian congregation. It also was the first meeting place in 1883 for Bellevue College.

(2) OMAHA

St. Cecilia's Cathedral

Twin towers rising high over Omaha at 40th and Burt streets mark the headquarters of the Roman Catholic Archdiocese of Omaha. Unusual and original art treasures are contained in St. Cecilia's Cathedral, which was begun in 1905 and completed in 1955. Over 50 stained-glass windows range from 16th-century imported originals to contemporary style. Nine kinds of marble have been incorporated into the structure of Spanish architecture with its baroque scrolls and massive buttresses. Above the main altar of Cararra marble is an original 6-foot crucifix, with Christ looking up to pray, "Father, forgive them for they know not what they do," rather than a Christ looking down in grief and suffering, as most portray. Still higher on the curving surface of the half dome is a painting of Cecilia, patron saint.

In the Lady of Nebraska Chapel there is an original statue of the Blessed Virgin Mary holding a stalk and ear of corn, as patroness of Nebraska. Stations of the cross in the main sanctuary are done in exquisite bronze medallions.

Boys Town

The traveler now turns west on U.S. 6 to Boys Town, a "city of little men." Rev. Edward Flanagan, Roman Catholic priest, established the first home in 1917 when he discovered several homeless boys. The present location, now comprising 1,645 acres, was secured in 1921 as many more boys needed homes. Though originated by a Catholic, the home is nonsectarian and presently a Lutheran and a Methodist are serving also as chaplains. More than half of the 500 boys are non-Catholics. Boys Town is typical of many similar social agencies founded by churches.

The lovely Gothic stone Dowd Memorial Chapel is the place of Catholic worship and is the resting place of Boys Town's founder. The Nativity

Boys Town, Air View

Chapel at the Field House is the place for Protestant service. Jewish youngsters attend a synagogue in Omaha.

Probably the most famous activity is the choir, which has just finished its 29th concert tour, singing in 40 cities within 22 states. Tours begin at the Visitors' Center where a cafeteria and museum are available to guests. On leaving, pause a moment at the poignant statue of a boy carrying his sleeping younger brother. "He ain't heavy, Father, he's my brother," probably wraps up the Boys Town philosophy, which has helped over 13,000 of its citizens.

(3) LINCOLN

First–Plymouth Congregational Church

Next stop on the eastern tour is south in the capital city, Lincoln. Six members organized First Congregational Church in 1866 when the town consisted of only seven buildings. Growth in town was such that in 1887 Plymouth Church was organized. In 1923, these two congregations merged. The contemporary church, which reflects the pioneer spirit of the plains, was dedicated in 1931. Entrance is through a spacious forecourt, with the parish house forming part of the enclosure. A tower with 20 sides stands 171 feet high and has a carillon of 48 bells, cast in England. It reminds one that this is grain country and many tall silos store this treasure.

The interior is basilical, with plenty of light. The ceiling is marine blue, with stars in constellations. Over the chancel, the stars are arranged as they were at the time of the nativity. The Star of Bethlehem is directly over the pulpit. The Southern Cross is at the southern end, and constellations familiar to readers of Psalms appear elsewhere on the valuted ceiling. In the floor of the sanctuary, between the pulpit and the lecturn, is a stone from Bethlehem.

Visitors will want to see this structure from many angles, then step into the forecourt to look at the Pilgrim Stone, which represents the beginnings of Congregationalism and which was a gift from Plymouth, England. The Martin Luther Stone was taken from his birthplace in Eisleben and given as a reminder of the beginning of Protestantism.

(4) NEBRASKA CITY

St. Mary's Church

Turning east on Route 2, we complete our tour of this section with a stop at the oldest Episcopal parish in Nebraska. It was organized by Rev. Eli Adams, who came to this community in 1857. The lovely English Gothic St. Mary's Church is a reminder of the country where the roots of this denomination began. Memorial windows are particularly beautiful.

Central Nebraska

(5) GRAND ISLAND

Stuhr Museum of the Prairie

Just off Route 80 proceeding westward, the traveler will come on a shining, white, flat-topped building which seems to float on a lake. The Stuhr Museum of the Prairie, designed in contemporary idiom by Edward Durell Stone, by contrast is filled with relics of pioneer days. Outside on the 267-acre tract is an outdoor museum consisting of over 55 buildings which have been moved here. A western-style Main Street, old depot, post office, and blacksmith shop take the traveler back to the days when the state was young.

The Danish Lutheran Church, built in 1888, sits somewhat apart from the other buildings. It is white frame and of country-Gothic design. The entrance is through a tower, whose striped steeple is unique.

(6) MINDEN

Harold Warp Pioneer Village

Another of the reminders of bygone days is found southwest of Grand Island on Route 6. America's progress since 1830 is shown on the 20-acre site of Harold Warp Pioneer Village. Authenticity is the village's pride, whether in prairie schooners, Duryea autos, wood-burning locomotives, or antique vacuum cleaners. Over 30,000 items can be seen, ranging from paintings to planes. Of special interest is an old log, mud-chinked fort prepared for Indian raids.

The little Lutheran church was used from 1884 to 1950 in Minden and became the chapel of the village when the congregation built a larger church. It is a white-frame building with tower entrance. The interior is quite elaborate with a circular apse over a Gothic altar.

WYOMING

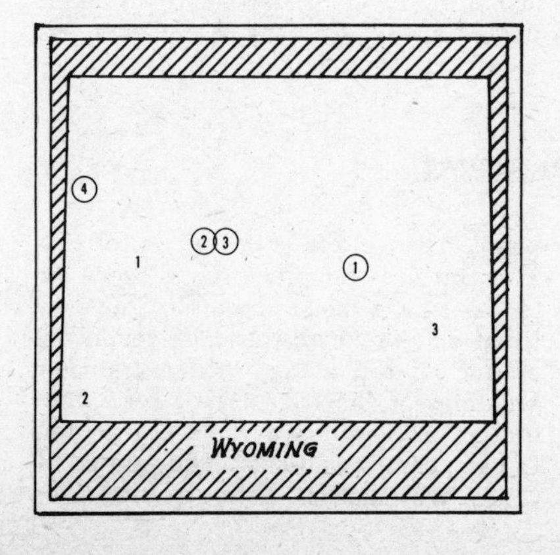

High, wide, and windy, Wyoming has been called—and so it must have seemed to those first explorers, traders, missionaries, and pioneers when they covered the vast grasslands and saw the high peaks of the Tetons. This last frontier of the United States was a passageway for many following the Oregon Trail west. The multitudinous pioneer wagons left marks 5 feet deep in the limestone that can still be seen today at Guernsey. Proof of the number of travelers is at Independence Rock, that "Great Record of the Desert" that rises 193 feet and covers 27 acres. On it thousands of travelers have inscribed their names, including many who followed the Oregon Trail.

Settlement began with the trading posts and increased rapidly when the railroad came. Fort Laramie, the first permanent white town, began as the trading post Fort William in 1834. Such was the population explosion that when Cheyenne was settled in 1867, by the end of that year it had 6,000 inhabitants.

The sudden influx of whites was a blow to the Indians, who saw their lands melting away. They battled intermittently between several treaties. By 1880, all the tribes had been removed except the Shoshone and Arapaho. Statehood came in 1890.

Jesuit Father Pierre de Smet is credited with saying the first Mass in Wyoming Territory when he came from St. Louis to minister to the Flathead tribes. A delegation of braves met the "black robe" (Jesuit) Father de Smet and held a service "under a lodge of buffalo hides." The Green River site has a historic marker.

Episcopalians sent missionaries and Mormons pased through to their Promised Land. The Christian Church, with headquarters at Dayton, Ohio, had a brief impact when it established Jirah College and Christian Community on homestead land in 1909. For ten years higher education was available to the youth from the lonesome sagebrush prairie before lack of funds canceled out the community.

Present-day steeples of all major denominations point heavenward amid religious rites, like the Sun Dance, that extend back into prehistory.

Eastern Wyoming

1 CASPER

Natrona County Pioneer Museum

After a side trip to see the ruts of prairie schooners that still scar the limestone plain, the traveler should continue west to the fairgrounds at Casper. Here, in a church built in 1891, is a museum of pioneer artifacts that portray the lives of the homesteaders. Many settled in sod huts and used most primitive utensils and tools.

After browsing among the exhibits, the traveler might like to take a side trip a few miles southwest to see that monolith of the desert, Independence Rock, where so many early travelers inscribed their names.

Western Wyoming

2 FORT WASHAKIE

Wind River Indian Reservation

East of the Continental Divide is the reservation of the Shoshone and Arapaho tribes. The 70- by 55-mile tract was set aside in 1869 when the celebrated Chief Washakie helped his people keep peace with the white man. The traveler can proceed up Route 28 to the agency headquarters of the new tribal offices, where there are reminders of the old fort along with several new buildings of the tribe. Maps for camping and exploring may be secured from Indian game wardens. The grave of Chief Washakie is here. In the Shoshone Cemetery also is the grave of Sacajawea, girl guide of the Lewis and Clark expedition, who spent her last years on the reservation.

Sightseers will enjoy the scenic drives and panoramic views. Traditional Indian dancing can be seen nightly during the summer months at nearby Lander and Riverton. Arapahos hold a Powwow in July and in August. Annual Sun Dances are held at Fort Washakie and Ethete in July. The Sun Dance is a ritual lasting 72 hours, during which the dancers eat no food and drink no water. Prayers chanted to the Supreme Being are sent on the rays of the Sun. Partakers do so for various reasons, including healing of disease, thanksgiving, repentence, forgiveness of sins, and spiritual resurrection.

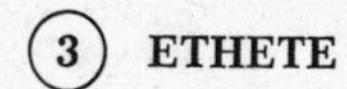

(3) ETHETE

St. Michael's Mission

The Episcopal St. Michael's Mission was established as a church and school for the northern Arapaho tribe in 1913. Several buildings include not only educational facilities but boarding homes for the young people. An exciting recent addition is the Wyoming Indian High School, which was made possible by a grant from the Bureau of Indian Affairs to the Wind River Education Association.

The log church is the oldest building in the mission complex. It is decorated with Indian symbols. The clear-glass chancel wall gives a view of the Wind River Mountains.

(4) MOOSE

Church of the Transfiguration

After leaving the nature's paradise of the Indians, continue northwest to discover more of Wyoming's grandeur. Before entering Grand Teton National Park, stop a moment at the tiny dark-brown log Episcopal chapel that nestles on a low plain at the foot of the Teton Range. The rustic house of worship blends perfectly into the landscape. Nature's beauty is its backdrop, for behind the altar is a wall of glass framing the jagged mountain peaks, with Grand Teton thrusting heavenward 13,770 feet. It is an inspiration to rest on the rustic seats and reflect on the unsurpassed beauty.

VIII.
THE FAR WEST

CALIFORNIA

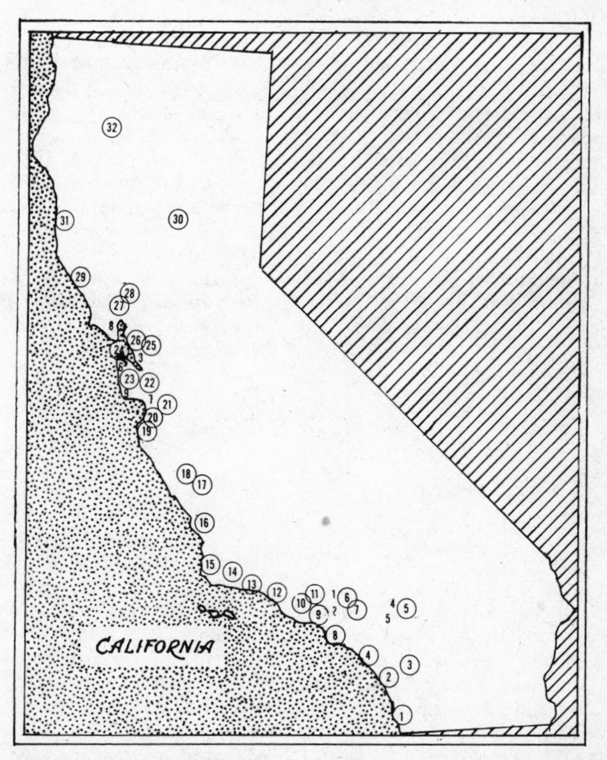

The far-reaching oceans were the first broad thoroughfares that led white men to the far west. They landed wherever the unceasing breakers pounded against the shores—in California, Alaska, and Hawaii. Their accompanying religions were as varied as their homelands—Catholics of Spain, Orthodox of Russia, and Congregationalists from America.

The Oregon-Washington territory, also bordering on the water world, was settled next, by fur traders and missionaries. Both Protestants and Catholics were drawn to minister to the vast number of natives.

Inland states—Nevada and Idaho—

were the last to feel the pioneer's plow. Mormons spilled over into Nevada and a gold strike brought instant cities to Idaho.

The widest spectrum of visible religious heritage is in the far west. A Buddhist Temple, a Chinese Joss House, an Indian Totem, and the onion dome of the Russian Orthodox may be seen along with the more familiar ancient and contemporary shapes.

Our tour begins in southern California, where the indefatigable gray-robed Franciscan friars established a chain of missions along the southern coast.

Spain held undisputed sway in California from the time Juan Rodriguez Carbillo sailed up its shores in 1542 through the mission era. When Russians ventured south from Alaska and planted a farming community at Fort Ross in 1812, Spain hastened to push its mission chain still farther north to ensure its empire.

When Spain relinquished her rights to Mexico and in turn our south-of-the border neighbor gave her rights to the United States, Americans arrived. Indians, Spanish, Americans, and Orientals fitted into the scene.

John Marshall's pick struck gold in 1848 and electrified the world. The gold rush was on. Ships and farms were abandoned for the gold mines. Wagon trains, clipper ships, and puffing locomotives brought thousands of hopefuls to the diggings.

As the excitement subsided along with the gold veins, and pioneers found other pathways to livelihood, the burgeoning population settled into towns and religious heritage sites began. Along with the ancient Indian tribal rites and traditional Masses could be heard oriental temple gongs and church bells of transplanted eastern residents. A variety of sites evolved that are today as diverse as the state's natural features.

Our travels begin in the south in the steps of Franciscan fathers Junipero Serra and Ferman Lausen. With tireless zeal, they established 18 Spanish Catholic missions. Between 1769 and 1823, there were 21 mission settlements approximately a day's journey apart. These formed El Camino Real, Spain's Royal Road, which extended from San Diego to Sonoma.

Southern California

(1) SAN DIEGO

Adobe Chapel

Immerse yourself in Old Town, oldest part of San Diego, to find the Spanish flavor of California's earliest mission town. Off Route 5 in the heart of the city, the charming settlement has ancient adobe buildings clustered around a quaint plaza. Once called Cosoy by the Indians, it was the original site of Father Junipero Serra's first mission, established in July 1769. Casa de Estudillo, a restored adobe has Spanish and early American artifacts. Casa de Lopez, a long house built around 1835, features a candle shop and museum. The Presidio, on a nearby hill, overlooks the city and once enclosed the house of the commandante as well as quarters for the military men.

A low, Spanish-style chapel facing the plaza was built in 1850 and dedicated in 1858. "Father Gaspara," the priest in *Ramona,* was in reality Father Antonio D. Ulbach of this chapel. Helen Hunt Jackson set her story in Old Town and characters in the novel were married in this tiny sanctuary.

Mission San Diego de Alcala

The mother mission of Mission Trail is located on San Diego Mission Road, about 6 miles north of Old Town. First located at the Presidio, the Mission San Diego de Alcala was moved here in 1774. The white Spanish-style building is redolent with age and the fragrance of candles. A side court with an old bell wall stands in a Spanish garden. Indians destroyed the mission in 1780; it was restored then and again in 1941, but the patina of antiquity still surrounds the adobe complex. On the surrounding fields the first irrigation dam and ditches in the state were dug when Franciscans sought to help Indians with agriculture.

(2) OCEANSIDE

Mission San Luis Rey de Francia

Franciscan Father Fermin Lausen is responsible for this large and outstandingly beautiful mission church, founded in 1798 and named for Louis IX, king of France. The high-ceilinged interior has original decorations painted by the Indians. A complete restoration was made in 1892 when the misison was chosen as a Franciscan Order house of study for priests.

At its zenith, the mission had about 3,000 Indian converts living within its extensive walls. A laundry built by them can be seen. A museum containing many relics of early days explains life in a mission settlement. Travelers will enjoy visiting during fiesta time in July, or in August at the Indian Dance Festival.

PALA

Mission San Antonio de Pala

Indian children still learn reading and writing at the only one of the original Spanish California missions to survive in its purpose of serving the Indian community. Today, however, 170 white and Indian children learn together, taught by the Sisters of the Blessed Sacrament, a missionary order dedicated to serve Indians and blacks. Franciscan Father Peyri established the chapel in 1816 as an *asistencia* to that of San Luis Rey in Oceanside. He wished to start an island chain of chapels for each of the native towns located far from the shore. Mission De Pala was therefore located near a sizable Indian village. When the Mexican government took over the mission lands, the many activities ceased and buildings decayed, though church services were still continued.

The Verona Fathers, who also work with Indians and blacks, began an ambitious rebuilding program in 1954. Work in the original quadrangle demonstrates the old California way of building. Walls are of handmade adobe, trusses and rafters are of roughly hewn cedar logs, and tiles of the roof and floor are made with soil of the Pala valley. Visitors will want to stroll in the old cemetery, by the original viaduct, to the free-standing bell tower and into the fascinating gift shop where colorful Christmas cards made by the children are on sale.

(4) SAN JUAN CAPISTRANO

Mission San Juan Capistrano

Midway between San Diego and Los Angeles on Highway 101, is the "Jewel or Alhambra of the Pacific coast." The same year as the Declaration of Independence, Father Junipero Serra proclaimed the freedom of Indians from any superstitious past by setting up the cross at Capistrano on November 1, 1776. Since then the bells have pealed forth the angelus daily amid gardens and cloisters. The visitor steps into Old Spain when entering the Mission walls, for repair work has been done with great care to preserve the original.

Above: Ruins of Mission Church
Below: Shrine of Our Lady of Gratitude, San Juan Capistrano

Beside the massive ruins of the great stone church, begun in 1797, is the oldest building in California and the only remaining church where Father Serra officiated at Mass. Two original confessionals, old stations of the cross, candlesticks, torches, and processional cross date from the mission's early days. The building is extremely narrow because long beams were unobtainable.

Intriguing remains of the workshops portray candlemaking, tanning, dyeing, and weaving. A smelter where metal was prepared for making locks, keys, and iron bars is nearby. It is altogether a most comprehensive place to learn about the way of life in the old mission towns.

Greater Los Angeles

(5) FOREST FALLS

Forest Home

About 15 miles northeast of Redlands on Route 38 is an outstanding camp and conference center dedicated to meeting the needs of local churches. Since 1938, the ecumenical center has been the camping arm of hundreds of churches, representing 40 different denominations. Family camping in a setting of mountain grandeur and with a Christ-centered emphasis is stressed in summer. Indian Village has tribes of juniors, Camp Rancho houses the junior highs, while seniors revel in the Youth Corps. Adults are housed year round in Lakeside, and special weeks are devoted to college students.

On a bank overlooking Lake Mears is the startingly contemporary Sermon on the Mount Chapel. The roof thrusts upward toward majestic Mt. San Bernardino, while the triangular glass sides allow panoramic views of the mountains. Since Forest Home is set into a bowl of mountains, views from any of the five camp areas are breathtaking. With accommodations for ten to 1,000, the center can answer many needs.

(6) PASADENA

The Children's Campus

Congregational and Unitarian fellowships have joined in the Neighborhood Church in South Pasadena. The new children's chapel and educational complex is geared to making religion such a vital and absorbing experience that it becomes a natural part of their world. All buildings have been integrated with the outdoors. The chapel has both an oriental and a New England flavor. Vertical windows alternate with plaster walls to give a windowless effect. No wide views to distract attention can be seen from inside.

The chapel fronts on a plaza leading to the other buildings under covered walks. The chapel door has touchable ashwood sculptures of religious themes. Latticed entrance walls give a no-wall effect.

(7) SAN GABRIEL

Mission San Gabriel Arcangel

The oldest cemetery in Los Angeles County is found within the walls of the old Mission San Gabriel Arcangel, which was established in 1771. A tall crucifix stands as a memorial to 6,000 Indians buried here. The cemetery is also the burial place for the Claretian Missionaries, Sons of the Immaculate Heart of Mary, who now conduct the mission.

The San Gabriel Mission Church is of cut stone, brick, and mortar and is unique among mission structures for its Moorish design. Vaulted roof and buttressed walls create a fortress-like appearance. Original walls are 4 feet thick. The main altar was made in Mexico City and brought here in the 1970s. Wooden polychromed statues were hand-carved in Spain. The 300-year-old painting "Our Lady of Sorrows" is on display.

After visiting other parts of the extensive grounds, the traveler will be enthralled with the museum, originally sleeping quarters for the mission fathers. The Art and Literature Room contains priceless books, one of which dates to 1489. A Spanish bedroom set dates to 1623 and Aboriginal paintings of the 14 stations of the cross are probably the oldest Indian sacred pictorial art in the state. Olive oil was the paint base, with colors derived from wild flowers.

(8) PALOS VERDES

Wayfarers Chapel

At 5755 Palos Verdes Drive, overlooking the expansive Pacific, is the "Glass Church," a memorial to Emanuel Swe-

denborg, 18th-century mystic. Architect Frank Lloyd Wright used Swedenborg's vision of a sanctuary made of living trees to design the building for the Swedenborgian Church of the New Jerusalem. The frame is of redwood, and walls and ceiling are of glass, so the evergreens outside seem part of the structure. The 3½-acre plot is beautifully landscaped and biblical plants are featured. A 50-foot stone tower is surmounted by a cross which is a landmark to seagoers, and known as "God's candle." Visitors should stroll down Meditation Walk to the "answer house" with its special Bible dioramas and book corner.

(9) LOS ANGELES

Old Mission Church

The village of Our Lady, the Queen of Angels of Porciuncula, was founded in 1781 by Spaniards and later was capital of the Mexican province until 1847. The original settlement around North Main and Los Angeles streets is now a historic park. Overlooking the ancient plaza is the Nuestra la Reina de Los Angeles Mission Church. The original part of the adobe building was begun in 1814 and is the city's oldest continuously used church. Franciscans founded the church, which is noted for its earthen floor and bell tower.

On Olvera Street, the city's oldest thoroughfare, the Las Posadas is held at Christmastime. From December 16 to 24, it is fiesta, and sidewalk shops, artists' booths, and restaurant cafés celebrate the season.

Wilshire Boulevard Temple

Less than 100 Jews lived in the sleepy little pueblo of Los Angeles when the Congregation B'nai B'rith had its origins in 1847. The crowning feature of the present temple, at 3663 Wilshire Boulevard, is a massive 125-foot dome inlaid with mosaics. The interior has marble and wood mosaics, stained-glass windows, and Belgian marble columns. Wall paintings tell the story of the Jewish people from the time of Abraham to Columbus. Rare possessions are

gold- and silver-embroidered Ark curtains from early European synagogues.

A religious school and temple camps outside Malibu teach the noblest expression of Judaism and American citizenship.

St. Sophia Cathedral

On September 28, 1952, in a centuries-old ceremony of Opening of Doors, the rapping of the archbishop's golden crozier on the massive oak panels signaled the opening and dedication of the Cathedral Church of the Divine Wisdom of God—St. Sophia. The structure was then consecrated to the service of God in Christ in the 2,000-year-old tradition of the Eastern Orthodox Church. The Greek Orthodox house of worship, located at 1324 South Normandie Avenue, is considered to be the most "brilliant gem" in the Western hemisphere.

Patterned after the Hagia Sophia of Justinian in Istanbul, it is of Byzantine style, yet not a slavish imitation of the original. The exterior, set in 4½ acres of handsome gardens, is devoid of architectural decoration. The interior, however, is a sumptuous ornamentation of wood, stone, crystal, and paint, producing glowing beauty. The ceiling of the apse has a painting of the Blessed Virgin and the Christ Child. The interior of the soaring dome represents Christ as Lord of All. Paintings and illuminations fill nearly every available space. A cathedral lecturer is always available to answer questions.

First Baptist Church

Baptists arrived in Los Angeles as early as 1853, but the first organized group, of 11 members, was not formed until 1874. The Southern Gothic edifice, at 760 South Westmoreland Avenue, was dedicated in 1927. Two of its three rose windows are copied from Chartres Cathedral in France. The tallest tower rises 155 feet. The mammoth structure has 100 rooms and includes a Good Neighbor Center, gymnasium-theater, and Francis Chapel. The tremendous sanctuary seats 1,950 and has an 88-rank organ.

Los Angeles Mormon Temple

The stately Mormon Temple at 10777 Santa Monica Boulevard stands on a knoll in a 20-acre tract. Its gleaming white 275-foot tower can be seen far out to sea. It is topped by a 15-foot cast-aluminum and gold-leaf statue of Angel Moroni. The Visitors' Center, spacious and beautiful, has back-lighted reproductions of noted artists' portrayals of the life of Christ. A Carrara marble statue of Jesus Christ, first displayed at the New York World's Fair, is in the entrance. Documents, dioramas, and movies tell the Mormon story and show the temple interior, which is open only to Mormons.

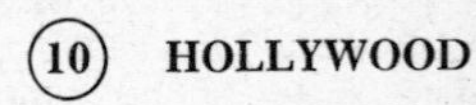

(10) HOLLYWOOD

Hollywood Temple

Onion-top domes on a sparkling white structure mark the location at 1946 Vedanta Place of the Vedanta Society of Southern California. The Society, a nonprofit religious corporation, was begun in 1934 and maintains, in addition to this Hindu-style temple, a convent and a monastery. It also has a similar complex in Santa Barbara and a monastery in Trabuco.

Visitors who drop in at this center will find a book store and a public-lecture schedule. Personal instruction is given by the Swami in prayer and meditation. The California Society is one of several in the country that resulted from the visit of Swami Vivekananda to the World's Fair Parliament of Religions in Chicago in 1893. Though connected with the Ramakrishna Math and Mission of India, it operates as a separate unit.

(11) SAN FERNANDO

Mission San Fernando Rey de Espana

One of the restored Spanish missions can be found at 15151 San Fernando Mission Boulevard. A military party and Franciscan friars established Mission San Fernando, another in the mission chain, in 1797. This was one of the most flourishing, but after 1846 it was dissolved and the buildings gradually decayed. Now the school, convento, church, and workrooms have been restored and give an insight into early California life. A historical museum, Indian craft room, and old gardens with plants from the other 20 missions give a pleasant few hours of browsing under the California sun.

Central California

(12) VENTURA

Mission San Buenaventura

After leaving the sprawling megalopolis, the traveler should follow Route 101 north to the coast and to another church on the Mission Trail. Founded in 1782, Mission San Buenaventura was particularly noted for fine gardens and vast grazing lands. It was Father Serra's ninth and last mission. The church dates to 1809 and is of adobe, stone, and tile. Though carved doors are replicas, the rafters and baptismal font are original, as are the Indian paintings. Patron saint is Bonaventura, whose statue is over the main altar. The Spansh crucifix is believed to date back 400 years.

The museum has baptismal and death records signed by Father Serra and an exquisitely carved confessional made by Indians.

SANTA BARBARA

Mission Santa Barbara

Padre Fermin Lausen raised the cross here in 1786, making it the tenth in

the mission chain. Original buildings were of adobe and unpretentious. This is the fourth and largest church. It was dedicated in 1820, and stands impressively on a hill overlooking the town. The twin-towered tile-roofed church is one of the best preserved and is often called "Queen of the Missions."

Chumash Indians made up the first congregation. Franciscans built a special Indian town near the mission for those who wished to become Christian. Franciscans taught them agriculture, building a dam 2 miles upstream and bringing water via aqueduct to assist in farming. Orange and olive trees were planted and vines cultivated. Wheat, barley, corn, beans, and peas were grown in the fields. Ruins of an old mill, tanning vats, storage reservoir, and filter can still be seen. The old Indian cemetery holds 4,000 graves.

Presently the church is used by the Santa Barbara Parish, but Indian artifacts, tools, relics, and art work are on display in a museum. An interesting Moorish fountain graces the front of the mission. The Indian Dance Festival held in July and the Little Fiesta in August will interest tourists.

Santa Barbara Temple

The Vedanta Society of California maintains a temple at 927 Ladera Lane. A convent and monastery are included in the complex as well as the Spanish mission-style temple. A wide entrance, tile roof, and adobe-type exterior form an interesting East-West combination. It is surrounded by low hills, giving a pleasing atmosphere for contemplation.

The Vedanta Society now has a membership of 700 and is open to those, regardless of creed or religious affiliation, who are seriously interested in Vedanta teachings. Religious festivals such as Ram Nam and ancient Hindu song services are held throughout the year for members.

(14) SOLVANG

Old Mission Santa Ines

Still on Route 101 but inland, we next come to Little Denmark, a town founded for Danes in 1911. Settlers came from all over the country, as well as from Denmark, and built Scandinavian-style. The church, college, school, and shops with Scandinavian handcrafts seem a sharp contrast to the old mission.

In 1804, another in the mission chain was begun by the Franciscans to serve the Indian communities. It was almost destroyed in an uprising in 1824 and abandoned in 1836 with the secularization. Now it has been restored, through efforts of the archdiocese of Los Angeles. A historical museum preserves Indian and mission relics and vestments. An 18th-century Mexican polychrome of St. Agnes is in the altar niche. Other carvings and paintings of the period decorate the sanctuary.

(15) LOMPAC

La Purisima Mission State Historic Park

This will be a fun stop on the Mission Trail, for a garden and corral have burros and sheep, something lively to see after a session with the antiquities. The original mission of 1787 was demolished by earthquake in 1812. Franciscan priests rebuilt it the next year. Eight buildings and the water system have been faithfully re-created, making this one of the most complete restorations. The museum holds valuable relics. Indian crafts are demonstrated in the summer and tourists can walk through a padre's residence, church, and guardhouse.

(16) SAN LUIS OBISPO

San Luis Obispo de Tolosa

Father Junipero Serra personally founded this fifth mission in the chain of 21 in 1772. It was dedicated to St. Louis, bishop of Toulouse, France, and has a relic of the saint enshrined in the altar. The 14 stations of the cross in the sanctuary are originals used by the church since 1812. Bells, tiled roofs, whitewashed walls, and surrounding greenery paint a picture of the old Spanish era of those first decades.

Chumash Indians, specialists in basket-making and seaworthy canoes, comprised the congregations. In the most flourishing period (1803-1806), 800 converts lived either at the mission or on one of its ranchos where grain was grown and livestock kept. The vast quadrangle included church, sacristy, padre's dwelling, hospital, women's quarters, and gardens—all built around a patio.

When the missions were secularized, this was sold, but later given back to the bishop for a parish church. Restoration of the decaying buildings began in 1933 and presently there is much activity, including mission schools, staff quarters, and an excellent museum. An extensive picture collection presents a vivid image of mission life and the history of the city that surrounds the mission.

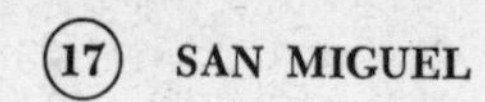

(17) SAN MIGUEL

Mission San Miguel Arcangel

Driving northward on Spain's Royal Road, the traveler turns inland. This attractive structure, founded in 1797 as a mission, is now a parish church and therefore well preserved. Special features are the decorations. Frescoes done by Esteban Munras and Indian assistants are bright and beautiful. Paintings from Spain and a brightly painted wall pulpit are noteworthy. Probably most unusual, however, are the vaulted corridors. Visitors walking beneath can find many different types of arches. An Indian dance festival in June and an annual fiesta in mid-September are enjoyable affairs for tourists.

(18) JOLON

Mission San Antonio

Still farther north, in the Valley of the Oaks, is found one of the best places to step back into the past. Franciscan fathers still maintain the 1771 Mission San Antonio de Padua, only now they

San Antonio Mission

guide tourists and explain the old Indian mission days. Beehive ovens, used for baking bread and foodstuffs by Indian women, the ancient water-powered gristmill, wells preserved in the Indian village, and original wine vats conjure up activities of former days.

After mission secularization and the 4,651st baptism, there was an 84-year interval before the Franciscans came back. Now, after extensive restoration, the mission and museum are open not only for tourists but also for retreat for individuals or groups up to 30 in number. The peace and quiet are most conducive to spiritual growth. The 1813 chapel is restored to its former charm and beauty.

 CARMEL

Mission San Carlos Borromeo Del Rio Carmelo

The "Great Conquistador of the Cross," Father Junipero Serra, lies buried here along with three other mission padres. Father Serra founded the mission at Monterey in 1770, but moved it to Carmel the following year where good soil made it a better location. From here, Father Serra made his many journeys to establish other missions. When he passed away in 1784, his title of Presidente of Missions of Upper and Lower California passed on to Padre Lausen.

The restoration of the mission began in 1884, and it became a parish church in 1933. Pope John XXIII made it a Minor Basilica in 1960. It is one of two in the western United States.

 MONTEREY

Royal Presidio Chapel

Mass was first said in this area under a large oak tree in 1602 at the Viscaino landing. The mission was founded, however, in 1770 when Carlos III of Spain sent the Portola expedition from Mexico to colonize and Christianize California. Franciscans assigned were Fathers Junipero Serra and Juan Crespi. The following year the mission was transferred to Carmel, only the Presidio remaining. In 1794, Royal Presidio Chapel was erected with Indian labor. Material was sandstone plastered over. The façade and doorway are originals. In 1858, the church was increased in size with the addition of transepts and a larger sanctuary. In the rear of the church is part of the old oak trunk which grew at the site of the 1602 Mass.

(21) SAN JUAN BAUTISTA

San Juan Bautista Mission

The last stop before the San Francisco area is San Juan Bautista, the 15th mission, which was most fortunate to have clergy continuously in residence since its founding June 24, 1798. That day Padre Lausen, in the presence of priests, soldiers, and Indians, blessed the water, the place, and the cross. The largest of mission churches was built here, from 1803 to 1812, to accommodate the several-thousand-member Indian congregation. Mission boundaries included 25 to 27 native villages, whose occupants soon moved close to the padres. Here the men were taught farming, masonry, and carpentry and the women weaving, cooking, and candlemaking. It was a different life from when they lived off the land on acorns, seeds, rabbits, squirrels, and birds.

Musical talents of Father Estevan Tapisa, president of the Spanish Missions, were passed along to the natives when he developed a choir. Samples of the large sheets with colored notes may be seen in the mission museum along with a rare barrel organ. Other instruments of sticks, hollow balls, and whistles were used by Indians for vigorous accompaniment to the hymns.

Greater San Francisco

 SANTA CLARA

Mission Santa Clara de Assis

Still traveling northward, as did those untiring friars, we next come to the remains of an old mission on the University of Santa Clara campus. Each of the 21 missions seems to have a unique work of its own. Santa Clara's is many-faceted education, for during its first century it ministered to thousands of Indians and during its last century it has housed a college and university program. When the travelers turn into the main drive, they immediately see a replica of the mission cross, which contains original fragments under glass inside its beams.

A replica of the original church is across the street and is roofed with 12,000 tiles made by Indians for the first mission. Site of Padre's quarters is marked with a plaque, and a walled cemetery is close to the church. Adobe Lodge, built in 1822 as a granary, is now the Faculty Club. Over 30 buildings comprise this modern educational facility which still pays tribute to the founding padres.

 PALO ALTO

Stanford Memorial Church

The brilliantly colored mosaic façade of the church is the dominant feature of Stanford University campus, as travelers turn up Palm Drive. The Sermon on the Mount is the subject of the striking Italian mosaic over the entrance. Mosaic motif was continued inside when donor Jane Stanford obtained papal permission to have the Rosselli fresco of "The Last Supper" in the Vatican's Sistine Chapel copied.

The Leland Stanfords gave the university in memory of their son and Mrs. Stanford built the church in memory of her senator-husband. The church was erected in 1899-1903 and nearly destroyed in the 1906 earthquake. Fortunately its art treasures were preserved, and Italian mosaic workers came from Italy to restore them. The church was reopened in 1913.

Visitors will find a nonsectarian emphasis, yet a strong devotional impact in the church, which is open from sunrise to sunset for spiritual comfort and reflection. Do spend enough time to examine the Venetian mosaics done in Byzantine style from 15th-century models. Stained-glass windows chronicle the life of Christ. The 28 inscriptions on interior walls are Mrs. Stanford's paraphrases of biblical quotations.

 SAN FRANCISCO

Mission Dolores

Fast-moving freeways bring the traveler up the peninsula on Route 101 into the sparkling white city of San Francisco, famous for cable cars and mountain peaks.

Keeping a wary eye for traffic, travelers should turn off onto Dolores Street and the sixth mission established by Father Serra. Founded June 29, 1776, its birthday is five days before that of our country. Mission Dolores, known also as Mission San Francisco de Asis, is one of the city's oldest buildings and is quite different in style from the others. Moorish, Mission, and Corinthian are combined in the massive building. The white façade has two-story round pillars and bell niches close to the roof. Rough-hewn wood timbers are still lashed with rawhide. Wooden pegs of manzanita hold it together. The ceiling remains as it was decorated by the Indians with vegetable coloring. The hand-carved altars and statues came from Mexico in 1780.

Cemetery browsers will come upon

a replica of the Grotto of Lourdes and an enormous statue of the larger-than-life Padre Serra. The setting in Mission Dolores Park is quite a contrast to the hustle of the surrounding city.

Buddha's Universal Church

Volunteers of all faiths and classes helped to build the Buddhist church at 720 Washington Street. Here in the largest Chinese community outside of Asia, a bit of the Orient is capsuled. The altar in the gold-hued main chapel is in the form of a ship, which is the Buddhist vessel of truth. The altarpiece is Buddha in a 6-foot mosaic. There are other small sanctuaries for meditation as well as a roof-garden quiet place.

WALNUT CREEK

Trinity Lutheran Church

East of Oakland, in Walnut Creek, is a contemporary church which uses the outdoors in its building complex exceptionally well. A meditation court is on one side of Trinity Lutheran Church and a social court on the other. The approach signifies worship, for three free-standing towering crosses are planted in the driveway circle. These were hand-hewn from telephone poles by church members.

The sanctuary, when approached from the side, blends into the foliage almost like an American barn. This effect is carried out inside by the roof contours. The utterly simple and serene design has an enormous glass mosaic cross against a redwood backdrop. Muted colors of wood used throughout give a restrained, elegant effect.

(26) BERKELEY

Pacific School of Religion

Turning westward again, toward the bay, the traveler comes to one of the largest concentrations of student life and the most complex set of educational buildings in the country. The School of Religion, founded in 1866, is the oldest seminary, or theological school, west of the Mississippi. It prepares students representing 25 denominations for the ministry, religious education, teaching, and counseling fields. Its connections, though interdenominational, are with United Church of Christ, Christian Church (Disciples), and the United Methodist Church. A contemporary chapel is the focal point on the campus.

Palestine Institute and Howell Bible Collection

Also on the grounds of the Pacific School of Religion, at 1798 Scenic Avenue, is a museum with "unwritten documents" such as coins, seals, religious talismans, cooking pots, lamps, and jewelry that vividly illustrate Bible history. Most were excavated from the ancient Hebrew town of Mizpah, scene of Pacific's expeditions from 1926 to 1935. This Bade collection and many archeological books are biblical treasures to be "mined" by visits. Here, too, is the Howell Bible collection which illustrates the fascinating development of the Scriptures over 2,000 years. Since 1938, its exhibits have assisted scholars and Bible students. A facsimile of the 1456 Gutenberg Bible as well as time charts and other manuscripts are worth perusing.

Northern California

SONOMA

Mission San Francisco Solano

Around the tree-shaded plaza of Sonoma, a typical sleepy Spanish-style town, are buildings now protected in the Sonoma State Historical Park. The northernmost mission in the chain was founded in 1823 by the Franciscans. Just 12 years later Mexican Gen. Mariano Vallejo established the town.

His palatial home on the outskirts, as well as the old barracks, may be seen.

The old mission sits serenely overlooking the square and the colorful shops. It bears the Christian name of Sem-Yeto, handsome chief of the Suisune Indians, who was a valuable ally to the whites. The original church was wooden and was built in 1840-1841 so the town could have a parish church. Now the complex is owned by the state, and the restoration is most authentic. A collection of paintings of all the missions are on display as well as many artifacts, clothing, and tools of early years.

It was in Sonoma that first resistance to Mexico by Americans came when the Mexican flag was pulled down and the star-and-grizzly-bear emblem of California was raised in 1846.

ST. HELENA

Elmshaven

Continuing north through the Valley of the Moon, across a tortuous mountain pass and down country lanes, one comes to the home of Ellen White, prophetess of the Seventh-day Adventists. Converted to the movement in 1842 in Portland, Maine, she was extruded from the Methodist Church. She married Elder James White in 1846, received visions and transports, and began writing about them in a steady stream of pamphlets and books. When Battle Creek, Michigan, became Adventist headquarters in 1855, the Whites resided there, then did mission work in Australia. In 1903, the church moved its offices to Washington, D.C., and continued to expand, with Mrs. White's nine-volume *Testimonies* as a unifying factor.

Elmshaven was her home from about 1900 to 1915, where she continued her writing. The Victorian house sits on a knoll in a wooded valley. Most memories of the prophetess can be evoked in the second story study. In an ample rocker with footstool, she sat in a sunny, 7-windowed tower to write. A lapdesk stands as if she had just put it down. Around the room are cases containing her books, letters, and other documents of Adventist interest. Her book *Steps to Christ*, still in constant demand, can be seen in many of the 78-language editions.

On a nearby hill is Pacific Union College and a large sanitarium operated by the Adventists.

JENNER

Fort Ross Historic State Park

Now spiritual heritage pilgrims should turn west toward the coast to view the first Russian Orthodox settlement in the continental United States. The Russians had long been in Alaska and felt the need of an agricultural outpost to supply food for their northern colonies. It was their arrival in 1812, which spurred the Spanish king to send conquistadors and friars north to plant settlements to protect Spanish lands.

For 29 years Fort Ross was an agricultural, trade, and commercial post. Vallejo, commander of Spain's northernmost post at Sonora, got along well with the Russians but was relieved when they abandoned their outpost in 1841. John Sutter, of gold-rush fame, bought it and later earthquake-damaged buildings were restored for a state park.

The wooden palisaded fort sits high on a bluff overlooking the Pacific on a 350-acre site. A Russian Orthodox chapel forms part of the wall and its two towers, the larger topped with a cross, seem strange in its California setting. The complex also has blockhouses and a commandant's home, which had an amazing amount of refinement and comfort.

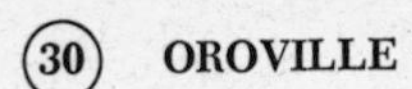

OROVILLE

Chinese Temple

Turning inland again, we travel northeast to Route 70. Over 10,000 Chinese lived in Oroville in the 1860s, drawn by the veins of gold and the need for help in the mines. A place of worship was needed and a temple was erected in 1863. The structure included a room each for Taoists, Confucianists, and Buddhists, and a council hall where non-English-speaking Chinese could be assisted in their business affairs. Help was needed in settling arguments, writing letters, and arranging for bones from bodies of the deceased to be sent back to China.

The Feather River flood in 1907, which washed out most of Chinatown, and the use of dredgers in mining forced the Chinese to leave. Now the authentic complex is a museum of Oriental treasures including the best tapestry collection in the Western world.

MENDOCINO

Mendocino Presbyterian Church

Back to the coast, we head north zigzag fashion. High above the Pacific on a bluff is Mendocino Presbyterian Church constructed of native redwood in 1868. A 90-foot bell tower is the outstanding feature of the English Gothic building. The surf was so loud that a bell weighing 1,000 pounds was installed to call people to worship over the sound of the sea. Original kerosene lamps, and a square grand piano built in 1850, are worth seeing.

(32) WEAVERVILLE

Joss House

The last stop in California is northwest on Route 299 where the oldest Chinese temple in the state is preserved by the California Park System. In July 1848, gold was found in a sandbar on Trinity River and a gold rush was on, bringing Chinese along with others. By 1849, there were 55 Chinese and by 1852 there were 2,500, mostly from the province of Kwang Tung. When mining faded, the Chinese worked on the railroads. When Weaverville Chinatown burned in 1906, many more departed.

The Chinese Temple of the Forest and the Clouds was erected for Taoist worship in 1852-1853 and is still in use. When a fire destroyed most of the building and furnishings in 1873, the present temple was immediately erected. The ornate wooden gate and fanciful gables and cornices set the Oriental theme. Inside is a set of second doors, called "spirit screens," to keep out evil spirits. Three ornately carved wooden canopies, with images of gods, stand behind an altar with candles, incense, fortune sticks, and an oracle book. A small wooden table and a stone urn are ready to hold food offerings.

Worshipers come alone, with their families, or with small groups to pray, and to place incense, candles, and food offerings before the gods of health, decision, and mercy. An adjacent building houses a conference room and temple attendants' quarters.

ALASKA

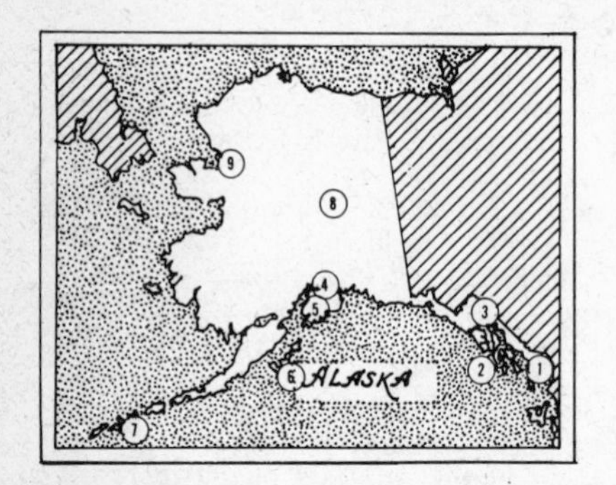

The midnight sun, 5,000 glaciers, majestic Mt. McKinley, and the vapor clouds in the Valley of Ten Thousand Smokes can all be seen in Alaska, the 49th and largest state. This great primeval land was unknown until Russian ships under Vitus Bering explored its southern shores along the Aleutian Island chain in 1741. Recognizing the great wealth in furs and skins, the Russians created the Russian-American Company and made an initial settlement at Three Saints Bay on Kodiak Island in 1783. When a tidal wave washed away most of the tiny town, it was rebuilt at Kodiak in 1791. Other towns were planted along the coast at Kenai in 1791 and its later capital, New Archangel (Sitka), in 1799.

Natives who greeted the Russians were the Aleuts of the Aleutian Islands and the Tlingit and Haida Indians of the southeastern panhandle. Eskimos lived in northern Alaska mostly within the Arctic Circle. The Aleuts became converts of the Russian Orthodox Church through ministrations of the priests who accompanied the colonizing party.

Indians of the panhandle were totemic societies and have perpetuated their totems and religious ceremonies, though many became adherents of Russian Orthodoxy or of later arriving mission churches, such as Friends and Presbyterians. Missionaries traveled to the Eskimos also, though shamans or medicine men still perpetuated their ancient ceremonies.

Russian influence waned as the American and British colonies grew on the west coast. In 1876, Alaska was formally turned over to the United States at ceremonies in Sitka. Later gold strikes and today's "black gold" reserves prove it was a bargain at $7,200,000, or 2 cents an acre.

Alaska's history is now being updated daily with the whirlwind developments accompanying oil pipelines in America's last frontier. So too is its religious heritage. As new residents pour in, so do their churches. Many are erected in startlingly contemporary style and contrast vividly with onion-domed Orthodox buildings, log churches, and stark mission structures. Old Believers, refugees from present-day Russia, have also found a private haven.

The usual pathways to Alaska are via plane, rail, or boat up the scenic southeastern coast, with its fjords, glaciers, and mountains, so that is where our heritage trail begins.

Southeastern Panhandle, Alaska

 KETCHIKAN

Totem Bight Historical Site

In old Haida Indian territory can be found a remarkable collection of totem poles, many found by deserted villages and restored. Tallest were for ceremonial feasts (potlaches). Others are crests connected with certain families. Guardian animals or their symbols are seen on the poles and are also painted on house fronts, boxes, and objects of daily wear and ceremonial use. The ornate ceremonial house is a true object of art.

Saxman Totem Park

South of Ketchikan is the Saxman Indian Village and Totem Park where colorfully clad Tlingit Indians perform traditional ceremonial dances in the Alaskan Native Brotherhood/Sisterhood Hall. Here, too, are many more totems with their grotesque painted faces.

A visit to the Tongass Historical Society Museum at 629 Dock Street will also be helpful. Here are artifacts of southeast Alaska Indian tribes, Czarist Russian relics, pioneering equipment, and old photographs which help to reconstruct the early heritage so unfamiliar to most continental Americans.

SITKA

Totem Square

Once the site of an ancient Indian town, Sitka was next the capital of Russian America and called New Archangel. The Tlingit Indians, who occupied the island when the Russians arrived in 1799, fought bitterly for their land. Their complex thousand-year-old culture was allied to forces of nature and the land. They protested its exploitation by the Russian hunters and trappers by massacring the settlement of St. Michael in 1802. The Russians returned in force with Aleut allies and crushed the Tlingits at the 1804 Battle of Alaska. New Archangel then became a fortified town and capital.

On the hill above the central Totem Square is a Russian blockhouse, a copy of those that were along the stockade walls in the early 1800s. One can imagine Gov. Aleksandr Baranov's palatial home within the stockade which once resounded to the strains of a piano as he entertained the shipmasters and military men that called at New Archangel. The cemetery with its Russian headstones poignantly reveals this heritage of another century.

Sitka National Historic Park

The 107-acre park east of Sitka is the site of the Battle of Alaska and a trail leads to the Tlingit fort. Along the path are 18 totems that record family and tribal history—the ancient way of proudly displaying one's genealogy. "Fog Woman," a 59-foot totem pole, largest in the state, guards the Visitors' Center. First stop should be here where an audiovisual program explains the significance of the monument.

St. Michael's Cathedral

The beautifully reconstructed St. Michael's Cathedral (Russian Orthodox) at Lincoln and Maksoutoff streets is a replica of the first 1848 structure. Vestments, chalices, wedding crowns, and other precious relics were saved when a disastrous fire leveled the building in 1963. Also saved were elaborate icons, including one painted like the Kazan Mother of God icon. The artist Borovikovsky, who lived from 1757 to 1825, was the creator of this Sitka Mother of God icon.

Translations of the Holy Bible in the Tlingit language can be seen in the cathedral museum, along with church service books printed in Tlingit. Church relics from the short-term settlement of Fort Ross in California are also on display.

Sheldon Jackson College and Museum

The oldest school in Alaska was founded in 1895 and is a memorial to Rev. Sheldon Jackson, Presbyterian missionary. After setting the pace for home missions between the Mississippi and the Rockies, he spent 25 industrious years in Alaska. "Short, be-whiskered, spectacled, but by inside measurement a giant" was the characterization of a newspaperman. The school museum has on display Eskimo handwork as well as Indian and Russian artifacts, tools, and utensils. The ceremonial masks and kayaks are an important part of Alaska's cultural heritage.

3 JUNEAU

St. Nicholas Church

Back to the mainland along the spectacular coastline, we proceed to Juneau, the capital since 1900. Begun by a gold strike in 1880 and crowded on a narrow shore between snow-capped mountains and the Gastineau Channel, it is a splendid sight. The St. Nicholas Church (Russian Orthodox), built in 1894 and located at 326 Fifth Street, is the oldest in southeastern Alaska. Tlingit Indian converts built the octagonal wood-frame church which is dedicated to the patron saint of fishermen. Until 1917, the predominately native congregation was supported by missionary funds from Moscow. The interior has ancient icons brought from Russia in the 19th century, and old vestments, books, and church furnishings.

Complete the trip with a visit to Alaska State Museum on Whittier Street.

Western Alaska

4 ANCHORAGE

Eklutna Indian Village

The largest city in Alaska and an international travel center, Anchorage, is located on Cook Inlet and framed in snow peaks. Modern skyscrapers and a jet port sit alongside ancient Indian burial grounds. Eskimo dancers perform ceremonials amid liturgies of the white man's churches.

About 25 miles north on Glenn Highway is the Indian community of Eklutna. The old Russian Orthodox church building is the result of missionary activity. Its nearby burial ground has brightly painted diminutive "spirit houses" covering the graves. From a distance they look like tiny dollhouses, and are temporary residences for the spirits of the dead. Many are quite complete with tiny doors and windows. Others are more fragile tent coverings. All are part of the north's fast-fading past.

5 KENAI

Russian Orthodox Church and Chapel

The first missionary to arrive in Kenai was one of the original delegation of ten monks who disembarked at Kodiak with the colonizing party. In 1796-1797, Father Juvenaly wintered at Kenai and reported he "baptized all local inhabitants." The first building of the Holy

Assumption of the Virgin Mary Russian Orthodox Church was where the St. Nicholas Chapel now stands. The second was the present Russian-style church which was built in 1896. Its circular bell tower and tiny onion dome were added in 1908. The simple wood-frame exterior belies the elaborate and ornate interior, which has a remarkable collection of icons and a candelabra once in the Kodiak church. Two wedding crowns used in the Orthodox marriage service are intricately made.

The tiny dark wood chapel was built in 1911 as a memorial to the first resident priest, Abbot Nicholas, who served here 20 years.

A visit to the Fort Kenay complex will shed further light on this second oldest Alaskan community established in 1791 as a Russian trading post.

Old Believers

A bit of present-day Russia has taken root on the Kenai Peninsula, where Old Believers (or Old Ritualists) have created the village of Nikolaevsk. Amid rolling hills covered with spruce and birch, the peasant-costumed men and women seem to have dropped out of 17th-century Russia. Actually, they fled in the 1920s, stopping first in Hong Kong, Brazil, and Oregon. When civilization threatened their Christian communistic society, they retreated to the virgin territory of Alaska.

Old Believers are remnants of a people excommunicated 300 years ago when they refused to accept reforms of the Russian Orthodox church. Many were martyred for their faith. Here in the small community begun in 1968, they built their church, and continue the age-old customs. High point of the religious year is Easter (Julian calendar) Sunday, after which a feast ends Lenten fasting. Colored hard-boiled eggs and *braga* highlight the festival.

Though travelers probably will not see the Old Believers unless they pass in their colorful costumes on Kenai streets, it is well to know of a still developing Alaskan religious heritage; also, small colonies of Old Believers are in New York, New Jersey, and Oregon.

 KODIAK

Holy Resurrection Church

Russian missionary monks from Valaam Monastery in Russian Finland established the first Russian Orthodox church in Alaska at Kodiak in 1794. Two buildings preceded the present contemporary Holy Resurrection structure which houses the spiritual descendants of that first congregation. In the 1945 building are icons that date from the earliest times as well as a metal Gospel cover dating from 1793 that was brought to the New World by the missionary monks. Also found here is the reliquary of St. Herman of Alaska, one of the first monks, who spent most of his life on Spruce Island and was canonized by the Orthodox Church in America at Kodiak in 1970.

 UNALASKA

Russian Orthodox Church

Visitors lucky enough to fly or sail part way down the Aleutian Island chain to the island community of Unalaska will be rewarded by the saga of Ionann Veniaminov, later Bishop Innocent, whose first missionary years were in Unalaska. The remarkable priest set the tone for mission work when he decreed natives should be helped and educated, with no coercing for conversion. While directing the building of the Holy Ascension of Christ Orthodox Cathedral in 1826, he also revolutionized the natives' lives by teaching them skills and trades like carpentry, metalwork, and brick-making. His school soon had 100 boys and girls with many courses, including navigation. Veniaminov also instituted a course in the local dialect, Aleutian-Fox, composing a dictionary, grammar, and primer. He kept up his scientific hobbies and wrote a three-volume compendium on the region which is still a basic text.

(8) FAIRBANKS

St. Matthew's Episcopal Church

Leaving the southern shores, and traveling north, one comes to the golden heart of Alaska, for it was here in 1902 that Felix Pedro struck gold and mining camp became the nucleus of today's modern city. A second boom followed—discovery of North America's greatest oilfields in 1969. About 130 miles south of the Arctic Circle, it is the stepping-off place for trips to the interior. It is a one-day trip to the base of the highest peak on the continent, Mt. McKinley.

Representative of those early congregations that followed the populace is St. Matthew's Episcopal Church built of logs in 1948. It was intended to be a symbol of pioneer Alaska in a city where skyscrapers are rising. The intricately carved altar made of native Alaska birch in 1906 is a noteworthy feature.

(9) KOTZEBUE

Friends Mission

An Alaskan trip is not complete without a flight to Kotzebue, second largest Eskimo village inside the Arctic Circle. Amazingly the Eskimos are 130 miles from Siberia and in the same time zone as tropical Hawaii. The primitive main street is the gravel beach fronting the village. In the Utukkuktukagvik (place having old things) is a museum portraying the culture and activities which include polar-bear hunting.

The Friends established the oldest mission, school, and hospital here in 1879. In the *Alaskan Diary* of Martha Hadley, Quaker missionary, there is an amazing record of mission development. Her northern odyssey took place from 1899 to 1903. A birthright Quaker, she was sponsored by the California Yearly Meeting of Friends, though others also contributed medicines and supplies to her work. The isolation of the mission, the customs and foods of the Eskimos, as well as their eagerness to learn, are all found in the day-to-day account of teaching, doctoring, and loving the little congregation. The white-frame mission church, dating from 1897, has a huge bell mounted in front on a timbered tower. It is adjacent to the school and the hospital.

HAWAII

Once a royal kingdom, Hawaii now has the only royal palace in the United States as well as the most varied of spiritual heritages.

Long before white men stepped on the lava shores of these volcanic islands, Polynesians from the Marquesas and Tahiti arrived by outrigger canoe. They came about A.D. 500-900, bringing their families and their lesser gods. One Supreme Being was over all, they believed, and his four major helpers were Kane, Lono, Ku, and Kaneola. Life was lived in accord with nature, but native priests insisted on the keeping of many taboos.

A thousand years later the feudal island kingdoms that had developed were welded together by Kamehameha the Great, the Alexander of the Pacific. After Kamehameha's death, the ensuing struggle for power and the chaos stirred by white traders and whalers destroyed faith in the old gods and the wooden idols were burned.

At this propitious moment in April 1820, the brig *Thaddeus* dropped anchor off the High Islands. Aboard were Congregational missionaries and their families, sent by the American Board of Commissioners for Foreign Missions "to give [Hawaiians] the Bible, with skill to read it . . . to make men of every class wise, good, and happy."

King Kamehameha II remarked at their audience: "We have just got rid of one religion. I am not sure we want another." Nevertheless, permisison for a year's trial was granted, and Rev. Hiram Bingham preached the first Christian message in a pili-grass house in Honolulu to Governor Boki while commoners jostled by the doorway and crowded into the yard.

Three decades later Hawaii was on the threshold of becoming one of the world's great Christian nations. By 1852, Hawaiian Christians were launching their own missionaries to the westward islands of Micronesia.

Growth and progress made Honolulu the crossroads of the Pacific and brought people of every race. Waves of Japanese, Spanish, Chinese, and Portuguese arrived and were assimilated into the population. Their churches came too: Catholic, Mormon, Buddhist, Episcopalian. Father Damien answered the lepers' need with a colony on Molokai.

By the time the monarchy was abolished for territorial status and statehood was achieved in 1959, a profusion of congregations were meeting on the largest islands—and the curving roofs of Buddhist temples, glistening white Mormon towers, and steepled cathedrals rose among the palm trees, hibiscus flowers, and aging monuments of the primitive faith.

The first view of this island paradise is usually from the Pacific skies as the jetliner swoops down over Diamond Head and Waikiki Beach on Oahu.

Oahu

(1) HONOLULU

Mission Houses Museum

A fascinating walk through Hawaiian history begins in a shaded courtyard in downtown Honolulu. A white-frame New England-style cottage built in 1821 is the oldest wooden house in Hawaii. It was erected when King Kamehameha II recognized the value of the missions and gave approval to the missionaries to remain. As one steps into the house that was home to so many families, one comes upon a desk with quill pen and Hawaiian translations of the Bible. The sitting room table has a teapot and cups seemingly ready for use. In the cool basement, a large trestle table is ready to accommodate a dozen or so inhabitants and whoever may be visiting. Doll furniture and children's clothing remind us that small tots were part of the mission band.

The old printing house next door has a working replica of the Ramage Printing Press which first printed the

Hawaiian language in 1822. Also fronting on the courtyard is the Visitors' Center and gift shop, made of cut coral and originally designed for a depository and additional living quarters.

An old stone bench in the yard provides a place for rest and reflection, when seemingly one hears the swish of long gowns and the thump of the presses. The Research Library, with its thousands of unpublished books and pamphlets on early Hawaii (first called the Sandwich Islands), is constantly in use by scholars.

Kawaiahao Church

Across the street the traveler will find the Westminster Abbey of Hawaii, Kawaiahao Church, the church of commoners and kings, built in 1840. Earlier there had been grass chapels—four, one after the other—the first in 1821. The first congregation, however, began when the missionaries arrived in 1820 and met in the grass homes. At first called the house of prayer, the King's Chapel, it was given its present name in 1863.

The edifice is of coral and the third oldest church in the islands, with Molokai and Kailua-Kona buildings predating it. Made a National Historic Landmark in 1965, it has a museum-like quality, with its wall plaques and oil paintings of Hawaiian royalty. In the rear are the royal boxes with their colorful feather insignias.

Sunday visitors will be enthralled with the part-Hawaiian, part-English service with its magnificent choir. Afterward there is a tour of the church, book store, and grounds as well as a local luncheon menu complete, of course, with poi.

Cathedral Church of St. Andrew

On Queen Emma Square is St. Andrew's, one of the oldest Episcopal churches in the United States. The cornerstone was laid in 1867 by King Kamehameha V; and Queen Emma, consort of Kamehameha IV, raised most of the money for the original section. The early French Gothic style was the result of Episcopal church beginnings in 1862, with the arrival of two clergy families. Ninety-six years later, in 1958, with the construction of additional bays and the great west window, the church was completed. The whole west end of St. Andrew's is a brilliant wall of intricately patterned stained glass measuring 50 by 20 feet. This largest window, constructed in the United States, depicts Christian church history. Outside, the approach is by a long fountain court with a statue of St. Andrew and carrying out the fisherman theme.

Soto Mission of Hawaii

A Zen temple was erected at 1708 Nuuanu Avenue in 1952 and officially dedicated in 1953. The triple-towered palatial structure is modeled after a temple in India. The central tower rises in layers from a columned doorway to crowned peak. Gold flowers and an 800-year-old statue of Buddha highlight the interior. Buddhist priests explain beliefs and ceremonies for visitors who will also appreciate the landscaped gardens patterned after Japan's Kyoto Gardens.

Honpa Hongwanji Mission

Centuries of Buddhist philosophy are evidenced in the large temple at 1721 Pali Highway. The superb statue of the spiritual Buddha over the altar is of lacquer and gold leaf. Believed to be the work of a famed 12th-century Japanese artist, the standing figure has golden rays of light emanating from a cloud symbol behind the head. Images of St. Honen, founder of Judo Shu, and St. Shinran, founder of Shin Buddhism, flank the altar.

KANEOHE

Byodo-in-Temple

In the Valley of the Temples Memorial Park on Kahekili Highway is a replica of a 900-year-old Buddhist temple in Kyoto, Japan. Dedicated in 1968 to the first Japanese immigrants, the temple is a pleasing array of curved pagoda roofs, erected on stilts to give an airy feeling. An 18-foot statue of Buddha in gold stands below a screen depicting his 52 followers. Gold phoenixes perch on the steep roof. A bell house and ceremonial teahouse adjoin the temple. The foreground is a lake surrounded by landscaped gardens; a background of jagged lava mountains complete the unusual setting.

LAIE

Mormon Temple

After riding along miles of beaches pounding with surf, where volcanic mountains rise steeply from the shores, one comes to the northeastern point of Oahu and the magnificent Hawaiian Mormon Temple. The first built outside the American mainland, it was dedicated in 1919 and is of contemporary block architecture fronted by the vast blue Pacific and backed by plantations of sugar cane. The setting of terraced gardens and reflecting pools will be enjoyed by visitors, though only Mormons may enter the temple.

Adjacent to the Mormon Brigham Young University is a 15-acre authentic cluster of six South Sea Island villages also maintained by the Mormons, where customs, arts, and crafts of the island cultures are illustrated in a living museum.

(4) PEARL HARBOR

Pearl Harbor Memorial Church

Separate Lutheran and United Church of Christ congregations share this magnificent memorial to the men and women of the armed services. A quonset hut in 1946 saw the beginnings of the United Church congregation and the present contemporary building was erected in 1958. The Lutheran church of Pearl Harbor began in 1950 with several military families. Each congregation maintains its own identity, having separate Sunday services, but many Christian programs are held in common.

The church is near the Arizona Memorial at Pearl Harbor as well as Hickham and Pearl Harbor military bases.

The front wall of the sanctuary is a 44- by 30-foot A-frame of 140 individual sections each having 12-20 pieces of stained European glass. Central figure is of Christ, with people of all nations being drawn to him. Intriguing from the street, it is overpowering when seen from inside where indirect sunlight brings out dazzling colors and intricate detail. The thread of oneness with other religions is portrayed with the Judaism's star of David, Hinduism's "OM," Buddhism's wheel, Confucianism's symbol of cosmic power, and Islam's emblem of one God. Included also is a salute to American patriotism with scenes of the country's early history shown on the four entrance doors.

Kauai

KILAUEA

St. Sylvester's Roman Catholic Church

An eight-sided church in the round sits by the village stream. St. Sylvester's, constructed of lava and wood, has a central altar with benches surrounding it. Exposed beams slant upward. Hawaiian artist Jean Charlot has created decorative frescoes.

Catholic fathers came to the islands

in 1840 and one of their first missions was at Koloa (1841).

(6) WAILUA

Holo-Holo-Ku Heiau

On the southeast coast of Kauai is one of the island's oldest temples where human sacrifices were once offered. The Kauai Historical Society and the Bishop Museum in Honolulu have restored the complex. The grass house is a re-creation of one used by the kahuna, or priest, who performed the religious ceremonies. Birthstones outside the enclosure were touched by women of royal blood before birth of a child to ensure its royalty.

Molokai

(7) KALAUPAPA

Church of the Healing Spring

Our island hopping next is southeast to the home of Father Damien's colony for victims of Hansen's Disease (leprosy). Here the dedicated Roman Catholic priest devoted his life, dying of the disease in 1889. The Kalaupapa Peninsula is reserved for sufferers of the disease, still, although modern medicine has cut the population and has made the area safe for tourists. While visitors must not photograph the patients, they are welcome to see the colony.

Siloma, the Church of the Healing Spring, was built in 1871 on the east side of the peninsula to serve Potestant patients and for special services.

Maui

(8) HANA

Wananalua Church

Another flight will take the traveler farther southeast to the "Valley Isle," an island formed by two volcanoes with a fertile isthmus between. The Congregational Church, now affiliated with the United Church of Christ, was established in 1838. The first church building was of grass; the more permanent structure begun in 1842 took 20 years to finish. Built of volcanic rock, the structure is held together by pulverized coral cement. When one stands and gazes up at the massive tower, one wonders how the natives, without modern tools, could have built such an edifice.

Ministers are secured by a unique "minister of the month" plan, whereby mainland ministers take turns spending a month in Hana, holding services and vacationing.

St. Mary's Catholic Church and the Church of Jesus Christ Latter-Day Saints welcome visitors to their plants.

Hawaii

(9) KAILUA-KONA

The "big island" has more natural wonders than any other as well as the most active volcano in the world.

Mokuaikaua Church

The oldest church building in the state is found on Alii Drive. Since Kailua was where Kamehameha the Great was born, ruled, and died, it was where the missionaries arriving on the brig *Thaddeus* first met the reigning Kamehameha II in 1820. While the Binghams went to Honolulu, the Thurstons remained in Kailua until the royal family moved to Honolulu. Coming back three years later, they found that the small band of

new Christians had erected a chapel. The delighted Thurstons saw seats around the walls, floors covered with mats, and "a decent painted pulpit." By 1824 the congregation averaged 600 to 1,000 in attendance.

When there was no room for the people, every man went into the woods to gather materials for a new church. The "largest and most elegant native building" erected was dedicated in 1826, but destroyed by fire in 1835. Governor Kuakini came to the aid of the congregation and the present stone church was built in 1837. At the dedication 3,000 were present and a visitor counted 210 canoes leaving the beach after service. Gallery pews and pulpit paneling are of koa wood. In 1919, a memorial arch was built at the entrance of the grounds to commemorate the centennial of the arrival of the first missionaries.

St. Michael's Church

The first Catholic priests, Picpus fathers, were sent to Hawaii in 1827, and the first permanent mission was established in 1839. In 1840, two priests arrived on Big Island and celebrated the first Mass. Governor Kuakani gave land for the church, which at first was a grass chapel. St. Michael's, oldest Catholic church on this island, was completed in 1850 and restored in 1935. The Coral Grotto was built over an old water well in 1940. Father Benno's orphan boys and parishioners dived off the Kona coast to get 2,500 pieces of coral for the grotto. A lovely memorial chapel was erected in the cemetery in 1941 and stands on the location of the first grass church. The present parish of North Kona includes five churches and is administered by the Maryknoll fathers.

St. Peter's Chapel

One of the churches connected with St. Michael's is the lovely little Blue Church found about 4 miles south of Kailua village. It was first erected in 1880 at Laaloa Beach and was moved to its present location in 1912. Backed by the blue sea, its own blue roof, tower and trim make a charming picture. Beside it is a square pond used by natives to wash clothes by day and wash themselves by night. The church has twice been moved off its foundation by tidal waves, but each time has been tenderly replaced. Porch and belfry were added in 1938.

(10) HONAUNAU

City of Refuge National Historical Park

On the southeastern side of the island is one of the sacred spots established in the early 15th century. Breakers of *kapu* (religious laws) could flee here until purified by the priests. Also, women, children, and defeated warriors were protected within its walls in time of war.

The natural fortress was built on a 6-acre shelf of ancient lava and the ocean bounds it on north, west, and south. The Great Wall is on the south and east. Remains of the first temple are close to the sea. About 1550, its stones were used to build the second temple, which is the large temple platform inside the wall. The third temple was used from about 1650 to 1819, when the *kapu* system was abandoned and practice of the old religion forbidden. Bones of kings and important chiefs were placed here and their combined supernatural powers kept the refuge sanctified and inviolate.

City of Refuge

At the Visitors' Center, orientation talks are given and self-guiding tour leaflets distributed.

(11) HILO

Lyman House Memorial Museum

Continuing south and west on Route 11, one passes the volcano district and smoking Kilauea Crater to arrive at Hawaii's second largest city. At 276 Haili Street awaits a bit of old New England. Rev. David Lyman built the two-story white-frame home in 1839 when he and his family arrived in the fifth company of missionaries from Boston. A four-poster bed, Victorian rocker, music boxes, china, and other furnishings of the Lyman family convey their way of life. Original koa board floors and lighting fixtures from whaling ships are reminders of the exotic setting.

Connected to the old house is a modern museum dedicated in 1973 to the culture of the major ethnic groups making up Hawaii's population. Hawaiian grass houses, feather work, and religious artifacts are here, along with a Chinese Taoist shrine and Japanese costumes.

OREGON

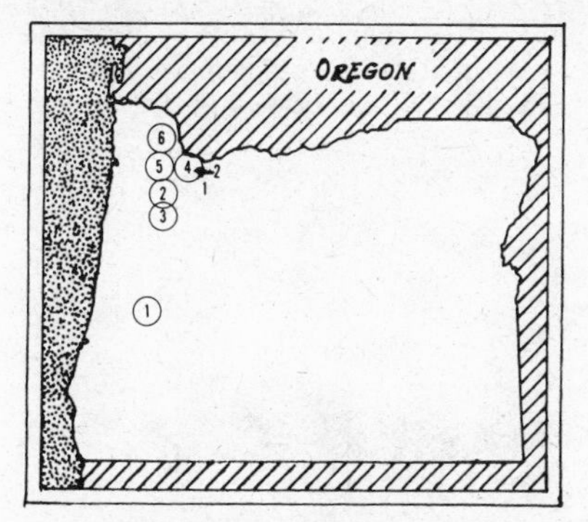

A kaleidoscope of contrasts is found in Oregon, from snow-capped Mt. Hood to Haystock Rock on the rugged coast. Part of the old northwest, it was one of the last areas in the country to be tamed. Indians of the Shoshone and Paiute tribes ranged its woodlands, shores, and mountains while occasional ships of white men briefly dropped anchor. The trappers and explorers sought pelts and mapped the land.

Astoria, trading post of John Jacob Astor's Pacific Fur Company, begun in 1811, was the first settlement and the place of first religious services. Post directors read Sunday services from the Church of England and Catholic prayer books before clergymen arrived. Then pioneers came overland, drawn by tales of the magnificent land.

In 1832, when four Indian chiefs of the northwest startled St. Louis by emerging from the wilderness in search of the white man's "Book of Heaven" and "Black Robes," missionary zeal of all denominations was aroused. Methodist missionaries Jason and Daniel Lee arrived in 1834 to establish missions in the Willamette valley. With the support of the American Board for Commissioners of Foreign Missions, Presbyterian Rev. Samuel Parker came the following year. When Dr. Marcus Whitman, a physician, and Rev. Henry Spalding brought their wives in 1836, the women became the first white women to cross the country. In 1938, Jason Lee returned to the east and brought back by sea a party of 50 missionaries and families. That same year Catholic missionaries arrived in Oregon. Whitman eventually settled in Washington and Spalding in Idaho.

The great immigration of 1843 was the beginning of a steady flow of pioneers to the Columbia valley, which brought the inevitable conflict with the Indians, who saw their lands disappearing. After constant turmoil and the Moduc Indian War, the remaining tribes were given reservations. Statehood came in 1850.

One of the largest reservations today is Warm Springs Indian Reservation where a tribal confederation owns the land and operates the unusual resort of Kay-Nee-Ta (Gift of the Gods). Guests can stay in cottages, in hand-sewn teepees, or in their own campers in this land of the Indian. Spiritual heritage sites of our native Americans are not as prolific here as in many other states.

Major denominations pioneered in education: Presbyterians at Albany College in 1867, Roman Catholics at Columbia University in 1901, United Evangelical at Dallas College in 1853, Congregationalists at Pacific University in 1853, Baptists at McMinnville College in 1858, Friends at Pacific College in 1885, United Brethren at Philomath College in 1866, and Methodists at Willamette University in 1844.

Recent comers to the religious scene have been the Vedanta Society and the new Shiloh Houses which are Christian communal groups arising from youth and charismatic movements.

Our tour is in the populated plains of the west and leads from south to north.

Western Oregon

(1) COTTAGE GROVE

First Presbyterian Church

A complete departure from traditional ecclesiastical architecture is found in this neighborhood Presbyterian church. Since Cottage Grove is located in the center of fir lumber industry, material is entirely of fir planking, reminiscent of Oregon's "barn architecture." Though dating back to 1855, the congregation looked to the future in this 1951 contemporary structure.

Situated around a courtyard which contains several polished rocks set into Japanese-style gardens, the complex consists of a one-story chapel, taller square sanctuary with simple cross on the wall over the communion table, and adjacent parish house. The bell stands on a supporting frame of redwood, carved with Christian symbols. Large windows flood interior rooms with radiance from outside. Rose-tinted glass in the north chancel casts warm pink and lavender shades, creating a devotional atmosphere.

 ST. PAUL

St. Paul's Catholic Church

In the great bend of the Willamette River is a town referred to as "French Prairie," which was settled in 1830 by retired French Canadian trappers. They petitioned the bishop of Red River, in Canada, for a priest, who sent Fathers Francis Blanchet and Modeste Demers in 1838. On arriving, they found the French and Iroquois settlers had built a log chapel. The priests immediately held a three-week mission in the chapel, baptizing dozens of half-blood children and their Indian mothers, marrying their parents, and establishing a cemetery.

The present lovely brick church, St. Paul's, which has been twice enlarged and beautified, was erected in 1846. It is believed to be the oldest brick building west of the Rockies as well as the oldest church in Oregon. For many years it was the cathedral for Father Blanchet, who became archbishop. His grave, marked with an ornate cross and impressive monument, can be seen in the nearby cemetery. Nestled close to the church is a tiny replica of the original log chapel. Its square tower over the entrance is topped with a fancy white cupola and cross.

(3) SALEM

Mission Hill Museum

After a pleasant trip up the coast past busy harbors and scenic marvels, the way lies inland via Route 20 to Salem, the state's capital. On Mill Street is a complex which includes the home and parsonage of Jason Lee, pioneer Methodist missionary. Both buildings were erected in 1841. The parsonage is furnished in 19th-century style, much as it was when the energetic missionary used it as home base. A five-room slab house built in 1847 by another Methodist minister, John D. Boon, can also be seen.

(4) PORTLAND

Zion Lutheran Church

Though elegant and modern, Zion Lutheran Church at S.W. 18th Avenue and Salmon Street conveys the effect of a village church. Built in 1950, it is made of brick and wood and was designed by Pietro Belluschi. Bronze entrance doors have an angel design. Interior arches lend a Gothic touch. A copper altar and cross are lighted by varying effects through the stained glass.

This is the mother church of the Missouri Synod's northwest district and the congregation dates to 1871. The form of the church with its simple spire recalls the village churches of peasant Europe as well as wood adaptations of the early Protestant northwest. The rough-sawn board and batten exterior has an old-country somber effect, lightened by the shining copper entrance.

Vedanta Society

The Portland Vedanta Society was founded in 1925 as a religious organization. The swami (teacher) and American lay people constitute the governing board. Since 1968, its headquarters have been a wood-frame building at 1157 S.E. 55th Avenue near Mt. Tabor Park. The heart of the movement is meditation, and a shrine is always open in the temple headquarters for devotees and friends. Lectures, classes, books, and conversation are always available so people may learn more about the Society, which is an outgrowth of teachings of Sri Ramakrishna, 19th-century Hindu saint.

(5) FOREST GROVE

Old College Hall

East of Portland on the grounds of Pacific University is the oldest structure in continuous educational use west of the Mississippi. A community building-bee was held in 1850 to raise the clapboard structure. Settlers for miles around camped here for two weeks while the men framed the hall, women served the meals, and the children played. The building, which began the Congregational school, now contains a chapel, meeting room, and museum. Indian artifacts, pioneer mementos, and relics of other ethnic groups can be seen.

(6) SCAPPOSE

Vedanta Retreat

Close to the northwest boundary is the Hindu-style retreat of the Portland Vedanta Society. Set on a 120-acre tract overlooking the Columbia River, the center is open to members and friends during the warm months of the year as a place of reflection and meditation. Permission must be secured from the swami-in-charge. The octagonal building with its white onion dome is an intriguing sight when viewed against the background of tall pines.

WASHINGTON

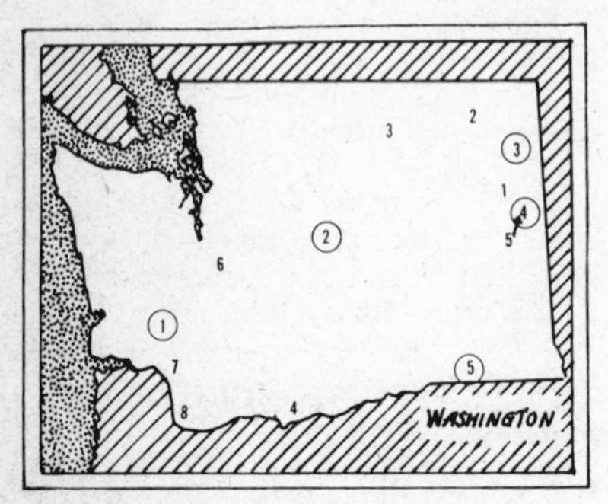

The white man's religion came to Washington with the Hudson's Bay Company posts, when Fort Vancouver was completed in 1825. Dr. John McLoughlin continued the Sunday custom, begun earlier in Astoria (Fort George), of reading from the Church of England Book of Common Prayer and holding services in French for Catholics.

Since Canada and the United States were vying for this vast game preserve, missionaries came from both countries. Protestant Dr. Marcus Whitman came overland, an emissary of the American Board of Commissioners of Foreign Missions, to open Waiilatpu mission to the Cayuse Indians near Walla Walla in 1836. Meanwhile French Canadian Fathers Modeste Demers and Francis Blanchet celebrated the first Mass north of the Columbia River in 1838 and began a long chain of Catholic missions. Father de Smet, approaching through Montana, held a Mass in 1844 at the famous caves of the Kalispel Indians.

The full flow of the great emigration brought foreign-born as well as American pioneers. Miners of Orthodox and Lutheran extraction arrived, along with Russo-German Volga families who moved on from an initial settlement in Nebraska after several dry seasons. German Congregational and German Lutheran churches resulted.

Though the Whitman Massacre and disastrous Indian Wars curtailed religious outreach temporarily, peace, establishment of reservations, and a new influx of settlers brought still more denominations to the breathtakingly beautiful state of towering Mt. Rainier and the alpine Cascade Range. Congregationalists established Whitman College, Catholics began Gonzaga College, Presbyterians started Whitworth College, and Methodists opened the University of Puget Sound between 1866 and 1903.

Western Washington

CHEHALIS

Claquato Church

Three miles west of Chehalis is the last of the early territorial churches remaining in its original form. Claquato Church, the third oldest church building in Washington, was built by the Methodist Missionary Society in 1858 for the use of all denominations. Homesteader Lewis Davis conveyed the land and donated the first lumber from his sawmill for the 20- by 30-foot structure. The belfry is surmounted by a symbolic crown of thorns made of white pinnacles placed on a louvered octagon.

With the coming of the railroad to Chehalis, people moved away, leaving the church building to decay. Fortunately the county protected it, and in 1953 American Legion members restored it and the unique building was rededicated as a pioneer memorial. It is now on the National Register of Historic Properties.

2 CASHMERE

Pioneer Village and Museum

Turning north through the Wenatchee and Cashmere valleys which lie east of the Cascade Peaks, the traveler will find apple orchards with tantalizing fruits along the way, as well as a taste of ripe apricots in season. After a visit to a fruit stand, the pilgrim should continue on Route 2 to a restored typical western community. Original buildings from various parts of Chelan County were moved here by the Chelan County Historical Society and in 1959 the museum was dedicated. The Willis Carey collection of Indian artifacts and pioneer relics was the nucleus of the museum's still growing memorabilia.

At the head of Main Street is a log mission, replica of the one built between 1856 and 1863 by the Oblate fathers. This first Christian mission in north central Washington was originally located south of Cashmere. In 1873, Father Urban Grassi rebuilt it near Indian territory and named it St. Francis Xavier. In 1888, the log structure was replaced by a frame building which stood as late as 1915. The replica with its bell tower and cross stands near a store, assay office, school, and log cabins of the 1800s.

Eastern Washington

3 CUSICK

Kalispel Caves

On the Kalispel Indian Reservation are caves rich in legends and precious to the Indian heritage. It is believed that Father de Smet, first missionary to the Kalispels, said Mass here in 1844. He then founded the St. Ignatius Mission, which stood on the reservation from 1845 to 1854. Because frequent floods and shortage of game made it difficult to support such a large number of people, Chief Voctor asked that the mission be moved to a better location. So in 1854, the mission and most of the hundreds of natives moved to the present Montana site.

Early in September each year, the Kalispel tribe gathers at the caves for an annual pilgrimage and memorial Mass.

4 SPOKANE

Cathedral of St. John the Evangelist

The Episcopal stone cathedral at 127 East 12th Avenue was begun in 1925 for a congregation that started much earlier. Designed in English Gothic with some French touches, the enormous structure is an impressive sight. The interior has wood carvings, stone carvings, and stained-glass windows. A carillon designed in England has 49 bells that weigh more than 40 tons. The organ has over 5,000 pipes. Occasional recitals are given on both instruments and draw music lovers from afar.

5 WALLA WALLA

Whitman Mission

When the call was sounded for volunteers for northwest mission work among the Indians, the American Board of Commissioners of Foreign missions sent Rev. Samuel Parker and Dr. Marcus Whitman. Arriving at the fur traders' rendezvous at Green River, the men consulted with Flathead and Nez Percé Indians and were convinced of the promising field. Parker continued on to explore possible sites, while Whitman returned to recruit workers. In 1836, Whitman, Rev. Henry Spalding, and their wives journeyed by wagon and cart to Fort Vancouver.

The Spaldings returned to the Nez Percé of Idaho, and the Whitmans built a mission house among the Cayuse at Waiilatpu. After learning the language and devising an alphabet, the mission-

aries printed books in the Indian language, first books published in the Pacific northwest. Agriculture was begun as the Indians were urged to give up nomadic life. Reports of dissension among the natives and a lack of money caused the Board to order the work closed, but Whitman returned east and persuaded the Board to reverse their decision. On returning in 1843, he was a valuable guide and physician to the great migration, and the mission soon became a welcome stop on the Oregon Trail.

For 11 years the Whitmans labored among the Indians until the Cayuse were convinced their way of life was in danger. Seeing their lands disappearing, and concerned over a measles epidemic spread by whites, the Cayuse attacked in force November 29, 1847, killing the Whitmans and 11 others. The 50 who were taken captive were ransomed a month later by the Hudson's Bay Company. The massacre ended Protestant mission work here and led to a war between natives and settlers.

Religious pilgrims to the 98-acre site should begin at the Visitors' Center and museum, then follow the self-guiding trail to the Great Grave, Whitman Memorial Shaft, and the mission buildings. The latter includes the site of small log lean-to Whitman hastily constructed for his bride, the elaborate T-shaped mission house built in 1838, and the Emigrant House used for weary travelers of the Oregon Trail.

NEVADA

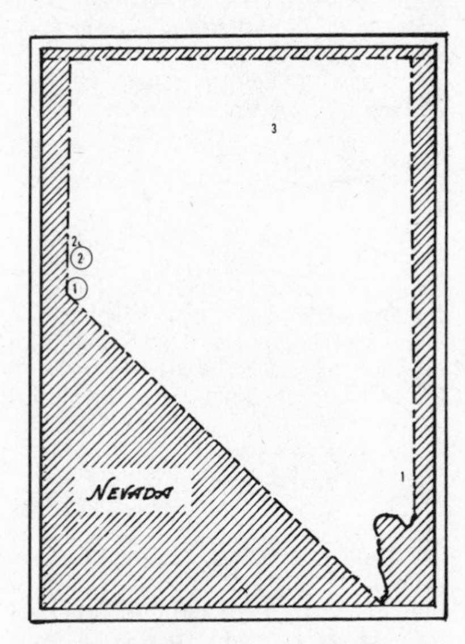

The Sagebrush state, with most of its lands in the arid Great Basin, is understandably thinly populated and has fewer spiritual heritage sites.

Franciscan friars first traversed the alkaline deserts in the early 1700s, followed by explorers and trappers.

Mormon settlers were responsible for the first permanent settlement when seven men from Salt Lake City established Mormon Station (now Genoa) in 1849, to sell supplies to emigrants passing through to California. Other Mormons and gentiles followed, and in 1851 they petitioned Congress for territorial governments. Statehood came with increased population in 1864.

The young Paiute Indian medicine man Wovoka began another facet of spiritual heritage in 1888 when he experienced his visions at Pyramid Lake. This is now within one of the approximately six Indian reservations in Nevada. Wovoka, the Indian Messiah, called native Americans to perform the Ghost Dance and other ceremonials. If they would don the white cloaks and dance this Spirit Dance, he said, they would be rid of the white man. The rituals soon spread to other tribes. The frenzied activity was misconstrued by whites as a war dance and triggered the Sioux Indian War.

Our tour begins on the northwest border of Nevada, where its earliest settlement can be found understandably near a cluster of lakes.

Northwestern Nevada

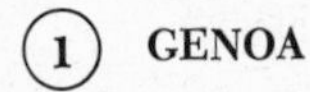

GENOA

Mormon Station Historic State Monument

Mormon Hampden Beatie established Mormon Station trading post in 1849. The Reese brothers, also of Salt Lake City took over the buildings in 1851, supplying meat, grains and perishables to prospectors traveling to California gold fields. It became a stop on the Pony Express and the Overland Telegraph. On the 2½ acre site is a log replica of the stockade and Mormon post as well as a museum.

 VIRGINIA CITY

St. Mary's in the Mountains

Highways 50 and 17 lead through the capital of Carson City and on to the community that was once the west's mining metropolis. The Comstock Lode, one of the richest ever discovered in silver and gold, brought a population of 30,000 in the 1870s. A reminder of the six churches is the impressive Gothic building on D Street. The present deep red church with large white bell tower and 4 small steeples was built in 1868, replacing a wooden structure.

IDAHO

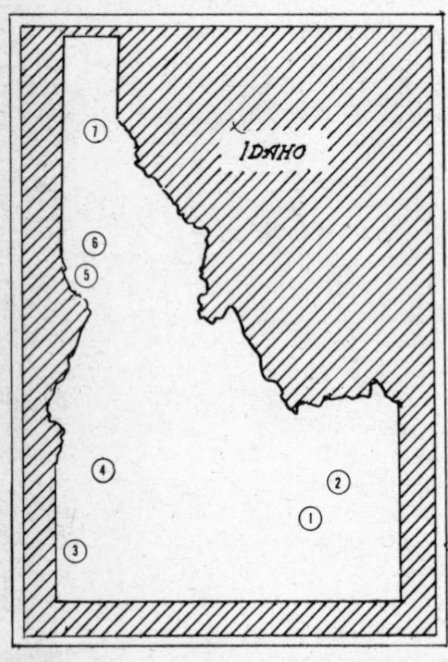

The land of the Sawtooth Mountains, Snake River, sparkling waterfalls, and Indian heritage is still primitive—a backpacker's paradise.

Until the gold rush of 1860, the great forests of the north were inhabited by Indians, trappers, and missionaries, while southern plains were dotted with Mormon agricultural settlements. With the influx of white men after the glittering metal was discovered in the Boise Basin, civilization came fast and statehood followed in 1890.

First years of the young state were turbulent, however, with miners' strikes and Indian troubles. The Nez Percé refused to be confined to part of their original reservation and, led by their brilliant chief, Joseph, resisted fiercely. After several defeats of troops, Joseph led a masterly retreat through 2,000 miles of enemy country into Montana, shepherding his noncombatants. He was captured just 30 miles south of the Canadian border and the Nez Percé were finally removed to Indian territory. Today native Americans, owning three major reservations, contribute much to our heritage.

Our tour begins in the south at Fort Hall, oldest white settlement begun in 1834, strategic meeting place of pioneer trails west.

Southern Idaho

 FORT HALL

Indian Tribal Building

Shoshone and Bannock Indian headquarters are in Fort Hall, Idaho's earliest permanent white settlement, just off Route 15 above Pocatello. Progressive Indian cattlemen and farmers take care of tribal business here. Buckskin and bead handcrafts are sold and information on activities may be obtained. Indian Sun Dances, their traditional religious ceremonies, are held close by in late July or early August. Spectators without cameras are allowed during the three days of dancing and the fourth day which is a feast day.

(2) IDAHO FALLS

Mormon Temple

North on Route 15 is a visible reminder of the Mormons who spread north into Idaho from their Utah promised land. Agricultural settlements were needed to care for the growing population around Great Salt Lake, so nearby Idaho was the answer. The glistening structure stands by the Snake River and overlooks the falls for which the city was named. It serves church members in eastern Idaho, Wyoming, and Montana. Slim white towers rise together to a climax, almost like a gigantic fountain when seen from a distance. Visitors are welcome to tour the grounds and enjoy films of the interior at the Visitors' Center.

(3) SILVER CITY

Ghost Town Church

After retracing Route 15 westward, the traveler comes to Idaho's largest ghost town, mostly deserted except in summer. Set amid sage-covered hills, Silver City can be found west of Mountain Home. About 40 of the earliest structures survive, reminding us that once this was the center of the second largest silver-producing area in the country.

On a bleak little byway is a wooden church with square bell tower. Two glass-less Gothic windows flank the boarded-up entrance door. If there was any paint, it has long disappeared. Men who once attended services here fought an underground war in 1868 when claim jumpers broke into shafts of the Golden Chariot Mine.

(4) BOISE

First United Methodist Cathedral

We leave the old for the new at Boise, capital of Idaho, when we drive up to the Cathedral of the Rockies, 1110 Franklin Street. Completed in 1960, the Gothic-style building encompasses a city block and seats 1,000. Arizona

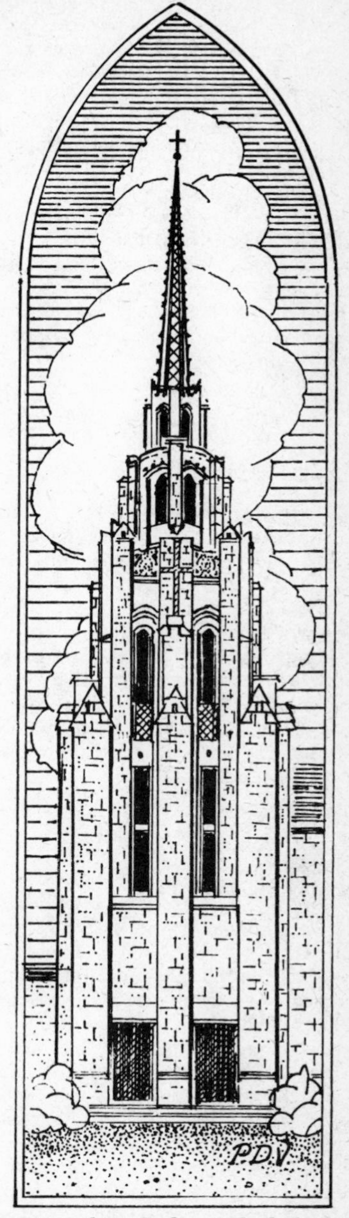

First United Methodist Cathedral, Boise

flagstone with Indiana sandstone trim is the exterior finish. The crowning feature is the soaring 135-foot tower, which is beautiful by day but magnificent at night when floodlights show the intricate tracery of the stone-and-metal patterns to the tip of the 8-foot cross which climaxes the spire.

Pioneer families worshiped in homes until 1875, when their first brick structure was completed. Now the 64 adjacent rooms in the cathedral house the many activities of a busy parish that serves all ages and a wide geographic area.

St. Michael's Cathedral

The sturdy Roman Catholic cathedral at 518 North Eighth Street was dedicated in 1902, and reminds us that Catholics were early arrivals in the state, beginning with Father de Smet as early as 1842. The sandstone building of today is English Gothic in style and is noted for a beautiful Tiffany stained-glass window. The tower added later is a memorial to soldiers killed in World War II.

Northern Idaho

(5) SLICKPOO

St. Joseph's Mission

Father Joseph Cataldo worked to convert the Nez Percé Indians to Catholicism and helped them build St. Joseph's Mission in 1874. It is found off Route 95, southeast of Lewiston. The white-frame building with its gleaming cross over the bell tower remains as a memorial to that early mission work. Nez Percé Indians gather the last Sunday of May each year for a memorial mass. It is part of the Nez Percé Historical Park.

(6) SPALDING

Spalding Memorial Park

At the headquarters of the Nez Percé National Historical Park is found the site of the second mission to the Indians founded by Presbyterian missionary Henry Spalding. He and his wife, Eliza, journeyed west with the Whitmans in 1836, then began their work in Idaho. A church, school, and mills were built. Traces of the 1840 saw- and flour-mills are still visible. On the grounds also can be seen the graves and monuments to the missionaries. The first printing press in Idaho territory turned out Indian and white literature here.

(7) KELLOGG

Coeur d'Alene Mission of the Sacred Heart

Jesuit missionaries and a band of Indians built the picturesque mission church at Kellogg between 1848 and 1853. The oldest building in the state, it was constructed with simple tools like the auger, broad ax, pulley, penknife, and a few ropes. Walls were originally plastered with mud from the Coeur d'Alene River. Large hand-pegged timbers can still be seen in the sanctuary, and the hand-carved altar, statues, and panels show the dedication and craftsmanship of the Indians and priests. The imposing exterior has six pillars reminiscent of Greek Revival architecture. Its façade has a sunburst design below the high cross.

APPENDIX

The numbers which precede each site indicate the location of the site on the appropriate state map in the body of the book.

ALABAMA

1 Athens
Founders Hall Chapel Athens College campus, life-sized carvings of New Testament on altar.

2 Florence
Ceremonial Indian Mound South Court St., Museum of Native American Culture.

3 Greensboro
Presbyterian Church Organized in 1823 by veterans of American Revolution.

ARIZONA

1 Yarnell
Shrine of St. Joseph Highway 89, memorial to war dead of Catholic Action League, statues by Felix Lucero.

ARKANSAS

1 Arkansas Post
Arkansas Post National Memorial 1686 site of state's first settlement, fort, fur-trading post and mission.

2 Augusta
Presbyterian Church Woodrow Wilson worshipped here as a youth.

3 Bull Shoals
Mountain Village 1890 Restored Ozark town includes church.

4 Eureka Springs
Hillspeak Route 23S, Headquarters of Episcopal Book Club and *Anglican Digest,* also tours of editorial facilities.

Hillspeak 3000 acre headquarters Episcopal Book Club *St. Elizabeth's Catholic Church* like St. Sophia, Austria-Hungary.

5 Murfreesboro

Caddo Burial Mound Route 27, prehistoric Indian settlement and museum.

CALIFORNIA

1 Glendale

Forest Lawn Memorial Park Griffiths Park, replicas of three famous churches and large painting of crucifixion.

2 Los Angeles

Hebrew Union College Campus of University of Southern California, Rosenberg Archives on American Jewish Life.

Holmes Memorial Chapel 6th and Berendo Streets, international office of United Church of Religious Science.

St. John's Episcopal Church 514 West Adams Blvd., re-creation of elaborate church in Toscanella, Italy.

3 Oakland

Oakland Mormon Temple 1964 white towered temple of Church of Jesus Christ Latter-Day Saints.

4 Redlands

San Bernardino Asistencia Barton Road, 1830 mission, restored, now a museum.

5 Riverside

Mission Inn 3649 Seventh St., historical hotel with chapels, cloister walk & bell collection.

Mt. Rubidoux Huntington Park, cement cross memorial to Father Junipero Serra.

6 San Francisco

Grace Episcopal Cathedral 1051 Taylor St., 60 spectacular stained-glass windows.

Old St. Mary's 660 California St., 1854 gothic-style church, art objects, Chinese mission.

St. Mary's Cathedral Geary and Gough Sts., poured concrete 1970 church, multi-colored stained-glass cross.

Temple Emanue-El Arguello Blvd., levantine, richly decorated temple with colonnaded courtyard.

7 San Jose

Mission San Jose de Guadalupe Adobe *padre's* quarters now museum of 1797 mission.

8 San Rafael

Mission San Rafael Arcangel 1104 Fifth Ave., founded 1817 now restored, once a mission hospital.

9 Santa Cruz

The Last Supper 526 Broadway, art gallery with Leonardo da Vinci's masterpiece in life-sized wax figures.
Mission Santa Cruz 126 High St., reproduction of 1794 mission has exhibits in chapel wing.

CONNECTICUT

1 Brooklyn
First Ecclesiastical Society Unitarian church in village center is a gem of colonial-style design.
Old Trinity Church East of Brooklyn off Route 6, Episcopal "hip roof" church.
2 Cornwall
Site of Foreign mission school Across from First Church of Christ, from 1817 to 1826 trained youth of other races for mission work.
Grave of Henry Obookiah Cornwall Cemetery, Hawaiian youth whose death launched Hawaiian mission movement.
3 Farmington
Congregational Church Main St., 1652 architectural gem, only offshoot of Thomas Hooker's church.

DELAWARE

Middletown
Old St. Anne's Episcopal Church South on Rt. 896, 1786 colonial-style brick on site of log chapel.

DISTRICT OF COLUMBIA

The sites are so compacted here, it is best for the traveler to obtain a detailed street guide.

Christ Church 620 G St. SE, first Episcopal parish in city, "Folk Gothic" design by Benjamin Latrobe.
Convent of Mercy 3525 N St. NW, first Roman Catholic church in area built 1791–95, originally named Trinity Church.
Convent of Visitation of the Holy Mary 1500 35th St. NW, founded 1799, Poor Clare nuns, 1821 chapel.
Memorial Evangelical Lutheran Church Thomas Circle NW, church leaders depicted in stained-glass, built 1864.
Metropolitan Memorial United Methodist Church Nebraska and New Mexico Aves. NW, 1932, English Gothic.
National City Christian Church Thomas Circle NW, 1930, church of President James Garfield (an ordained minister).

Notre Dame Chapel Trinity College campus NE, award winning church, ceiling mosaics, stained-glass windows.

St. John's Episcopal Church 16th & H Sts. NW, stained-glass windows feature statesmen.

St. Matthew's Roman Catholic Cathedral 1725 Rhode Island Ave. NW, Renaissance style, altar and font from India.

St. Paul's Episcopal Church Rock Creek Church Rd. NW, parish dates from 1712, fine sculptures.

FLORIDA

1 Boca Raton
Bibletown Off Route 1, conference center and Community Church in campus setting.

2 Chipley
Methodist Mission Moss Hill settlements, log schoolhouse where court sessions also were held.

3 Clearwater
Church of Christ South Hercules Ave., luminous interior from gold metallic cloth and plastic roof.

4 Fort George Island
Site of 1567 Spanish Mission Kingsley Plantation, State Historic Site, bird and plant sanctuary.

5 Fort Lauderdale
Coral Ridge Presbyterian Church 555 No. Federal St., magnificent contemporary design, seats 2500.

6 Fort Walton Beach
Temple Mound Museum Route 98, Temple mound and archeological site dating to A.D. 1250.

7 Hibernia
St. Margaret's Episcopal Church English Gothic-style church built 1875–77.

8 Jacksonville
Riverside Baptist Church 2650 Park St., 1925, Spanish and Byzantine architecture.

9 Key West
Convent of Mary Immaculate Truman St., native stone building, hospital in Spanish-American war.

10 Miami
Plymouth Congregational Church 3429 Devon Rd., mission-style coral building, 350 year old door.

11 Ocala
First Christian Church Contemporary design with free-standing cross.

12 Palm Beach

Bethesda-by-the-Sea South County Rd. & Barton Blvd., 15th century Gothic design, cloister, paintings.

13 Pensacola

Old Christ Church 407 South Jefferson St., now historical museum of early Florida.

14 St. Augustine

St. Joseph Academy 241 George St., school for blacks founded after Civil War.

St. Photios Shrine Greek Orthodox center memorial for Greek immigrant colony of 1768–1778.

Trinity Episcopal Church St. George St., has both Anglican and Spanish Catholic history.

15 Tallahassee

Trinity Methodist Church off Park Ave., result of first Methodist mission to area.

16 Tarpon Springs

Universalist Church Grand Blvd. and Read St., religious art by George Innes Jr. with "mystic brush."

17 West Palm Beach

First Church of Christ, Scientist Classical design with Ionic-columned portico.

GEORGIA

1 Cartersville

Etowah Indian Mounds Route 41, ceremonial mounds, museum about mound dwellers.

2 Chatsworth

Chief Vann House Route 76, home of Cherokee Indian who sponsored Moravian mission.

3 Pine Mountain

Ida Carson Callaway Memorial Chapel Callaway Gardens, noted for stained-glass windows.

4 Savannah

Evangelical Lutheran Church of the Ascension Bull and State Sts., 16 miniature historical scenes, Norman-Gothic style.

Independent Presbyterian Church Bull St., replica of St. Martin-in-the-Field, London.

HAWAII

1 Honolulu

Makiki Christian Church 829 Pensacola St., designed like Osaka Castle, Japan.

2 Honaumau
St. Benedict's Catholic Church Off Route 16, painted church gives illusion of space inside.

3 Kilauea
Christ Memorial Episcopal Church Off Route 56, of native stone with hand-carved altar.

ILLINOIS

1 Andover
Jenny Lind Chapel Swedish Lutherans settled here in 1850, brick chapel built 1854.

2 Chicago
Queen of All Saints Basilica 6280 North Sauganash Ave., magnificent Gothic cathedral.

3 LaSalle
Starved Rock State Park Off Route 71, site of Father Marquette's 1675 mission.

4 Mundelein
Benedictine Sanctuary of Perpetual Adoration Memorial to 1926 International Eucharistic Congress.

5 Oak Park
Unity Temple 875 Lake Street, a Unitarian-Universalist church by Frank Lloyd Wright.

6 Peoria
Jubilee College State Memorial Off Route 50, chapel and buildings built by Bishop Chase.

INDIANA

1 Anderson
Mounds State Park Route 32, ceremonial mounds of Mound-building Indians, dig and artifacts.

2 Indianapolis
Carmelite Monastery Cold Spring Road, designed like European castle.
Tabernacle Presbyterian Church 418 East 34th St., stained-glass windows depict Biblical scenes.

3 Jasper
St. Joseph's Roman Catholic Church 1121 North Newton St., Romanesque design, mosaics.

4 Munster
Carmelite Shrine 1628 Ridge Rd., built of sponge rock, interior chapels decorated with rocks.

5 Valparaiso
Seven Dolors Shrine On Franciscan grounds, shrine to Mary and service men of Slavic origin.

IOWA

1 Council Bluffs
Mormon Memorial Boulder Bayliss Park, commemorates 1846–1847 stop on westward trek.

2 Dyersville
Basilica of St. Francis Xavier 1889 Catholic church with fine ceiling fresco.

3 Grinnell
Herrick Chapel Grinnell College campus, carbon prints of Sistine Chapel's prophets and sibyls.

4 Guttenberg
Gutenberg Press Facsimiles of Gutenberg Bible on display.

5 McGregor
Effigy Mounds National Monument Off Route 52, Indian burial mounds in shape of bears and birds.

6 Oskaloosa
William Penn College 1875 Quakers established college, chapel, library with Quaker publications.

7 West Branch
Herbert Hoover National Historic Site Off Rte. I80 restored Quaker meeting house attended by Hoovers.

KANSAS

1 Atchison
St. Benedict's Abbey College, prep-school and Abbey Chapel with 31 frescoes and 31 altars.

2 Council Grove
St. Mary's Chapel On grounds of original post, 1855 chapel was once school, now Catholic

3 Leavenworth
Memorial Chapel Fort Leavenworth, 1878 post chapel of limestone, national cemetery.

4 Newton
Kauffman Museum Bethel College campus, Mennonite settlers' farm, cabin, artifacts.

5 Osawatomie
Old Stone Church 6th and Parker Sts., pioneer church, oldest in continuous use.

6 Wichita

All Indian Center National museum and library focuses on religions and culture of natives.

Pioneer Church Cow Town of 1870s, 1870 Protestant church, now Catholic.

KENTUCKY

1 Auburn

Shaker Museum Off Route 68, Shaker culture graphically portrayed, 2,500 items.

2 Bardstown

St. Joseph's Cathedral 310 Stephen Foster St., neoclassical designed Catholic edifice, art masterpieces.

3 Covington

Cathedral Basilica of the Assumption 12th St. and Madison Ave., Catholic "Cathedral of Glass."

4 Tompkinsville

Old Mulky Meeting House State Shrine Oldest log church in Kentucky, site of revivals.

5 Wickliffe

Ancient Buried City Route 62, excavations of Moundbuilders show temple mounds, exhibits.

MAINE

1 Norridgewock

Memorial Marker Off Route 201, 1688 grave of Father Sebastian Rasle, Jesuit missionary.

2 Popham Beach

Fort Popham Memorial Off Route 1, 1607 site of first English settlement, 1861 fort ruins.

MARYLAND

1 Baltimore

Cathedral of Mary Our Queen 5200 North Charles St., impressive Gothic-style Catholic edifice.

Greek Orthodox Church of the Annunciation 22 Preston St., once Congregational, 1963 renovations.

2 Columbia

Interfaith Centers at Wilde Lake and Oakland Mills, Catholics, Jews, and Protestants share facilities.

3 Emmitsburg

Mount Saint Mary's College founded 1808, stone convent, early school room.

4 Warwick

Marker for Cokesbury College Route 40, site of first Methodist college in country.

5 Wye Mills

Old Wye Church Route 50, 1712 colonial-style brick building erected as "chapel of ease."

MASSACHUSETTS

1 Amesbury

Mary Baker Eddy Home 277 Main St., founder of Christian Science lived here 1868–1870.

John Greenleaf Whittier Home 86 Friends St., Quaker poet, hymn writer lived here 1836–1892.

2 Boston

Cathedral of Holy Cross 1400 Washington St., archdiocese headquarters, one of world's largest churches.

Chinese Christian Church 54 Harvard St., 1946 church ministers to large Chinese community.

Temple Ohabei Shalom 1187 Beacon St., domed edifice of Baroque-Romanesque style.

3 Concord

Old Manse Monument St., home of Ralph Waldo Emerson, clergyman, essayist and Transcendentalist.

4 Danvers

Wadsworth Parsonage Site 69 Center St., servant Tibatha's ghost stories began witchcraft troubles.

5 Duxbury

John Alden House 105 Alden St., last home of Pilgrim Alden, built in 1673 by son Jonathan.

6 Gloucester

Sargent-Murray-Gilman Hough House Middle St., home of Rev. John Murray, founder American Universalism.

7 Lexington

Hancock-Clarke House 35 Hanover St., parsonage sheltered patriots on April 18, 1775.

8 Marblehead

St. Michael's Church Pleasants St., oldest Episcopal church in continuous use in New England.

9 New Marlboro

United Church of New Marlboro, Christ Congregational Elihu Burritt organized League of Universal Brotherhood.

10 Orleans

Community of Jesus Rock Harbor, Cape Cod abbey-like Christian community, chapel, retreat house.

11 Salem

Essex Institute 132 Essex St., old Quaker meeting house on grounds, museum exhibits.

Pioneers' Village Forest River Park, replica of original Puritan settlement includes governor's house.

12 South Boston

St. Augustine Chapel 181 Dorchester St., New England's oldest Catholic church.

13 Springfield

Old First Church Court Square, 1819, Congregational parish dates to 1637.

14 Williamstown

Haystack Monument Mission Park, Williams College site of prayer meeting where foreign missions began.

MICHIGAN

1 Bloomfield Hills

Christ Church Cranbrook 470 Church Rd., English Gothic edifice, art galleries, gardens, science institute.

2 Detroit

Jefferson Avenue Presbyterian Church 8625 Jefferson Ave., 1926, Gothic stone edifice, carved wood.

3 Ludington

Illuminated Cross At mouth of Pere Marquette River, site of Father Marquette's death in 1675.

4 Mio

Our Lady of the Woods Shrine Route 72, shrine-grotto consisting of many Marian shrines.

5 Royal Oak

Shrine of the Little Flower Woodward Ave., Ohio limestone edifice, site of Father Coughlin broadcasts.

6 St. Louis

Bethany Indian Lutheran Cemetery Route 27, Lutheran mission here 1848–1869.

7 Vermontville

First Congregational Church Vermont Congregationalists settled town in 1836, New England style church.

MINNESOTA

1 Duluth

Bible House 715 West Superior St., collection of Bibles and scrolls includes Torah and Koran.

2 Garden City

Log Cabin Seminary Route 169, replica of Missouri seminary at fairgrounds.

3 Isle

Father Hennepin State Memorial Wayside Mille Lacs Lake, Father Hennepin captured here.

MISSISSIPPI

1 Columbus

Annunciation Catholic Church 808 College St., stained-glass windows, decorated ceiling.

First United Methodist Church 602 Main St., 1860 brick edifice, slave balcony.

2 Port Gibson

Presbyterian Church Church and Walnut Sts., steamboat chandeliers, pointing finger on steeple.

MISSOURI

1 Branson

Williams Chapel College of the Ozarks campus, Gothic church resembles European cathedrals.

2 Liberty

Charles Haddon Spurgeon Collection William Jewell College Library, Puritan and Anabaptist books.

3 St. Louis

Vedanta Society 205 South Sinker Blvd., Hindu temple, library, book shop.

MONTANA

1 Browning

Museum of the Plains Indians Route 2 and 89, history, culture and current information.

NEBRASKA

1 Grand Island

Cathedral of the Nativity of St. Mary Virgin 204 South Cedar St., 1928 Gothic edifice.

2 Omaha

Pioneer Park Mormon Cemetery Memorial to 600 deaths, winter 1846–1847.

NEVADA

1 Overton
Lost City Museum Route 12 Indian relics and ceremonials.
2 Reno
Center for Religion and Life University of Nevada campus, non denominational.
3 Tuscarora
Tuscarora Museum Chinese settlement when mines operated, artifacts and exhibits.

NEW HAMPSHIRE

1 Enfield
La Salette Shrine Route 4, replica of Marian Shrine at La Salette, France.
2 North Salem
Mystery Hill Route 111, archeological, megalithic site dating about 2000 B.C.
3 Rumney
Mary Baker Eddy Home Residence of founder of Christian Science from 1860–1862.
4 West Claremont
Old St. Mary's Church First Catholic church in state, built 1823–24, also housed first Catholic school.
Union Church Oldest standing Episcopal church in state begun 1771, completed 1789.

NEW JERSEY

1 Hackensack
Old Church on the Green 42 Court St., 1696 Dutch Reformed Gothic-Colonial edifice.
2 Hopewell
Old School Baptist Church West Broad St., 1748 brick Baptist meeting house, hospital in Revolution.
3 Newark
Cathedral of Sacred Heart Clifton and Park Aves., French Gothic architecture, 200 stained-glass windows.
4 Smithville
Historic Town of Smithville Route 9, reconstructed 19th century village, 60 buildings including church.
5 Somerville
Old Dutch Parsonage 65 Washington Place, residence of Rev. Jacob Hardenburgh founder of Rutgers.

6 Stanhope
Waterloo Village off Route 206, restored prerevolutionary town of Andover Forge includes church.
7 Trenton
Friends Meeting House East Hanover and Montgomery Sts., plain 1680 building has original construction.

NEW MEXICO

1 Santa Fe
Our Lady of Lights Chapel 219 Old Santa Fe Trail, unsupported spiral staircase in 1878 church.

NEW YORK

1 Albany
St. Peter's Episcopal Church State and Lodge Sts., French Gothic, stained-glass windows.
2 Allegany
St. Bonaventure University Library Rare manuscripts include 1368 Vulgate Bible.
3 Buffalo
Our Lady of Victory Basilica Routes 62 and 18, 1926 Renaissance shrine.
Temple Beth Zion 804 Delaware Ave., Ben Shahn stained-glass windows.
4 Clinton
Hamilton College Chapel Only early three story church remaining in America, 1827.
5 Fishkill
Old Dutch Church Route 52, 1716 church was briefly prison for Revolutionary spy Enoch Crosby.
Trinity Episcopal Church Route 52, hospital for American troops in Revolution.
6 Garden City
Cathedral of the Incarnation Cathedral Ave., Episcopal, Gothic style, centennial bells.
7 Kings Point
U.S. Merchant Marine Memorial Chapel 68 acre, 40 building complex, 1000 midshipmen.
8 Mohawk
Fort Herkimer Church German Palatines built church in 1730, used twice as a fort.
9 Moravia

St. Matthew's Episcopal Church 16 Church St., Oberammergau carvings by Hans Mayer.

10 New York City

Church of the Transfiguration 1 East 29th St., "Little Church Around the Corner," Episcopal.

Hebrew Union College and Jewish Institute 40 West 68th St., Rabbinical school, Reform Temple.

St. Mark's in the Bowery 2nd Ave. and 10th St., 1799, grave of Peter Stuyvesant.

St. Mary's Catholic Church 246 East 15th St., Byzantine rite, Greek style mosaics, icons.

St. Thomas' Episcopal Church 5th Ave. and 53rd St., Gothic style, 60 sculptures of saints and churchmen.

Seamen's Church Institute of New York 15 State St. Episcopal agency serving active merchant seamen; begun as a floating chapel in 1834 in New York harbor; serves all nationalities with educational, recreational and counselling facilities; Conrad library, chapel.

11 Onchiota

Six Nation Indian Museum North of Saranac off Route 33, authentic miniature village, exhibits.

12 Ossining

Maryknoll Shrine Headquarters of Roman Catholic Foreign Mission Society of America, museums.

13 Richmond

Richmondtown Restoration Staten Island, 40-building restoration, 1695 church-school.

14 Schenectady

St. George's Episcopal Church 30 North Ferry St., Mohawk valley's oldest, barracks during Revolution.

15 Schoharie

Old Stone Fort German Lutherans built fort-church in 1772, library and museum.

16 Youngstown

Our Lady of Fatima Shrine Barnabite Fathers administer shrine of penance and prayer, 90 statues.

NORTH CAROLINA

1 Asheville

St. Lawrence Catholic Church 97 Haywood St., Spanish Baroque-style tile and brick edifice.

2 Bethabara

Bethabara Park 1788 Moravian church built by first settlers, houses, reconstructed stockade.

3 Fayetteville
First Prebyterian Church Bow and Ann Sts., colonial style building, exceptional furnishings.

4 Manteo
Fort Raleigh National Historic Site Lost Colony memorial, drama, exhibits.

5 Pinehurst
Village Chapel Routes 401 and 211, near 5 golf courses, nondenominational, early service for golfers.

6 Raleigh
Christ Episcopal Church 120 East Edentown St., Neo-Gothic medieval parish style church, cloister.

7 Snow Camp
Cane Creek Meeting Quakers settled region in 1749, old mill and store, drama "The Sword of Peace."

NORTH DAKOTA

1 Devils Lake
Fort Totten Historic Park Route 57, 1865 chaplain's quarters, museum, native dances.

2 Fargo
Bonanzaville, U.S.A. Cass County Agricultural Park, 19th-century recreated village, church.

3 Jamestown
Frontier Village Route 94, 1883 frame church in pioneer-town reconstruction.

4 New Town
Three Affiliated Tribes Museum Four Bears Memorial Park, Mandan Indian earth mounds, exhibits.

5 Rugby
Pioneer Village Museum Route 2, reconstruction includes church, nation's geographical center.

OHIO

1 Burton
Century Village Routes 87 and 700, restored Western Reserve community, 20 buildings, church.

2 Carey
National Shrine of Our Lady of Consolation Image, copy of original in Luxembourg.

3 Cincinnati
Klau Library and Balsheimer Rare Books University of Cincinnati, Hebrew Union College.

4 Cleveland
National Shrine of Our Lady of Lourdes Rock grotto resembles Lourdes, France.

5 Granville
St. Luke's Church New Englanders settled town, 1837 church has original furnishings.

6 Kirtland
Kirtland Temple 9020 Chillicothe Rd., original Mormon temple restored, three story stone edifice.

7 Marietta
Campus Martius State Memorial Museum Contains possessions of 48 Congregational pioneers.

8 Miamisburg
Miamisburg Mound State Memorial Routes 25 and 175, 68 foot conical mound, prehistoric earthworks.

9 Mt. Pleasant
Friends Meeting House Near Ohio River, restored Quaker structure.

10 Oxford
Kumler Memorial Chapel Western College campus, reproduction of 11th-century Norman church.

11 Toledo
Rosary Cathedral 2561 Collingwood Blvd., limestone and granite 16th-century Spanish edifice.

OKLAHOMA

1 Norman
W. B. Bizzell Memorial Library University of Oklahoma campus, comprehensive Bible collection.

2 Oklahoma City
St. Luke's Methodist Church 222 N.W. 15th St., comtemporary edifice, stained-glass panels.

3 Okmulgee
Old Creek Indian Council House 1878 capitol of Creeks, museum of culture and history.

4 Tulsa
Boston Avenue Methodist Church Boston Ave. at 13th St., skyscraper style combines business and church appearance.

OREGON

1 Oregon City
Atkinsin Memorial Church 6th and John Sts., Gothic, oldest Congregational Church in west, 1844.

2 Portland
Old Church 1422 S.W. 11th Ave., 1883 Carpenter-Gothic church, former Presbyterian, now hall.
National Sanctuary of Our Sorrowful Mother 1924 Catholic shrine, Order of the Servants of Mary.

PENNSYLVANIA

1 Camp Hill
Peace Church 1793 edifice, state historic site, built for separate German Lutheran and Reformed parishes.
2 Harrisburg
State Capitol Capitol Hill, murals in dome highlight Penn's invitation to religiously persecuted.
3 Loretto
Prince Gallitzin Chapel House (Catholic) Russian Prince Father Gallitzin founded town.
4 Newtown
Quaker Meeting House George School campus, 1755 timbers in 1812 building, moved from Philadelphia.
5 Philadelphia
Cathedral of Saints Peter and Paul (Catholic) 18th St., replica of Lombard Church of St. Charles, Rome.
6 Pittsburgh
Heinz Memorial Chapel University of Pittsburgh, French Gothic style, seals of early colleges.
7 Watsontown
Warrior Run Church Route 147, 1835 brick structure begun by Scotch-Irish settlers.
8 Womelsdorf
Conrad Weiser Park Route 422, home of judge, diplomat, religious layman, Indian peacemaker.

RHODE ISLAND

1 Middletown
Whitehall Berkley and Paradise Aves., 1729 home of Dean Berkley, Irish Bishop, philosopher.
2 Newport
Sabbatarian Meeting House Newport Historical Society includes 1729 Seventh-day Baptist edifice.
3 Portsmouth
St. Gregory's Chapel Portmouth Abbey grounds, octagonal church of Italian inspiration.

SOUTH CAROLINA

1 Charleston
Unitarian Church 8 Archdale St., First Independent, became south's first Unitarian church, Gothic tracery.
2 Clemson
Hanover House Clemson University campus, built in 1716 by fleeing French Huguenots.
3 Columbia
Trinity Episcopal Church 1100 Sumter St., replica, Cathedral of St. Peter, York, England.
4 Stateburg
Church of the Holy Cross (Episcopal) gift of Countess Natalie DeLarge, Gothic-Revival style, 1852.
5 Summerville
Old Dorchester Historical State Park Route 642, 1695 Congregational town ruins, church bell tower.

SOUTH DAKOTA

1 Bethlehem
Shrine of Nativity Off routes 168 and 137 from Piedmont, Benedictine shrine, candles for United Nations Members.
2 Rapid City
Sioux Indian Museum and Craft Center Hadley Park, displays of past and present culture.

TENNESSEE

1 Hermitage
Old Hermitage Church President Andrew Jackson contributed to building of handmade brick church.
2 Rugby
Christ Church Once part of 1880 Christian Socialist village begun by Thomas Hughes, 1849 rosewood organ.

TEXAS

1 Bracketville
Alamo Village Route 674, replica of Alamo and area, circa 1836.
2 Castroville
St. Louis Catholic Church Alsatian settlers founded town in 1844, church erected 1869.

3 El Paso
Nuestra Senora de la Concepcion del Cocorro Lower Valley, pueblo and mission complex.
San Elizario Presidio Chapel 1777 Spanish military garrison chapel now parish church.

4 Goliad
Goliad State Historic Park Routes 77A and 183, restored 1749 mission, Spanish architecture.

5 Houston
St. John's Church Sam Houston Park, Bagby St., recreated pioneer village, clapboard church.

6 San Antonio
San Fernando Cathedral Main Plaza, Canary Island colonists began parish in 1849.
Temple Beth El 211 Belknap Place, Spanish-style edifice has stained-glass symbols.
Our Lady of Mt. Carmel and St. Therese Off Route 181, national shrine, replica of Shrine of Little Flower, France.

7 San Marcos
Robinson Chapel Tower of Prayer San Marcos Baptist Academy campus, wood and glass structure.

UTAH

1 Cove Fort
Old Cove Fort Routes 4 and 15, stone Mormon fort, exhibits.

2 Logan
Cache Valley Historical Museum 52 West 2nd St. N., pioneer Mormon artifacts.

3 Salt Lake City
This Is The Place Monument Pioneer Trail State Park, 60 foot spire, visitors' center.

VERMONT

1 Arlington
St. James Church Route 7, oldest Episcopal parish in Vermont, 1829 Gothic, granite and wood.

2 Highgate
Marker of First Church in State Built by Jesuit priests and Abnaki Indians.

3 Middlebury
Congregational Church Pleasant and Main Sts., intricate decorations, palladian windows.

4 Proctor
Marble Exhibit Route 3, bas-relief copy of Last Supper by Leonardo Da Vinci carved from one block.
5 Richmond
Old Round Church Unique 16-sided edifice built in 1812–1814 for 5 denominations, now town owned.
6 South Stratford
Universalist Church First Universalist church in America, built in 1868.
7 Stowe
Blessed Sacrament Catholic Church Rustic chapel memorial to Joseph Dutton who served lepers on Molokai.

VIRGINIA

1 Lancaster
Christ Church Routes 3 and 222, restored 1732 edifice, Carter family had 14 distinguished citizens.
2 Lynchburg
Quaker Memorial Presbyterian Church 1798 South River Meeting of Friends, now Presbyterian.
3 Petersburg
Blandford Church Crater Rd., 1734–1737, 15 Tiffany windows given by Confederate States.
4 Smithfield
St. Luke's Church Route 10, "The Old Brick Church," 1632, was Church of England, now national shrine.
5 Waterford
Waterford Historic District 1740 Quaker town now restored, craft center.
6 Winchester
Old Lutheran Church Ruins 226 West Amherst St., reminder of early settlers of Fairfax Grant, 1764.

WASHINGTON

1 Ford
Site of Tshimakain Mission Granite marker where Congregationalists clergy began work with Indians.
2 Kettle Falls
St. Paul's Mission Restored second Catholic mission in Washington begun by Father de Smet in 1845.
3 Omak
St. Mary's Mission Off Route 97, 1905 white frame church on campus of school for Indians.

4 Maryhill
Stonehenge Route 14, replica of ancient 2000 B.C. ceremonial worship center in Wiltshire, England.

5 Spokane
Pacific Northwest Indian Center Gonzaga University campus, Jesuit missionary manuscripts, Indian artifacts.
St. Charles Parish Church 4514 Alberta St., contemporary Catholic edifice, copper bell tower.

6 Tacoma
Tacoma Totem Pole 9th and A Sts., Alaskan Indian heritage reminder at beginning of Historic Trail.
Washington State Museum North Stadium Way, contains journal of missionary, Mrs. Marcus Whitman.

7 Toledo
Cowlitz Mission 1838 site of oldest Catholic mission in state, St. Francis Church and Academy.

8 Vancouver
Fort Vancouver National Historic Site East Evergreen Blvd., monument to first sermon of Jesse Lee.

WEST VIRGINIA

1 Charles Town
Ruins of St. George Chapel Route 51, 1769 Church of England not used after the Revolution.

2 Grafton
Mother's Day Shrine Former Andrews Methodist Church, now international shrine to Mother's Day.

3 Lewisburg
Old Stone Church Route 51, Scotch-Irish Presbyterians settled area in 1783, slave balcony.

WISCONSIN

1 Dickeyville
Grotto of Christ the King and Mary His Mother Shrine of stone, glass and shells from around the world.

2 Green Bay
Christ Episcopal Church Cherry and Madison Sts., Oldest permanent church site in state, 1829.

3 Hubertus
Shrine of Mary-Help of Christians Route 167, Carmelite friars maintain Romanesque church.

4 La Crosse
Christ Episcopal Church 111 North Ninth Street, Interior has elaborate wood carvings.

5 Milwaukee
Marquette University Art Collection Flemish Italian Renaissance religious art.

WYOMING

1 Daniel
Monument to Jesuit Pierre de Smet 2 miles southeast of Daniel, site of first mass June 5, 1840.

2 Fort Bridger
Fort Bridger State Historic Site Route 30 S., 1834 trading post was Mormon headquarters, museum.

3 Guernsey
Fort Laramie National Monument Route 26, post and fort restoration, site of Father de Smet's treaty.

PICTURE CREDITS

PICTURE CREDITS BY PAGES

Massachusetts: **2.** Plymouth Plantation, **3.** D.C. Mahoney, **4.** Witch House, **6.** Christian Science Publishing House, **8.** Courtesy Longyear Historical Society, **13.** Brandeis University

New Hampshire: **19.** Shaker Community

Connecticut: **26.** Sketch by John Wadda, courtesy The Unitarian Church

Vermont: **27.** Old First Church photo by Fred M. Dole

New York: **30.** Marble Collegiate Church, **31.** Middle Collegiate Church, **34.** Joseph Molitor photo courtesy Plymouth Church of the Pilgrims, **37.** New Paltz Huguenot Society, **38.** First Church in Albany, **40.** Church of Jesus Christ Latter-Day Saints

New Jersey: **42.** David Beardslee photo courtesy New Brunswick Seminary

Virginia: **47.** (top) Association for Research and Enlightenment, **47.** (bottom) Courtesy Norfolk Convention & Visitor's Bureau, **48.** Thomas L. Williams photo courtesy Jamestown Foundation, **49.** Photos courtesy Abingdon Episcopal Church, **50.** Old Presbyterian Meeting House, **51.** (left) Photo by Marler courtesy Christ Church, **51.** (right) Photo by Allen Studios courtesy Trinity Episcopal Church, **53.** National Park Service photo by Richard Frear

Maryland: **55.** U. S. Naval Academy, **56.** L. Aubrey Bodine photo, **57.** Mount Vernon Place Methodist Church

Delaware: **59.** Custom Studios courtesy Holy Trinity Episcopal Church

Pennsylvania: **63.** Society of Friends, **65.** Ralph S. Humphreys photo, **67.** American Baptist News Service photo, **68.** Jacob Stelman photo, **71.** Photo by Rath, **73.** Courtesy Old Economy Village

West Virginia: **76.** Courtesy Bethany College

District of Columbia: **78.** National Presbyterian Church, **79.** J. Alexander photo courtesy General Conference of Seventh-day Adventists

Florida: **82.** Florida News Bureau Dept. of Commerce, **84.** Florida News Bureau, **85.** Florida News Bureau

Georgia: **86.** Courtesy Christ Church, **88.** Midway Museum, **89.** Photo by B. Berg, Park Tech. Courtesy National Park Service

North Carolina: **92.** Courtesy Brunswick Town State Historic Site, **93.** Duke University, **94.** Thyatira Presbyterian Church

South Carolina: **98.** Photo Louis Schwartz, **100** & **101.** Bob Jones University Collection

Mississippi: **103.** Audrey Murphy photo, **104.** National Park Service

Alabama: **106.** Andy Russell photo courtesy News Bureau University of Alabama, **107.** (left) courtesy of Bureau of Publicity and Information, Alabama, **107.** (right) Bureau of Publicity & Information State Capitol, Montgomery, Alabama

Louisiana: **108.** Greater New Orleans Tourist and Convention Committee, **109.** Grace Episcopal Church

Tennessee: **111.** Nashville Banner photo by Jack Gunther courtesy Office of Public Relations, University of the South, **112.** (top) Office of Public Relations, University of the South, **112.** (bottom) Downtown Presbyterian Church

Kentucky: **115.** Division of Publicity, Frankfort, Ky., **117.** Friends of South Union, Shakertown

Arkansas: **119.** Courtesy Passion Play

Wisconsin: **122.** Courtesy Anderson Store, **123.** Photos courtesy Annunciation Greek Orthodox Church, **125.** (left) Courtesy Little Norway, **125.** (right) Photo Ezra Stoller from Architectural Forum magazine

Michigan: **127.** Courtesy Fort Michilimackinac Historic Park, **129.** Chapel photo courtesy St. Augustine's House, **130.** Harry J. Wolf photo courtesy Mariner's Church, **130.** Photo New Covenant Magazine, **131.** Photo Joel's Studio, Holland, Michigan

Illinois: **133.** Courtesy Oblates of Mary Immaculate, **135.** (left) Produced by Audio-Visual Services Reorganized Church of Jesus Christ of Latter-Day Saints, Independence, Missouri, **135.** (right) Photo by State of Illinois Department of Conservation, **136.** Courtesy University of Chicago Office of Public Relations, **137.** National Baha'i Public Information Office

Indiana: **139.** Indiana Department of Commerce, **140.** Ray Hartill photo courtesy Public Relations Office St. Meinrad Seminary, **141.** First Christian Church, **142.** Church of God, **143.** Courtesy University of Notre Dame, **144.** News Bureau Valparaiso University

Iowa: **145.** Courtesy Vesterheim Center

Ohio: **150.** Wyandott Mission Shrine, **152.** Kellar Studio photo

Minnesota: **154.** News Bureau Augsburg College, **155.** Gustavus Adolphus College, **156.** Courtesy St. John's Abbey

New Mexico: **159.** Glorieta Baptist Assembly, **160.** (left) Mission St. Francis of Assisi, **160.** (right) Courtesy Aztec Ruins National Monument, **162.** National Park Service photos by Fred Mang, Jr.

Texas: **168.** Courtesy Awani Press

Arizona: **170.** Courtesy Tumacacori National Monument, **171.** P. E. Huth photo, **175.** Courtesy Pipe Spring National Monument

Missouri: **176.** Photo by Arteaga, **177.** Blessed Rose Philippine Duchesne Shrine, **178.** Hardy photo, **180.** Courtesy Reorganized Church of Jesus Christ of Latter-Day Saints

Kansas: **182.** Courtesy Eisenhower Center, **183.** Courtesy Rice County Historical Society, Lyons

Oklahoma: **185.** Oral Roberts University information bureau photos

South Dakota: **190.** Buechel Memorial Museum photo

Utah: **196.** Courtesy Latter-Day Saints Graphic Library, **196.** Courtesy Box Elder Tabernacle

Colorado: **200.** Stewarts Commercial Photographers, **201.** Photos courtesy U.S. Air Force Academy, **202.** Courtesy Association Camp, **204.** Courtesy United States Dept. of Interior, National Park Service

Nebraska: **206.** Walter S. Craig Film Productions photo

Wyoming: **208.** W. H. Jackson photo from D. Howell Collection

California: **213.** Courtesy Mission De Pala, **214.** Courtesy Mission San Juan Capistrano, **216.** Photos by Wiener of Torrance, **217.** (top) Courtesy Wilshire Blvd. Temple, **217.** (bottom) Courtesy Vedanta Society of So. Calif., **218.** Courtesy Santa Barbara Mission, **219.** Courtesy Vedanta Society of So. Calif., **220.** Courtesy Mission San Antonio

Hawaii: Courtesy Soto Museum of Hawaii (Zen), **235.** Hawaii Visitors Bureau Photo, **236.** (top) Courtesy National Park Service, **236.** (bottom) Photos courtesy Lyman House Memorial Museum

Oregon: **238.** St. Paul Catholic Church photo

Washington: **242.** Courtesy Whitman Mission

INDEX

(EPIS) Episcopal (RC) Roman Catholic (UCC) United Church of Christ